Prioritizing Integration

Bertelsmann Stiftung, Migration Policy Institute (eds.)

Prioritizing Integration

The Transatlantic Council on Migration

| Verlag Bertelsmann**Stiftung**

Bibliographic information published by the Deutsche Nationalbibliothek

The Deutsche Nationalbibliothek lists this publication in the
Deutsche Nationalbibliografie; detailed bibliographic data
is available on the Internet at http://dnb.d-nb.de.

© 2010 Verlag Bertelsmann Stiftung, Gütersloh
Responsible: Dr. Christal Morehouse
Copy editor: Michelle Mittelstadt
Production editor: Christiane Raffel
Cover design: Nadine Humann
Cover illustration: Thomas Kunsch, Bielefeld
Typesetting and Printing: Hans Kock Buch- und Offsetdruck GmbH, Bielefeld
ISBN 978-3-86793-071-0

www.bertelsmann-stiftung.org/publications

Contents

Introduction

The Transatlantic Council on Migration

First convened in 2008, the Transatlantic Council on Migration is a unique deliberative and advisory body that aims to have a tangible, measurable impact on migration and immigrant integration policy on both sides of the Atlantic. The Council's principal policy partner in this effort is the Bertelsmann Stiftung. The Council, an initiative led by the Migration Policy Institute and convened by MPI President Demetrios G. Papademetriou, is generously supported by the Carnegie Corporation of New York, the Open Society Institute, the Bertelsmann Stiftung, the Rockefeller Foundation, the Ford Foundation, the Barrow Cadbury Trust, the Luso-American Development Foundation, the Calouste Gulbenkian Foundation and the governments of Germany, the Netherlands and Norway. More information about the Council's membership, operations and publications can be found at: www.migrationpolicy.org/transatlantic.

In the wake of the "Great Recession," countries on both sides of the Atlantic must confront two competing realities: increased integration needs and vastly reduced spending capacity. What's more, there is little public appetite for investing in immigrants at a time when many native-born citizens are experiencing soaring unemployment and there is ever greater competition for society's resources. Yet, as immigration continues to shape our societies, better integration is a critical component for future economic growth.

At its fourth plenary meeting, held in Bellagio, Italy, in May 2010, the Transatlantic Council on Migration deliberated on how to make smart investments in immigrant integration at a time of reduced budgets by assessing where the greatest needs and opportunities are. Where have immigrants been hit the hardest? At what point in the immigration arc are investments most effective? How should politicians speak about immigrant integration in order to garner public support? And what effect will reduced funding have on the laws and practices that shape immigration and immigrant integration?

To answer these questions, the Council convened senior policymakers and experts from Europe and North America to come up with a series of strategies and recommendations that can help farsighted policymakers rebuild robust economies and improve social cohesion during the long recovery ahead. The Council also convened a high-level education symposium in advance of its plenary meeting to hone in on specific recommendations for optimizing mainstream school reforms.

This volume—the fourth major publication of the Transatlantic Council on Migration—is based on these discussions and the research commissioned for the Council's May 2010 meeting. All the contributions are original work. The book joins the first three Transatlantic Council books—*Delivering Citizenship* (November 2008), *Talent, Competitiveness and Migration* (April 2009) and *Migration, Public Opinion and Politics* (November 2009)—in offering an evidence-based, pragmatic approach to the most complex and controversial policy debates surrounding migration.

There are three sections to this volume. Part One begins with the Council Statement on "Immigrant Integration—Priorities for the Next Decade," which synthesizes the primary recommendations to emerge from the fourth meeting of the Transatlantic Council on Migration from May 5–7, 2010 in Bellagio, Italy. Although the Statement reflects the deliberations of the Council, the final responsibility for its contents rests with its authors.

Part Two analyzes where and how immigrants have been affected by the economic crisis. On both sides of the Atlantic, deep recession and the threat of a protracted recovery with ongoing high unemployment are having profound implications for immigration, immigrants and whole communities. This section maps out what we know about the recession's impact on immigrants, covering areas such as employment outcomes, educational performance, government investments in integration and political extremism.

Demetrios G. Papademetriou, Madeleine Sumption and Aaron Terrazas begin Part Two with their chapter on "Recovering from Recession: Immigrants and Immigrant Integration in the Transatlantic Economy." In many countries, the years of economic expansion prior to the recession witnessed a greater openness toward immigration. In particular, some countries saw large inflows of immigrants into lower-skilled occupations, policies that are now being thrown into question. With contributions from Carola Burkert, Stephen Loyal and Ruth Ferrero-Turrión, this chapter explores five country case studies—Germany, Ireland, Spain, the United Kingdom and the United States—and illustrates the very wide variation among advanced industrialized nations, both in terms of macroeconomic impacts and outcomes for different immigrant groups. At the same time, immigration-receiving countries in the transatlantic sphere face many of the same integration challenges as they move beyond the global economic crisis.

Aaron Terrazas, Michael Fix and Margie McHugh explore effects on US education in chapter two, entitled "Immigrant Students in US Schools and the Recession of 2007–2009." They find emerging evidence that the economic crisis has prompted a period of both painful adjustment and promising innovation in the nation's elementary and secondary schools due to state-level fiscal crises and an unprecedented fiscal stimulus package. This chapter also focuses on how immigrant and limited English proficient (LEP) students were faring in US schools prior to the recession and how primary and secondary school education policies have evolved over the last few years.

The third chapter, by Miho Taguma and entitled "Immigrant Students in OECD Countries during a Recession-Inspired Era of Resource Constraints," compares the educational outcomes of immigrant children to those of natives in Organisation for Economic Co-operation and Development (OECD) countries. The chapter highlights the importance of a whole-school approach—engaging teachers, school leaders, parents, communities and students—to improve equal opportunity and standards of excellence in schools and the long-term benefits of careful investments in education. This paper concludes with several points of action on how to improve education outcomes for students of immigrant origin.

Chapter four, entitled "The Economic Crisis and Funding for Immigrant Integration in the United States," was co-authored by Randy Capps and Margie McHugh, with contributions by Monica Arciga, Michael Fix and Laureen Laglagaron. This chapter explores the impact of the crisis on funding for key services and programs that support the integration of immigrants and their families in the United States. It focuses on the five most populous US states—California, Texas, New York, Florida and Illinois—to understand their potential impact on prospects for furthering the integration of immigrants and their children.

The fifth chapter, the work of Elizabeth Collett and Sheena McLoughlin, is entitled "Government Investment in Integration and Fiscal Uncertainty: Reactions in Europe." It takes a first look at government reactions to integration policy-making, financing and programming in select countries across Europe, with a particular study of integration programming in post-crisis Ireland, and finds that governments have responded in a variety of ways to new and potential fiscal constraints. It concludes by identifying areas of potential concern over the coming decade with respect to maintaining sustainable investments in integration.

Chapter six, entitled "The Relationship between Immigration and Nativism in Europe and North America," was authored by Cas Mudde. The chapter highlights the complex and frequently unclear relationship between immigration and extremism. Higher levels of immigration in the three regions examined in this chapter—North America, Western Europe and Central and Eastern Europe—do not automatically correlate to more votes for radical-right parties, though nativist parties in government have affected immigration policies. This chapter concludes by demonstrating what sort of impact nativist and radical-right parties have had on immigration debates and policies.

The final chapter in Part Two is called "Investing in School and Labor Market Preparedness: A Silver Lining to the Economic Crisis?" This chapter, by Maurice Crul, examines how second-generation migrants in seven European countries (Austria, Belgium, France, Germany, the Netherlands, Sweden and Switzerland) have been faring in education and jobs, based on a Europe-wide survey called TIES. It concludes with recommendations on how governments can prioritize policies that will allow second-generation migrants to improve their skill levels and employment prospects, especially during the slow economic recovery.

Part Three of this book is a summary of the discussion at the Council's meeting in May 2010. It contains the key deliberations of the Council members and experts who attended the meeting. It is written in accordance with the Chatham House Rule—intended to foster free and uninhibited discussion—and, hence, does not reveal the speakers' identities.

All chapters contained in this book are original contributions from leading academics and thinkers on international migration. Readers will also find a summary of Council-related migration and integration resources on the Web as well as information about the Transatlantic Council on Migration.

The Council believes that recent rates of immigration growth, which are projected to increase further, demand that governments, employers, civil society and immigrants themselves make investments that create stronger families, contribute to economic growth and build stronger communities. With this book, the Transatlantic Council on Migration aims to provide practical strategies and tools to help these actors invest wisely.

Demetrios G. Papademetriou
Migration Policy Institute

Gunter Thielen
Bertelsmann Stiftung

13

Part I: The Transatlantic Council on Migration

Council Statement: Immigrant Integration— Priorities for the Next Decade

May 5–7, 2010, Bellagio Conference Center, Italy

Demetrios G. Papademetriou and Annette Heuser

Introduction and Context

Immigrant integration is both very complex and costly. To succeed, it must be constantly evaluated and adapted to the ever-changing realities on the ground. Yet, while the true benefits of successful integration emerge gradually—over decades and even generations—our political culture demands virtually instant results from our public investments. And, despite rhetoric about integration as a "two-way street," what most people and all but the most thoughtful of politicians actually expect is near-assimilation rather than the mutual accommodations true integration entails.

As countries grapple with the legacy of the Great Recession—in most instances, soaring unemployment for immigrants, minorities and youth; competition for society's resources; and spikes in anti-immigrant sentiment—the consequences of our actions today will be felt for decades during the long recovery that lies ahead. Considering the continuing—and, in many instances, rising—need for immigrants, losing momentum on integration is not an option.

The goal of this meeting of the Transatlantic Council on Migration, held in May 2010, was to show how to shift our focus back onto integration as a continuous and interactive process—and to do so amidst the tumult of a persistent economic crisis. In doing so, participants considered the critical question of how to invest smartly in a new world that confronts two competing realities: increased integration needs with reduced spending capacity. The Council convened se-

17

nior political leaders, seasoned policymakers and global experts to deliberate on how to make investments—including whom to target and when to invest—that promise to deliver the best outcomes.

The Great Recession and Immigrant Integration

The recession's most distinctive feature has been the diversity of its effects across countries. Unemployment rates have ranged from 3 percent in Norway to nearly 20 percent in Spain, where over 30 percent of nonnationals are unemployed. But while some categories of immigrants have fared poorly—particularly men (reflecting the recession's decimation of workforces in the manufacturing sectors), youth (who are always the most marginally attached to the labor force and, hence, are the most expendable workers) and minorities (especially African-born ones)—immigrants as a group have actually outperformed natives in some Organisation for Economic Co-operation and Development (OECD) countries. And immigrant women have fared much better than men, as they have been disproportionately represented in the growing health and care-giving sectors.

Those on temporary work permits and less-regulated worker channels have served as welcome "flexible valves" in the labor market, with flows responding most directly to the decreased demand for jobs. In some countries, these workers and many immigrants have also been more willing to relocate and switch sectors in order to find work. However, most of those who lack an explicit right to return (e.g., unauthorized immigrants, European Union [EU] Member State nationals with temporary work restrictions or permanent residents penalized for long stays abroad) have chosen to stay put, even during the most severe phase of the economic crisis. This is an unintended natural experiment that clearly argues for greater flexibility to be built both into labor markets and immigration systems so they are able to react more nimbly to business-cycle fluctuations.

Looking forward, the Council's analyses and discussions made clear that policymakers must be prepared for more funding shortfalls ahead. National and subnational budget crises are far from over, and extraordinary and sustained job creation will be necessary before unemployment begins to approach pre-Great Recession levels. The economy will also be appreciably different, with many employers in the manufacturing sector demanding workers with better skills relative to those needed prior to the recession (a product of capital investments and other production-process adjustments made during the downturn) and with construction (among other sectors) claiming a smaller share of the job market in countries such as the United States, the United Kingdom, Spain and Ireland.

What does this mean for immigrants in the labor market? As noted, unemployment has been particularly vicious for minority and immigrant youth, and the danger of substantial and long-term "economic scarring" is great; that is, workers who either attempt to enter the labor market or who lose their jobs during a recession are likely to suffer permanent income and mobility disadvantages relative to the rest of the workforce. Yet there is little appetite for increased investments to bridge these gaps; the winding-down of stimulus funds and growing concern in many countries about high levels of public debt are likely to exacerbate concerns that immigrants compete with natives for diminishing public expenditures designed to cushion the effects of the recession for workers and families.

Public Opinion and Politics in the Recession

The public's views on immigration are neither simple nor linear. While the crisis has not yet led to acute negative reactions, it has created space in the public discourse for more hostile political rhetoric and has strengthened the political fortunes of parties that are more explicitly skeptical about immigration, in some instances propelling anti-immigration parties to electoral success. The growing prominence of anti-immigration sentiment in some countries is aided by the fact that immigration-related views tend to be intensely held. For instance, in the United States, 80 percent of the public considers illegal immigration to be a problem, and three-quarters of those consider it to be a "very serious" one; in the United Kingdom, 77 percent of the public says net immigration should decrease or that no immigration should be allowed at all.

Public opinion on immigration is also marked by ample ambiguity: Voters might oppose reform while simultaneously abhorring the status quo. In the same vein, people might enjoy the benefits of legal and illegal immigration while expecting others to deal with its adverse consequences. This paradox lies at the heart of the political challenge. Public attitudes speak to the reality that many of the fears about immigration are not, in fact, about the immigrants themselves: Anti-immigration sentiment is frequently a proxy for the pace of social, economic and cultural change more broadly, to which immigration contributes mightily, and the growing sense of lack of control over that change. The composition of recent flows, that is, the perception of "distance" and "difference," further contributes to the discomfort.

Public attitudes might be managed better if leaders understand the importance of "priming" public opinion. This may require emphasizing the importance of orderly immigration, including immigration controls and enforcement. Furthermore, the public must be assured that economic-stream immigrants are admitted only in response to measurable labor market needs and/or as part of explicit economic-growth and competitiveness policies. Both the challenge and the opportunity is to present orderliness and strict selection criteria in immigration as the means through which immigrants become the economic (and social) assets they typically are rather than the liabilities they are often (and somtimes correctly) portrayed to be.

Adding to the issue's complexity is that widespread discrimination continues to plague many immigrant-receiving countries, a phenomenon not conclusively tied to the recession, although it may be exacerbated by it. This is particularly troublesome because minorities often do not report discriminatory incidents or even violence due in great part to the belief that filing a complaint will change nothing. This level of resignation among minorities and immigrants suggests they themselves believe public attitudes toward visible difference are deeply rooted.

But what is the effect on politics? Many far-right politicians have exploited an alternative narrative based on a "clash of civilizations," discussing immigration in the context of the supposed unassimilability of certain groups and the "ownership" of a country based on history and blood ties. However, it is difficult to assess how much extremist groups are capitalizing on real fears concerning jobs or whether they are simply employing savvy—though short-sighted—politicking strategies. There is also evidence that some mainstream politicians, finding themselves rather powerless to effectively manage the financial and economic maelstrom unleashed by the recession, are seizing on immigration as a way to prove that they can be in control of at least one large phenomenon: immigration-induced social change. This is evident most starkly in the American state of Arizona, with its new immigration law, and in the recent statements (for instance) of UK Labour Party leadership candidate Ed Balls.

Thinking Long Term Even in the Short Term: Rewriting the Political Narrative

While the economic crisis preoccupies governments, less visible long-term trends and needs must be incorporated into public thinking. Demographic change and aging workforces are on a collision course with the high living standards and social protections of modern life. Thus, focusing squarely on labor market needs and reforms—through a combination of policy actions, such as encouraging more women (and others who are not in the workforce, most notably immigrants) to work; lengthening work lives; increasing productivity through better education and training programs; and increasing immigration levels in orderly fashions—is critical to continuing prosperity and future growth. This realization is hard to act on at the best of times; but, in a context of high unemployment and uncertainty, it may be particularly difficult to implement.

21

How can this new political discourse be framed? The narrative told by politicians is very important. While the current narrative, including a focus on deportations, resonates with many in the public, it misjudges the complexity of public concerns about immigration while also promising much more than it can deliver. The result is the further erosion of public trust in governments. Thus, it is critical to articulate a compelling new story about immigration that resonates with the public, is based on the facts and sets forth a realistic vision for the way forward. The Council believes that a focus on immigrant integration is an indispensable component of such an approach, especially if it sets realistic and hence achievable goals.

Smarter Investments in Immigrant Integration

Just as the crisis impacted different countries in different ways and to differing degrees, its effects on government budgets—and the fiscal reactions of governments—have been equally diverse. While some countries have slashed spending on integration for newly arrived immigrants, others have redoubled their focus on language training and on facilitating immigrant access to the labor market. Regardless of their initial responses, however, one thing is clear: The bulk of the fiscal tightening on both sides of the Atlantic is yet to come. Governments—city, regional and national—will be looking for more and more ways to save money.

Integration policies can easily become the soft target. Pressure to focus public investments first and foremost on citizens, particularly the most vulnerable ones, is strong and likely to get stronger. Yet, failure to also invest in immigrants and their families at such a crucial time will have a generational impact with much larger long-term fiscal and societal consequences. Put simply: Governments can neither afford to play "beggar thy neighbor" games with their public investments nor to "save" money on immigrant integration if for no other reason than they will need strong and well-prepared workers in order to be ready for (and react to) the onset of robust economic growth.

However, money must be spent smartly. As detailed in the strategies below, the Council believes that how governments prioritize limited resources and how they structure necessary reforms—as well as how they communicate these changes to the public—can have as much of an impact as the policies they pursue.

Reconceptualizing Integration Strategies

- *A new immigration framework.* Developing a new, fact-based narrative on the role of immigration in modern society and the policies that can support it is necessary to reduce the frequently dramatic access and achievement gaps between immigrant groups (and their progeny) and natives. From education and employment rates to income and mobility projections, these gaps are wide in many countries. Immigration, well-conceived and carried out, can become a central element of the economic future of countries on both sides of the Atlantic, whether in boom times or in downturns. Investing in anti-discrimination policies—and informing vulnerable groups of their rights—must be an integral part of this plan. At the same time, any narrative must honestly and forthrightly address fears of immigration's consequences.
- *Mainstream services.* Although many immigrants are more vulnerable during a recession, the challenges they face—particularly in the areas of education and skills development—are similar to those faced by all disadvantaged natives and, typically, minorities. This means that while certain services and programs have to be designed to address the unique needs of immigrants and other vulnerable groups, they should be made available to all who need and qualify for them. For example, including the needs of immigrant children under mainstream, systemic education reforms—and thus making schools accountable for the performance of immigrants—is an effective way to improve outcomes. Such efforts can also "fly under the political radar," thus disarming those opposed to targeting resources to immigrants in times of crisis. So that funding for immigrants does not

get lost if placed in a bigger purse, accountability structures are needed to ensure that resources are allocated fairly and effectively.

- *Willingness and built-in capability to adapt.* Governments must become more open to learning proper lessons from others' experiences and much more nimble in adopting innovative new ideas. Clearinghouses that can undertake meaningful evaluation of ideas and establish which are clearly effective—and transferable to different contexts—are a critical investment. Governments must also commence and/or make significant progress in monitoring how their investments are impacting vulnerable groups and be always ready to adapt programs accordingly. This requires building flexibility into programs that allow public and private service-delivery groups to rethink and adapt their strategies in the face of new knowledge and ideas.

Worthwhile Priorities

- *Invest early.* Too often, human capital is needlessly wasted in the early stages of immigration, when newcomers' education, skills and experiences are most up-to-date and hence relevant. Early interventions in the economic integration of immigrants—via orientation classes, language programs, skills identification and augmentation, and assistance with essential labor market information—will facilitate early entry into the labor market at a level that reflects and builds upon existing skills. This can be more cost-effective in the long term, even if the stay in the destination country turns out to be a short one. For those who return home, the investment will continue to pay dividends in terms of opening up better personal opportunities and reducing the need to reemigrate.
- *Improve access to the labor market.* Successful long-term integration hinges upon the adoption of policies that ease immigrants' early access (and reentry) into the labor market. This applies to all immigrants, regardless of nationality or generation. Some effective policies in this regard are:

- *Individualized assessments.* Interviewing immigrants upon arrival to assess their existing skills, language proficiency and the most helpful and cost-effective additional education and training needed can help determine the appropriate integration support and can facilitate effective entry into the labor market. And, while such assessments are easier for countries with such systems already in place for natives—and with relatively small numbers of immigrants—the concept is one that deserves careful emulation.
- *Apprenticeships and wage subsidies.* Programs designed to offer immigrants a chance to get work experience in-country while also allowing employers to assess and build skills on-site can be critical policy tools. Such programs, which target those who need support in entering or reentering the labor market, are relevant to immigrants and natives alike.
- *Vocational training.* Many immigrants arrive with skills and experiences needed in the labor market but require "bridging" education and training assistance in order to match the specific requirements of the host country's labor market. Employers and government agencies alike need to include immigrants in their programs to develop and improve upon existing skills.

- *Optimize recognition of skills.* Developing and investing in systems for recognizing existing skills and qualifications is critical; no country currently manages to do this well, and there is a systematic underutilization of skills among immigrant populations on both sides of the Atlantic. Investments in common standards for skills recognition would not only bring economies of scale for governments but also ensure that immigrants can contribute to the host economy and society in the fullest way possible.
- *Engage civil society and the private sector.* Effective public-private cooperation on skills development for immigrants can act as a multiplier for public budgets, generating better outcomes with fewer resources. Similarly, partnering with civil society in imaginative ways can lubricate the process of integration and complete the whole-of-society approach that is at the heart of societies that suc-

ceed with immigration—and thus change the narrative about it. When governments work hand-in-glove with the private sector and civil society, they can ease and facilitate the social and economic integration of immigrants while also mitigating discrimination and anti-immigrant sentiment.

- *Focus on the next generation.* Smart investments in the education of immigrant children will create multiplier effects and avoid creating a "lost generation." Priorities should include improving early childhood education, parental engagement and teacher quality. Specifically:

  - *Teacher quality.* Countries must first elevate the status of teaching in society and assign the most qualified teachers to work with the neediest children, an approach that does not require more resources but, rather, simply a smarter allocation of them.

  - *School content.* Curricula should strike a balance between the needs of society and those of immigrant children. As with most aspects of integration, this is a two-way street: Children need to be integrated into the culture of the host country, but curricula should also be responsive to the specific needs, values and assets that immigrant children bring with them. Furthermore, curricula should integrate language-learning with subject-matter content so that nonnative speakers do not fall behind in school.

  - *A greater focus on skills.* Innovative methods should be explored, including focusing on apprenticeships or vocational training, so that students graduate with the skills they need to succeed in the labor market.

Conclusion

While the recession might be over, the economic crisis for individuals, families and communities continues—and threatens to get worse as stimulus funds are withdrawn. The Transatlantic Council on Migration underscores not only the critical role integration plays in helping families weather the economic crisis, but also the role that smart investments in integration will play in helping immigrant-destination countries be better prepared to grow and compete once the economic recovery takes off.

The Council thus urges governments to make sustained, focused investments in five key areas:

- Making early and sustained integration investments in language training;
- Improving newcomers' access to the labor market, for example, through workforce training and skills-bridging programs;
- Optimizing recognition of skills, credentials and experiences;
- Focusing on the next generation by improving education for immigrant youth;
- Engaging often overlooked actors, such as civil society and the private sector in all aspects of integration.

Reshaping immigration policies based on a positive, but fact-based, political narrative is the first step toward realistically achieving these goals. At the same time, building flexibility and adaptability into the immigrant-integration system and targeting all disadvantaged groups will improve the effectiveness of these efforts.

Part II:
Integration Policies in the Postrecession Era

Recovering from Recession: Immigrants and Immigrant Integration in the Transatlantic Economy

Demetrios G. Papademetriou, Madeleine Sumption and Aaron Terrazas with Carola Burkert, Steven Loyal and Ruth Ferrero-Turrión

Introduction: The Global Economic Crisis

From Boom to Bust: A Dramatic and Unexpected Economic Crisis

Few observers imagined in 2007 that the bursting of the construction bubble in the United States, Spain, the United Kingdom and Ireland during the course of that year would create ripple effects large enough to shake the very foundations of the global financial system and plunge the industrial world into its severest economic crisis since World War II. Yet, with the demise of Lehman Brothers in September 2008, a full-throated economic crisis ensued and spread quickly from the United States to much of Europe and the developing world—although its impact in emerging economies proved to be much less virulent and lasting.

The resulting recession was dramatic. Industrialized countries in the North Atlantic region had experienced two decades of nearly un-interrupted growth and, in many cases, low unemployment.[1] Sustained global integration, including the movement of goods, information, ideas and—critically—people, created wealth and lifted millions in the industrialized and developing worlds out of poverty. Robust employment growth during the boom years and the expectation that

---

1 Growth in the 1990s and 2000s varied by country, but many countries experienced brief recessions or periods of rising unemployment in around 1991 and 2001.

it would continue led to very tight labor markets in many fast-growing countries—particularly in booming sectors, such as construction, finance, health care and information and communications technology. Inequality increased despite rapid growth: Between the mid-1980s and the mid-2000s, the Gini coefficient—a composite measure of income inequality—increased by 0.021 points in Organisation for Economic Co-operation and Development (OECD) countries (excluding Mexico and Turkey) (OECD 2008).

Policymakers attributed this period of unprecedented prosperity to a combination of private-sector innovation and sound public policy-making (Blanchard, Dell'Ariccia and Mauro 2010; Islam and Nallari 2010). But, in retrospect, the long boom obscured structural weaknesses in many industrialized and emerging economies. Early signs of turmoil in certain industries and regional economies were dismissed as localized phenomena. When the global financial system spectacularly unraveled in the fall of 2008, the severity of the crisis caught policymakers by surprise. As Figure 1 illustrates, the International Monetary Fund (IMF) did not foresee any slowdown in industrialized countries' economic growth in October 2007; as late as October 2008, it did not expect growth to dip below zero. (Tellingly, the IMF also underestimated the pace of economic growth as country after country exited the recession.) Adding insult to injury, "the size and speed of the collapse created a situation of extreme uncertainty," prompting investors and consumers to sharply curtail spending (Commission on Growth and Development 2010: 6–7). Sudden investor aversion to risk and low consumer confidence contributed to deepening the recession.

The recession has also forced a reconsideration of assumptions about the modern economy that had become mainstream. The idea of a "great moderation" for example, the theory that a fundamental shift in economic dynamics, together with good policy, had essentially brought the business cycle under control by the end of the 20th century—began to look somewhat naïve (Stock and Watson 2002), as did the notion that the strength of the relatively unregulated US labor market prevented unemployment from reaching European levels.

32

Figure 1: Declining gross domestic product (GDP) growth forecasts for industrialized economies, 2007 to 2010

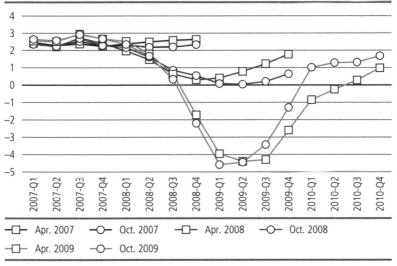

Data are the projected annual growth rates as a percentage of GDP.

Source: International Monetary Fund, World Economic Outlook, various years

Unemployment in the European Union had been on a relatively steady downward trajectory since the early 1990s and had almost halved by the end of 2007. Joblessness in the United States has been considerably lower than in Europe for more than 20 years: From 1998 to 2000, US unemployment hovered at around 4 percent.[2] Brief recessions in the early 1990s and early 2000s witnessed significant cyclical upticks, but unemployment remained well below European levels. But, in the two years from the end of 2007 to the end of 2009, unemployment shot up 5 percentage points in the United States, from under 5 percent to nearly 10 percent; in Europe, it jumped by a more modest

---

2   The United States had the highest unemployment rate in the OECD in the early 1960s when unemployment rates in Europe and many other developed countries were particularly low. But this began to change in the 1970s and, more recently, the United States has had consistently lower unemployment than the European Union (Nickell, Nuzianta and Ochel 2005).

2.5 percent, to 8.8 percent.[3] The recent recession, therefore, over-turned US-EU unemployment trends for the first time in decades (see Figure 2).

With the advantage of hindsight, it is now clear that the basis of growth varied across countries and industries. Some industries grew due to innovation and expanding markets, while others grew due to asset price bubbles or public subsidies. Both types of growth created jobs and attracted immigrants to fill rapidly expanding labor needs. Once the economic downturn began, some of these newly created jobs proved more durable than others. Meanwhile, the countries that have seen the most savage reductions in production have not necessarily suffered the harshest labor market impact. For example, the United States has experienced a larger-than-average increase in unemploy-ment (relative to other OECD countries) despite a smaller-than-aver-

Figure 2: Unemployment rate, United States and the European Union, quarterly, 2000 to 2009

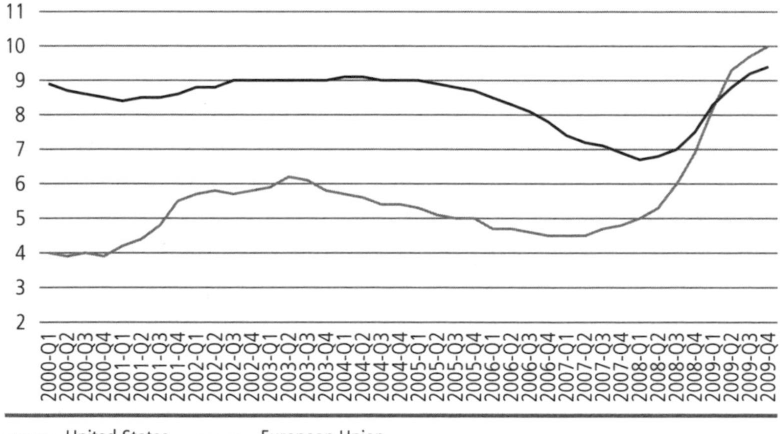

United States ——— European Union

All data in percent

Source: OECD, Labor Force Statistics, Harmonized Unemployment Rates and Levels

---

3 Unemployment data are from the OECD, Labor Force Statistics, Harmonized Un-employment Rates and Levels.

age GDP hit, while Germany has seen the opposite—a lower-than-average unemployment rise despite a substantial shock to GDP (Moeller 2010).

These differences arise in part from the nature of the recession (e.g., whether it involved a financial crisis or a house-price bust), from labor market institutions (e.g., subsidies for part-time working and labor market flexibility) and from the skill level of employees in sectors that bore the brunt of economic contraction. Germany's recession, for example, was driven not by a financial crisis or housing bust but by the reduction in demand for exports, which is thought to have dampened the shock to employment (International Monetary Fund 2010a). In addition, some employers were much more likely to hold on to qualified workers who would be expensive to replace once the recession ended, even if these decisions implied a short-term reduction in productivity. This "labor hoarding" has been more common in some countries than others. In 2009, for example, productivity per hour worked shot up 3.7 percent in the United States, but in the United Kingdom and Germany, where unemployment increases were more moderate, productivity decreased by 1.9 percent and 1.1 percent, respectively (US Bureau of Labor Statistics 2010; UK Office of National Statistics 2010; Statistisches Bundesamt Deutschland 2010).

The global recovery is now underway, and advanced economies are expected to grow by an average of 2.3 percent in 2010 (IMF 2010a). But, for the most part, the jobs crisis continues. In the United States, the legacy of the recession could be stubbornly high unemployment (if recent recessions are anything to go by) and, in Europe, fiscal tightening necessary to ease sovereign debt concerns may prolong the employment crisis. A huge amount of slack remains in the labor market in the form of part-time workers who would prefer to work full time, or underutilized employees who were "hoarded" by firms during the crisis. Many employers will not need to hire new employees for some time.

Meanwhile, several countries have experienced increases in long-term unemployment over the past year precisely because flows *out of* unemployment are so low (see country case studies in this report and

Elsby, Hobijn and Sahin 2010). Recessions tend to speed up economic restructuring, leading to the rapid decline of industries that already struggled to remain competitive. As a result, laid-off workers may find that their skills have become obsolete and that they must retrain for an entirely new industry or resign themselves to entry-level employment. This increases the time it takes them to get back to work and the likely wage cut they will take in a new job (Congressional Budget Office 2010). Furthermore, unemployment rates are proving stubborn even as employment levels rise amid an economic recovery because discouraged and other inactive workers who are not counted in official unemployment rates are beginning to reenter the labor force, actively seeking jobs once more.

Immigration Policy Challenges for the Postcrisis Period

In many countries, the years of economic expansion prior to the recession witnessed a greater opening to immigration (if only grudgingly, in some cases), driven overwhelmingly by labor shortages and demographic change. Over the past 30 years, the immigrant share of the population in developed regions of the world nearly doubled, from 5.4 percent, in 1980, to 10.5 percent, in 2010, according to United Nations estimates.[4] The size of the immigration inflows varied substantially by country. Most notably, former countries of emigration, such as Ireland and Spain, experienced dramatic increases in their foreign-born populations from the mid-1990s onward. Growth was large but more moderate (as a proportion of the existing population) in the United States and the United Kingdom. Others, such as Germany and France, saw relatively little immigration growth during the boom. In some countries, the period also saw large inflows of immigrants into less-skilled occupations. Immigration policies and geographical proximity to lower-income countries meant that Greece,

4 "More developed regions" comprise all regions of Europe and North America, Australia, New Zealand and Japan (United Nations Population Division 2008).

Italy, the United States and Spain, for example, experienced large increases in illegal immigration. By contrast, immigration to Ireland (and, to a lesser extent, the United Kingdom) comprised a large proportion of European migrants even before EU enlargement and the opening of labor markets to new EU nationals. These workers fueled economic growth by meeting labor demand and helping to moderate inflation (Blanchflower, Saleheen and Shadforth 2007).

The general opening to immigration was not without controversy. Immigrant populations grew rapidly and unexpectedly. Some countries with very small foreign-born populations were transformed into significant immigration destinations over the course of just a few years, while foreign-born workers in some of the countries more accustomed to immigration (notably, the United States and the United Kingdom) began to move to new areas that were largely unused to the phenomenon. As a result, immigration drove highly visible changes to local communities, in some cases creating concerns about social integration and strains on public services. And, inevitably, many questioned the impact of these new immigrants on native workers. Indeed, aggregate economic growth was accompanied by wage stagnation for less-skilled workers—attributable in part to immigration (as well as to trade liberalization and other economic and policy drivers). Populist politicians seized on the issue in regions where immigration fed into broader concerns about globalization and the changing fortunes of the world's major economies. But, on balance, there was a clear trend toward embracing the benefits of openness.

The crisis changes these dynamics in various ways. On the one hand, it marks an interruption in (and perhaps an end to) this period of sustained growth and prosperity in which immigrants were an important driving force. Whether the coming years will witness a return to the prerecession status quo or a more fundamental shift in economic trajectories remains highly uncertain. On the other hand, the economic crisis has strengthened the voices of those who have always been skeptical of immigration's benefits and those who have been critical of what they view as unexamined support for openness. According to the German Marshall Fund's survey of transatlantic trends, the share of people who considered immigration more of a problem than an opportunity increased by between four and nine percentage points between 2008 and 2009 in France, Germany, Italy, the Netherlands, the United States and the United Kingdom (German Marshall Fund of the United States 2009). Over one-third of Americans considered immigration a "bad thing" for the country in 2009, according to the Gallup Organization—a higher share than at any point since the recession of 2001–2002 (Morales 2009).

Concerns about immigrants consuming too many publicly funded benefits or competing with natives for jobs have loomed large in the public debates. As a result, some governments have found the idea of return migration attractive. In Spain, the Czech Republic, Denmark and Japan, this has taken the form of "pay-to-go" schemes that provide unemployed immigrant workers some form of financial compensation in return for leaving the country. In other countries, such as the United Kingdom and Ireland, politicians have preferred to emphasize (and publicize) the volume of voluntary return migration, particularly among new EU nationals. The desire to encourage return migration has not always been realistic, however, especially where immigrants' "home" countries were as deeply mired in economic crisis as the host country and where immigrants have no guarantee that they will be able to return to the host country when economic conditions improve.

Yet, overall, the policy response to the recession has been relatively moderate. Several countries have taken steps to reduce labor migration in the short term (e.g., by reducing the number of occupations that qualify for visas in strategic or shortage industries, or by raising the bar for entry under a points system). But, despite the now widespread comparisons between the recent recession and the Great Depression, the world has seen nothing like the protectionism of the 1930s. It has, of course, helped that, in many cases, immigration inflows to OECD countries have fallen of their own accord—chiefly on the "unregulated" margins,[5] such as illegal immigration to the United

5   We owe this observation to economist Giovanni Peri.

States and Europe and Eastern European immigration to the United Kingdom and Ireland. Demand for temporary workers has also fallen. It is no coincidence that these same channels helped fuel the immigration boom in the mid-2000s.

Politicians welcomed the recent immigration "pause" (or at least slowdown) because it took the pressure out of public fear and anger over immigration at a time when jobs are scarce and because it demonstrated the contested point that at least some immigration flows respond to the economic cycle. Declining inflows are also welcome because of emerging evidence that confirms what many already suspected: In times of economic weakness, the economy does not have the same capacity to "absorb" immigrants without reductions in wages or job prospects for the existing population (Peri 2010). At the same time, immigrants face the very real possibility of "economic scarring." Just as college students who graduate into a recession and experienced workers who lose their jobs during downturns face long-term setbacks in the labor market, immigrants who arrive when jobs are scarce are thought to take many years to catch up with their counterparts who arrived in times of economic well-being (Aydemir 2003; McDonald and Worswick 1999; Aslund and Rooth 2007). Studies that document this phenomenon typically do not distinguish between groups of immigrants arriving through different entry channels; but it seems likely that the impact falls primarily (perhaps almost exclusively) on those who arrive without a job offer, such as family and humanitarian immigrants and labor migrants selected through points systems.

The current environment is one of considerable uncertainty. Looking forward toward the recovery, does the current climate of high unemployment and slow employment growth represent a cyclical aberration that will eventually return to the precrisis equilibrium? Or has there been a longer-term shift in labor market demand in developed countries? How will the crisis shape the medium- and long-term pressures for emigration from sending countries? And how will it affect behavior among groups on the margins of the labor force whose decisions determine the overall supply of workers—that is, less-educated workers, discouraged workers, the urban poor, disadvantaged older workers, women who had voluntarily left the labor force but want to return to it, retirement-age individuals returning to work or postponing retirement, and those who had shunned certain occupations as too hard, too dangerous or too lacking in prestige? All of these groups' decisions will shape how many immigrants countries will "need" in the coming years. The future remains riddled with uncertainties. In the months and years ahead, immigration policymakers will face the challenge of offering credible responses in largely uncharted territory.

Immigrants and the Labor Market in the Recent Economic Crisis

Recessions can take an extraordinary human toll that extends well beyond temporary earnings losses for unemployed workers. Job loss during a downturn is thought to result in long-term employment and wage setbacks, deteriorating health and higher divorce rates, increasing poverty and child poverty, and lower educational attainment for children in low-income areas (CBO 2010; Isaacs 2009; Ochsen 2010). These impacts are most troubling for low-income households that are less well-positioned to buffer earnings losses during a recession and are more likely to fall into poverty as a result.

Immigrants and their families merit particular attention. Statistical analysis shows that immigrants are more vulnerable to cyclical swings in the macroeconomy and overrepresented among vulnerable groups who are likely to experience the setbacks described above (Dustmann, Glitz and Vogel 2009; Orrenius and Zavodny 2009). They tend to have lower incomes and are more likely to experience poverty at any point in the business cycle, and low-income immigrant children (especially second language learners) face particular challenges at school. This observation, based on the experience of past recessions, appears to be true for the recent recession as well. In 12 of 19 European and North American countries for which data are available,[6] unemployment increased faster among immigrants than among natives between the third quarter of 2007 and the third quarter of 2009.[7] (It increased proportionately for both groups in six countries, and it increased less for immigrants than for natives in two countries.[8])

Immigrants' greater vulnerability to unemployment is typically attributed to a complex and interrelated set of reasons, including the following:

- *Immigrants disproportionately share the demographic characteristics of the groups most likely to lose jobs during economic downturns.* Immigrant workers in most immigrant-receiving OECD countries are overrepresented among the low skilled. Language barriers and difficulty translating credentials among the better skilled exacerbate their relative disadvantage. During a time of recession, employers tend to shed their least-productive workers and those who are easiest to replace (e.g., because they have not received costly training).

- *Immigrants are more likely to work in cyclical industries.* More mobile and flexible than long-term residents or the native born, immigrants (and particularly recent immigrants) often respond most quickly to economic conditions, moving into cyclical industries (e.g., construction) or occupations (including a wide range of service jobs) during economic expansion. In many cases, additional workers are attracted to the country by the very existence of these cyclical jobs. Of course, the corollary is their increased vulnerability when these jobs are lost.

- *Immigrants are more likely to work as a contingent labor force.* Immigrants provide an important source of temporary labor when the economy is growing, for example, through temp agencies, short-

---

6 Data compiled from Eurostat, European Labor Force Survey; US Census Bureau, Current Population Survey; and Statistics Canada, Labor Force Survey. For a similar analysis, cf. Fix et al. 2009.

7 Austria, Belgium, Canada, Estonia, Finland, Greece, Italy, Luxembourg, Portugal, Spain, Sweden and the United States. Includes only noncitizens.

8 Unemployment increased proportionately for both groups in Cyprus, France, Germany, the Netherlands, Norway and the United Kingdom. Unemployment increased more for natives than for immigrants in the Czech Republic and Denmark.

term contracts or day-labor arrangements. These working structures are often used to bypass stricter labor regulations that make it difficult to fire permanent employees; countries with stricter employment protection legislation for permanent jobs tend to have higher shares of workers on fixed-term contracts (IMF 2010a). The temporary work sector tends to lose a greater proportion of its jobs when unemployment rises.

- *"Last hired, first fired" approaches tend to disadvantage immigrants.* Recent hires can be more vulnerable to job losses, primarily because they have less firm-specific knowledge or have received less employer-provided training. This makes them less expensive to replace. Recently arrived immigrants will likely have shorter tenure at their current job, and various immigrants also experience greater "churn" between jobs. All of this suggests that immigrants should be more vulnerable to job cuts (Dustmann, Glitz and Vogel 2009).

Of course, not all immigrant groups experience the same impacts. Unauthorized immigrants, for example, are particularly vulnerable; they tend to represent the most "contingent" workforce, often with the lowest education levels, the greatest language barriers and the greatest reliance on day labor or other temporary work arrangements. By contrast, highly skilled immigrants (similar to highly skilled native workers) are protected from the brunt of the recession's job losses—particularly when employers have made substantial investments in order to bring them to the country. In addition, differences between countries' institutional, policy and economic contexts affect how their immigrants fare. For example, the widespread use of fixed-term contracts has probably exacerbated the immigrant-native unemployment gap in Spain, while the relatively high education levels of the average immigrant in the United Kingdom may have helped to keep the UK gap relatively small.

This chapter comprises a series of studies on the experiences of five countries with substantial immigrant and second-generation populations—the United States, the United Kingdom, Germany, Ireland

42

and Spain. It represents an initial attempt to consolidate the evidence of how immigrants fared in labor markets over the course of the recession and to synthesize what policymakers can learn from the experience as they begin thinking beyond the stabilization and recovery. The five countries illustrate the huge variation between advanced industrialized nations in terms of both immigrants' outcomes and the impact of the global economic crisis. They also show how economic and institutional differences across countries have shaped immigrant integration and their vulnerability to the recession.

As the case studies show, immigrants' vulnerability has varied substantially both within and between countries. Focusing briefly on unemployment rates, several differences emerge. In Ireland, the United States and especially Spain, the recession has undoubtedly hit immigrants harder than the native born, leading to a widening unemployment gap. US immigrants entered the recession with comparable or even slightly lower unemployment than natives, while those in Ireland and Spain faced a moderate structural disadvantage even before the recession. But, overall, a similar story can be told: In all three cases, less-skilled immigrants concentrated in cyclical industries (particularly construction) saw rapid declines in job opportunities.

The UK and German experiences are somewhat different. While the United Kingdom faced some of the same economic problems as the United States and Ireland (in particular, a credit crunch and falling house prices), unemployment increases were relatively moderate, and the overall gap between immigrants and the UK born has remained essentially unchanged. A division emerged, however, between less-skilled workers from non-EU sending countries, who did see rapid unemployment increases, and their counterparts from Eastern Europe, who have fared remarkably well despite a concentration in less-skilled work. Finally, as of early 2010, immigrants in Germany had not been hit particularly hard by the recession, which—contrary to previous German and current international experience—primarily affected skilled workers. Here, the overwhelming challenge is not the impact of the recession but, rather, the huge structural barriers that have faced German immigrants for some time.

Whatever the fallout from the recession, one thing remains certain: The challenge of immigrant integration—a challenge that existed before the recession and has become all the more pressing over the past two years—will not disappear. Countries that saw unprecedented immigration inflows during the boom now have large foreign-born populations; it will take time and concerted investments to ensure their integration. Even some of the countries that did not throw open their doors—Germany, for example, has maintained a ban on almost all labor migration since the oil crisis of the 1970s—face huge inequalities between immigrant and native populations that continue into the second generation and sometimes beyond.

Now that the worst of the recession is over, governments must shift from crisis management to picking up the pieces: assessing the damage to workers and families, consolidating whatever lessons can be drawn and shaping policies to ensure a sustainable recovery. This will occur in the context of tighter public finances. As the recent turmoil in eurozone bond markets has shown, a fiscal crisis has rapidly joined the continuing jobs crisis as one of the top challenges facing policymakers. Public debt has surged in advanced nations, the result of a collapse in government tax revenues and (to a lesser extent) the decisive fiscal policies that prevented a more dramatic collapse.[9] In particular, several European economies that had rapidly growing immigrant populations prior to the recession (particularly Spain, but also Greece, Ireland and Portugal) now face large budget deficits and are finding it increasingly expensive to finance their debt. Austerity measures to tackle deficits are being introduced at varying rates (most notably in Greece, but also in France, Ireland, Portugal and Spain). These circumstances will make the challenge of immigrant integration all the more difficult.

---

9 About half of the debt increase in advanced G-20 economies is driven by revenue losses; one-tenth results from fiscal stimulus packages (IMF 2010b).

Immigrant Integration in the US Labor Market: The Recession and Its Aftermath

Demetrios G. Papademetriou and Aaron Terrazas

The Economic Crisis of 2007–2009

The recession officially began in the United States in December 2007, but as early as 2006, some indicators in several industries and regional economies foreshadowed the impending turmoil. Residential construction activity began declining rapidly in the South and West during the second half of 2006. By mid-2008, the crisis had spread to the financial sector and then more broadly throughout the economy. Between the end of 2007 and the middle of 2009, real GDP contracted by 4 percent (Bureau of Economic Analysis 2010) and the US labor market lost nearly 7 million jobs (Bureau of Labor Statistics 2010).[1] Most of the damage—over 80 percent of the decline in real GDP and nearly 60 percent of the total fall in employment—occurred during the severe phase of the recession, which ran from the third quarter of 2008 to the first quarter of 2009 (Eichengreen and O'Rourke 2009).

Immigrants in the US Labor Market

Over the past two decades, a rapidly growing US economy attracted large numbers of immigrants. Between 1990 and 2007, the immigrant population grew from 7.9 percent to 12.6 percent of the total

---

1   Data reflect the change between the fourth quarter of 2007 and the second quarter
    of 2009.

Figure US-1: Unemployment rate of native- and foreign-born workers, 2000 to 2009

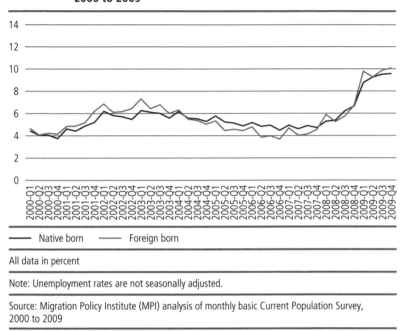

—— Native born   —— Foreign born

All data in percent

Note: Unemployment rates are not seasonally adjusted.

Source: Migration Policy Institute (MPI) analysis of monthly basic Current Population Survey, 2000 to 2009

population—a share not recorded since the tail end of the last great wave of immigration in the 1920s. Unemployment among immigrants in the United States is somewhat more cyclical than among natives (Orrenius and Zavodny 2009). But, in contrast to many European countries, US immigrant and native unemployment track each other very closely and almost never diverge by more than one percentage point. The current recession has been no exception, as Figure US-1 shows.[2] Severe job losses hit both groups, with a slightly higher

2 The data for this and other charts on the United States are taken from the Monthly Basic Current Population Survey (CPS) microdata made available by the US Census Bureau. The data are pooled into quarters. This analysis comes with the caveat that CPS is known to undercount immigrants, many of whom are not sampled because they move frequently, live in nonstandard housing or are hesitant to interact with US government representatives. However, CPS remains the most useful and detailed periodic source of information on immigrants in the US labor market.

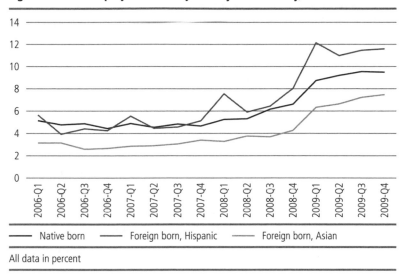

—— Native born   —— Foreign born, Hispanic   —— Foreign born, Asian

All data in percent

Note: Unemployment rates are not seasonally adjusted.

Source: MPI analysis of monthly basic Current Population Survey, 2006 to 2009

increase for immigrants. Since the first quarter of 2009, unemployment has stabilized for both groups.

But the immigrant population in the United States is incredibly diverse, and the aggregate data hide substantial differences in the experiences of various segments of the foreign-born population over the course of the recession. Figure US-2 shows how unemployment has evolved for Hispanic and Asian immigrants compared to the US born.[3] Hispanic immigrants have fared significantly worse than natives, while Asians have fared significantly better.

What has driven the differences in native and immigrant groups' labor market outcomes during the recession? Why have Hispanic immigrants been hardest hit, while Asian immigrants have for the most

3 Throughout this case study, we use race and ethnicity as self-reported in the CPS. We include as "Asian" those who self-identify as non-Hispanic and as "Asian only," "Hawaiian/Pacific Islander only," "White-Asian," "White-Hawaiian," "Black-Asian," "Black-Hawaiian," "American-Indian-Asian" or "Asian-Hawaiian/Pacific Islander."

part fared better than natives? Youth, males and the less educated have been among the hardest-hit workers during the recession and, in the fourth quarter of 2009, faced record unemployment rates (dating to 1948, when the data first became available).[4] On average, immigrants—and particularly Hispanic immigrants—tend to share these demographic characteristics:

- The median age of native-born workers in the labor force in 2008 and 2009 was 41, compared to 42 for Asian immigrants and 38 for Hispanic immigrants.
- About half of the native-born and Asian-immigrant labor force was male, compared to two-thirds of the Hispanic immigrant labor force.
- The median native-born worker in the labor force had some college education, whereas the median Asian immigrant in the labor force had a bachelor's degree and the median Hispanic immigrant had a high school degree or less.

But can we attribute the "immigrant penalty" in the labor market to these demographic characteristics alone? How have immigrants fared in terms of unemployment relative to comparable natives, controlling for education, gender and age?

Education[5]

Unemployment among less-educated workers is consistently higher than for better-educated workers, and the less educated are also more vulnerable to job loss during economic downturns.[6] Unemployment

---

4 Youth is defined as ages 16 to 26. US Department of Labor, Bureau of Labor Statistics, Labor Force Statistics.
5 The analysis of unemployment rates by education is limited to the population age 25 and older.
6 For the purpose of this case study, "less educated" includes individuals with a high school degree or less, and "highly educated" includes individuals with a bachelor's degree or more. The terms "highly educated" and "better educated" are used interchangeably.

Figure US-3: Unemployment rate, native and foreign born, by ethnicity and education, 2006 to 2009

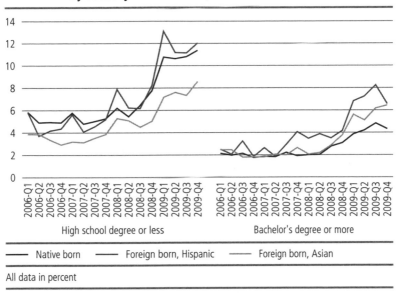

High school degree or less | Bachelor's degree or more

—— Native born —— Foreign born, Hispanic —— Foreign born, Asian

All data in percent

Note: Data are not seasonally adjusted. The unemployment rate represents unemployed as a share of the labor force (employed plus unemployed).

Source: MPI analysis of monthly basic Current Population Survey, 2006 to 2009

among less-educated natives and Hispanic immigrants has increased dramatically since the recession began, rising from around 5 percent in the fourth quarter of 2007 to nearly 12 percent in the fourth quarter of 2009 (see Figure US-3). Less-educated Asian immigrants faced lower unemployment prior to the recession and have fared somewhat better since the economic crisis began, with unemployment rising from 4 percent to 8 percent over the same period. However, less-educated Asian immigrants are also less likely to participate in the labor force, and their labor force participation rate has declined since the recession began. By contrast, labor force participation has remained stable for natives and Hispanic immigrants. Among workers with a bachelor's degree or higher, unemployment has increased more for both Hispanic and Asian immigrants than for natives.

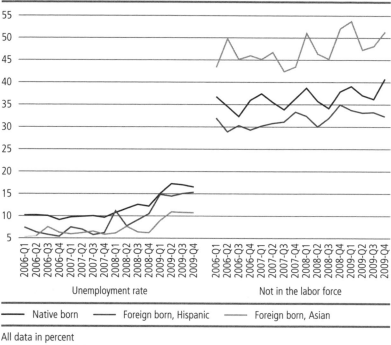

Figure US-4: Unemployment and labor force participation rate for youth age 16 to 26 by nativity and ethnicity, 2006 to 2009

Unemployment rate · Not in the labor force

—— Native born —— Foreign born, Hispanic —— Foreign born, Asian

All data in percent

Note: Data are not seasonally adjusted. The unemployment rate represents unemployed as a share of the labor force (employed plus unemployed). The labor force nonparticipation rate represents the share of all individuals age 16 and older who are not in the labor force.

Source: MPI analysis of monthly basic Current Population Survey, 2006 to 2009

Youth

The labor force behavior of both immigrant and native youth is an important focus of policymakers. Youth often move fluidly between employment, study and leisure (and, in some extreme cases, incarceration) as their individual preferences or life circumstances change. Research shows that youth is a formative period during which individuals develop lifetime work habits and attitudes. Weak labor market attachment or periods of extended unemployment during youth have long-term implications.

During recessions, youth are historically more susceptible to losing their jobs given their limited work experience and the strong seniority systems that dominate some industries. In the best of circumstances, losing a job may prompt youth to enter a new industry, start a business or return to school. However, youth who must work, often because of family obligations, face more daunting challenges. Others simply exit from the labor force with no alternative plans, joining the ranks of the so-called disconnected youth who neither work nor study.

Prior to the recession, unemployment among immigrant youth was lower than for native-born youth. It has risen for all groups since the recession began, but more for Hispanic immigrant youth than for either native youth or Asian immigrant youth (see Figure US-4). Meanwhile, labor force participation has declined more for Asian immigrant youth than for native-born or Hispanic immigrant youth. This suggests that, on average, Hispanic immigrant youth are choosing to remain in the labor force while Asian immigrant youth are pursuing other options.

Gender

The current recession has not been gender neutral, leading some pundits to label it the "mancession" (Rampell 2009; Thompson 2009; Cook 2009). Unemployment has risen much faster for men as a result of their high concentration in industries that have fared particularly poorly, notably, in construction and finance. The inverse is also true: Women tend to be concentrated in industries, such as health care, that have continued to grow despite the broader economic downturn.

However, this trend appears to be largely driven by the native born. Among Asian immigrants, unemployment has increased similarly for both men and women (see Figure US-5). Among Hispanic immigrants, male unemployment has increased dramatically since the recession began. But Hispanic immigrant women faced higher

Figure US-5: Unemployment rate by nativity, ethnicity and gender, 2006 to 2009

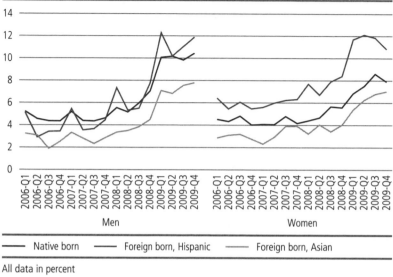

Men   Women

—— Native born   —— Foreign born, Hispanic   —— Foreign born, Asian

All data in percent

Note: Data are not seasonally adjusted. The unemployment rate represents unemployed as a share of the labor force (employed plus unemployed).

Source: MPI analysis of monthly basic Current Population Survey, 2006 to 2009

unemployment prior to the recession, and the two rates have now converged. Although it is too early to identify a trend, unemployment among Hispanic immigrant women began declining in late 2009, while it continued to increase for Hispanic immigrant men, suggesting that the labor market for Hispanic immigrant women might recover sooner than for Hispanic immigrant men.

Underemployment and Labor Force Marginalization

Official unemployment and labor force participation rates do not tell the full story of how workers fare in the labor market during recessions. Unemployment rates measure the numbers of workers who are not currently employed but who have actively searched for employment during the previous four weeks. As a result, the data may overlook other forms of labor market hardship or vulnerability, including *underemployment* and *labor force marginalization* (i.e., long-term unemployment and exit from the labor force due to the perception that no jobs are available). Underemployment is principally a concern for immigrants with high labor force attachment (e.g., youth, unauthorized immigrants), while labor force marginalization is more of a concern for workers with lower labor force attachment (e.g., less-skilled natives, naturalized citizens) (Slack and Jensen 2007; De Jong and Madamba 2001; Layard, Nickell and Jackman 2005).

US-born workers are typically more likely to work in part-time jobs (before the recession, about 18 percent of employed US-born workers held part-time jobs, compared to about 13 percent of employed immigrants). However, this gap has narrowed during the recession as a result of the substantial increase in part-time working among Hispanic immigrants. Meanwhile, Asian immigrants have seen essentially no change in part-time work trends (MPI analysis of monthly basic Current Population Survey, 2006 to 2009).

Some workers may prefer to work part time, and the decision to forego full-time employment is often voluntary (e.g., students, new parents and workers moving incrementally toward full retirement). However, many workers also accept part-time work because they are unable to find full-time employment. These workers are known as *involuntary part-time workers*. The share of part-time workers who would have preferred to work full-time is much higher for Hispanic immigrants than for the US born. By late 2009, more than half of part-time Hispanic immigrant workers could be considered underemployed (Figure US-6). Asian immigrants, by contrast, were roughly comparable to natives until the severe stages of the recession, when they saw a moderate spike in involuntary part-time employment.

Since the recession began, the average duration of unemployment has increased for all groups in the United States. Long-term unemployment, lasting 27 weeks or more, is of particular concern for policymakers because, in most states, workers lose unemployment bene-

Figure US-6: Involuntary part-time workers as a share of all part-time workers by nativity and ethnicity, 2006 to 2009

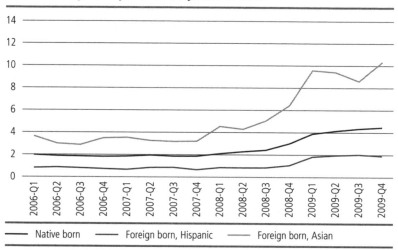

All data in percent

Note: Includes employed workers age 16 and older. Data are not seasonally adjusted. Involuntary part-time workers include those who worked part-time due to slack work or business conditions or because they could only find part-time work.

Source: MPI analysis of monthly basic Current Population Survey, 2006 to 2009

fits after 26 weeks.[7] Similar to overall unemployment rates, long-term unemployment rates among the native and foreign born track each other fairly closely. But Asian immigrants face higher long-term unemployment than Hispanic immigrants (see Figure US-7). As of late 2009, more than one of every four unemployed Asian immigrants and about one-third of Hispanic immigrants had been out of work for 27 weeks or longer. The number of discouraged workers (individuals who are not currently employed and are available for work, but who

7   During periods of high unemployment, the US government can extend this period, as it did in February and November 2009 and March and April 2010. Eligibility requirements for unemployment insurance are determined at the state level. Among other criteria, it is based on time spent in formal employment and is limited to those whose employment is involuntarily terminated. States may include additional criteria. The legally employed foreign born are eligible for unemployment insurance in all states.

Figure US-7: Long-term unemployed as a share of total unemployment by nativity and ethnicity, 2006 to 2009

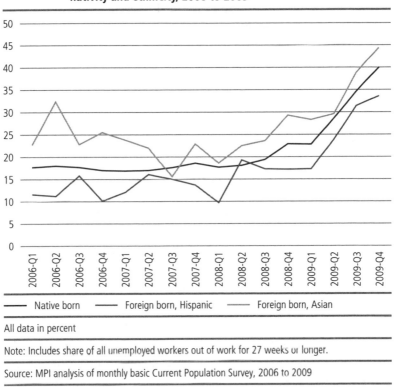

Native born ——— Foreign born, Hispanic ——— Foreign born, Asian

All data in percent

Note: Includes share of all unemployed workers out of work for 27 weeks or longer.

Source: MPI analysis of monthly basic Current Population Survey, 2006 to 2009

have given up actively searching for a job because they feel that none is available to match their skills) has also grown faster among Hispanic and Asian immigrants than among natives.

Policy Responses: Is Doing Nothing Doing Enough?

On the immigration policy front, the recession has proven to be neither the catastrophe that many pessimists predicted nor the catalyst for reform that many advocates desired. Fears of an anti-immigrant backlash did not materialize, and the political dialogue on immigration has moderated in some respects (Migration Information Source 2009). State legislatures, which became increasingly active on immigration during the years leading up to the recession, have been remarkably quiet, presumably occupied with the task of balancing contracting state budgets.[8] Immigration reform has not advanced in the US Congress and has been subordinated to other policy priorities, such as health-care reform and financial regulation. Early attempts by the 111th Congress to prohibit financial institutions receiving public support under the Troubled Assets Relief Program (TARP) from hiring foreign workers on temporary visas quickly faded away. Bureaucratic changes in the administration of immigration policies—notably, moves by the Department of Homeland Security toward a greater emphasis on employer enforcement and apprehension of criminal aliens—are widely considered the result of the power shift in Washington associated with the 2008 elections, independent of the economic crisis (Migration Information Source 2009a).

If anything, the recession has coincided with a shift in the immigration policy debate away from immigration reform toward social policy and immigrants' access to the safety net for low-income workers. Most famously, the question of legal and unauthorized immigrants' access to publicly subsidized medical attention briefly dominated the debate on health-care reform in the fall of 2009 (Capps, Rosenblum and Fix 2009). At the state level, budget cuts have eliminated many services to low-income populations, including immigrants.[9] Other federal initiatives, such as pending reforms to the country's major student aid and higher education, elementary and secondary education and workforce training laws hold important implications for how immigrants (and especially less-educated immigrants) will fare in the US labor market over the course of the recovery.

8 See the Migration Policy Institute's National Center for Immigrant Integration Policy's database of state immigration-related legislation.
9 The Center on Budget and Policy Priorities (CBPP) has closely tracked the evolution of state budget cuts in a series of reports. Cf., for instance, Johnson, Oliff and Williams 2010. The California Immigrant Policy Center provides occasional updates on immigrant-relevant budget cuts in California; cf. www.caimmigrant.org.

A substantial portion of immigration flows appears to have responded relatively quickly to the changing labor market. In 2009, it took about nine months to fill the annual quota for highly skilled temporary worker (H-1B) visas for the next fiscal year—a sharp increase over the days or weeks it typically took in prior years to fill the quota. Perhaps more remarkably, the inflow of unauthorized immigrants slowed substantially starting in 2007, almost in sync with the decline of the US residential housing market.[10] However, the outflow of unauthorized immigrants appears to have remained constant. Analysis of return-migration flows to Mexico suggests that outflows from the United States declined in 2007 but then returned to long-term trends in early 2008 (Rendall, Brownell and Kups 2009). Presumably this slowdown in return migration was due, in part, to the prospect of a legalization program as Congress debated immigration reform in early 2007. Return migration to Mexico slowed again during the severe phase of the recession, in the third and fourth quarters of 2008, as individuals held off on a wide range of long-term decisions, but it has since returned to normal.

On balance, the flexibility of unauthorized immigrant inflows likely contributed to moderating the increase in unemployment among Hispanic immigrants observed in this section. On the other hand, the relative rigidity of outflows probably contributed to the rapidly rising unemployment rate among Hispanic immigrants. This is in stark contrast to the United Kingdom, where both inflows and outflows of less-skilled workers are more responsive to labor market conditions in the framework of European labor mobility liberalization.

What Explains the "Hispanic Recession"?

The data presented in the preceding sections describe the diversity of experiences within the immigrant population over the course of the recession. However, they overwhelmingly point to the daunting chal-

10 The authors are indebted to Pia Orrenius of the Federal Reserve Bank of Dallas for this observation.

lenges facing Hispanic immigrants in the US labor market. Unemployment and underemployment have increased more dramatically among Hispanic immigrants than among natives or Asian immigrants. (One exception is long-term unemployment, which has grown dramatically among the Asian immigrant population, but this likely reflects Hispanics' strong attachment to the labor force out of necessity rather than preference.) In some cases, this reflected Hispanic immigrants' relative youth, low levels of formal education and concentration in male-dominated industries. For others, including many highly skilled immigrants, limited English proficiency and difficulty translating credentials obtained abroad slowed upward occupational and wage mobility (Batalova and Fix 2008). For unauthorized immigrants, the lack of legal immigration status was (and still is) a seemingly insurmountable barrier to advancing beyond the low-wage labor market.

The poor labor market performance of Hispanic immigrants over the course of the recession is most likely the result of both demography and policy. Hispanic immigrants' demographic and labor force characteristics group them among the workers most vulnerable to job loss during a downturn. As has been widely observed, it is also the result of US immigration policies that "lock in" unauthorized immigrants, effectively limiting the flexibility of the low-skilled labor market. But US social welfare policies that exclude many legal and unauthorized immigrants from basic labor market protections also contribute to this vulnerability.

Challenges to Immigrants' Labor Market Integration

Historically, the workforce has been a powerful immigrant-integrating institution in the United States, enabling immigrants to earn family-sustaining wages, escape from poverty and achieve upward socioeconomic mobility. During the years immediately prior to the recession, the story of immigrants' integration into the US labor force was more mixed. In general, the foreign born had high labor force participation, but they were also more likely to occupy low-paying jobs. Moreover, since 1996, noncitizens have been excluded from most of the federal means-tested public benefits (i.e., mandatory public support provided by the federal government to low-income households) that moderate poverty and promote intergenerational economic mobility among native-born households.[11] Despite many challenges, a growing economy during the 1990s and early 2000s provided ample opportunity for immigrants and especially their children to gradually improve their status over time (Haskins 2008).

The recession has reversed many of these gains, especially for Hispanic immigrants. Poverty increased 2.5 percentage points among immigrants (from 15.3 percent to 17.8 percent) between 2006 and 2008, compared to an increase of 0.7 percentage points among natives (from 12.0 percent to 12.7 percent).[12] Poverty data through the severe phase of the recession, which started in late 2008, are not yet available, but if the data presented in this case study are considered an advance indicator, it likely increased markedly in 2009. Perhaps more critically, the recession has exposed an underlying weakness in the longstanding assumption that, as in the past, a dynamic labor market alone would effectively integrate the latest wave of immigrants into the United States. A growing body of research points to the importance of the social safety net in limiting the intergenerational transmission of poverty among less-educated natives (cf. the work of the Economic Mobility Project; also Haskins, Isaacs and Sawhill 2008). The role of policy in ensuring (or hindering) immigrants' success in the labor market is less understood.

Recent evidence suggests that the recession most likely ended toward the end of 2009 (Bureau of Economic Analysis 2010). But the recovery is still fragile, and there are credible fears of a second con-

11 In the past, some states allocated state funds to provide some means-tested benefits to legal permanent immigrants, but state fiscal crises, notably in California, have forced cuts to these supplemental programs. On immigrants' vulnerability to the business cycle, cf. Orrenius and Zavodny 2009. On immigrants' access to the social safety net, cf. Fix 2009.

12 MPI analysis of the March Socio-economic Supplements to the 2007 and 2009 Current Population Surveys.

traction (Roubini 2010). Economists estimate that the United States must create about 100,000 jobs each month if employment is to keep pace with demographic growth (Bernanke 2009). As of February 2010, the US economy continued to lose jobs, albeit at a much slower pace than in 2009. With 14.9 million unemployed in February 2010 compared to 7.7 million in December 2007, it will likely take years before the unemployment rate returns to precrisis levels. When it does arrive, the recovery is expected to be slow with stubbornly high unemployment. *The Wall Street Journal's* economic forecasting service recently estimated that about one-quarter of the jobs lost between December 2007 and December 2008 will not return (Izzo 2010).

The evidence presented in this case study points to broader labor market challenges for immigrants in the United States, even after job creation begins anew. In recent decades, Hispanic immigrants tended to fill low-wage jobs at the bottom of the labor market. But the less-skilled labor market has been stagnant for years, and the recession has further limited the prospects for these workers (cf. US Department of Labor, Bureau of Labor Statistics 2009). The booming economy of the past decade hid many of these longstanding tensions that the recession has now exposed.

Recession in the United Kingdom: Effects on Immigrant Workers and Integration

Madeleine Sumption

Introduction

Immigration in the United Kingdom

The global recession hit the United Kingdom at an interesting moment in the nation's immigration history. After decades of low immigration,[1] the United Kingdom experienced a significant uptick as the result of two trends: a greater openness to economic migration beginning in 1997, which facilitated a 10-year boom in immigrant numbers, and EU enlargement in 2004, which led to a dramatic and unexpected inflow of workers from Eastern Europe. All told, the foreign born grew steadily from under 9 percent of the population in the mid-1990s to 13 percent on the eve of the recession in 2007.[2]

---

1   A wave of immigration from British Commonwealth countries during the 1950s and 1960s came to an end in the 1970s with the introduction of restrictive policies aiming to achieve zero net immigration. For more background on UK immigration history, cf. Somerville, Sriskandarajah and Latorre 2009.
2   Immigrants are defined in this case study by place of birth, not by nationality. The data for this and other charts on the United Kingdom are taken from the Quarterly Labour Force Survey (LFS) microdata, made available by the UK Data Archive. The most recent data available at the time of writing was the first quarter of 2010. The analysis comes with the caveat that the LFS is known to undercount migrants, many of whom are not sampled because they move frequently or live in public or nonprofit communal accommodation. However, the LFS remains the most useful and detailed source of information on immigrant workers.

Despite sustained economic growth, public concerns about immigration grew with the size of the inflows. In response, the Labour government introduced a series of structural reforms. These included a points-based system for admitting skilled immigrants and students, the phasing-out of low-skilled immigration from outside the European Union and the introduction of an independent committee of economists with a mandate to advise the government on the economics of immigration and identify labor market shortages. The election of a new Conservative-Liberal Democrat coalition in May 2010 promises yet more changes to the UK immigration system, including, most notably, the introduction of a cap on non-EU economic migration.

At the onset of the economic crisis in mid-2008, about 30 percent of the foreign-born population came from old and new EU Member States, about one-fifth was from the Indian subcontinent (Bangladesh, India, Pakistan and Sri Lanka) and just under a fifth came from African countries.[3] On the whole, immigrants are more highly educated than the UK born.[4] However, wage rates do not reflect this additional education, and employed immigrants earn roughly comparable wages to the UK born. The gap between immigrant and native hourly wages has moved from slightly positive to slightly negative for immigrants in recent years, in part due to the arrival of EU nationals concentrated in less-skilled occupations. At the end of 2009, the median hourly wage for A8-born[5] workers was about two-thirds that of natives.[6]

---

3 Author's calculations from the Labour Force Survey.
4 Foreign-born labor-force participants between the ages of 25 and 65 had, on average, left school at the age of 20, compared to 17 for their UK-born counterparts. Author's calculations from the Labour Force Survey.
5 A8 refers to the eight Eastern European countries that joined the European Union in May 2004: the Czech Republic, Estonia, Hungary, Latvia, Lithuania, Poland, Slovakia and Slovenia.
6 Author's calculations from the LFS. The sample includes all individuals with non-zero wages.

The 2008–2009 Recession

The UK recession began in early 2008, accompanied by a particularly severe banking crisis and the end of a long housing-market boom. GDP contracted more sharply than in the United States or the EU eurozone, falling by 6 percent from the beginning of 2008 to mid-2009, and house prices fell by 7.4 percent in 2009 alone (Whiffin and Pimlott 2010). A 0.1 percent GDP increase barely pulled the United Kingdom out of recession in the fourth quarter of 2009. As of mid-2010, economic recovery was expected to be relatively slow for at least 18 months, outpacing the European Union but lagging behind the United States (International Monetary Fund [IMF] 2010).

Nonetheless, the recession's impact on the labor market has been relatively modest and much lower than feared. Employment fell by 2.8 percent from the spring of 2008 to the end of 2009, much less than the contraction in GDP (Office for National Statistics 2010a). Unemployment rose to 8 percent in early 2010 from a 2005 low of just under 5 percent, and long-term unemployment rose from just over one-third of the unemployed to just under one-half over the same period.[7] Young workers and the least skilled were worst affected, with unemployment reaching 18 percent among 18- to 24-year-olds in early 2010 (Office for National Statistics 2010b).

The relatively modest labor market impact appears to result at least in part from the fact that cutbacks have been shared across the workforce, with fewer people holding multiple jobs, more part-time working, pay freezes for 35 percent of private-sector workers, greater use of voluntary unpaid leave and short-time working, and a decline in labor productivity (Chamberlain 2010). "Labor hoarding" has been more common in this recession than in previous downturns, perhaps because increasing education levels in the UK workforce, the growth in the proportion of highly skilled occupations and an increase in skill requirements within occupations appear to have made the average em-

---

7 Author's calculations from the LFS, 2005–2010. Long-term unemployment rates over the period are about the same for immigrants and the UK born.

63

ployer more willing to retain staff even at the cost of low productivity (Lambert 2010). As employers take up the slack that has accumulated during the recession, employment growth is likely to remain slow.

In addition, the outlook for economic growth in the coming years is unclear, primarily because of the United Kingdom's large fiscal deficit and the advent of policies designed to reduce it. Sharp cuts in government spending are being introduced, the bulk of which will take effect in or after the spring of 2011, while some public spending has already been cancelled. Economists remain divided over the speed with which the United Kingdom can cut the deficit without hurting the economic recovery. As of mid-2010, forecasts suggested that unemployment would not drop substantially even by the end of 2011 (HM Treasury 2010) and that the labor market recovery will depend to a large extent on whether the United Kingdom can maintain reasonable growth despite the fiscal consolidation.

The Impact of the Recession on Immigrants

This case study examines the labor market performance of various immigrant groups over the past few years, focusing on unemployment.[8] Immigrants have historically experienced higher unemployment than UK-born workers, regardless of economic conditions. During the boom of the early- to mid-2000s, immigrants' unemployment rate averaged 2–3 percentage points higher than the rate for natives, as shown in Figure UK-1. With the onset of the recession, unemployment rose among both groups. The size of the gap between them, however, remained essentially unchanged. In other words, when we consider immigrants as a single group, the crisis does not appear to have affected immigrants disproportionately.

---

8   Unemployment is not, of course, the only measure of how hard the recession has hit UK workers in the labor market. Employment, labor force participation, wages and underemployment all provide different angles on this question. However, in the interest of brevity, and to facilitate comparisons across groups, this case study focuses exclusively on unemployment rates.

Figure UK-1: UK native and immigrant unemployment rates, 2004 to 2009

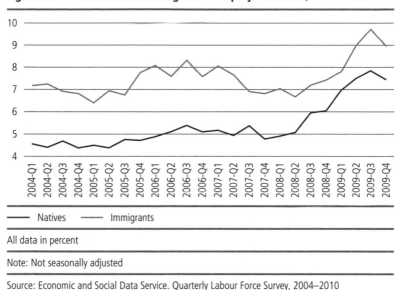

All data in percent

Note: Not seasonally adjusted

Source: Economic and Social Data Service. Quarterly Labour Force Survey, 2004–2010

These aggregate trends mask some substantial differences between groups. Some immigrant groups had much higher prerecession unemployment than others, and not all saw increases of the same magnitude. For example, unemployment rose more, from a higher base, for immigrants from Africa and the Indian subcontinent, reaching approximately 15 percent and 12 percent, respectively, in the third quarter of 2009 (together, these regions make up almost two-fifths of the UK foreign-born population). On the other hand, recent immigrants from the A8 countries (which had lower incomes than the EU average)[9] as well as some advanced industrialized nations in the EU-15[10] and North America fared as well as or better than the UK born (see Figure UK-2).

9 The data do not include the higher-income accession countries Cyprus and Malta. They also do not include Romania and Bulgaria, which joined the European Union in 2007 and still face significant restrictions on their labor market access in the United Kingdom.

10 EU-15 countries are those that were Member States prior to EU enlargement: Austria, Belgium, Denmark, Finland, France, Germany, Greece, Ireland, Italy, Luxembourg, the Netherlands, Portugal, Spain, Sweden and the United Kingdom.

Figure UK-2: UK unemployment in Q3 2007 and Q3 2009 by selected region of origin

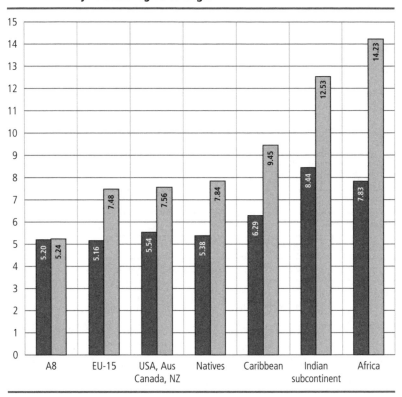

Q3 2007 ■   Q3 2009 □

All data in percent

Note: Due to sample-size limitations, small to moderate changes in the unemployment rate for immigrant groups are not necessarily statistically significant.

Source: Economic and Social Data Service. Quarterly Labour Force Survey, July–September 2006 and 2009

What drives these large differences between groups? Why have workers from Africa and the Indian subcontinent fared least well, while EU and North American immigrants have escaped the worst of the recession's impact? In the following section, we explore some factors that have driven immigrants' vulnerability to the economic cycle and that might explain some of these differences. The data show that education, language, minority status, age, gender and the level of economic development in source countries have all shaped immigrant workers' unemployment over the past two years. Less-educated immigrants, those from less-wealthy source countries, workers who do not speak English at home and those belonging to ethnic minorities have experienced high and often sharply increasing unemployment during the economic crisis. In general, the workers who struggled most in the UK labor market before the recession have been the same groups that lost most ground during its course, while those who fared well during the boom have been more insulated from the recession's impact. Modes of entry (whether through family, employment-based or humanitarian channels) also appear to be important, but data limitations mean that only suggestive evidence is available to show this.

Characteristics of the Country of Origin

The level of economic development in an immigrant's country of origin has tracked unemployment rates remarkably closely over the past two years, as shown in Figure UK-3.[11] This trend is probably less a reflection of economic development per se and more about the characteristics of immigrants who gain entry from different source regions and the circumstances under which they come.

Wealthier countries have been the beneficiaries of more relaxed immigration policies. Twenty-five EU Member States receive free labor market access, while skilled workers from wealthy Organisation for Economic Co-operation and Development (OECD) countries can migrate with relative ease. By contrast, workers from less-wealthy

11 Income data is purchasing power parity-adjusted, from the IMF World Economic Outlook Database 2009. Calculations using this data do not include a small fraction of immigrants for whom precise countries of origin are not specified in the LFS (e.g., "Caribbean"). Countries not ranked in the 2009 IMF calculations are assigned to income groups, where possible, based on estimates in the *CIA World Factbook* (CIA 2010).

Figure UK-3: UK unemployment in Q3 2007 and Q3 2009 by 2009 per capita GDP of country of origin

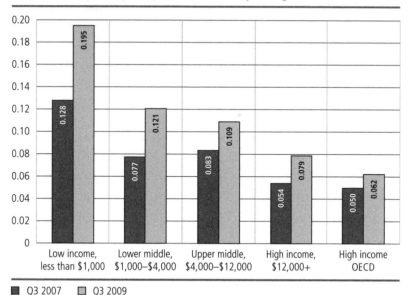

	Low income, less than $1,000	Lower middle, $1,000–$4,000	Upper middle, $4,000–$12,000	High income, $12,000+	High income OECD
Q3 2007	0.128	0.077	0.083	0.054	0.050
Q3 2009	0.195	0.121	0.109	0.079	0.062

■ Q3 2007   □ Q3 2009

All data in proportion unemployed

Source: Author's calculations from the Labour Force Survey using International Monetary Fund (IMF) and Central Intelligence Agency (CIA) data on GDP, adjusted for purchasing power differences.

countries are more likely to be illegally resident—a factor that may have hurt their labor market prospects. Meanwhile, a greater proportion of immigrants from poorer source countries are humanitarian entrants, a group that tends to face particular difficulties in the labor market (not least because of rules that forbid asylum seekers from working). While the data do not identify refugee status, it is telling that some of the national groups with the highest unemployment rates are among the largest refugee and asylum-seeker groups in the United Kingdom. Of the countries that are large enough to analyze individually in the Labour Force Survey, two stand out: immigrants born in Somalia and Iraq (two substantial humanitarian source countries). Both experienced unemployment of over 30 percent in the second and third quarters of 2009.[12]

In addition, some of this trend almost certainly results from differences in human capital. Less-wealthy source countries tend to have less-developed educational institutions, so that the same years of schooling do not generate the same returns; curricula and work experiences in those source countries are less likely to be aligned to employers' needs in an advanced industrialized economy, such as the United Kingdom; and immigrants from these countries are more likely to lack English language skills.[13] Meanwhile, a much greater proportion of immigrants from low-income countries belong to visible minority groups that may fall victim to employer discrimination (over 90 percent of immigrants from "lower-middle-income" countries with per capita GDP of $1,000 to $4,000 are minorities, compared to about 5 percent of those from high-income OECD countries, for example. The impact of minority status is discussed shortly).

Education

A second undeniable trend emerging from the crisis is that less-educated workers have fared worse within all major groups, whether native or immigrant. Figure UK-4 shows unemployment for natives and all immigrants in a low- and high-education category (defined as those who left school at 16 years or less or 18 years or more, respectively).[14]

By late 2009, less-educated immigrants had the highest unemployment rates of the four groups shown: approximately 12 percent. Within

12 About 50 percent of grants of settlement to Iraqi immigrants in 2008 were made on humanitarian grounds. Somalia also has a longstanding humanitarian population in the United Kingdom (Home Office 2009).
13 Under the World Bank classification system used here, "lower-middle-income" countries with per capita GDP of $1,000 to $4,000 had the highest proportion of immigrants who spoke a language other than English at home (50 percent); the proportion was lowest for high-income OECD immigrants (about one-quarter).
14 Since the LFS does not contain reliable educational information for immigrants, we use the age at which the individual left full-time education as a proxy.

Figure UK-4: UK unemployment rate by education level and birth status, 2004 to 2009

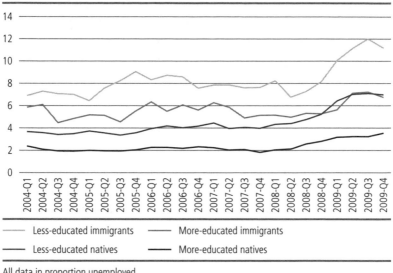

Less-educated immigrants ——— More-educated immigrants
Less-educated natives ——— More-educated natives

All data in proportion unemployed

Note: "Less educated" comprises workers who left full-time education at the age of 16 or earlier; "more educated" comprises those who left full-time education at 18 years or older.

Source: Economic and Social Data Service. Quarterly Labour Force Survey, 2004–2009

both the immigrant and native populations, less-educated workers fared worse; and within both the high and low education groups, immigrants fared worse. This education effect may help to explain why the highly educated Eastern European migrants have maintained such low unemployment rates.

Of course, educational attainment or school-leaving ages do not necessarily mean the same thing across countries. Even in the complete absence of discrimination, immigrants educated abroad may "need" more years of schooling in order to reach the same level of UK-relevant human capital as a worker educated in the United Kingdom. This means that educational attainment does not necessarily explain differences between national groups with much accuracy; but it does explain differences within groups—that is, how Germans fare relative to other Germans or Indians relative to other Indians. (Indeed, workers from the Indian subcontinent and Africa have a higher median school-leaving age than EU-15 immigrants but have experienced significantly higher unemployment.)

Language

Differences between immigrant groups also arise from trends in language ability. The Labour Force Survey identifies individuals who speak a language other than English at home.[15] We can therefore compare unemployment and the change in unemployment from the peak of the economic expansion to the depths of the recession in late 2009.

In both 2006 and 2009, unemployment was higher for immigrants who spoke a language other than English at home. In 2009, over 11 percent of immigrants who spoke another language at home were unemployed, compared to between 8 percent and 9 percent for English speakers. Immigrants who came from low-income countries *and* spoke another language at home saw unemployment approaching an estimated 30 percent (author's calculations from the LFS). However, the *change* in unemployment between 2006 and 2009 did not differ significantly by language spoken.

Minority Status

Members of visible ethnic minorities—both immigrants and natives—had higher precrisis unemployment than white ethnic groups and also saw steeper increases in unemployment during the recession.[16]

---

15 Unfortunately, the data do not indicate language *ability*. We assume, for the purposes of this analysis, that immigrants who speak another language at home have, on average, lower language ability, although this of course will not be universally the case.

16 Minorities are defined as ethnic Asian, black, ethnic Chinese or mixed race, as reported in the LFS. The "other ethnic group" category is excluded from the analysis, as it includes many immigrants from countries with overwhelmingly white ethnic populations, who did not self-report as white.

Figure UK-5: UK unemployment by minority status and nativity, 2004 to 2009

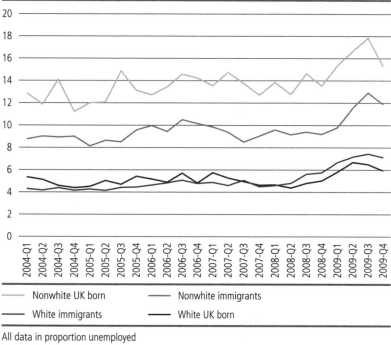

— Nonwhite UK born   — Nonwhite immigrants

— White immigrants   — White UK born

All data in proportion unemployed

Note: Excludes individuals who identify their ethnicity as "other race." Not seasonally adjusted.

Source: Economic and Social Data Service. Quarterly Labour Force Survey, 2004–2009

However, the most striking trend is that native-born visible minorities were more likely to experience high unemployment than immigrants.[17] UK-born minorities, a group that largely comprises second-generation children of immigrants who arrived from former colonies in the post-World War II period, saw the highest unemployment rates of all groups. Nonwhite immigrants have fared somewhat better but still reached unemployment levels of over 12 percent. Meanwhile, white workers have fared comparably, whether native or immigrant,

17 This mirrors trends found in the United States, among other countries.

so there does not appear to be an "immigrant penalty" for workers who are white.

The reasons for these differences are, of course, highly complex. A substantial volume of research shows that higher unemployment among second-generation workers from black African, black Caribbean and Indian/Pakistani/Bangladeshi ethnic groups cannot be explained by differences in demographic and educational characteristics and that higher education levels do not translate as effectively into better labor market prospects for many ethnic minorities as they do for white British groups.[18] Some of this disadvantage arises from employer discrimination.[19] But it also likely reflects persisting inequality between generations in a country with relatively low income mobility (D'Addio 2007): nonwhite groups are more likely to hail from low-income source countries. Even within income groups, however, minorities have higher unemployment rates than white workers.[20]

Age and Gender

Young workers and men have faced particularly high unemployment rates during the crisis. How has this affected the immigrant-native gap in employment prospects in the United Kingdom? Two interesting trends become clear when we disaggregate the data by gender and age.

First, the immigrant-native gap in unemployment during the recession essentially disappears if we limit the analysis to men. In mid-2009, immigrant and native men both saw unemployment of approximately 9 percent, as did immigrant women. UK-born women, on the other hand, were unemployed at a significantly lower rate, of 6.4 percent.

18 For a summary, cf. National Equality Panel 2010.
19 Resume testing experiments have shown that job applicants with names associated with a minority ethnic group are less likely to be called to interview than those with "white-sounding" names. Cf. ibid.: 234.
20 For example, white workers from upper-middle and high-income countries have similar unemployment rates, of approximately 8 percent, while minorities from the same countries have unemployment rates of over 12 percent. Author's calculations from the LFS, third quarter of 2009.

Second, the "immigrant penalty" in unemployment rates also disappears when we consider only youth. About 18 percent of young workers (defined here as 16- to 26-year-olds) were unemployed regardless of their place of birth. For older workers (age 27 and above), the immigrant-native gap remained roughly constant, at about 3 percentage points, before and during the recession.

UK Immigration Policy during the Recession

The UK government has essentially no control over immigration flows from EU Member States, which made up around half of all labor immigration to the United Kingdom at the peak of the economic expansion (Migration Advisory Committee [MAC] 2008). (It still retains discretion over immigration from Romania and Bulgaria, although nationals from these two countries must gain full labor market access to all EU Member States by 2014.) However, immigration from Eastern Europe collapsed of its own accord with the onset of the economic crisis. Other inflows have also seen modest declines, although it is difficult to differentiate the impact of the recession from that of the newly reformed UK immigration system, which became fully operational in 2008.

In response to the economic turmoil (and the less-forgiving public attitudes toward immigration that came with it), the government introduced policies to reduce immigration in some of the areas over which it has genuine discretion. It adjusted the criteria for entry under the highly skilled migrant program—an entry route that does not require a job offer and, hence, creates concern over "scarring" effects, whereby workers who immigrate into a weak labor market suffer longer-term setbacks.[21] The government also added regulations to

---

21 Beginning on March 31, 2009, applicants under "Tier 1" of the points-based system required a master's degree, whereas a bachelor's degree was previously sufficient to be eligible for the program. In April 2010, this decision was reversed, allowing applicants to earn points for a bachelor's degree.

the Tier 2 employer-sponsored entry route,[22] requiring employers to advertise more jobs to UK workers; and it took up recommendations from the MAC that effectively reduced the number of "shortage" occupations for which workers can more easily qualify for a work permit. In December 2008, the government announced that restrictions on the right of Romanians and Bulgarians to work in the United Kingdom would remain in place (in a decision that was also based on a MAC recommendation).

Immigration loomed large in the spring 2010 election campaign, that ultimately brought an end to a 13-year-old Labour government, replacing it with a Conservative-Liberal Democrat coalition (a rare outcome in a country with a voting system that usually produces substantial one-party majorities). Soon after coming to power, the coalition government began a consultation on the implementation of an immigration cap. This policy was not presented as a response to the recession but, rather, as a response to the consistently high immigration levels of the previous decade. However, recession-related concerns may have fed into the cap policy's widespread popularity.

Tightening Public Finances and Government Spending on Integration

The United Kingdom faces a substantial budget deficit, and elevated unemployment could exert steady pressure on public finances for several years. The new government has pledged to cut the deficit substantially faster than its predecessor (in addition to the cuts proposed by the outgoing Labour government, the Conservative-Liberal Democrat government plans to cut more than half as much again) (Chote 2010). Likewise, in June 2010, the coalition's emergency budget outlined a fiscal consolidation of about 6 percent of GDP (Tetlow 2010), powered by cuts of up to 25 percent in the budgets of government departments, the details of which were expected to emerge from a

---

22 Under the UK points system, Tier 1 labor immigrants are selected on the basis of their skills alone, while Tier 2 labor immigrants require a job offer.

spending review in October 2010. The new approach has been described as the "longest, deepest sustained period of cuts to public services spending at least since World War II" (ibid.).

The United Kingdom devotes few hard funds to immigrant integration and, for historical reasons, most integration funding targets ethnic minorities rather than first-generation immigrants.[23] Immigration-specific funding is used primarily to support "social cohesion" in communities hosting high numbers of immigrants rather than the immigrants themselves (although some of these funds are spent on services such as English language instruction). Approximately £300 million ($465 million)[24] per year is devoted to funding language training for particularly vulnerable immigrant groups (Department for Innovation, Universities and Skills 2009). Spending such as this may be vulnerable to budget cuts that are likely to affect almost all departments over the next few years, given the significant public deficit the United Kingdom currently faces.

Meanwhile, welfare expenditures on immigrants during the recession have been limited to some extent by restrictions on benefit eligibility. New EU migrants must be continuously employed for 12 months in order to claim welfare payments, and most temporary migrants cannot receive benefits. The rates at which unemployed immigrants claim benefits has increased during the recession, though less than they have among the UK born (author's calculations from the LFS). As a result, welfare spending reductions announced in the June 2010 emergency budget may have a smaller impact on immigrants. However, A8, African and Indian subcontinent immigrants are over-represented among recipients of tax credits and child benefits (author's calculations from the LFS), two programs facing cuts or freezes, so they may feel the pain of reductions in these two areas slightly more.

---

23 For example, much of the spending on English as a Second Language programs is made through the Ethnic Minority Achievement Grant available to schools.
24 Converted at the current exchange rate of £1 = $1.52 (March 14, 2010).

Conclusions

Has the United Kingdom Escaped an Immigration Boom and Bust?

The United Kingdom saw a substantial increase in net immigration during the economic expansion. However, relative to some other major immigrant-receiving countries that experienced similar growth, the newcomers' rise in unemployment has been relatively contained. Since recent arrivals typically are expected to be most vulnerable to unemployment (since they have had less time to integrate into the labor market), the concern arises that an immigration boom during economic expansion can lead to a high-unemployment bust with the onset of a recession.

Recently arrived African and Indian subcontinent immigrants have indeed experienced particularly high unemployment.[25] However, the largest recent influx—Eastern Europeans—has fared relatively well, at least through late 2009, when A8 unemployment was approximately 5 percent on average and about 4 percent for more-educated workers.[26] The low unemployment in this group is surprising for two reasons: First, A8 workers were concentrated in the two sectors that shed most jobs during the recession: construction and manufacturing.[27] Second, their relative success stands in stark contrast to Eastern Europeans in Ireland, who have been among the *worst* affected during the recession. In both countries, Eastern Europeans had very high labor force participation before the recession (above 90 percent) (see the Ireland case study in this report; cf. also Sumption and Somerville 2010). Their flows appeared highly sensitive to economic conditions (inflows peaked during the boom and collapsed with the onset of the recession). In Ireland, the Eastern European

---

25 Immigrants from these two groups who immigrated in or after 2004 experienced unemployment rates of well over 15 percent. Author's calculations from the LFS, third quarter of 2009.

26 Those who left full-time education at the age of 18 or higher. Author's calculations from the LFS, third quarter of 2009.

27 For a more comprehensive analysis of Eastern European immigrants in the United Kingdom, cf. Sumption and Somerville 2010.

population has actually declined by 15–20 percent since its peak at the end of 2007,[28] while the rapid growth of the A8 population in the United Kingdom came to a halt at the beginning of 2008, after which point the population has remained roughly constant, at about 700,000.[29] In both countries, Eastern Europeans earned lower wages than other immigrant groups and were concentrated in low-skilled, cyclical industries (see analysis in this report; cf. also Barrett and McCarthy 2007). Exposure to the construction industry was slightly greater in Ireland (just over 20 percent of Eastern Europeans at the end of 2007, compared to 14 percent over the same period in the United Kingdom),[30] and employment reductions in Irish construction were much heavier (construction employment fell by almost half and about one-eighth, respectively).

One might attribute A8 workers' relative success in a recessionary UK labor market to high education levels, the greater prevalence of temporary or short-term migration among A8 workers (compared to other immigrant flows that are more permanent in nature) (Somerville and Sumption 2009) or EU freedom of movement, which has allowed immigration flows—particularly inflows, but also to some extent outflows—to respond to economic circumstances. But the huge contrast with Ireland suggests that the reasons for low A8 unemployment require more-detailed investigation.

Whatever the case, the available evidence for the United Kingdom suggests that the boom-time immigrant influx has not led to catastrophic immigrant unemployment, in large part thanks to Eastern European workers. However, there is no guarantee that these trends will last forever. Eastern European migration to the United Kingdom is still in flux, and it may not look the same 10 years from today. Indeed, there are already signs that Eastern European workers are putting down more permanent roots in the United Kingdom and estab-

28 Calculations from Central Statistics Office Ireland's Quarterly National Household Survey (QNHS), Table A1, *Estimated number of persons aged 15 years and older classified by nationality and ILO economic status*.
29 Author's calculations from the LFS, 2004–2009.
30 Both statistics refer to the 12 new Member States that joined the European Union in 2004 and 2007: the A8, Romania, Bulgaria, Cyprus and Malta.

lishing families there in contrast to the prevailing image of the young, single and highly labor-motivated Eastern European worker (Sumption and Somerville 2010). Any changes to the nature of the A8 population in the United Kingdom will likely affect integration and the vulnerability to future economic cycles.

Other uncertainties cloud the future outlook. First, the impact of institutional reforms, including the introduction of a points-based immigration system, also remains to be seen, and policymakers will need to monitor its effect on immigrant integration. For example, how will the new Tier 1 highly skilled workers fare as they arrive in the United Kingdom without a job offer? How will the new system affect the composition of immigrants to the country, and with what implications? Second, UK policymakers will need to remain sensitive to the potential growth of increasingly transient forms of migration— from circular migration from EU Member States to short-term flows from outside the European Union and particularly India, which is now the origin of a large number of workers coming to the United Kingdom temporarily to work in sectors such as IT. These forms of migration may have declined somewhat during the recession, but in the long run, they are likely to become more widespread. The labor-integration process for these transient migrants does not follow the standard model (whereby workers gradually improve their labor market position over a period of many years). This could create new challenges to policymakers' efforts to sustain social cohesion and make the most of immigration to the United Kingdom.

Migration, Integration and the Labor Market after the Recession in Germany

Carola Burkert

Introduction

Although the world recession hit Germany more deeply than the average country in the Organisation for Economic Co-operation and Development (OECD), its effect on employment proved unexpectedly moderate. Through early 2010, the increase in unemployment in Germany was the lowest of all OECD countries. Three factors are responsible for the mild response: a huge reduction in working hours; a moderate reduction in productivity; and massive use of Germany's short-time working policy (*Kurzarbeit*), which provides subsidies when workers' hours are reduced for economic reasons.

Immigrants in Germany experienced much higher unemployment than natives before the recession, and the gap remains wide today. However, at first glance, the recession that began in 2008 has not hit migrants as hard as one might expect, and job losses have been moderate. One reason is that the recession primarily hit middle- and highly qualified people[1] and, among qualified workers, the share of migrants is low. Yet, on further review, it appears that the recession hit migrants worse in an indirect sense: They have a experienced a substantial increase in long-term unemployment.

---

1 High, middle and low qualifications refer respectively to those with a university degree, vocational training and no vocational training.

Before the crisis, many OECD countries considered increased migration as a way to remedy their labor market shortages and to compensate for declines in their population. Germany was an exception before the recession. Immigration—especially labor market immigration—was minimal even before the recession, both compared to Germany's past experience and to other countries. The inflow of highly qualified or self-employed immigrants obtaining a German permanent residence permit was already very low in 2008 (689) and increased only slightly in 2009 (896). The inflow of qualified immigrants granted a temporary residence permit did not change at all between 2008 and 2009, staying around 28,000 annually (Bundesagentur für Arbeit [BA] 2009a and 2010d).

This case study examines the global economic crisis, how it has affected the German labor market and why the impact of the recession has been so small. It analyzes the impact of the crisis on the labor market integration of migrants and on their employment and unemployment. It also discusses policy reactions to the recession and provides an outlook for the future and supplies some policy conclusions to address the structural barriers facing migrants in the labor market.

The Global Economic Crisis and the German Labor Market: Better than Expected?

The German economy was in good condition at the beginning of the crisis. In the years leading up to 2009, employment grew as a result of sustained economic growth, a moderate union wage-rate policy and labor market reforms. The global recession hit Germany harder than average in terms of GDP losses, but the effect on employment was unexpectedly mild, with Germany posting the lowest increase in unemployment of all OECD countries (see Figure DE-1).

The number of overall registered unemployed in Germany increased by around 155,000 in 2009, just 0.4 percentage points. This section analyzes the German labor market's surprisingly mild re-

Figure DE-1: Real GDP growth and change in unemployment rate for OECD countries, Q2 2008 to Q2 2009

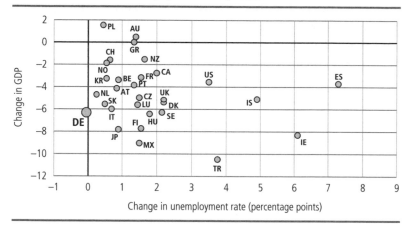

Change in unemployment rate (percentage points)

Note: Country abbreviations are: AT Austria, AU Australia, BE Belgium, CA Canada, CH Switzerland, CZ the Czech Republic, DK Denmark, ES Spain, FI Finland, FR France, DE Germany, GR Greece, HU Hungary, IE Ireland, IS Iceland, IT Italy, JP Japan, KR Korea, LU Luxembourg, MX Mexico, NL the Netherlands, NO Norway, NZ New Zealand, PL Poland, PT Portugal, SE Sweden, SK Slovakia, TR Turkey, UK the United Kingdom, US the United States.

Source: OECD, taken from Sachverständigenrat 2009, first presented in Moeller 2010.

sponse to the severe demand shock that occurred in the aftermath of the financial crisis. It draws on recent work by economist Joachim Moeller that aims to "demystify" what 2008 Nobel Prize winner Paul Krugman described as "Germany's jobs miracle" (Moeller 2010).

The 2008–2009 downturn was the sharpest in Germany since World War II. In the past, employment tracked declines in real GDP with a lag. By contrast, recent experience has been much more favorable than expected based on past experience (ibid.). Moeller discusses three main reasons for this:

First, the crisis primarily hit strong firms in economically strong regions—mainly export-oriented manufacturing firms in southern and western Germany. The rise in unemployment in these areas was early and sharp. The crisis also hit firms that had been suffering from a shortage of trained workers (*Fachkräftemangel*), which made them unwilling to lay off qualified workers.

Second, in the past, there had been increased use of flexible working hours through working-hours accounts. In the boom period, a surplus of working hours was accumulated on these accounts, and, at the beginning of the recession, a buffer stock was available. This channel of internal flexibility enabled those firms to reduce their working hours massively at a time when they were experiencing only moderate reductions in productivity. Both the sharp reduction in working hours as well as the reduction in productivity are known as "labor hoarding".

A third key factor in the mild labor market impact in Germany was the short-time working policy (*Kurzarbeit*), a subsidy program that supplements the wages of workers whose hours are reduced for economic reasons.[2] In the early 1990s, short-time work was used to dampen the structural shock from the reunification of Germany after the fall of the Soviet Union. During the recent crisis, the short-time work subsidy became a widespread instrument—mainly among export-oriented manufacturing firms in Germany's western regions. Use of the short-time work program in 2009 reached its highest level in the postreunification period. The state short-time allowance has saved jobs and thereby reduced unemployment.

Not all industrial sectors were equally affected by short-time work; it was most heavily used in manufacturing. For example, 35 percent of employees subject to social insurance contributions in the metal-production and -processing sector were short-time workers in June 2009. Engineering was strongly affected, with 24.7 percent of employees on short-time work, as was the manufacture of electrical equipment (21.9 percent) and the car industry (21.5 percent) (Bundesagentur für Arbeit 2009a).

---

2 Germany's Federal Employment Agency (Bundesagentur für Arbeit, or BA) provides funding for short-time work based on business-cycle or economic reasons under Section 170 of the Social Security Code (SGB III) if certain conditions are met (among other things, at least one-third of a company's staff must be affected by loan cuts of at least 10 percent of their monthly gross pay). If this is the case, the amount paid by BA for each eligible employee is based on 60 percent (or 67 percent for employees with children) of the flat-rate calculation of the missing net pay. Cf. Bundesministerium für Arbeit und Soziales 2010a.

The Effect of the Crisis on the Labor Market Integration of Migrants: As Bad as Expected?

Since autumn 2008, the global economic crisis has been clearly felt in the labor market statistics—particularly in the area of short-time work—although its effects are also notable in the figures for unemployment as well as employment subject to social insurance contributions.[3]

Development of Unemployment

As previously mentioned, immigrants experienced much higher unemployment than natives before the recession, and the gap remains wide today. Differences exist by gender, economic sectors, nationalities and regions. The unemployment rate was 8 percent for Germans and 17.1 percent for migrants (defined throughout this paper as foreign nationals) in February 2010 (Bundesagentur für Arbeit 2010b). The ratio between the two rates has been very stable over the last two decades, with migrant unemployment 2.5 to 2.7 times higher than the rate for natives.

In spite of the deep recession, there has been only a modest rise in overall unemployment: In the year between February 2009 to February 2010, unemployment rose from 16.9 percent to 17.1 percent for migrants (an increase of 2.5 percent, or 0.2 percentage points), and from 7.8 percent to 8.0 percent for natives (an increase of 2.6 percent, or 0.2 percentage points) (ibid.).

---

3 The data in this section are taken from BA and represent the most recent data available. The more detailed "Microcensus" data that would be necessary to examine subgroups are currently only available for 2008 and, thus, so are insufficient for our current purposes. Cf. Statistisches Bundesamt 2010. "Employment subject to social insurance contributions" comprises all employees who pay contributions to social insurance (unemployment, medical, pension). It does not include civil servants (*Beamte*), soldiers, self-employed persons and family workers (*mithelfende Familienangehörige*). The most recent data available for 2009 only covers employees subject to social insurance contributions.

Figures DE-2a and DE-2b show the enormous regional disparities in unemployment for natives as well as for migrants. Eastern Germany has far greater labor market problems than the western part. In some areas of Eastern Germany, foreign nationals' unemployment rate had reached more than 25 percent in early 2010. However, foreign-born employees are not distributed uniformly across Germany, and the highest shares of immigrant workers are in the west and south. In Germany as a whole, the foreign born make up 12.9 percent of the population. This figure includes the *Aussiedler*, that is, individuals of German descent who arrived in Germany between 1950 and 2005, primarily from Eastern Europe and the former Soviet Union. A further 6 percent have a "migration background"[4] but were born in Germany, making a total of almost 19 percent of the population with a migration background. In West Germany (including Berlin), however, individuals with a migration background make up 21.7 percent and, in East Germany, only 4.7 percent (Statistisches Bundesamt 2010). This unequal distribution is the legacy of the guest worker program operated in West Germany from 1955 to 1973. The recruitment program was designed to attract low-skilled workers. In Germany, most guest workers were employed in manufacturing, notably in the construction, mining and metal industries located in the west and south (Herbert 2001).[5]

These regions, with their export-driven industries, have been worst affected during the crisis. The rise in unemployment in southern and western Germany was early and sharp; Eastern Germany was less affected.

---

4 The term "migration background" (*Migrationshintergrund*) is a data category in German national statistics. It refers to people who immigrated to Germany after 1950 and to their descendants.
5 For immigration literature focused on the influence of ethnic enclaves on economic performance and/or language fluency, cf. Granato 2009 as well as Danzer and Yaman 2010.

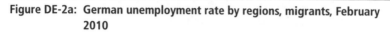

Figure DE-2a: German unemployment rate by regions, migrants, February 2010

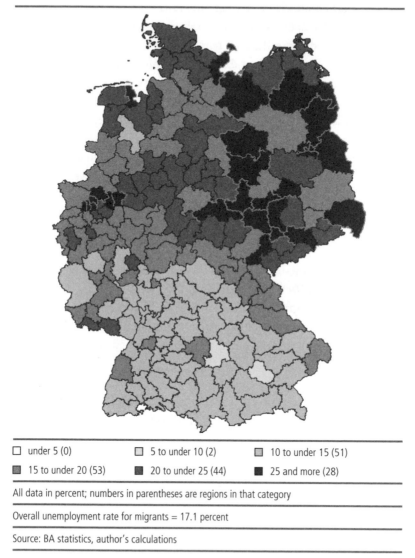

☐ under 5 (0)		☐ 5 to under 10 (2)		☐ 10 to under 15 (51)	
■ 15 to under 20 (53)		■ 20 to under 25 (44)		■ 25 and more (28)	

All data in percent; numbers in parentheses are regions in that category

Overall unemployment rate for migrants = 17.1 percent

Source: BA statistics, author's calculations

Figure DE-2b: German unemployment rate by regions, natives, February 2010

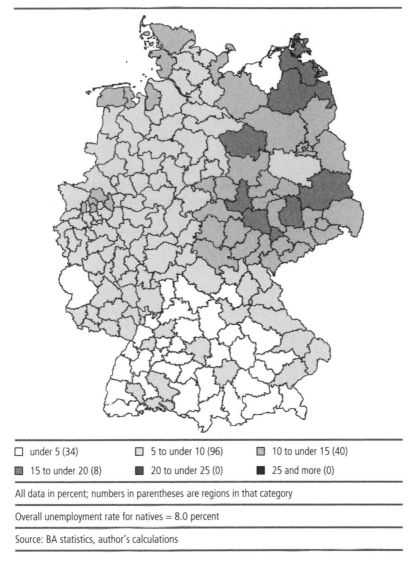

☐ under 5 (34)	☐ 5 to under 10 (96)	▨ 10 to under 15 (40)
▨ 15 to under 20 (8)	■ 20 to under 25 (0)	■ 25 and more (0)

All data in percent; numbers in parentheses are regions in that category

Overall unemployment rate for natives = 8.0 percent

Source: BA statistics, author's calculations

Unemployment Patterns between 2005 and 2010:
Differences Between Migrants and Germans

Overall, foreign nationals made up about 19 percent of all unemployed during the 2008–2010 period, and this proportion has stayed stable over time. Both Germans and migrants have suffered unemployment increases during the recent recession, but the increases and decreases have been larger in percentage terms for Germans. (Of course, migrants entered the recession with high unemployment, 2.5 times the rate of natives. This rate has been stable for the last two dec-

Figure DE-3: **Percent change in stock of unemployed in Germany since same month of previous year, migrants and natives, January 2005 to February 2010**

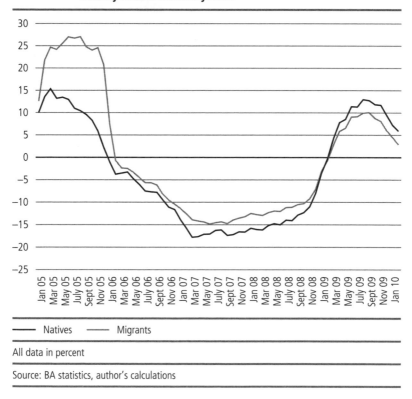

Natives — Migrants

All data in percent

Source: BA statistics, author's calculations

ades. The main increase occurred in the 1980s, and unemployment has remained at a high level ever since.)

Figure DE-3 shows the percent change in the stock of unemployed persons for migrants and natives as compared to the same month of the previous year. Until January 2009, migrants lost jobs faster when unemployment was rising and gained jobs more slowly when unemployment was falling. However, this trend changed at the beginning of 2009, when Germans began to join the ranks of the unemployed at a faster rate (in percentage terms).

Development of Unemployment by Qualification Level

More-educated workers tend to have higher employment, lower unemployment and better-paid, more stable jobs; qualifications are the main basis for smooth labor market integration. Migrants are overrepresented among the low-qualified in Germany. Around one-third of employed foreign nationals have low qualifications—around double the share for natives (29 percent versus 14.1 percent). About 60 out of 100 natives have vocational training (middle qualification), which is the main route into stable employment in Germany's occupationally segmented labor market. By contrast, only 30 out of every 100 migrants possess this main entrance ticket. Finally, just 7.6 percent of migrants possess high qualifications, compared to 10.6 percent of Germans. The qualification structure for migrants has not improved in the last decade, even if we only consider workers with jobs and not the unemployed or nonparticipants in the labor force (author's calculations from BA Statistics).

The low qualification level of migrants, even among their children, shows that integration policy in Germany can boast only the most modest of successes. Germany's almost impermeable education system has entrenched low qualification levels among migrants (OECD 2006; Geisler 2006). The education and qualification level of parents is still the strongest determinant of their children's educational opportunities—and migrant parents tend to have disproportionally low education levels.

During the recent recession, however, these facts have not translated into increased vulnerability for migrants. Table DE-1 shows clearly that, for both migrants and natives, middle- and highly qualified people made up an increasing share of the total unemployed population from 2009 to 2010 (rows 2, 3, 6 and 7).[6] These trends are quite unusual. In previous recessions, low-educated workers have been affected significantly worse by business cycles than the highly educated (Dustmann, Glitz and Vogel 2006).

The change in the number of unemployed from February 2009 to February 2010 was highest for highly qualified people (a 27.8 percent increase for Germans and a 26.7 percent increase for migrants) and lowest for low-qualified people (a 2.1 percent decrease for Germans and a 1.0 percent increase for migrants). Qualification structure, therefore, helps to explain why migrant unemployment has risen more slowly since 2009. In the recent recession, unemployment hit more middle- and highly qualified people, and migrants are underrepresented among these groups.

Unemployment by Duration/Type of Unemployment Benefits[7]

Two types of benefits are available to the unemployed in Germany, regardless of whether they are native or foreign born. Since the "Hartz IV" welfare reforms took effect in 2005, full unemployment insurance payments (*Arbeitslosengeld I*) are available for the first 12 months of unemployment (or the first 18 months for individuals over the age of 55). After 12 months, and if they meet the requirements, the unemployed receive basic social security (*Arbeitslosengeld II*), which is usually much lower.[8] Individuals on basic social security, therefore, have

6 Data for unemployment by qualification is only available since January 2009 due to data restrictions.
7 The unemployment insurance data in this section refer to West Germany, including Berlin.
8 *Arbeitslosengeld II* brought together the two former "unemployment benefits," unemployment benefits for the long-term unemployed (*Arbeitslosenhilfe*) and welfare benefits (*Sozialhilfe*), leaving them both at approximately the lower level of the former *Sozialhilfe* (SGBII).

Table DE-1: Development of unemployment in Germany by qualification, migrants and natives, 2009 to 2010

	Unemployed native Germans by qualification in percent				Unemployed migrants by qualification in percent			
	Low qualification	Middle qualification	High qualification	Not reported	Low qualification	Middle qualification	High qualification	Not reported
	1	2	3	4	5	6	7	8
Jan 2009	44.2	49.9	5.5	0.4	77.7	17.9	4.1	−2.2
Jan 2010	41.5	52.3	5.9	0.3	76.5	18.7	4.5	0.3
Feb 2010	41.1	52.9	5.7	0.4	76.3	18.8	4.4	0.4
Percent change in number of unemployed								
Jan 2010– Jan 2009	−2.3	16.4	23.7	−9.6	0.4	16.5	24.5	−0.6
Feb 2010– Feb 2009	−2.1	14.4	27.8	−19.0	1.0	16.1	26.7	−10.5
Feb 2010– Jan 2009	−3.0	12.4	24.4	−8.8	−0.3	12.4	22.8	1.6

Source: BA statistics, author's calculations

been unemployed for longer and have a smaller chance of being reintegrated into the labor market.

The distribution between these two types of benefits is quite different for migrants and native Germans. On average, 80 percent of unemployed migrants are long-term unemployed, compared to 60 percent of unemployed native Germans, and these numbers are very stable. Migrants experience more long-term unemployment for several reasons, including low educational and professional qualifications, insufficient language skills and the nonrecognition of foreign credentials (Bundesministerium für Arbeit und Soziales 2010b).

During the recession, the increase in unemployment was mainly concentrated in "short-term" unemployment insurance. This is the result of the high number of new cases of unemployment against the relatively small number of cases of people returning to work after unemployment. When we distinguish between short- and long-term unemployment, it becomes clear that the increase for Germans has been larger. The number of migrants receiving full unemployment benefits increased by "only" 1.3 percent (1,617) from February 2009 to February 2010, whereas for Germans the increase was 9.9 percent (40,842). Migrants were less hit by job losses and therefore made fewer new claims for unemployment insurance.

By contrast, the number of migrants receiving basic social security for the long-term unemployed increased by 3.3 percent, almost eight times more than the number receiving full unemployment insurance. For Germans, this measure of long-term unemployment increased by just 0.5 times more than "short-term" unemployment.

At first glance, the recession that started in 2008 has not hit migrants as hard as one might expect, and job losses were moderate. One reason is that the recession hit mainly qualified people, and the share of qualified migrants is low compared to qualified native Germans. But, on further review, migrants were hit harder in an indirect sense, experiencing a huge increase in long-term unemployment because they could not manage to return to work after 12 months of unemployment. The recession, in other words, has worsened the chances of *returning* to work—especially for low-qualified people.

The Impact of the Crisis on Employment
(Including Employment Subject to Social Insurance Contributions)

The slump in the economy has so far had a relatively moderate impact on employment, including employment subject to social insurance contributions. However, the impacts have varied significantly by sector, with industry and trade the most strongly affected. Given the low share of immigrant employees in East Germany and the fact that the crisis had its strongest impact in West Germany, the following analysis concentrates on West Germany, including Berlin.[9]

Figure DE-4 shows the impact of the crisis by branch of industry from March 2009 to June 2009 in West Germany and Berlin. As expected, the main loss for both groups has been in manufacturing, and job losses in manufacturing were higher (in percentage terms) for migrants. Migrants improved their situation in sectors that they already dominated, such as hospitality. Note that the absolute number of migrants is low compared to natives, so that a small absolute improvement means a large percentage increase.

Temporary work (*Leiharbeit*) is always considered a precursor of the mood in the labor market. And temporary work is controversial due to working conditions and the greater difficulty of entering the "primary" labor market and also because the share of immigrant temporary workers is double compared to that of nonmigrants (3.5 percent to 1.7 percent). Figure DE-5 shows the change in the number of employees in the temporary work sector compared to the previous quarter, for migrants and native Germans. Both groups were hit hard in the fourth quarter of 2008, but the impact was worse for migrants (−22.3 percent). The decline bottomed out in the first quarter of 2009 but it was still large—and larger for migrants. By the second quarter of 2009, there was an increase—but it was very small for both groups.

---

9   Berlin is located in East Germany, but its migrant population much more closely resembles that of West Germany (its population is 24.1 percent migrant, compared to 21.5 percent for West Germany but only 4.7 percent for East Germany) (Statistisches Bundesamt 2010).

Figure DE-4: Percentage change in total employment in selected sectors, migrants and natives, West Germany (including Berlin), March 2009 to March 2010

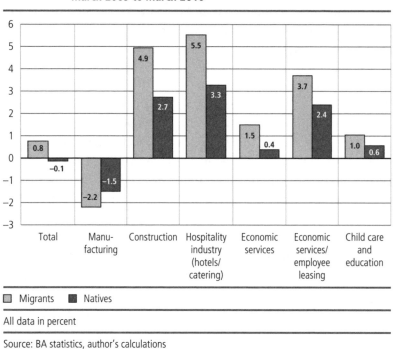

All data in percent

Source: BA statistics, author's calculations

Outlook and Conclusions

At first glance, the recession that began in 2008 has not hit migrants as hard as one might expect for several reasons. First, across the German labor market as a whole, a harsh recession had an unexpectedly mild impact on jobs, and German firms proved to have much more internal flexibility than in the past. Labor hoarding—that is, a massive reduction in working hours, a moderate reduction in productivity per hour worked and extensive use of the short-time work policy (*Kurzarbeit*)—appears to have driven this phenomenon. Rather than being forced by employment-protection policies, firms have so far de-

Figure DE-5: Impact of the crisis on temporary workers by change in jobs compared to previous quarter, migrants and natives, December 2007 to June 2009, West Germany (including Berlin)

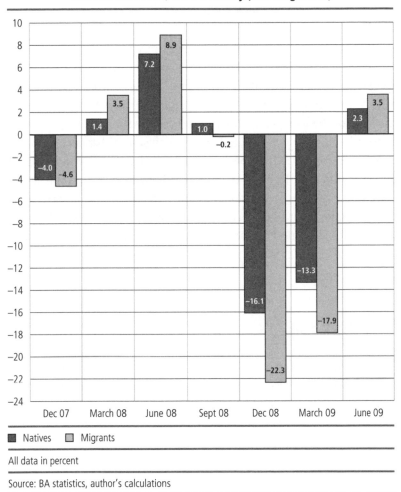

Natives ■   Migrants ▢

All data in percent

Source: BA statistics, author's calculations

liberately and voluntarily opted—and continue to opt—to avoid making a large wave of dismissals (Moeller 2010: 336).

Second, the crisis hit companies with relatively well-qualified employees, primarily exporters in Germany's economically robust regions.

Even here, job losses were moderate. Since job cuts would mean a huge loss of firm-specific knowledge, labor hoarding and short-time work were highly attractive for the companies. Moreover, the share of qualified migrants in these companies is low compared to that of qualified native Germans.

Still, upon further review, it becomes apparent that migrants have felt more indirect impacts. They have experienced a huge increase in long-term unemployment, as the recession has reduced the ease with which workers who were already unemployed can return to work, especially for the low qualified. Likewise, despite the mild impact of the recession on migrants in Germany, the structural barriers they face remain enormous. Unemployment was and remains much higher for migrants than for natives. Migrants have lower education levels, have less access to the vocational training that is the entrance ticket to stable employment in Germany and are concentrated in sectors (such as building cleaning and maintenance, employee leasing, hospitality and manufacturing) where jobs tend to pay less and have poor working conditions.

Policy Conclusions

There have not been any migrant-specific measures or policy reactions to the crisis because the crisis hit specific regions and specific branches rather than specific labor market groups.

There are several signs of stabilization in the economic situation. But early indicators make an unfavorable development in the labor market appear likely, particularly in the coming months.[10] On the other hand, there must be consideration that the unusual amount of

---

10 There will be long-terms impacts from the recession that we cannot predict now. Schmieder et al. show that workers displaced from stable jobs during mass layoffs amid the 1982 recession in Germany suffered long-term earnings losses of 10–15 percent for at least 15 years. They find that job displacements can lead to large and lasting reductions in income even in labor markets (like Germany) with tighter social safety nets and lower earnings inequality. Cf. Schmieder, Wachter and Bender 2010.

labor hoarding will put some stress on firms' financial situation and will increase unit labor costs. As Moeller points out, "the flip side of the employment stability is an extended period of jobless growth during the recovery" (Moeller 2010). This will make immigrant integration—and the reduction of the very high levels of migrant unemployment—particularly important.

Further training—especially for unemployed and low-qualified migrants as well as for migrants in short-time work—should be initiated. At the same time, the country needs a better system for recognizing foreign qualifications.[11] The problems of labor market integration of migrants are the same as before the crisis: On average, migrants have low educational and qualification levels and higher unemployment rates. Throughout what is expected to be an extended period of jobless growth during the recovery, the structural barriers facing migrants are likely to remain problematic. Many migrants will face significant difficulties reintegrating into the labor market; even if they have comparable education and qualifications to natives, it is much harder for them to get vocational training or a job. Therefore, it is absolutely necessary to prevent structural disadvantages, to foster measures of further education and to enhance participation in training and educational programs as well as in the workforce.

As Germany looks forward, policymakers will have to face up to the challenges posed by demographic change. As the native workforce ages and fertility rates decline, Germany will need qualified and highly qualified workers in the near future. As a result, it cannot afford to waste immigrants' potential—and must rely on efforts from all players, including employers, employment agencies, policymakers, educators and individuals themselves to more fully integrate the foreign born into the labor market.

---

11 A new law in Germany, which took effect in 2010, regulates the recognition of foreign qualifications. Cf. Bundesministerium für Bildung und Forschung 2009.

Migration and the Recession in Spain

Ruth Ferrero-Turrión

Introduction[1]

Over the past three decades, Spain enjoyed an era of unprecedented economic growth and prosperity. Between 1980 and 2007, per capita GDP—the broadest measure of a country's income relative to its population—grew almost without interruption, from \$8,215 to \$15,416.[2] However, Spain's economy began slowing in early 2008 and fell into recession by the third quarter of 2008 with the onset of the global economic crisis. Preexisting weaknesses in the Spanish economy, including heavy dependence on construction and consumer services and a strongly segmented labor market, contributed to deepening and prolonging the crisis. Exports contracted by 10 percent in the fourth quarter of 2008, and unemployment more than doubled (from 8 percent to 19 percent) between March 2007 and December 2009; 1.6 million jobs were lost during the same period, of which over 800,000 were in the construction sector (BBVA Servicio de Estudios 2010). Reflecting expectations of a sluggish recovery, Standard and Poor's lowered Spain's sovereign debt rating from AA+ to AA in April 2010, and, in May 2010, Fitch lowered Spain's rating from AAA to AA+.

---

1 This paper draws upon the author's previous research and analysis on the impact of the economic crisis on immigrants in Spain. Cf. Ferrero-Turrión and López-Sala 2009a, 2009b and (forthcoming) 2010; Cebolla-Boado, Ferrero-Turrión and Pinyol-Jiménez (forthcoming) 2010.
2 Per capita GDP in constant prices. International Monetary Fund 2009.

As Spain's economy grew, the country evolved from a net sender of migrants into one of the largest single destinations for immigrant flows in the world. Several interrelated factors explain this dramatic transformation. First, the country's rapid economic growth—which averaged 3.2 percent annually between 1985 and 2007, making Spain consistently the fastest-growing country among the original 15 European Union (EU) Member States—generated substantial *demand* in the Spanish labor market.[3] Second, the country experienced heavy demand for unskilled labor due to strong growth in low-skilled, labor–intensive sectors, such as construction and domestic services. Over the same period, Spain's labor market became strongly segmented, and the size of the informal economy grew to around 20 percent of GDP.[4]

Trends in labor *supply* also influenced immigration trends. The Spanish population, especially the economically active population, has aged rapidly: The share of youth age 16 to 24 among the economically active population has declined from 21 percent in 1977 and 1987 to 15 percent in 1997 and 11 percent in 2007.[5] Birth rates have also fallen rapidly over the past three decades, from 2.7 children per woman in 1977 to 1.4 children per woman in 2007; fertility in Spain has not equaled or exceeded the universal replacement rate of 2.1 children per woman since 1980.[6] Moreover, the Spanish population displays low levels of internal mobility, which results in an irregular, and often suboptimal, population distribution across regions of the country.

As a result of these supply and demand trends, Spain has attracted unprecedented numbers of immigrants in recent years. Three features have characterized immigration flows to Spain over the past decade: rapid growth, diversity of origins and diversity of motives.

3   GDP data from National Statistics Institute 2010. The 15 EU Member States (EU-15) are Austria, Belgium, Denmark, Finland, France, Germany, Greece, Ireland, Italy, Luxembourg, the Netherlands, Portugal, Spain, Sweden and the United Kingdom.
4   Estimates of the size of Spain's informal economy in 2009 varied from 19.5 percent (from the OECD) to 23.3 percent (from the Trade Union of Tax Technicians of the Ministry of the Economy, *Sindicato de Técnicos del Ministerio de Hacienda Gestha*).
5   Author's analysis of data from the Encuesta de Población Activa, 1977 to 2007.
6   National Statistics Institute, Indicadores Demográficos Básicos, "Número medio de hijos por mujer, 1975 to 2008," www.ine.es/jaxi/tabla.do.

Rapid Growth

Throughout the 1980s and 1990s, the immigrant population in Spain grew very slowly, from about 233,000 (0.6 percent of the population) in 1981 to 350,000 (0.9 percent of the population) in 1991 and 750,000 (1.9 percent of the population) in 1999.[7] But the immigrant population in Spain grew rapidly during the first decade of the 21st century, growing by an average of nearly 500,000 people each year between 1999 and 2008. By 2009, the immigrant population had grown to 5.6 million people, or 12.0 percent of Spain's population, as reported by the National Statistics Institute.[8] Growth was particularly intense between 2000 and 2003 (and again in 2005), when the year-on-year growth rate of the immigrant population ranged between 23 percent and 48 percent. Over the decade, Spain accounted for about one-third of all new migratory flows to Europe[9] and was the second-most-popular destination for immigrants to OECD countries, after the United States. As Figure ES-1 illustrates, the number of immigrants and their share of the total population grew almost exactly in parallel, suggesting that almost all population growth in Spain over the past 30 years has been due to immigration.

---

7   Throughout this report, stock data on the immigrant population in Spain refer to individuals with foreign nationality; they exclude immigrants who have acquired Spanish nationality. Data from the National Statistics Institute (INE) Municipal Register and from the 1981, 1991 and 2001 censuses. Data for 1981 to 2006 are presented in Izquicrdo 2006. Data for 2007 to 2009 are updated from the INE by the author.

8   Of these 5.6 million, less than half (2.3 million) are citizens of EU countries (National Statistics Institute 2009a).

9   References to migration flows to Europe include immigrants from Romania and Bulgaria prior to 2007; in subsequent years, immigrants from Romania and Bulgaria have been considered intra-European flows.

Figure ES-1: Foreign population, number and share of total population in Spain, 1981 to 2009

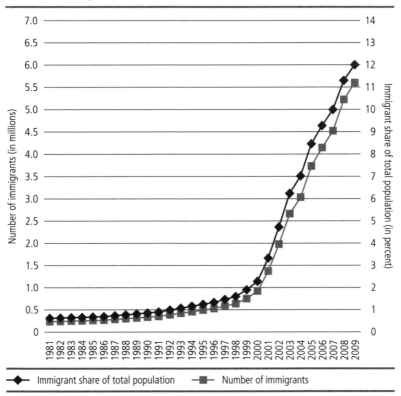

Sources: National Statistics Institute, Padrón Municipal de Habitantes; Censos de Población y Viviendas. Data for 1981 to 2006, Izquierdo 2006; data for 2007 to 2009 updated with National Statistics Institute, Padrón Municipal de Habitantes.

Diverse Origins

Spain's immigrant population is extremely diverse, and the top countries of origin as of 2009 include four European countries, four Latin American countries and one North African country (see Figure ES-2). In 2009, Romanians (758,823 or 13.4 percent) constituted the largest single group of foreigners in Spain, followed by Moroccans (627,858

Figure ES-2: Stock of foreign population in Spain by nationality, 2001 and 2009, in percent

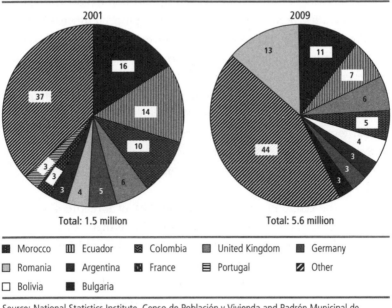

2001

Total: 1.5 million

2009

Total: 5.6 million

▨ Morocco	▥ Ecuador	▨ Colombia	▨ United Kingdom	■ Germany
▨ Romania	■ Argentina	▨ France	▤ Portugal	▨ Other
☐ Bolivia	■ Bulgaria			

Source: National Statistics Institute, Censo de Población y Vivienda and Padrón Municipal de Habitantes, in Ferrero-Turrión and López-Sala (forthcoming) 2010

or 11.1 percent), Ecuadoreans (409,328 or 7.2 percent), nationals of the United Kingdom (355,988 or 6.3 percent), Colombians (296,304 or 5.2 percent), Bolivians (223,455 or 4.0 percent), Argentines (195,572 or 3,4 percent), Germans (174,374 or 3.1 percent), and Bulgarians (158,110 or 2.8 percent). Though the rankings may have changed, these countries also were the top sending countries for immigrants to Spain in 2001. Among recent immigrants, the numbers of Paraguayans, Chinese, Peruvians, Brazilians, Ukrainians and Pakistanis have grown dramatically.

Diverse Motives

The wide variety of origins of the immigrant population in Spain—which includes both developed and developing countries—reflects the diverse reasons why immigrants move to Spain. A substantial portion of immigration to Spain was driven by labor market demand. However, Spain also receives a substantial amount of family-based and retirement migration.[10] Retirement migration is mainly composed of immigrants from the United Kingdom, Germany and France (which together account for two-thirds of foreigners from the EU-15 in Spain) as well as other northern European countries, who are attracted to Spain by the country's temperate climate, among other factors.

Since the economic crisis began, the *stock* of foreigners in Spain has continued to grow but at a much slower rate than before. As Figure ES-3 illustrates, data from the Ministry of Labor and Immigration on the number of foreigners holding residence permits show that the foreign population grew at a slower quarterly rate between 2008 and 2009 than at any point over the previous two years. Moreover, municipal population registers data compiled by the National Statistics Institute show that the share of new immigrants started declining, from 920,534 to 692,228, between 2007 and 2008. Finally, estimates of the number of foreigners residing abroad who are offered jobs in Spain—a process known as *contratación en origen* (CO)—declined dramatically, from 45,995 in 2006, 70,444 in 2007 and 48,693 in 2008 to 4,429 in 2009 (Ministry of Labour and Immigration 2010). Overall, data from these three sources support the thesis that although the economic crisis has reduced the appeal of Spain as a destination country, the number of immigrants continues to grow, mainly due to family reunification and existing migration networks.

---

10 There are no reliable estimates of the share of foreigners residing in Spain who are "retirement migrants" from EU-15 countries since there is no compulsory registration for EU nationals.

Figure ES-3: Year-on-year change in the number of foreigners with legal residence permits in Spain, by quarter, 2006 to 2009

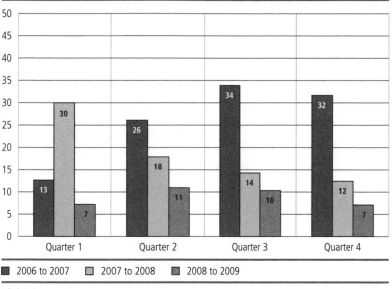

Legend: 2006 to 2007 ■ 2007 to 2008 ■ 2008 to 2009 ■

All data in percent

Source: Ministry of Labor and Immigration, Informes Trimestrales, 2006 to 2009, in Ferrero-Turrión and López-Sala (forthcoming) 2010

The Economic Crisis and Its Impact on Immigrants

The very fast development of the Spanish economy in such a short period of time was due to a variety of factors. During the 1980s and 1990s, economic growth in Spain was mainly due to economic liberalization and rapid investment, particularly in the context of European integration, as well as to the entry of women into the labor force and higher productivity as the Spanish population became more educated (Barro and Sala-i-Martin 2003). By the 2000s, however, Spain's economic growth came to rely more on a handful of labor-intensive sectors, including services, tourism and construction. Scholars and policymakers are increasingly concluding that Spain's dependence on these sectors structurally weakened the country's economy and created a growing productivity gap relative to other European economies. This dependence is also at the root of Spain's current malaise (cf. Cabrales et al. 2009; also papers presented at the March conference of the Fundación de Estudios de Economía Aplicada [FEDEA] 2010).

Over the past decade, immigrants filled jobs in many of the rapidly growing sectors. But immigrants also filled jobs in stagnating or contracting industries, such as agriculture, that were increasingly shunned by Spanish workers as education levels and employment expectations increased (Cachón 2009). Many formerly booming industries have contracted sharply over the course of the recession: of the 1.6 million jobs lost in Spain between March 2007 and December 2009, over half were in the construction sector (BBVA 2010). The agricultural sector actually has gained jobs during the recession and, in contrast to the past, emerging evidence suggests that many Spanish workers appear to be willing and available for these jobs. As a result, immigrants in the Spanish labor market have been particularly affected by the economic crisis.

Labor Force Participation

The labor force participation rate among immigrants is much higher than among natives. About 55 percent of Spaniards age 16 and older are in the labor force, compared to 80–85 percent of immigrants from Latin America and 70–75 percent of immigrants from other parts of the world. Immigrants' relative youth explains most of this difference. For instance, among the prime-working-age population (age 25 to 54), labor force participation rates range between 80–85 percent for both native-born Spaniards and foreigners alike, although there are some differences among immigrants. Prime-working-age foreigners from Latin America have very high labor force participation rates (consistently around 90 percent), while prime-working-age foreigners from the "rest of the world"—a residual category of Asians and Africans that is dominated by Moroccan immigrants—has comparatively low labor force participation rates.

The relatively low labor force participation among immigrants from the "rest of the world" is primarily driven by gender differences, especially among Moroccan women (cf. Cebolla-Boado, Ferrero-Turrión and Pinyol-Jiménez (forthcoming) 2010). Among men between the ages of 25 and 54, immigrants of all origins and native-born Spaniards have very similar labor force participation rates. Immigrant men of all origins and Spanish men of prime working age have very similar labor force participation rates; but among prime working-age women, participation rates vary widely. Nearly 90 percent of prime-working-age immigrant women from Latin America are in the labor force, compared to 75–80 percent of immigrant women from Europe (both EU and non-EU citizens) and native-born Spanish women. However, among prime-working-age immigrant women from the "rest of the world," only about half are in the labor force.

Figure ES-4 shows how the number of immigrants in the Spanish labor market has evolved since the recession began. (The rapid increase in labor force participation among EU immigrants and rapid decrease in labor force participation among other European immigrants in early 2007 is due to the accession of Romania and Bulgaria to the European Union in January 2007.) Overall, the number of immigrants in the Spanish labor force continued to grow throughout 2008 but stabilized in 2009; among Latin American immigrants, the number appears to have stabilized earlier, in mid-2008, and declined modestly in 2009. However, Latin American men have been hit harder than Latin American women: The number of Latin American men in the labor force declined by about 46,000 workers (6 percent) between the fourth quarter of 2008 and the fourth quarter of 2009 compared to a decline of 17,000 workers (2 percent) among Latin American women over the same period. Prior to the recession, Latin American men were heavily concentrated in construction, which likely explains much of this difference.

Figure ES-4: Foreign labor force participants in Spain, by world region of origin, 2005 to 2009

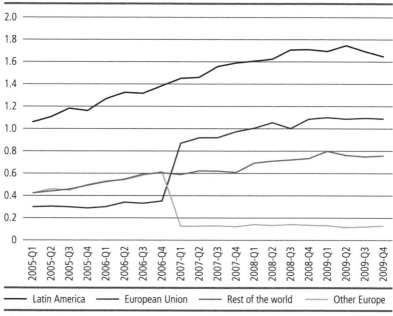

Latin America — European Union — Rest of the world — Other Europe

All data in millions foreigners

Note: Foreigners from Romania and Bulgaria were categorized with "other Europe" prior to the first quarter of 2007 and are grouped with "European Union" for subsequent quarters.

Source: Author's tabulations of data from the National Statistics Institute, *Encuesta de Población Activa*, 2005 to 2009

Unemployment

The number of unemployed workers in Spain increased by nearly 2.3 million (from 1.7 million to 4.0 million) between the fourth quarter of 2007 and the fourth quarter of 2009; over the same period, the unemployment rate more than doubled, from 8.6 percent in the fourth quarter of 2007 to 18.8 percent in the fourth quarter of 2009. Job losses were particularly severe during the fourth quarter of 2008 and the first quarter of 2009.

Rising unemployment has had profound impacts on the immigrant population. Between the fourth quarter of 2007 and the fourth quarter of 2009, the immigrant unemployment rate increased from 12.4 percent to 29.7 percent, while it increased from 7.9 percent to 16.6 percent among native-born Spaniards. Prior to the recession, unemployment among immigrants was higher than among natives, and the gap has grown since the recession began, particularly during the first year of the recession. Immigrants now account for more than one in four unemployed in Spain (compared to about one in eight for natives). All immigrant groups have experienced rising unemploy-

Figure ES-5: Unemployment rates, by nativity, 2005 to 2009

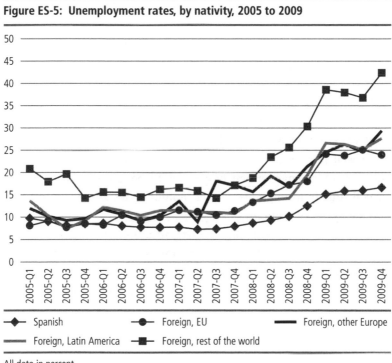

◆ Spanish	● Foreign, EU	▬ Foreign, other Europe
▬ Foreign, Latin America	■ Foreign, rest of the world	

All data in percent

Note: Foreigners from Romania and Bulgaria were categorized with "other Europe" prior to the first quarter of 2007 and are grouped with "European Union" for subsequent quarters.

Source: Author's tabulations of data from the National Statistics Institute, *Encuesta de Población Activa*, 2005 to 2009

ment, but the increase has been particularly severe among immigrants from the "rest of the world," who saw unemployment increase from 17.1 percent to 42.4 percent (see Figure ES-5).

Data from the Ministry of Labor and Immigration on workers receiving unemployment benefits provide further support for the observation that certain groups of immigrants have fared far worse than others. In particular, the number of Moroccan, Ecuadorean and Colombian immigrants receiving unemployment benefits has grown dramatically since 2007 (see Figure ES-6).[11]

Sectoral Differences

Certain sectors of the Spanish economy, including several industries that attracted substantial numbers of immigrants in recent years, have experienced greater turmoil than others during the recession. In particular, total employment in construction decreased, but so did the share of immigrants among all construction-sector workers (see Figure ES-7c). A similar, but much smaller, trend is observable in industry as well (Figure ES-7b). This is largely due to the fact that immigrants were among the first employees to be laid off; but it is also partially due to immigrants' higher mobility rates among sectors and into the informal economy.

On balance, it appears unemployment among immigrants is due to an increase in labor force participation, intersectoral mobility and new arrivals, whereas unemployment among natives is due to job destruction. As a result, unemployment is expected to fall faster among immigrants than among natives as Spain's economy gradually recovers from the recession.

11 In order to be eligible for unemployment benefits, workers (both natives and immigrants) must be registered with the Social Security Administration, formally unemployed and actively searching for a new job, and they must have contributed to the social security system for a minimum of 12 months over the previous six years. Retirees are excluded from unemployment benefits. Data from the Ministry of Labor and Immigration show that the number of immigrants working in Spain legally has increased in recent years, as has the number receiving unemployment benefits.

Figure ES-6: Persons receiving unemployment benefits in Spain by nationality, 2007 to 2009

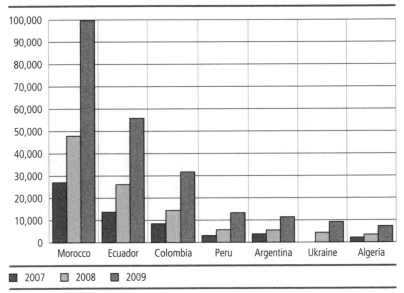

All data in number of people

Source: Ministry of Labor and Immigration, 2006 to 2009, in Ferrero-Turrión and López-Sala (forthcoming) 2010

Gender Segmentation

Foreign men and women have fared differently over the course of the crisis, largely due to the disproportionate job losses suffered by the construction industry and the relative stability in sectors traditionally dominated by immigrant women, such as domestic work. At the onset of the recession, the unemployment rate among immigrant women was higher than among immigrant men, but that has since reversed (see Figure ES-8). By contrast, unemployment among native men has increased faster than among native women but remains lower overall. The only exception to that rule is unemployment among Moroccan women (cf. Cebolla-Boado, Ferrero-Turrión and Pinyol-Jiménez 2010 (forthcoming).

Figure ES-7a–b: Total native and foreign employment in Spain, by sector, 2008 to 2009

Primary sector

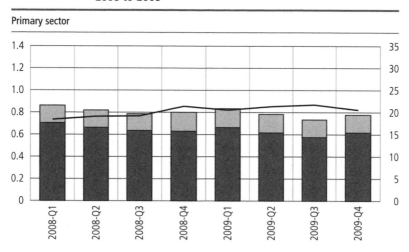

Industry

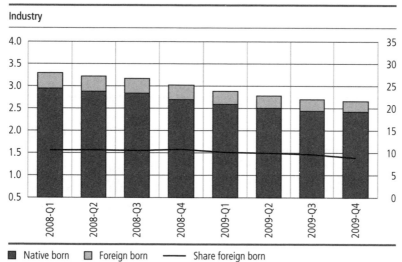

◼ Native born   ☐ Foreign born   —— Share foreign born

Notes: The number of native- and foreign-born workers in a given industry is displayed in millions on the right-hand axis; scales vary across charts. The share of foreign born in a given industry is displayed on the left-hand axis and includes uniform scales.

Source: Author's tabulations of National Statistics Institute, *Encuesta de Población Activa*, various years

Figure ES-7c–d: Total native and foreign employment in Spain, by sector, 2008 to 2009

Construction sector

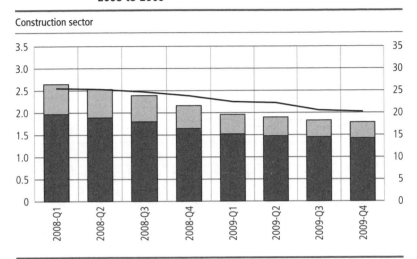

Services sector

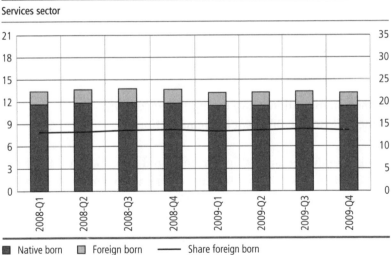

■ Native born　☐ Foreign born　—— Share foreign born

Notes: The number of native- and foreign-born workers in a given industry is displayed in millions on the right-hand axis; scales vary across charts. The share of foreign born in a given industry is displayed on the left-hand axis and includes uniform scales.

Source: Author's tabulations of National Statistics Institute, *Encuesta de Población Activa*, various years

Figure ES-8: Unemployment rates, by nativity and gender, 2005 to 2009

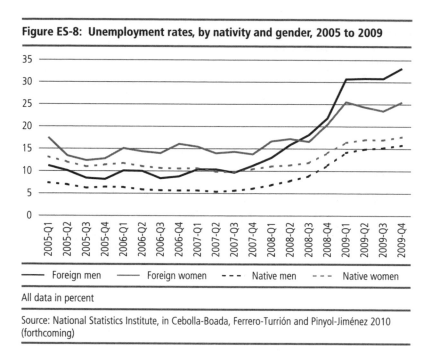

All data in percent

Source: National Statistics Institute, in Cebolla-Boada, Ferrero-Turrión and Pinyol-Jiménez 2010 (forthcoming)

Spanish Immigration Policy during the Recession: Same Philosophy, Different Implementation

Until recently, the Spanish government did little to coordinate labor immigration flows. An ad hoc arrangement—whereby immigrants would enter Spain illegally, obtain informal employment and later receive legal status through regularization programs—managed to meet most low-skilled labor needs in the past. Over the past decade, new policy measures were enacted to limit illegal migration and increase border security through programs such as Plan Greco in 2000. However, these programs to fight illegal migration without managing flows were not effective, and Spain passed a number of new regulations between 2000 and 2005 (Arango and Jacimowicz 2005; Ferrero-Turrión and Pinyol-Jiménez 2007).

Since the publication of new regulations governing immigrant inflows in 2005, Spanish migration policy has become more proactive in several important ways:

- *Adjustment of status prohibited.* Spain's quota system for admitting foreign workers changed in 2000 to prohibit individuals currently residing in the country from taking part in what was ostensibly a labor recruitment program. Migrants can no longer convert their status from within Spain, and all recruitment of foreign workers by Spanish employers must take place abroad. Also, in 2006, the quota system was again modified, allowing flexibility over the year in order to cover demands of entrepreneurs.

- *Stakeholder input.* The new regulations encouraged active participation by local governments, employers and trade unions in identifying labor market needs. In particular, what was then called the Ministry of Labor and Social Affairs (and now the Ministry of Labor and Immigration) worked with employers, regional employment agencies and regional governments to develop a Directory of Labor Needs (*Catálogo de ocupaciones de difícil cobertura*). The directory is a regularly updated catalogue of occupations for which Spanish employers are unable to find sufficient qualified candidates.

- *Workplace regulation.* The ministry began more-effective enforcement of labor regulations through workplace inspections.

- *Seasonal worker enforcement.* The government began greater monitoring of seasonal work permits to ensure that temporary workers do not overstay the terms of their visas and implemented new seasonal worker programs promoting circular migration.

- *Bilateral agreements.* Spain negotiated and signed a number of bilateral agreements with Latin American, Eastern European and African countries to ensure cooperation with countries of origin on managing labor immigration flows (cf. Ferrero-Turrión and López-Sala 2009).

- *Manage and facilitate highly skilled immigration.* Finally, in February 2007, the Ministry of Labor and Immigration created a Division of Large Employers (*Unidad de Grandes Empresas*, UGE), an office responsible for allocating work authorizations and residence permits for highly skilled immigrants, such as business executives, Internet technology workers, scientists, university professors and internationally renowned artists. The UGE represents one of the Spanish government's first initiatives to manage the flow of highly skilled workers. In 2009, the UGE approved over 2,000 work authorizations. This figure is similar to what it had been in previous years, which suggests that demand for highly skilled workers continues in Spain despite the recession.

Since the economic crisis began, the Spanish government has undertaken several reforms to the country's immigration laws and regulations. Some of these reforms are directly linked to the recession while others represent longer-term initiatives independent of the economic crisis.

Reform of Immigration Regulations

Expanded Intersectoral Mobility

In July 2009, the Spanish government responded to the recession by implementing regulations granting greater intersectoral mobility to foreigners holding residence permits. In the past, work permits were tied to specific autonomous communities and industries. However, the new reforms allow greater intersectoral mobility for foreign workers, for instance, from self-employment to salaried employment and vice versa. The government hopes that this change will promote the reallocation of labor across the country as demand changes. The change will also facilitate the renewal of residence permits for workers who can prove continuous employment (nine months over the previous year) and for those with family ties in the country.

In December 2009, the government proposed further changes to the country's immigration laws to grant labor market access to the spouses and children (age 16 and older) of immigrants who enter through family-reunification channels. This reform aimed to reduce household dependence on a single earner. The reforms also included provisions to promote labor market integration, a new residence and work permit for highly skilled workers (the so-called "blue card") and the granting of new responsibilities for the processing of work permits to some autonomous communities (e.g., Catalonia).

"Pay-to-Go" Programs

As the Spanish economy deteriorated rapidly in late 2008, the Spanish government began exploring mechanisms to encourage immigrants to return to their countries of origin. Although these voluntary return programs received substantial attention, they are not new. Other countries, such as France and Germany, have operated voluntary return programs for decades, and Spain has offered return incentives since 2003 under the aegis of the Voluntary Return Program for Immigrants in Socially Precarious Situations (PREVIE).[12] Voluntary return programs in Spain and elsewhere have historically had a wide range of impacts and vary dramatically by local circumstances. But they typically do not increase voluntary returns.

---

12 PREVIE targets immigrants in several legal status categories, including refugees, asylum seekers, legal immigrants with work authorization and unauthorized immigrants. In order to participate, immigrants must be in a precarious economic situation or be otherwise socially vulnerable (e.g., unaccompanied minors). They must also have been in Spain for at least six months. The program provides information and advice on returning, one-way airfare to the country of origin, a small stipend for ground transportation and moving expenses, and psychological counselling. The International Organization for Migration (IOM) manages the program on behalf of the Spanish government.

In November 2008, the Spanish government approved a new voluntary return initiative called the Program for Early Payment of Unemployment Benefits to Foreigners (APRE). Under the program, foreigners who had worked in Spain and were eligible for social security could receive a single lump-sum payout from the Spanish social security system upon returning to their countries of origin for at least three years. On average, participants receive about €9,149, the equivalent of about ten months of unemployment benefits. Not all immigrants qualified for the program. Among other limitations, the program was restricted to nationals of a dozen countries that had (a) signed bilateral repatriation agreements with Spain and (b) had registered as unemployed with Spain's public employment agency.[13]

Data published in November 2009 showed that 8,724 immigrant workers plus 1,581 family members applied for the program during its first year.[14] The applications were mainly from Madrid (1,857), Catalonia (1,432) and Valencia (1,234). Citizens from Latin-American countries—such as Ecuador (44 percent), Colombia (18 percent), Argentina (9.7 percent), Peru (8.6 percent) and Brazil (5.3 percent)—were the top applicants. It is noticeable that Moroccans were not applying, though they are the oldest community in Spain and, thus, have the most potential candidates.

The government has concluded that the program has been a success, citing the statistic that 10 percent of potential participants (around 120,000 people) have applied. Still, this is well below the government's early estimates of participation levels. Critics point to the small number of participants in the program relative to the overall foreign population. Regardless of the arguments for and against the program, participation is fully voluntary.

---

13 Nationals of the following countries are eligible for the program: Andorra, Argentina, Australia, Brazil, Canada, Chile, Colombia, the Dominican Republic, Ecuador, Morocco, Peru, the Philippines, Ukraine, the United States and Uruguay.

14 These data were the most current publicly available figures for participation in Spain's voluntary return program at the time of publication.

Budget Cuts to Immigrant Integration Programs

In 2005, the Spanish government created a Social Integration Fund (*Fondo de Acogia e Integración*) to provide grants to autonomous communities to support immigrant integration in the areas of education, social services, employment services, housing, health care, civic participation, gender equality and community awareness. Autonomous communities must re-grant at least 40 percent of the funds received from the central government to municipalities, but only those where foreigners account for at least 5 percent of the total population are eligible. The fund is funded annually as part of the national budget, and it has increased from €120 million, in 2005, to €200 million, in 2009. Grants are allocated to autonomous communities based on the number of resident, working and educated third-country nationals. There are additional criteria based on some special situations, such as supplemental grants to autonomous communities with particularly large numbers of arrivals or unaccompanied minor immigrants.

Facing growing fiscal pressures, the government has tried to cut this fund on several occasions over the past two years. In February 2009, the government attempted to cut the fund to €59 million but faced strong opposition from the autonomous communities and political parties. In April 2009, the cut was rescinded. But the government again tried to cut the fund in December 2009 and succeeded at reducing it to €100 million. A new round of budget cuts in January 2010 reduced the fund by an additional €30 million. Negotiations over the fund continue between the government and political parties, and the outcome remains unclear. In April 2010, Spain's parliament passed a resolution appealing to the government to rescind the January 2010 cuts and maintain the fund at €100 million. However, in mid-May 2010, the government ratified the €70 million fund, distributing the grants among autonomous communities for three purposes: welcoming and integration (€41.2 million), education (€27.4 million) and unaccompanied minor immigrants (€1.3 million).

Migration and Recession in Ireland

Steven Loyal

Introduction and Economic Background

Ireland has historically been a country of emigration. However, 1996 marked a great turning point, as Ireland became a country of net immigration for the first time in decades. The onset of the recession in 2008 marked another shift in migration patterns, and this case study examines how the recession has affected immigration and whether immigrants have fared worse than natives in the Irish labor market. Data from the Central Statistics Office (CSO) tends to confirm that they have. However, immigrants in Ireland, despite being comparatively well-educated and young as a group, have been differentially affected by the recession, with immigrants from the accession states[1] suffering most adversely while those from the EU-15[2] less so.

Over the last 15 years, high and sustained levels of immigration have transformed Irish society. Given the recent nature of this immigration, the category of immigrants and non-Irish nationals will be treated synonymously in this case study. Between 1999 and 2008, Ireland's population increased by 18 percent—the highest rate in the

---

1 Cyprus, the Czech Republic, Estonia, Hungary, Latvia, Lithuania, Malta, Poland, Slovakia and Slovenia joined the European Union in 2004, followed in 2007 by Bulgaria and Romania.
2 The first 15 EU Member States: Austria, Belgium, Denmark, France, Finland, Germany, Greece, Ireland, Italy, Luxembourg, the Netherlands, Portugal, Spain, Sweden and the United Kingdom.

27 countries comprising the European Union. The vast majority of this increase was a result of immigration.[3]

Before the recession, Ireland was the fourth-most-affluent country in the Organisation for Economic Co-operation and Development (OECD). Notwithstanding an initial policy shift toward economic liberalization in the 1960s and Irish membership in the European Economic Community in the 1970s, the major factor responsible for Ireland's rapid economic growth in the mid-1990s—which earned it the moniker of the "Celtic Tiger"—was the huge increase in American foreign direct investment (FDI). The arrival of US investment and transnational corporations (TNCs) symbolized a shift in national production from agribusiness and traditional manufacturing to an economy increasingly based on technology and services.[4]

Employment growth was engendered by and concentrated in the services and construction sectors. Between 2001 and 2006 alone, the Irish labor force grew by 17 percent, increasing from 1.8 million to 2.1 million workers. The property boom was a major factor accounting for labor market expansion, especially after 2001. In order to escape an economic downturn, the government deregulated and stimulated high levels of investment in the property and housing market. This, in turn, created an enormous bubble in property prices, which increased more rapidly in Ireland in the decade leading up to 2007 than in any other developed world economy (cf. Central Intelligence Agency 2010). The result was a rapid overall expansion in the construction sector, including massive growth in the number of properties built. In addition to increased consumerism, higher standards of living and a drop in unemployment to 4.3 percent in 2006 (cf. CSO

---

3 The rate of natural increase of the population in Ireland was 9.8 per 1,000 in 2007, compared with an EU-27 average of just 1.0. Cf. Central Statistics Office (CSO) 2009a. The 2006 census recorded 4.2 million people in Ireland. The most recent figures, for April 2009, estimated a population of 4.6 million. Cf. CSO 2009b.

4 FDI in Ireland in 2006 was high, especially from the United States. Many major US companies had set up operations in Ireland, including Intel, Dell, Microsoft, IBM, Pfizer, Abbot Laboratories, Citigroup, Bristol-Myers Squibb and Bausch & Lomb. Cf. Killeen 2006.

2007a), there was a significant rise in wages. According to the National Employment Survey 2007, average annual earnings rose from €31,333, in 2002, to €37,200, in 2006 (CSO 2007b).

Immigrants' Demographic Background

The number of immigrants entering Ireland has grown rapidly over a very short period. The 2002 census recorded that non-Irish nationals made up just under 6 percent of the population. The most recent census, in 2006, which is probably the most accurate measure of the non-Irish population so far, recorded 419,733 non-Irish nationals, constituting about 10 percent of the population.

Unlike in many other developed countries experiencing mass immigration, the majority of non-Irish nationals come from the European Union and are, on the whole, well qualified. The census estimates that 275,775 individuals from the EU-25 were resident in Ireland in 2006, making up 66 percent of the non-Irish population. Almost 120,000 of these were from the accession states that joined the European Union in 2004. The European nationals who had migrated to Ireland were followed by nationals from Asia (11 percent), Africa (6 percent) and North and South America (5 percent).

Although 188 different nationalities are estimated to be residing in Ireland, 82 percent are estimated to be from just ten countries (CSO 2008). According to the 2006 census, the largest—and paradoxically least discussed—group of non-Irish nationals was from the United Kingdom (see Table IE-1).

The predominance of European migrants was reflected in the census question on ethnic and cultural background. Ninety-five percent of the population identified themselves as white while only 1.3 percent identified themselves as Asian and 1 percent as black (though these figures are open to question and most would consider them to underestimate racial diversity).

Table IE-1: Source countries of non-Irish nationals, 2006

Country	Number of non-Irish nationals	Percent of all non-Irish nationals
United Kingdom	112,548	26.8
Poland	63,276	15.1
Lithuania	24,628	5.9
Nigeria	16,300	3.9
Latvia	13,319	3.2
USA	12,475	3.0
China	11,161	2.7
Germany	10,289	2.5
Philippines	9,548	2.3
France	9,046	2.2

Source: CSO, n.d.

How Do Non-Irish Nationals Differ From the Irish Population?

The population of non-Irish nationals is predominantly of working age. Only 12 percent of immigrants are children while the number of those over the age of 65 stands at about 3.5 percent. The vast majority, 83 percent, are of working age (15 to 64 years of age).

In all, 53 percent of non-Irish nationals recorded in the census were male, while 47 percent were female. However, the gender ratio varies quite markedly by nationality. Thus, 64 percent of the 63,090 Poles are men compared to only 37.4 percent of the 1,812 Swedes. Ireland is still predominantly Catholic, with the latter accounting for 87 percent of the population, down from 88 percent in 2002 and 92 percent in 1991. However, although 92 percent of Irish nationals said they were Catholics in 2006, a relatively large number (51 percent) of non-Irish nationals did, too (CSO 2008). The increase in the number of Muslims—from 19,000, in 2002, to 33,000, in 2006—made Islam the third-largest religion in the state, with more Muslims than Presbyterians.

Non-Irish nationals are, on the whole, very well qualified. While they reported higher overall levels of education than the Irish population—38 percent were thought to have tertiary education compared to 28 percent of Irish nationals (CSO 2006)—this was primarily a demographic effect caused by the older age profile of the Irish population. When those aged 15 to 44 from both groups are compared, educational differences on the whole disappear; about 31 percent have tertiary education (CSO 2008). However, it should be noted that there are wide differences between nationalities. Census data indicates that approximately three-quarters of people from the EU-15, excluding Ireland and the United Kingdom, were educated to the tertiary level. The equivalent figure for people from the rest of the world was just under 50 percent (CSO 2006, Table 31).

Modes of Entry

Immigrants can come to live and work in Ireland through a number of channels. The majority arrived as EU nationals following the 2004 expansion of the European Union. More than 120,000 people from the 10 new accession states were present in 2006. Non-EU/European Economic Area (EEA)[5] nationals have entered into Ireland through various migration mechanisms. In order to work, they can enter through a work-permit system (from 1999 to 2010, about 130,000 work permits were issued, not including renewals) or the work authorization/visa system (in which 11,000 were issued between 2000 and 2005); the latter system, which was geared toward high-skilled immigrants, was replaced by a "green card" system in February 2007. Only immigrants earning over €60,000 can apply for a green card while those earning between €30,000 and €59,000 in selected occupations

5 The EEA includes European Union Member States plus Norway, Iceland and Liechtenstein.

may also apply. Given their restricted eligibility, fewer than 4,000 green cards have been issued since 2007.

Non-Irish nationals can also enter as asylum seekers (from 1992 to the end of 2006, there were 72,728 applications for asylum). Asylum seekers are not, however, entitled to work. Others immigrants arrive as students. In 2004, there were 21,270 non-EEA students registered in Ireland. Students who are registered for higher education courses can work part-time, for 20 hours per week, and full-time during holiday periods. Finally, dependents and spouses of work-permit holders have also immigrated to Ireland. However, figures for family reunification remain generally low.

Characteristics of the Current Recession

The Irish economy officially went into recession in September 2008, for the first time since 1983. The downturn was caused by a number of intertwined international and domestic factors.

First, Ireland is a small, open and highly globalized economy. According to the AT Kearney Globalization Index, Ireland is the second-most-globalized economy in the world (Allen 2007). The Irish economy relied strongly on foreign-owned firms, responsible for over 90 percent of exports in the country (cf. Finfacts Ireland 2008); these firms dramatically reduced their investment in 2008 (United Nations Conference on Trade and Development [UNCTAD] 2009). A further causal determinant was an overdependence on property and construction.

The decline in the construction sector—which currently contains about 30,000 newly built and unsold homes and where property prices have fallen by as much as 50 percent—also had repercussions for the Irish banking industry. Banks had given 60 percent of their loans toward property by the end of 2005; many of these loans could not be paid back when the recession hit (Kearns and Woods 2006). Third, the government's policy of maintaining light financial regulation in order to attract international financial services and investment for the benefit of business interests also played a role in the recession. Finally, as is the case with a number of other developed OECD countries, there had been a general long-term decline in manufacturing.

Low levels of savings and debt-burdened consumers exacerbated the economic problems ensuing from the recession: a collapse in the property sector, an acute credit crunch, a systemic banking and financial crisis, and a shortfall in public finances resulting in part from one of the lowest corporation taxes in Europe (12.5 percent).

The recession has been widespread and prevalent in most sectors of the economy. However, certain occupational sectors have been especially affected (see Table IE-2). Curtailed construction and manufacturing output and employment have been matched by a contraction in employment in the industrial and agricultural sectors.

Table IE-2: Change in employment in selected sectors of the Irish economy, Q4 2008 to Q4 2009

Sector	Percent change in employment
Construction	−37
Agriculture	−23
Industry	−11
Wholesale and Retail	−9
Admin and Support	−7
Accommodation and Food	4
Information and Communications	6

Source: CSO, Quarterly National Household Survey, 2008–2009

The scale and rapidity of job losses in the recession has been extraordinary. In the Quarterly National Household Survey (QNHS) covering the fourth quarter of 2008, there were 2,052,000 persons employed, an annual decrease of 86,900 or 4.1 percent, from 2007. This represented the largest annual decrease in employment since the Labor Force Survey was first undertaken, in 1975. In the fourth quarter of 2009, employment over the year fell by another 8.1 percent, to just

1,887,700. More than 60 percent of the drop in male employment is attributable to a 77,000-person fall in the number of males employed in the construction sector (CSO 2010a). The number of unemployed now stands at 12.4 percent, compared to just over 4 percent in 2004.

Impact of Recession on Immigrants and Immigration

The recession has brought about a dramatic slowdown in the volume of immigration. There was an enormous 40 percent drop in immigration from the new EU Member States in 2009 compared to 2008, as well as a steep fall in the number of work permits and Public Personal Service Numbers (PPSNs) issued.[6] In 2008, 127,695 PPSNs were allocated to foreign nationals, down almost a third compared to 2006 (CSO 2009c). In the first two months of 2010, the number of work permits was more than 60 percent lower than in the first two months of 2008 (1,441 compared to 3,837).

The recession has also led to the re-emergence of patterns of Irish emigration (see Figure IE-1). In September 2009, more people began to leave Ireland than to enter it for the first time in 15 years. The number of emigrants in the year leading up to April 2009 was estimated to have increased by over 40 percent. Of the 65,100 who emigrated during that time period, almost half were accession-state nationals, and almost 30 percent were Irish nationals. Immigration of all non-Irish groups showed a decline, with those from EU-12 countries showing the biggest fall.[7]

Figures in Ireland indicate that more than half the foreign nationals who registered for PPSN numbers in 2004 no longer appeared in

6 The PPSN number is a unique reference number that helps a holder gain access to social welfare benefits, public services and information in Ireland. State agencies that use PPSN numbers to identify individuals include the Department of Social and Family Affairs and the Revenue Commissioners.
7 Immigration from EU-12 countries dropped from 33,700, in April 2008, to 13,500, in April 2009, according to CSO 2009b. The EU-12 are the ten countries that joined the European Union in 2004 plus Bulgaria and Romania, which joined in 2007.

Figure IE-1: Migration flows to and from Ireland, 1987 to 2009

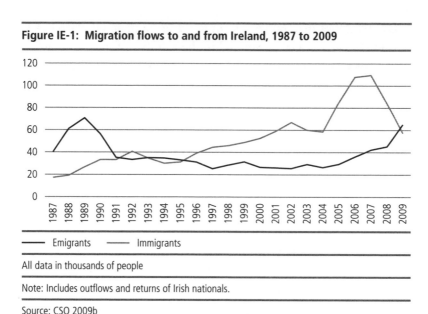

───── Emigrants   ───── Immigrants

All data in thousands of people

Note: Includes outflows and returns of Irish nationals.

Source: CSO 2009b

employment or welfare statistics in 2008, suggesting that many had left the country (CSO 2009c). Despite some return migration, however, a large number of migrants are here to stay. The global nature of the recession has meant that even many of the EU nationals who can leave and reenter without restrictions are unwilling to do so. In other cases, migrants have brought their families with them. Over 43,000 pupils of different nationalities attended primary school in 2007/2008 (Office of the Ministry of State for Integration 2010). Many of these workers wish to become part of Irish society, to which they have contributed. This desire is reflected in the dramatic increase in recent years in the number of applications for naturalization and long-term residency permits. For example, over the last decade, there have been almost 50,000 applications for naturalization.

Labor Force Participation and Employment

Labor market participation has varied by mode of entry and nationality. According to the 2006 census, nationals from the new EU-10 accession states had a labor participation rate of 93 percent compared with 68 percent for non-EU nationals and 62.5 percent for the population as a whole. Between the fourth quarters of 2007 and 2009, participation rates declined by about 2 percentage points (from 62 percent to 60 percent) for Irish nationals and by almost 4 percentage points (from 76 percent to 72 percent) for non-Irish nationals. Employment rates fell for Irish nationals by over 6 percentage points (from 59 percent to 53 percent), compared to 11 percentage points (from 71 percent to 60 percent) for nonnationals. In other words, the impact on nonnationals' employment and participation was about twice that of Irish nationals.[8]

Unemployment

Since the recession, unemployment has risen sharply—from 4 percent from just over a few years ago to over 12 percent at the end of 2009—and generalized fear has emerged about future employment prospects and the threat of job losses. Unemployment is somewhat higher for non-Irish nationals, and this gap widened substantially during 2009 (Figure IE-2).

Various factors account for immigrants' overrepresentation in unemployment figures. The concentration in specific sectors and in low-pay occupations means that they were the hardest hit during the recession. This was particularly the case for accession-state nationals who were heavily concentrated in construction, hotels and restaurants, and industry. Three-quarters of all nationals from the EU accession states, for example, were concentrated in four industries: manufacturing, construction, wholesale and retail trades, and hotels and restaurants.

---

8 Calculations from CSO, Quarterly National Household Survey (QNHS), Table A1, *Estimated number of persons aged 15 years and older classified by nationality and ILO economic status* (CSO 2010b).

Figure IE-2: Unemployment rates for Irish and non-Irish nationals, 2004 to 2009

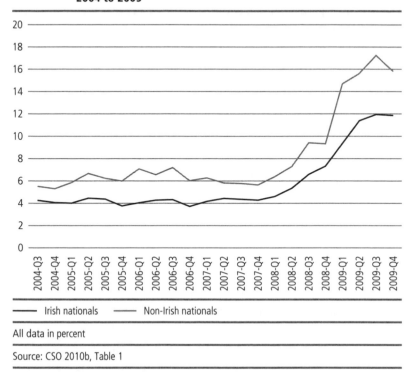

——— Irish nationals ——— Non-Irish nationals

All data in percent

Source: CSO 2010b, Table 1

Over half of Polish and Lithuanian males, two of the biggest groups of non-Irish nationals in the country, are in construction and manufacturing, many working as building laborers or in factories, while half of all females are in shops, hotels and restaurants. There have been large decreases in employment for non-Irish nationals in several of these sectors. In 2009, the employment of non-Irish nationals in construction more than halved; in the wholesale and retail trade, employment fell by 18 percent.[9] In addition, factors such as nonnation-

9 Calculations from CSO 2010b, Table A2, *Estimated number of persons aged 15 years and older in employment (ILO) classified by nationality and NACE economic sector.* Among the 39,000 non-Irish nationals making new applications for unemployment benefits in the first quarter of 2009, manufacturing workers accounted for about one-fifth, and workers from a further three sectors—wholesale and retail, construc-

130

als' concentration in cyclically sensitive industries, nonunionization, language barriers and a policy of "last hired, first fired" have led to layoffs.

Nationals from the EU-15, who have been concentrated in different employment sectors, tend to have been less adversely affected by the recession than other immigrants. Data on UK nationals remains opaque. Their geographic distribution and demographic details are very similar to Irish nationals. Immigrants from outside the European Union have also experienced high levels of unemployment (see Figure IE-3).

Figure IE-3: Unemployment rates in Ireland by nationality, 2007 and 2009

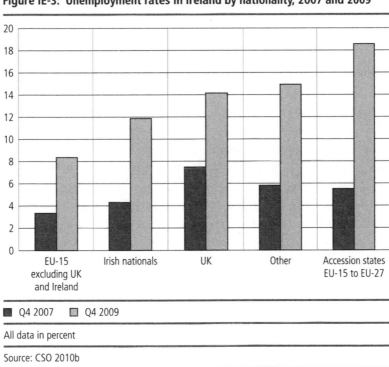

■ Q4 2007   ▨ Q4 2009

All data in percent

Source: CSO 2010b

tion and transportation—accounted for 14 percent each. Finance and insurance accounted for another fifth of the total. Statistics provided to the author by the Central Statistics Office.

Immigrants who have been made unemployed have, like Irish nationals, found it difficult to reaccess jobs. However, their take-up of jobs has been slightly higher than that of Irish nationals. Around 19 percent of immigrants who lost their jobs between January 1 and March 31, 2009 had managed to find a new job by the end of June 2009 compared with 17 percent of Irish nationals (CSO 2009d). There certainly is evidence of problems in accessing employment, especially for black immigrants. Recent studies have also shown that non-Irish nationals were three times more likely to face discrimination while looking for work while black people were seven times more likely (O'Connell and McGinnity 2008).

Labor Market Policies before and during the Recession

Social Protection

Although the numbers of people claiming either jobseeker's allowance or jobseeker's benefit[10] rose by more than half for Irish nationals, it tripled—from 8,000 to 25,000—for non-Irish nationals in the year leading up to December 2008. Migrants do not have automatic entitlement to social welfare. The Irish social welfare system has two programs: social insurance and social assistance. The former is on the basis of pay-related social insurance (PRSI) contributions and permit job-seeker benefits. To qualify, workers must have made the required number of payments into the program; immigrants are eligible if they have done so and if their residence stamp is still valid. If migrant workers build up a sufficient quantity of stamps over a num-

---

10 Jobseeker's benefit (JB) is a social insurance program. It is paid weekly to insured persons who are out of work. Jobseeker's allowance (JA) is a means-tested payment made to unemployed people who do not qualify for JB or whose entitlement to JB has expired.

ber of years, they may become eligible for jobseeker benefits. Social assistance is means-tested and does not depend on PRSI.

However, the Habitual Residence Condition (HRC) means that many migrants remain ineligible for social welfare payments and social assistance. The governments of Ireland and the United Kingdom introduced HRC in 2004 to prevent "welfare tourism." Individuals have to demonstrate that they have been habitually resident in Ireland—usually for over two years—and that they intend to remain here. These requirements also apply to Irish nationals who have lived abroad as well as to European Economic Area (EEA) and non-EEA nationals.[11] Many unemployed migrants are refused welfare benefits because they do not conform to the HRC. Fewer than 5,000 individuals were refused in 2005, but more than 10,500 were refused in 2009. As a result, a large number of migrant workers who lose their jobs will experience acute financial hardship, poverty and social exclusion. Moreover, claiming social welfare often means that an application for citizenship or long-term residency is refused (Immigrant Council 2009). For this reason, many migrants do not apply.

Immigration Policies

Fear of job losses, increasing competition for resources and heightened feelings of insecurity have led to scapegoating and increased racism toward migrants for "taking Irish jobs." The government initially responded to the recession by increasing restrictions on both the entry of work-permit holders and their rights and entitlements once they arrive. New permits for jobs paying less than €30,000 have not been given since June 1, 2009. In addition, the number of job categories ineligible for work permits was expanded, and the duration of the labor market test was also doubled: A job now has to be advertised

11 Applicability is based on the discretion of social welfare officers, who tend to permit returning Irish and some EEA workers greater access to welfare (though this is based on anecdotal evidence). EEA includes all EU Member States plus Iceland, Liechtenstein and Norway.

with the public employment services, FAS, and its EU counterpart, EURES, for at least eight weeks and in a national press advertisement for six days. Migrants made redundant were ineligible to apply for a new work permit unless the job had been advertised for two months. The government justified the increased work-permit restrictions by arguing that Irish nationals needed to be prioritized for jobs. However, this policy change affected only those on work permits—that is, about 1.5 percent of the workers in the country—and, therefore, was more symbolic than practical.

The call for a clampdown on work permits and the creation of tougher permit rules came from a vociferous group of populist politicians. As Fianna Fail Member of Parliament Noel O'Flynn remarked: "What in the name of God are we doing bringing workers in when we haven't work for our own people?" (Molony 2009). Along with Fianna Fail politician Ned O'Keeffe, he also called for greater checks to detect fraudulent claims for social welfare. Another opposition politician, Leo Varadkar, suggested that migrants be paid to leave the country. In November 2009, the Fianna Gael mayor of Limerick called for the cutting of social welfare payments and the deportation of immigrants, including EU nationals, who were abusing Ireland's generous welfare system or who could not find work in Ireland (*Irish Examiner* 2009).

This rhetoric was supplemented with real policy change. The government also cut back heavily on spending on its equality infrastructure and on its protection of migrant rights in Ireland generally. Although many departments saw some cuts, they were particularly acute in the equality sector. The Ministry of Integration's budget was effectively cut by 26 percent, the National Consultative Committee on Racism and Interculturalism was shut down, the Equality Authority was stripped of 43 percent of its resources, and the Irish Human Rights Commission lost 23 percent of its budget.

However, policies and practices have been contradictory, and not all have been restrictionist (Crowley 2010). Work-permit restrictions introduced in June were dropped in September 2009. The length of time migrants had to find a new job was doubled, from three to six months, in August 2009. Moreover, those who had worked for over five years in the work-permit system did not have to renew their permit but could instead apply for permission to live and work in Ireland on a yearly basis without acquiring a new permit (as long as they were in employment and could support themselves) (Irish Naturalisation and Immigration Service 2009a). In addition, after persistent lobbying by various nongovernmental organizations and interest groups, a bridging visa was introduced in October 2009 so that unauthorized migrant workers who had become unemployed because they were made redundant or suffered workplace exploitation could apply for four months' residence permission in order to reenter the permit system (Irish Naturalisation and Immigration Service 2009b).

Conclusion and Recommendations

Since reaching its peak of wealth creation in the first quarter of 2007, Ireland's economy has contracted by almost one-quarter. Since January 2008, government debt has doubled, to €75 billion, and it is expected to double again, to €150 billion, by 2014. An average of 18 companies a day have closed over the past two years (McConnell 2010). Job losses are still mounting, and unemployment increasing. Immigrants have also been disproportionately affected by the recession, especially those from the accession states. Given the acute nature of the economic crisis in Ireland, the likelihood is that unemployment will remain high for the foreseeable future.

A recession has meant a slowdown in immigration, at least in the short run, and it is likely to affect the kind of immigrants who arrive and leave. However, a large number of migrants are here to stay. The Irish government needs to acknowledge this and to facilitate their integration.

Moreover, in the long run, pressures for migration will remain. In its recent Population and Labor Force Projections 2041, the CSO noted that, by 2041, 25 percent of the population will be 65 and over and that, without sufficient net migration, the domestic labor market will not be able to supply enough workers to support the economy's long-run growth potential, even up to 2021. The government needs to acknowledge that immigration will continue and provide an effective information campaign explaining why immigrants will still be necessary in the future.

Integration Policies

There needs to be social inclusion for all workers in Ireland. Policies cannot be solely aimed at migrants; simultaneous efforts are required to help native low-skilled workers. In particular:

- Greater work protection is needed for immigrant workers, especially in the recession. The National Employment Rights Authority (NERA) needs to be given a greater number of inspectors and more powers to fine and sanction employers. Its current policy is to seek redress rather than to penalize. This essentially means that employers operate on a "wait and see if we get caught" basis. Thus, the Employment Rights Compliance Bill that is currently in the Dail needs to be strengthened.[12]
- Non-EU nationals who have worked in Ireland should have access to FAS courses, and language training should also be provided for immigrant workers.
- A system that more effectively recognizes migrant qualifications should be set up.

Immigration and Social Welfare Policies

As a matter of urgency and fairness, the government should reduce the bureaucratic processing times for residency schemes and ease restrictions that disqualify applications because of workers' short-term access to welfare. As of April 2009, 16,847 naturalization applications

---

12 In addition to placing NERA on a statutory footing, the bill entails introducing greater sanctions and fines against errant employers. However, it is not without its weaknesses. Cf. Migrant Rights Centre Ireland 2010.

and 8,000 long-term residency applications were still waiting for a decision (Kildarestreet.com 2009). The length of time for processing an application in both schemes—two years on average—is inordinately long (cf. Irish Naturalisation and Immigration Service 2010). Indeed, many people have been waiting over three years for their application to be processed, in effect making the individual wait a total of eight years for a certificate of naturalization (since a five-year residence period is required for eligibility). Given the long processing times, a number of migrants in these changed economic circumstances are experiencing great distress and anxiety awaiting the outcome of their applications. Many are in a vulnerable position and may become redundant or unauthorized while the application is being processed. Moreover, there are concerns that migrants will not be able to claim social benefits to which they are entitled because of their tax contributions, since this will disqualify them or make them ineligible for citizenship and long-term residency.

In addition, work-permit holders should be given greater mobility between jobs and more rights and entitlements in changing employers and in seeking redress for workplace violations. The Irish government also needs to reinvest in its equality infrastructure, provide a positive vision of migration in the future and create more-humane migration policies that do not depend solely on economic criteria.

Works Cited

Recovering from Recession

Aslund, Olof, and Dan-Olof Rooth. Do When and Where Matter? Initial Labour Market Conditions and Immigrant Earnings. *Economic Journal* (117) 3: 442–488, 2007.

Aydemir, Abdurrahman. Effects of business cycles on the labour market assimilation of immigrants. Research paper no. 203, Family and Labour Studies Division, Statistics Canada, July 2003.

Blanchard, Olivier, Giovanni Dell'Ariccia and Paolo Mauro. Rethinking Macroeconomic Policy. International Monetary Fund Staff Position Note SPN/10/03, IMF, February 2010. www.imf.org/external/pubs/ft/spn/2010/spn1003.pdf (accessed July 14, 2010).

Blanchflower, David, Jumana Saleheen and Chris Shadforth. The Impact of the Recent Migration from Eastern Europe on the UK Economy. IZA Discussion paper 2615, February 2007. ftp://ftp.iza.org/dps/dp2615.pdf (accessed July 14, 2010).

Commission on Growth and Development. *Post-Crisis Growth in Developing Countries: A Special Report of the Commission on Growth and Development on the Implications of the 2008 Financial Crisis.* Washington, DC: The World Bank, 2010.

Congressional Budget Office (CBO). Losing a Job During a Recession. CBO Economic and Budget Issue Brief, April 22, 2010. www.cbo.gov/ftpdocs/114xx/doc11429/JobLoss_Brief.pdf (accessed July, 2010).

Dustmann, Christiann, Albrecht Glitz and Thorsten Vogel. Employment, Wages, and the Economic Cycle: Differences between Immigrants and Natives. CReAM discussion paper June 2009, updated September 2009. www.econ.ucl.ac.uk/cream/pages/CDP/CDP_09_06.pdf (accessed July 14, 2010).

Elsby, Michael, Bart Hobijn and Aysegul Sahin. The Labor Market in the Great Recession. Paper prepared for Brookings Panel on Economic Activity, March 18–19, 2010.

Fix, Michael, Demetrios G. Papademetriou, Jeanne Batalova, Aaron Terrazas, Serena Yi-Ying Lin and Michelle Mittelstadt. *Migration and the Global Recession.* Washington, DC and London: Migration Policy Institute and the British Broadcasting Corporation, 2009. www.migrationpolicy.org/pubs/MPI-BBCreport-Sept09.pdf (accessed July 14, 2010).

German Marshall Fund of the United States. *Transatlantic Trends: Immigration.* Washington, DC: GMFUS, 2009. www.gmfus.org/ trends/immigration/index.html (accessed July 14, 2010).

International Monetary Fund. *World Economic Outlook.* Washington, DC: IMF, 2010a. www.imf.org/external/pubs/ft/weo/2010/ update/01/pdf/0110.pdf (accessed July 14, 2010).

International Monetary Fund. *Navigating the Fiscal Challenges Ahead.* Washington, DC: IMF, 2010b. www.imf.org/external/pubs/ft/fm/ 2010/fm1001.pdf (accessed July 14, 2010).

Isaacs, Julia B. The Effects of the Recession on Child Poverty. Washington DC: Brookings Institution, 2009. www.brookings. edu/~/media/Files/rc/papers/2010/0104_child_poverty_isaacs/ 0104_child_poverty_isaacs.pdf (accessed July 14, 2010).

Islam, Roumeen, and Raj Nallari. *Of Floods and Droughts: The Economic and Financial Crisis of 2008.* Washington, DC: The World Bank, 2010.

McDonald, James Ted, and Christopher Worswick. The earnings of immigrant men in Australia: assimilation, cohort effects, and macroeconomic conditions. *Economic Record* (75) 228: 49–62, 1999.

Moeller, Joachim. The German labor market response in the world recession. *Zeitschrift für Arbeitsmarktforschung* (42) 4: 325–336, 2010.

Morales, Lymari. Americans Return to Tougher Immigration Stance. Washington, DC: Gallup, 2009. www.gallup.com/poll/122057/ Americans-Return-Tougher-Immigration-Stance.aspx.

Nickell, Stephen, Luca Nuzianta and Wolfgang Ochel. Unemployment in the OECD Since the 1960s: What Do We Know? *The Economic Journal* (115) 1: 1–27, 2005. www.res.org.uk/economic/ freearticles/january05.pdf.

Ochsen, Carsten. Are Recessions Good for Educational Attainment? DIW Berlin SOEP papers on Multidisciplinary Panel Data Research no 285, March 2010. www.diw.de/documents/publikationen/73/diw_01.c.354663.de/diw_sp0285.pdf (accessed July 14, 2010).

OECD. *Growing Unequal: Income Distribution and Poverty in OECD Countries.* Paris: OECD, 2008.

Orrenius, Pia, and Madeline Zavodny. *Tied to the Business Cycle: How Immigrants Fare in Good and Bad Economic Times.* Washington, DC: MPI, 2009. www.migrationpolicy.org/pubs/orrenius-Nov09.pdf (accessed July 14, 2010).

Peri, Giovanni. *The Impact of Immigrants in Recession and Economic Expansion.* Washington, DC: MPI, 2010. www.migrationpolicy.org/pubs/Peri-June2010.pdf (accessed July 14, 2010).

Statistisches Bundesamt Deutschland. Detailed results on the economic performance in the 4th quarter of 2009. Statistisches Bundesamt press release no 061, February 24, 2010. www.destatis.de/jetspeed/portal/cms/Sites/destatis/Internet/EN/press/pr/2010/02/PE10__061__811.psml (accessed July 14, 2010).

Stock, James, and Mark Watson. Has the Business Cycle Changed and Why? NBER working paper 9127, August 2002. www.nber.org/papers/w9127 (accessed July 14, 2010).

UK Office of National Statistics. UK Whole Economy: Output per hour worked (data release LZVD), 2010. www.statistics.gov.uk/statbase/tsdtables1.asp?vlnk=prdy (accessed May 13, 2010).

United Nations Population Division. Trends in International Migrant Stock: The 2008 Revision. United Nations database, POP/DB/MIG/Stock/Rev.2008. 2008.

US Bureau of Labor Statistics. Major Sector Productivity and Costs Index (series ID PRS85006092). www.bls.gov/lpc/(accessed May 13, 2010).

Immigrant Integration in the US Labor Market:
The Recession and Its Aftermath

Batalova, Jeanne, and Michael Fix with Peter A. Creticos. *Uneven Progress: The Employment Pathways of Skilled Immigrants in the United States*. Washington, DC: MPI, 2008. www.migrationpolicy.org/pubs/BrainWasteOct08.pdf (accessed July 14, 2010).

Bernanke, Ben S. On the Outlook for the Economy and Policy. Speech at the Economic Club of New York, November 16, 2009. www.federalreserve.gov/newsevents/speech/bernanke20091116a.htm (accessed July 14, 2010).

Bureau of Economic Analysis. National Income and Product Account Tables, 2010. www.bea.gov/national/Index.htm (accessed July 14, 2010).

Bureau of Labor Statistics. Current Employment Statistics. Washington, DC, 2010. www.bls.gov/ces (accessed July 14, 2010).

Capps, Randy, Marc R. Rosenblum and Michael Fix. *Immigrants and Health Care Reform: What's Really at Stake?* Washington, DC: MPI, 2009. www.migrationpolicy.org/pubs/healthcare-Oct09.pdf (accessed July 14, 2010).

Cook, Nancy. What Mancession? *Newsweek* July 16, 2009. www.newsweek.com/id/206917 (accessed July 14, 2010).

Current Population Survey. MPI analysis of the March Socio-economic Supplements to the 2007 and 2009 Current Population Surveys, 2010. www.census.gov/cps (accessed July 14, 2010).

De Jong, Gordon F., and Anna B. Madamba. A Double Disadvantage? Minority Group, Immigrant Status and Underemployment in the United States. *Social Science Quarterly* (82) 1: 117–130, 2001.

Eichengreen, Barry, and Kevin O'Rourke. A Tale of Two Depressions. *VoxEU* September 1, 2009. www.voxeu.org/index.php?q=node/3421 (accessed July 14, 2010).

Federal Reserve Bank. Remarks at the Economic Club of New York. November 16, 2009. www.federalreserve.gov/newsevents/speech/bernanke20091116a.htm (accessed July 14, 2010).

Fix, Michael (ed.). *Immigrants and Welfare: The Impact of Welfare Reform on America's Newcomers.* New York: Russell Sage Foundation, 2009.

Haskins, Ron. *Economic Mobility of Immigrants in the United States.* Washington, DC: Economic Mobility Project, 2008. www.economic mobility.org/assets/pdfs/Pew_Economic_Mobility_Immigrants. pdf (accessed July 14, 2010).

Haskins, Ron, Julia B. Isaacs and Isabel V. Sawhill. *Getting Ahead or Losing Ground: Economic Mobility in America.* Washington, DC: Brookings Institution, Economic Mobility Project, 2008.

Izzo, Phil. Economists Expect Shifting Work Force. *The Wall Street Journal,* February 11, 2010.

Johnson, Nicholas, Phil Oliff and Erica Williams. *An Update on State Budget Cuts.* Washington, DC: Center on Budget and Policy Priorities, 2010. www.cbpp.org/files/3-13-08sfp.pdf (accessed July 14, 2010).

Layard, Richard, Stephen Nickell and Richard Jackman. *Unemployment: Macroeconomic Performance and the Labor Market.* London: Oxford University Press, 2005.

Migration Information Source. Enforcement Tactics Shift in the Obama Era—But What About Immigration Reform? Washington, DC: MPI, 2009a. www.migrationinformation.org/Feature/display. cfm?id=754 (accessed July 14, 2010).

Migration Information Source. What the Recession Wasn't. Washington, DC: MPI, 2009b. www.migrationinformation.org/Feature/ display.cfm?id=752 (accessed July 14, 2010).

Migration Policy Institute. National Center on Immigrant Integration Policy database of state immigration-related legislation, 2010. www.migrationinformation.org/datahub/statelaws_home.cfm (accessed July 14, 2010).

Orrenius, Pia, and Madeline Zavodny. *Tied to the Business Cycle: How Immigrants Fare in Good and Bad Economic Times.* Washington, DC: MPI, 2009. www.migrationpolicy.org/pubs/orrenius-Nov09. pdf (accessed July 14, 2010).

Rampell, Catherine. The Mancession. *New York Times Economix Blog,*
August 10, 2009. http://economix.blogs.nytimes.com/2009/08/
10/the-mancession/ (accessed July 14, 2010).

Rendall, Michael S., Peter Brownell and Sarah Kups. Declining Return Migration from the United States to Mexico in the Late 2000s
Recession. Working Paper WR-720, RAND Population and Labor,
2009. www.rand.org/pubs/working_papers/2010/RAND_WR720-1.
pdf (accessed July 14, 2010).

Roubini Global Economics. *Global Economic Update: Q1 2010.*
New York: Roubini Global Economics, 2010. www.roubini.com/
analysis/100594.php (accessed July 14, 2010).

Slack, Tim, and Leif Jensen. Underemployment across immigrant
generations. *Social Science Research* (36) 4: 1415–1430, 2007.

Somerville, Will, and Madeleine Sumption. *Immigration in the United
Kingdom: The Recession and Beyond.* London: Equality and Human
Rights Commission, 2009. www.migrationpolicy.org/pubs/
Immigration-in-the-UK-The-Recession-and-Beyond.pdf (accessed
July 14, 2010).

Sumption, Madeleine, and Will Somerville. *The UK's New Europeans:
Progress and Challenges Five Years After Accession.* London: Equality
and Human Rights Commission, 2010. www.equalityhuman
rights.com/uploaded_files/new_europeans.pdf (accessed July 14,
2010).

Thompson, Derek. It's Not Just a Recession. It's a Mancession! *The
Atlantic.* July 9, 2009. www.theatlantic.com/business/archive/
2009/07/its-not-just-a-recession-its-a-mancession/20991 (accessed
July 14, 2010).

US Department of Labor Bureau of Labor Statistics. Occupational
Projections 2008–18. Press release, December 2009. www.bls.gov/
news.release/pdf/ecopro.pdf (accessed July 14, 2010).

Recession in the United Kingdom:
Effects on Immigrant Workers and Integration

Barrett, Alan, and Yvonne McCarthy. The Earnings of Immigrants in Ireland: Results from the 2005 EU Survey of Income and Living Conditions. Bonn: Institute for the Study of Labor (IZA), 2007. http://ftp.iza.org/dp2990.pdf (accessed July 13, 2010).

Central Statistics Office Ireland. Quarterly National Household Survey. Cork: CSO. www.cso.ie/qnhs/calendar_quarters_qnhs.htm (accessed July 13, 2010).

Central Intelligence Agency. The World Factbook. Washington, DC: CIA, 2010. www.cia.gov/library/publications/the-world-factbook/rankorder/2004rank.html (accessed July 13, 2010).

Chamberlain, Graeme. Economic Review. February 2010. *Economic & Labour Market Review* (4) 2: 6–12, 2010. www.statistics.gov.uk/downloads/theme_economy/EconReview_0210.pdf (accessed July 13, 2010).

Chote, Robert. Post-budget Presentations: Opening Remarks. Presentation at the Institute for Fiscal Studies. June 23, 2010. www.ifs.org.uk/budgets/budgetjune2010/chote.pdf (accessed July 13, 2010).

D'Addio, Anna Cristina. Intergenerational Transmission of Disadvantage: Mobility or Immobility Across Generations? Paris: OECD, 2007. www.oecd.org/dataoecd/27/28/38335410.pdf (accessed July 13, 2010).

Department for Innovation, Universities and Skills. *A New Approach to English for Speakers of Other Languages (ESOL)*. London: Department for Innovation, Universities and Skills, 2009. www.bis.gov.uk/assets/biscore/corporate/migratedD/publications/E/esol_new_approach (accessed July 13, 2010).

Economic and Social Data Service. *Quarterly Labour Force Survey (LFS)*. 2010. www.esds.ac.uk/findingData/qlfs.asp.

HM Treasury. Forecast for the UK Economy. A comparison of independent forecasts. London: HM Treasury, June 2010. www.hm-treasury.gov.uk/d/201006forecomp.pdf (accessed July 13, 2010).

Home Office. Control of Immigration Statistics United Kingdom 2008. Supplementary excel tables. London: Home Office, 2009. http://rds.homeoffice.gov.uk/rds/immigration-asylum-stats.html (accessed July 13, 2010).

International Monetary Fund. World Economic Outlook Database, 2009. http://imf.org/external/pubs/ft/weo/2009/02/weodata/ weoselgr.aspx (accessed July 13, 2010).

International Monetary Fund. World Economic Outlook Update. Washington, DC: IMF, 2010. www.imf.org/external/pubs/ft/weo/ 2010/update/02/pdf/0710.pdf (accessed July 13, 2010).

Lambert, Richard. The Labour Market and Employer Relations Beyond the Recession. Warwick Papers in Industrial Relations no 93, 2010. www2.warwick.ac.uk/fac/soc/wbs/research/irru/wpir/ wpir_93.pdf (accessed July 13, 2010).

Migration Advisory Committee. Skilled, Shortage, Sensible: The recommended shortage occupation lists for the UK and Scotland. London: MAC, 2008. www.ukba.homeoffice.gov.uk/sitecontent/ documents/aboutus/workingwithus/mac/first-lists/0908/short ageoccupationlistreport?view=Binary (accessed July 13, 2010).

National Equality Panel. *An Anatomy of Economic Inequality in the UK.* London: National Equality Panel, 2010. www.equalities.gov.uk/pdf/ NEP%20Report%20bookmarkedfinal.pdf (accessed July 13, 2010).

Office for National Statistics. UK Workforce jobs seasonally adjusted, series DYDC, July 13, 2010. 2010a. www.statistics.gov.uk/ statbase/tsdintro.asp (accessed July 13, 2010).

Office for National Statistics. Economic & Labour Market Review— June 2010 Edition. Selected Labour Market Statistics. 2010b. www.statistics.gov.uk/elmr/06_10/2.asp (accessed July 13, 2010).

Office for National Statistics. Labour Force Survey, July 2010. 2010c. www.statistics.gov.uk/statbase/Source.asp?vlnk=358 (accessed July 13, 2010).

Somerville, Will, Dhananjayan Sriskandarajah and Maria Latorre. United Kingdom: A Reluctant Country of Immigration. *Migration Information Source,* March 2009. www.migrationinformation.org/ feature/display.cfm?ID=736 (accessed July 13, 2010).

Somerville, Will, and Madeleine Sumption. *Immigration in the United Kingdom: The Recession and Beyond*. London: Equality and Human Rights Commission, 2009. www.migrationpolicy.org/pubs/ Immigration-in-the-UK-The-Recession-and-Beyond.pdf (accessed July 13, 2010).

Sumption, Madeleine, and Will Somerville. *The UK's New Europeans: Progress and Challenges Five Years After Accession*. London: Equality and Human Rights Commission, 2010. www.equalityhuman rights.com/uploaded_files/new_europeans.pdf (accessed July 13, 2010).

Tetlow, Gemma. Public finances: more done, more quickly. Presentation at the Institute for Fiscal Studies, June 23, 2010. www.ifs. org.uk/budgets/budgetjune2010/tetlow.pdf (accessed July 13, 2010).

UK Data Archive. Quarterly Labour Force Survey (LFS), 2009. www.data-archive.ac.uk/findingData/lfstitles.asp (accessed July 13, 2010).

Whiffin, Andrew, and Daniel Pimlott. European housing hope despite gloom. *Financial Times* April 4, 2010. www.ft.com/cms/s/0/ c72b41a8-4007-11df-8d23-00144feabdc0.html?ftcamp=rss.

Migration, Integration and the Labor Market after the Recession in Germany

Bundesagentur für Arbeit. *Analyse des Arbeitsmarktes für Deutschland Dezember 2009*. Analytikreport der Statistik, Januar 2010. Nuremberg: BA, 2010a. www.pub.arbeitsagentur.de/hst/services/ statistik/000200/html/analytik/analytikreport_2009-12.pdf (accessed July 14, 2010).

Bundesagentur für Arbeit. *Analyse des Arbeitsmarktes für Ausländer Januar 2010*. Analytikreport der Statistik, Februar 2010. Nuremberg: BA, 2010b. www.pub.arbeitsagentur.de/hst/services/statistik/ 000200/html/analytik/auslaender-analytikreport_2010-01.pdf (accessed July 14, 2010).

Bundesagentur für Arbeit. *Analyse des Arbeitsmarktes für Ausländer Februar 2010*. Analytikreport der Statistik, März 2010. Nuremberg: BA, 2010c. www.pub.arbeitsagentur.de/hst/services/statistik/000200/html/analytik/auslaender-analytikreport_2010-02.pdf (accessed July 14, 2010).

Bundesagentur für Arbeit. *Arbeitsgenehmigungen und Zustimmungen 2009*. Arbeitsmarkt in Zahlen. Statistik der Bundesagentur für Arbeit. Nuremberg: BA, 2010d. www.pub.arbeitsagentur.de/hst/services/statistik/200912/iiia6/ae/aezu_d.pdf.

Bundesagentur für Arbeit. *Report on the labor market: The labor market in Germany—a year of crisis for the German labor market*. Nuremberg: BA, 2009a. www.pub.arbeitsagentur.de/hst/services/statistik/000100/html/sonder/a_year_of_crisis_for_the_german_labour_market.pdf (accessed July 14, 2010).

Bundesagentur für Arbeit. *Arbeitsgenehmigungen und Zustimmungen 2008*. Arbeitsmarkt in Zahlen. Statistik der Bundesagentur für Arbeit. Nuremberg: BA, 2009b. www.pub.arbeitsagentur.de/hst/services/statistik/200812/iiia6/ae/aezu_d.pdf (accessed July 14, 2010).

Bundesministerium für Arbeit und Soziales. *Mit Kurzarbeit die Krise meistern*. March 2010. Berlin: Bundesministerium für Arbeit und Soziales, 2010a. www.einsatz-fuer-arbeit.de/sites/generator/29874/Startseite.html (accessed July 14, 2010).

Bundesministerium für Arbeit und Soziales. *Wirkungen von SGB II auf Personen mit Migrationshintergrund*. Abschlussbericht, Hauptband. Berlin: Bundesministerium für Arbeit und Soziales, 2010b. www.bmas.de/portal/39948/property=pdf/f395__forschungs bericht.pdf (accessed July 14, 2010).

Bundesministerium für Bildung und Forschung. Eckpunke der Bundesregierung. Verbesserung der Feststellung und Anerkennung von im Ausland erworbenen beruflichen Qualifikationen und Berufsabschlüssen. Berlin: Bundesministerium für Bildung und Forschung, 2009. www.bmbf.de/pub/Pm1209-294Eckpunkte-Papier.pdf (accessed July 14, 2010).

Danzer, Alexander, and Firat Yaman. Ethnic Concentration and Language Fluency of Immigrants in Germany. IAB Discussion Paper 4742 2010. Nuremberg: Institute for Employment Research, 2010.

Dustmann, Christian, Albrecht Glitz and Thorsten Vogel. Employment, wage structure, and the economic cycle: differences between immigrants and natives in Germany and the UK. CReAM Discussion Paper (09) 06, 2006. www.econ.ucl.ac.uk/cream/pages/CDP/CDP_09_06.pdf (accessed July 14, 2010).

Geißler, Rainer. Bildungschancen und soziale Herkunft. *Archiv für Wissenschaft und Praxis der sozialen Arbeit* (37) 4: 34–49, 2006.

Granato, Nadia. Effekte der Gruppengröße auf die Arbeitsmarktintegration von Migranten. *Kölner Zeitschrift für Soziologie und Sozialpsychologie* (61) 3: 387–409, 2009.

Herbert, Ulrich. *Geschichte der Ausländerpolitik in Deutschland—Saisonarbeiter, Zwangsarbeiter, Gastarbeiter, Flüchtlinge.* Munich: Beck, 2001.

Krugman, Paul. Free to Lose. *New York Times*, November 12, 2009. www.nytimes.com/2009/11/13/opinion/13krugman.html (accessed July 14, 2010).

Moeller, Joachim. The German labor market response in the world recession—de-mystifying a miracle. *Zeitschrift für Arbeitsmarktforschung* (42) 4: 325–336, 2010.

Organisation for Economic Co-operation and Development (OECD). *Wo haben Schüler mit Migrationshintergrund die größten Erfolgschancen: Eine vergleichende Analyse von Leistung und Engagement in PISA 2003.* Paris: OECD, 2006.

Sachverständigenrat zur Begutachtung der gesamtwirtschaftlichen Entwicklung . *Die Zukunft nicht aufs Spiel setzen.* Jahresgutachten 2009/2010. Wiesbaden: Sachverstaendigenrat zur Begutachtung der gesamtwirtschaftlichen Entwicklung, 2009. www.sachverstaendigenrat-wirtschaft.de/gutacht/ga-content.php?gaid=55 (accessed July 14, 2010).

Schmieder, Johannes F., Till von Wachter and Stefan Bender. The long-term impact of job displacement in Germany during the 1982 recession on earnings, income, and employment. IAB Discussion Paper 01/2010. Nuremberg: Institute for Employment Research, 2010. http://doku.iab.de/discussionpapers/2010/ dp0110.pdf (accessed July 14, 2010).

Statistisches Bundesamt. Bevölkerung mit Migrationshintergrund. Ergebnisse des Mikrozensus 2008, Fachserie 1 Reihe 2.2, Wiesbaden: Statistisches Bundesamt, 2010. www.ec.destatis.de/csp/ shop/sfg/bpm.html.cms.cBroker.cls?cmspath=struktur,vollanzeige. csp&ID=1025212 (accessed July 14, 2010).

Migration and the Recession in Spain

Arango, Joaquin, and Maia Jachimowicz. Regularizing Immigrants in Spain: A New Approach. *Migration Information Source*, September 2005. www.migrationinformation.org/Feature/display.cfm?id=331 (accessed July 13 2010).

Barro, Roberto, and Xavier Sala-i-Martin. *Economic Growth*. Cambridge, Mass.: MIT University Press, 2003.

BBVA Servicio de Estudios. *Perspectivas para las economías española y madrileña 2010*. Bilbao: BBVA, March 2010. http://serviciode estudios.bbva.com/KETD/fbin/mult/100316_perspectivas_para_ las_economias_espanola_y_madrilena_2010_tcm346-216657. pdf?ts=1542010 (accessed July 13 2010).

Cabrales, Antonio, Juan José Dolado, Florentino Felgueroso and Pablo Vásquez (eds.). *La Crisis de la Economía Española: Lecciones y Propuestas*. Madrid: Fundación de Estudios de Economía Aplicada, FEDEA, 2009. www.crisis09.es/ebook (accessed July 13, 2010).

Cebolla-Boado, Hector, Ruth Ferrero-Turrión and Gemma Pinyol-Jiménez. *Analysis of Economic and Labour Market Indicators. Case Study: Spain*. Brussels: Independent Network of Labour Migration and Integration Experts (I-LISNET), (forthcoming) 2010.

Cachón, Lorenzo. La formación de la España inmigrante: Mercado de trabajo y ciudadanía. *Revista Española de Investigaciones Sociológicas* (97): 95–126, 2002.

Cachón, Lorenzo. *La España inmigrante: marco discriminatorio, mercado de trabajo y políticas de integración*. Barcelona: Anthropos, 2009.

Fundación de Estudios de Economía aplicada (FEDEA). *The Crisis of the Spanish economy*. Papers presented at FEDEA Annual Policy Conference Madrid, March 2010. www.crisis09.es/monografia 2009/descargas.html (accessed July 13, 2010).

Ferrero-Turrión, Ruth, and Ana López-Sala. Nuevas dinámicas de la gestión de las migraciones en España: el caso de los acuerdos bilaterales de trabajadores con los países de origen. *Revista del Ministerio de Trabajo e Inmigración* (80): 119–132, 2009a.

Ferrero-Turrión, Ruth, and Ana López-Sala. Economic Crisis and Migration Policies in Spain. The Big Dilemma. Unpublished paper presented at COMPAS Annual Conference "New Times? Economic Crisis, geo-political transformation and the emergent migration order." University of Oxford, September 21–23 2009. 2009b.

Ferrero-Turrión, Ruth, and Ana López-Sala. *Migration and the economic crisis: implications for policy in the European Union. Case Study: Spain*. Brussels: Independent Network of Labour Migration and Integration Experts (I-LISNET), (forthcoming) 2010.

Ferrero-Turrión, Ruth, and Gemma Pinyol-Jiménez. The regularization of undocumented migrants: A path to rights in the European Union. *Mediterranean Journal of Human Rights* (11) 2: 263–282, 2007.

International Monetary Fund. *World Economic Outlook 2009*. Washington, DC: IMF, 2009.

Izquierdo, Antonio. *Demografía de los Extranjeros: Incidencia en el crecimiento de la población*. Bilbao: Fundación BBVA, 2006.

Ministry of Labor and Immigration. Fondo de apoyo a la Acogida e Integración de Inmigrantes. Madrid 2009. www.mtin.es/es/ sec_emi/IntegraInmigrantes/contenidos/FondoAcogida.htm (accessed July 13, 2010).

National Statistics Institute. Producto Interior Bruto (PIB) Base 2000. Crecimiento en volumen. Madrid 2010. www.ine.es (accessed July 13, 2010).

National Statistics Institute. Indicadores Demográficos Básicos, Número medio de hijos por mujer, 1975–2008. www.ine.es/jaxi/tabla.do?per=12&type=db&divi=IDB&idtab=11&L=0 (accessed July 13, 2010).

National Statistics Institute. Encuestra de Población Activa. Madrid, various years. www.ine.es (accessed July 13, 2010).

Migration and Recession in Ireland

Allen, Kieran. *The Corporate Takeover of Ireland*. Dublin: Irish Academic Press, 2007.

Central Intelligence Agency. The World Factbook, Ireland. Washington, DC: CIA, 2010. www.cia.gov/library/publications/the-world-factbook/index.html (accessed July 15, 2010).

Central Statistics Office. *Persons usually resident and present in the state on census night, classified by nationality and age*. Cork: CSO, n.d. www.cso.ie/statistics/nationalityagegroup.htm.

Central Statistics Office. *Census 2006. Volume 10: Education and Qualifications*. Cork: CSO, 2006. http://beyond2020.cso.ie/Census/TableViewer/tableView.aspx?ReportId=76961 (accessed July 15, 2010).

Central Statistics Office. Measuring Ireland's Progress 2006. News release, April 30, 2007. Cork: CSO, 2007a. www.cso.ie/newsevents/pressrelease_measuringirelandsprogress2006.htm (accessed July 15, 2010).

Central Statistics Office. *National Employment Survey 2006*. Cork: CSO, 2007b. www.cso.ie/releasespublications/documents/earnings/nes2006/nes.pdf (accessed July 15, 2010).

Central Statistics Office. *Census 2006, Non-Irish Nationals Living in Ireland*. Cork: CSO, 2008. www.cso.ie/census/documents/NON%20IRISH%20NATONALS%20LIVING%20IN%20IRELAND.pdf (accessed July 15, 2010).

Central Statistics Office. *Measuring Ireland's Progress 2008*. Cork: CSO, 2009a. www.cso.ie/releasespublications/documents/other_

releases/2008/progress2008/measuringirelandsprogress.pdf (accessed July 15, 2010).

Central Statistics Office. Population and Migration Estimates. Cork: CSO, April 2009. 2009b. www.cso.ie/releasespublications/ documents/population/current/popmig.pdf (accessed July 15, 2010).

Central Statistics Office. *Foreign Nationals: PPSN Allocations, Employment and Social Welfare Activity 2008.* Cork: CSO, 2009c. www. cso.ie/releasespublications/documents/labour_market/current/ ppsn.pdf (accessed July 15, 2010).

Central Statistics Office. Analysis of Live Register Flows Q1 2009. Cork: CSO, 2009d. www.cso.ie/releasespublications/documents/ labour_market/current/alrf.pdf (accessed July 15, 2010).

Central Statistics Office. Quarterly National Household Survey, Q4, 2009. News release, March 24, 2010. Cork: CSO, 2010a. www.cso.ie/releasespublications/documents/labour_market/ current/qnhs.pdf (accessed July 15, 2010).

Central Statistics Office. Quarterly National Household Survey. Cork: CSO, 2010b. www.cso.ie/qnhs/calendar_quarters_qnhs.htm (accessed July 15, 2010).

Crowley, Niall. Hidden Messages, Overt Agendas. Dublin: Migrant Rights Centre Ireland, 2010. www.mrci.ie/news_events/ documents/HIDDEN_MESSAGES_OVERT_AGENDAS.pdf (accessed July 15, 2010).

Finfacts Ireland. Foreign-owned firms were responsible for 90.2 % of Irish exports in 2006—including both merchandise goods and internationally traded services. January 2008. www.finfacts.ie/ irishfinancenews/article_1012368.shtml (accessed July 15, 2010).

Immigrant Council. Citizenship processes in need of overhaul. News release, May 7, 2009. www.immigrantcouncil.ie/press_detail. php?id=9.1 (accessed July 15, 2010).

Irish Examiner. Limerick Mayor calls for deportations of unemployed immigrants. November 11, 2009. www.examiner.ie/breaking news/ireland/limerick-mayor-calls-for-deportations-of-unemployed-immigrants-433866.html (accessed July 15, 2010).

Irish Naturalisation and Immigration Service. New Provisions for Non-EEA workers who are made redundant. News release, August 28, 2009. 2009a. www.inis.gov.ie/en/INIS/Pages/New_Provisions_for_Non-EEA_workers (accessed July 15, 2010).

Irish Naturalisation and Immigration Service. Undocumented Workers Scheme. Irish Naturalization and Immigration Service, October 2009. 2009b. www.inis.gov.ie/en/INIS/Pages/Undocumented_Workers_Scheme (accessed July 15, 2010).

Irish Naturalisation and Immigration Service. Information on Application Processing Times. Dublin: Irish Naturalization and Immigration Service, 2010. www.inis.gov.ie/en/INIS/Pages/Citizenship_Processing_Times (accessed July 15, 2010).

Kearns, Allan, and Maria Woods. *The Concentration in Property-Related Lending: A Financial Stability Perspective.* Central Bank of Ireland Financial Stability Report 2006. www.centralbank.ie/data/FinStaRepFiles/The%20Concentration%20in%20Property-Related%20Lending%20-%20a%20Financial%20Stability%20Perspective.pdf (accessed July 15, 2010).

Kildarestreet.com. Dail debates; Written Answers. Kildarestreet.com, April 2, 2009. www.kildarestreet.com/wrans/?id=2009-04-02.1174.0&s=naturalisation+long+term+residency#g1178.0.r (accessed July 15, 2010).

Killeen, Tony. Speech by Minister of State for Labour Affairs at the launch of Jobs Ireland, New York, October 20, 2006. www.entemp.ie/press/2006/20061020c.htm (accessed July 15, 2010).

McConnell, Daniel. Our economy has fallen off a cliff. *Sunday Independent* March 28, 2010. www.independent.ie/national-news/our-economy-has-fallen-off-a-cliff-2114878.html (accessed July 15, 2010).

Migrant Rights Centre Ireland. Ending the Race to the Bottom. Dublin: Migrant Rights Centre Ireland 2010. www.mrci.ie/publications/documents/MRCIPPEndingtheRacetotheBottom-MigrantWorker-Exploitation.pdf (accessed July 15, 2010).

Moloney, Senan. Outspoken TD calls for work permit clampdown. *Irish Independent* February 7, 2009. www.independent.ie/national-

news/outspoken-td-calls-for-work-permit-clampdown-1631834.
html (accessed July 15, 2010).

O'Connell, Philip J., and Frances McGinnity. *Immigrants at Work: Ethnicity and Nationality in the Irish Labour Market.* Dublin: ESRI and Equality Authority, 2008. www.equality.ie/index.asp?docID= 737 (accessed July 15, 2010).

Office of the Minister of State for Integration. Overview of Key Statistics. 2010. www.integration.ie/website/omi/omiwebv6.nsf/page/ statistics-overview-en (accessed July 15, 2010).

RTE Business. Bank of Ireland Shares plummet to 83 percent. November 17, 2008. www.rte.ie/business/2008/1117/boi.html (accessed July 15, 2010).

United Nations Conference on Trade and Development (UNCTAD). *World Investment Report. Transnational Corporations, Agricultural Production and Development.* New York and Geneva: UNCTAD, 2009. www.unctad.org/en/docs/wir2009_en.pdf (accessed July 15, 2010).

Immigrant Students in US Schools and the Recession of 2007–2009

Aaron Terrazas, Michael Fix and Margie McHugh

Introduction[1]

The severe economic crisis that officially began in the United States in December 2007 has had profound implications for the nation's elementary and secondary schools. State fiscal crises have forced educators and administrators to reevaluate priorities and implement difficult budget cuts. Meanwhile, the unprecedented federal fiscal stimulus enacted in February 2009 provided a unique opportunity for policy innovation (in addition to a much-needed but temporary infusion of federal cash) and foreshadowed plans for more lasting changes in the federal role in K-12 education.

These changes occur at a critical juncture for US population trends. Sustained immigration to the United States in recent decades has reshaped the demographic profile of America's schools. Between 1990 and 2008, the number of children of immigrants doubled, from 8.2 million to 16.3 million, outpacing the growth of the number of US-born children with two US-born parents, which grew by only 2 percent, from 52.8 million to 53.7 million.[2] By 2008, children (both US and foreign born) of immigrants accounted for 23.2 percent of all children under age 18 compared to 13.4 percent in 1990.

---

1 The authors would like to thank MPI intern Christine Michelle Mechler for excellent research assistance.
2 We define *immigrant-origin children* or *children of immigrant origin* as children under age 18 (regardless of their own place of birth) who have at least one foreign-born parent.

155

Many immigrant students do extraordinarily well in US schools. But others face a wide range of barriers to success. Some of these barriers—poverty, limited parental engagement and de facto school segregation—are not unique to immigrant students but have a disproportionate impact in immigrant communities. Others, such as limited English proficiency and legal immigration status, are particular challenges for children in immigrant families.[3] The US K-12 education system also tends to reinforce existing socioeconomic inequalities. Strong local control over standards, teacher requirements and student assessment, among other key elements of schooling, mean that student outcomes vary widely. Heavy reliance on state and local financing (only roughly 10 percent of education funding is federally provided), combined with substantial de facto residential segregation, means that poorer districts face constant resource constraints and are vulnerable to rapid or unexpected contractions in local government revenues.

This chapter focuses on how immigrant and limited English proficient (LEP) students fared in US elementary and secondary schools prior to the recession and how K-12 education policies have evolved over the course of the recession. First, we describe how immigrant and LEP children were faring in US schools on the eve of the recession and the policies that shaped their academic outcomes. Since states play central roles in education policy, we also look at policy trends in five states that have historically received the largest numbers of immigrants—California, Florida, Illinois, New York and Texas—as well as several states that have recently attracted large numbers of immigrants, such as Arizona, Nevada and Maryland.

---

3 The term *limited English proficient* (LEP) refers to any person age 5 and older who reports speaking English "not at all," "not well" or "well." The term is used interchangeably with *English language learner* (ELL) throughout this report.

The Demography of Immigrant Students in US Schools

Immigration is changing the demographic profile of America's schools.[4] Sustained immigration to the United States in recent decades has re-shaped the demographic profile of America's schools. The number of children with immigrant parents is growing much faster than the number of US-born children with two US-born parents. As immigrant families settle in communities throughout the United States (rather than in a limited number of urban centers and major points of entry), their children are enrolling in schools not traditionally accustomed to educating immigrant students.

Growth. In 2008, nearly 16.3 million children under 18 lived in immigrant families, including 13.9 million US-born children (also known as "the second generation") and 2.3 million foreign-born children (or "the first generation"). Between 1990 and 2008, the number of children of immigrants doubled, from 8.2 million to 16.3 million, while US-born children with two US-born parents (or "the third-plus generation") grew from 52.8 million to 53.7 million (see Figure 1). Among young children age 6 and under, this trend is even more pronounced: In 2008, one-quarter of all children under age 6 had an immigrant parent compared to 13 percent in 1990. In California, nearly half of children under age 6 had an immigrant parent, as did more than a third of young children in Nevada, New York, New Jersey and Texas.

Geographic distribution. Immigrants have traditionally settled in a limited number of gateway states and cities. In 1990, two-thirds (68.7 percent) of children with immigrant parents resided in just five states: California, New York, Florida, Texas and Illinois. By 2008, the share of children with immigrant parents residing in these states had declined to 60.4 percent. (California and New York accounted for most of this decline, while the share increased in Texas and Illinois.) Driven by new job opportunities and escalating housing costs in coastal areas, many immigrants bypassed traditional destinations in favor of communities in the Southeast and Mountain West. The

---

4   This section draws on Batalova and Fix 2010.

Figure 1: Children of immigrants, 1990 to 2008

Number of children of immigrants

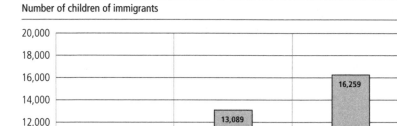

Percentage of all children under 18

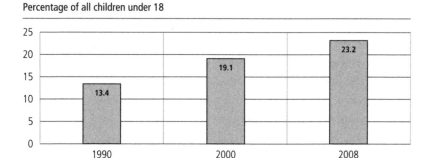

Data for top chart in thousands of individuals; data for lower chart in percent

Sources: MPI analysis of the US Census Bureau's 2008 American Community Survey and 1990 and 2000 Decennial Census

number of children with immigrant parents at least quadrupled in seven states—North Carolina, Georgia, Nevada, Arkansas, Tennessee, Nebraska and South Carolina—between 1990 and 2008 (see Map 1).

Map 1: Children of immigrants, by state, 1990 to 2008

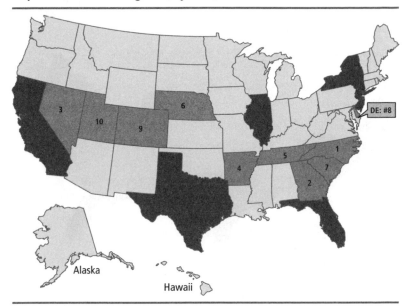

■ States with 500,000 or more children of immigrants (2008)

■ States (ranked) with more than 250 percent growth (1990 to 2008)

Sources: US Census Bureau, 1990 Decennial Census and 2008 American Community Survey.
Map: © Istockphoto/appleuzr

Children with immigrant parents face substantial barriers to academic success.[5] The US public education system has historically been a powerful force for immigrant integration, and many immigrant students do extraordinarily well in US schools (Fix (ed.) 2007; Haskins and Sawhill 2009). However, children with immigrant parents also face substantial barriers to academic success. Some of these barriers are unique to immigrant students; others reflect more general challenges to the US elementary and secondary education system.

5 Unless otherwise indicated, data presented in this section are based on Migration Policy Institute (MPI) analysis of pooled microdata from the 2007 and 2008 American Community Survey (ACS) made available through the Minnesota Population Center. Cf. Ruggles et al. 2010, http://usa.ipums.org/usa/. It includes children with immigrant parents—both first- and second-generation—who are enrolled in school.

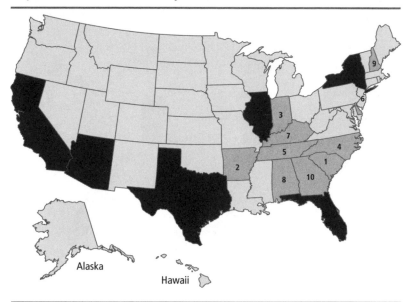

■ States with 150,000 or more ELL students (2005–2006)

☐ States (ranked) with more than 250 percent ELL growth (1996 to 2006)

Source: Office of English Language Acquisition, November 2008.
Map: © 2009 Istockphoto/appleuzr

English proficiency and English Language Learner (ELL) enrollment. In 2008, roughly one in 10 students in US schools was an English language learner. Between 1997 and 2008, the ELL population nationwide rose by 53 percent, while the overall student population grew by just 8 percent.[6] Reflecting the dispersion of immigrants throughout the United States, ELL enrollment has grown fastest in Southern and Midwestern states (see Map 2). Seventy-five percent of LEP children with immigrant parents speak Spanish.

6   MPI tabulation of data from State Title III Directors, Consolidated State Performance Reports to the US Department of Education and the Institute of Education Science's Core of Common Data.

Diversity of the ELL Population. According to 2008 American Community Survey (ACS) data, over three-quarters (78 percent) of elementary school students and over half (60 percent) of secondary school students who are English language learners were born (and presumably educated) in the United States. At the same time, a very large share of first-generation or immigrant students in both elementary (50 percent) and secondary (40 percent) schools are recently arrived—that is, having been in the United States less than three years. These patterns underscore the diversity of the ELL population in schools that includes both the recently arrived—many of whom have interrupted schooling in their home countries—and long-term US-born ELLs.

Poverty. Nearly half (48 percent) of children with immigrant parents live in families with total annual incomes below 200 percent of the federal poverty line, compared to about one-third (33 percent) of native-born children with native-born parents.

Segregation and concentration. Widespread de facto residential segregation in the United States results in most LEP children being concentrated in urban and high-poverty schools. According to the National Center for Education Statistics' *2007–08 Schools and Staffing Survey*, one of every five students in urban schools was an English language learner, compared to one of every 10 in suburban schools and one of every 18 in rural schools (see Figure 2).[7] Similarly, ELLs were nearly one-third of students in high-poverty schools compared to one-twentieth of students in low-poverty schools (see Figure 2).

Substantial evidence suggests that schools are not adequately meeting the academic needs of children with immigrant parents. Data on the academic outcomes of LEP, Hispanic and low-income students (of whom about 83 percent, 54 percent and 30 percent, respectively, are children of immigrants) indicate that children with immigrant parents and ELLs lag behind their peers on academic assessments, graduation rates and rates of matriculation in postsecondary education.

National academic assessments. The National Assessment of Educational Progress (NAEP) shows that ELLs score substantially below

7   Includes only public schools (Keigher and Gruber 2009).

Figure 2: ELL student concentration, 2007 to 2008

ELL share of students by community type

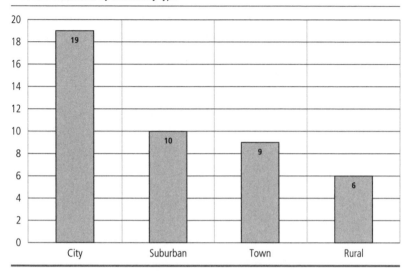

ELL share of students by free or reduced-price lunch eligibility

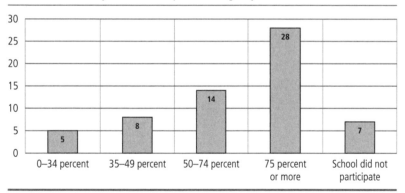

All data in percent

Note: Includes public schools only. For lower chart, low-poverty schools are those where fewer than 35 percent of students are eligible for free or reduced-price lunches. High-poverty schools are those where 75 percent or more of students are eligible.

Source: National Center for Education Statistics, Schools and Staffing Survey 2007–08

their peers and that the gap between ELLs and non-ELLs has remained remarkably stable in recent years. Furthermore, the academic performance of former ELLs (i.e., those deemed to have mastered English) falls sharply between the 4th and 8th grades, with former ELLs lagging behind English-proficient youth badly.

State academic assessments. A recent review of ELL student performance on state-administered exams suggests that ELLs are improving although the gains are more prominent for younger ELLs and are greater in mathematics than in reading (Chudowsky and Chudowsky 2010). In particular, ELLs made gains across the board in California, Texas, Florida and New York—states that account for over half of the nation's ELLs taking statewide assessments. However, the authors point to substantial differences between the state exams and caution is necessary when comparing the scores across states.

Secondary school completion. LEP youth ages 16 to 24 are three times more likely than their English-proficient peers to drop out of high school. Among LEP youth, the dropout rate is 24 percent, compared to 7 percent among English-proficient youth. Foreign-born youth who immigrate to the United States at a younger age are much less likely to drop out of high school than their late-arriving peers: The dropout rate among immigrant youth who arrived before age 14 is less than half the dropout rate among immigrant youth who arrived between the ages of 14 and 17 (13 percent versus 32 percent).

US Education Policy and Immigrant Students

Elementary and secondary education in the United States is primarily a state and local responsibility. However, the federal government has historically supported the establishment of national standards, promoted evaluation and innovation, and—since the 1965 Elementary and Secondary Education Act (ESEA)—subsidized the education of disadvantaged students (US Department of Education 2010). But the demographic profile of US students, and especially disadvantaged students, has changed dramatically in recent decades. Immigrant, second-generation and LEP children now account for a greater share of disadvantaged students than at any other point since ESEA was first enacted.

The most recent version of ESEA, the No Child Left Behind Act of 2001 (NCLB), made important advances toward ensuring that schools address the educational needs of LEP students. On balance, there is widespread consensus that NCLB represented a step in the right direction, at least when it comes to promoting greater school accountability for the performance of ELL students (Working Group on ELL Policy 2010). In particular, the law's requirement that LEP student performance be tracked and reported as a subgroup for school accountability purposes has focused greater attention on this historically overlooked population.

Federal education policy under NCLB represents a proactive attempt to improve the academic outcomes of immigrant and LEP students. NCLB is a complex, controversial law whose effects are still unfolding. Title I of the law provides grants to states for supporting the education of disadvantaged students, and Title III provides grants specifically targeted to ELLs. Both grants are formula-based (although, prior to NCLB, federal support for ELL education was channeled through competitive grants) and tie assessment and outcome conditions to the grants (Osorio-O'Dea 2001). Federal grants to states for disadvantaged students under Title I totaled $13.9 billion in 2008, about 20 times larger than federal grants for English language acquisition under Title III ($700 million). As a result, the conditions tied to Title I are far more powerful than those under Title III.

But NCLB also suffers from a number of flaws, and state implementation of the law has been uneven. NCLB has also been the object of extensive criticism. Some stakeholders fear that the law's emphasis on standardized tests and rigid sanctions unduly penalizes schools with large enrollments of disadvantaged and LEP children as well as jeopardizes the long-term success of these students by throwing schools subject to sanctions into turmoil (Ravitch 2010; Mintrop and Sunderman 2009). In the context of the economic crisis, three concerns are particularly relevant:

164

Federal funding to states for English language acquisition has declined in real terms under NCLB. In real terms (accounting for inflation), NCLB represented a substantial increase in federal education funding for both disadvantaged students (Title I) and English language acquisition (Title III under NCLB, prior Bilingual Education Act). However, since enactment in 2002, federal grants to states for disadvantaged students have stagnated, and grants for English language acquisition have declined, although these trends appear to have reversed under the Obama administration. Moreover, as discussed later in this report, federal stimulus spending under the American Recovery and Reinvestment Act (ARRA) channeled additional funds to Title I but overlooked Title III.

Emerging evidence suggests that state-level implementation of NCLB has been uneven. States have substantial discretion in setting achievement curriculum and standards, designing assessments and implementing sanctions for underperforming schools. This diversity is reflected in the wide range in reported outcomes and schools subject to sanctions. For example, the share of high school ELLs who test proficient in reading ranges across states between 6 percent and 87 percent; presumably this incredibly wide range reflects other factors in addition to student performance (Chudowsky and Chudowsky 2010). Some states have used several strategies—including watering-down standards, seeking loopholes to avoid reporting subgroups and encouraging underperforming students to drop out of school—to avoid implementing the most stringent sanctions, such as staff reorganization (for some of these strategies, see Chudowsky and Chudowsky 2005 and 2007).

NCLB provides support for the education of disadvantaged students, poor districts still rely overwhelmingly on state and local funding. Even as NCLB channeled greater federal funding to states to support the education of poor and LEP students and implemented more transparent outcome metrics to measure their progress, it continued to rely heavily on active support from state and (to a lesser extent) local governments. Federal funds have historically accounted for only about 10 percent of all K-12 education expenditures. Although districts with high ELL enrollments tend to rely somewhat more on federal revenues than other districts, they still depend overwhelmingly on state and local funding. Moreover, since ELLs are concentrated in low-income communities, high-ELL districts often have access to fewer local resources.

The Economic Crisis: Adjustment and Innovation

Government tax revenues have contracted sharply since the current economic crisis officially began in December 2007. Forty-eight of the nation's 50 states recently reported that they faced gaps in their 2010 budgets.[8] Federal, state and local policymakers have responded differently to these rapid contractions in revenues. State and local governments have been forced to dramatically cut services—including education—while the fiscal stimulus enacted by Congress under ARRA has allowed the federal government to temporarily expand its role in K-12 education.

The Obama administration has taken advantage of the financial crisis to introduce reforms that may benefit ELLs. The new administration seized upon the occasion of the economic crisis to implement far-reaching reforms, many of which had been on the table before the crisis. These included tying state funds to conditions that states establish longitudinal data systems to better track student outcomes, work toward establishing common standards and develop more meaningful academic requirements that better reflect the demands of postsecondary education and the labor force. As the Center on Education Policy has observed: "Although these reforms might have happened anyway, the stimulus package appears to have reinforced and in some ways advanced these efforts" (Kober et al. 2009).

American Recovery and Reinvestment Act of 2009. In February 2009, Congress enacted a record $787 billion economic stimulus bill known as ARRA. The bill included $115 billion in education spending, of which nearly half ($53.6 billion) was allocated to the State Fiscal Stabilization Fund (SFSF) and over a tenth ($13.0 billion) was allocated to

8 Inflation-adjusted total tax revenue. MPI tabulations of data from the US Census Bureau's Quarterly Summary of State and Local Government Tax Revenues; McNichol and Johnson 2010.

support the education of disadvantaged children under ESEA Title I.[9] *Importantly, ARRA did not include any supplemental funding for ESEA Title III, the main federal funding stream and program that supports English language acquisition.* In addition, ARRA included two notable competitive grant programs: (a) the Race to the Top competitive grant program offers $4.4 billion for states that commit to building longitudinal data systems to document student progress, improve outcomes at low-performing schools and design standards that better reflect the demands of postsecondary education and the workforce; and (b) the Investing in Innovation (i3) competitive grant program supports districts with a plan to close the achievement gap between underperforming students and their peers. (Cf. Box 1 for further information on the Race to the Top and i3 competitive grant programs.)

ARRA funds have primarily been used to prevent layoffs and, according to the Government Accountability Office (GAO), nearly two-thirds of school districts used more than half of their ARRA funding to retain jobs (Government Accountability Office 2010b). (Staff expenditures account for about 80 percent of local school expenditures.) The University of Washington's Center on Reinventing Public Education estimates that ARRA funds supported about 320,000 to 340,000 jobs in 2010 school year (5.5 percent of all K-12 jobs) (Roza, Lozier and Sepe 2010). Still, the GAO estimates that about half of school districts in Florida and California, about one-third in New York, one-fifth in Texas and one-tenth in Illinois continue to face likely staffing cuts. In California's Los Angeles Unified School District, the state's largest, officials estimate that ARRA funded at least 6,400 jobs, but the district still expects to cut 7,000 to 8,000 jobs to balance its budget for 2010–2011.[10]

---

9 Other programs receiving supplemental allocations under ARRA included Pell Grants for higher education ($15.6 billion), higher education tax credits ($13.9 billion), special education for children with learning disabilities ($12.2 billion), Head Start (a program that offers a wide range of developmental services to low-income children), child care development ($2 billion), technology ($900 million), vocational rehabilitation ($680 million), teacher quality ($400 million) and other programs ($620 million).

10 Statement of Linda Calbom, Western Regional Director for the Government Accountability Office, before the House Committee on Oversight and Government Reform (Government Accountability Office 2010a).

ARRA makes no specific reference to ELLs or language acquisition programs. For the most part, ARRA funds existing programs (and, above all, staff), so ELLs benefit only to the extent that mainstream programs, such as Title I, have been adapted to provide services that meet their needs. It is impossible to know the extent to which this has been the case. According to *Education Week* reporter Mary Ann Zehr, only a handful of school districts have been vocal about plans to use supplemental ESEA Title I funds under ARRA to benefit ELL students (Zehr 2009). These include Boston, Seattle, St. Paul and New York City. Most notably, Seattle, which has received criticism for pulling students out of regular classrooms to receive English instruction, plans to restructure its approach to include English instruction in the regular classroom setting.

Box 1: "Race to the Top" and "Investing in Innovation" competitive grants: Implications for immigrant and LEP students

Two competitive grant programs included in ARRA have attracted considerable attention from education policymakers: "Race to the Top" and "Investing in Innovation" (i3). Both aim to encourage states to undertake several core reforms in assessment and accountability practices, and the Obama administration has signaled its intent to model future reforms to the nation's elementary and secondary education systems on these two programs.

Race to the Top. Race to the Top will initially provide $4.4 billion in competitive grants to states that commit to key reforms in four specific areas (The administration has requested $1.4 billion in the 2011 budget to continue Race to the Top.):

- Adopting rigorous academic standards and assessments that are aligned to labor market needs in collaboration with other states (Duncan 2009c);
- Building statewide longitudinal data systems to track student progress from preschool through postsecondary education (P-20) (Duncan 2009d);

- Developing a professional teaching cadre that allows merit-based rewards based on student outcomes (Duncan 2009a);
- Intervening directly in underperforming schools by reorganizing schools, replacing staff, developing more-effective instructional materials, or linking staff pay to student outcomes (Duncan 2009b).

Investing in Innovation. The i3 Fund provides three types of competitive grants to new or innovative programs that demonstrate promise in addressing Race to the Top objectives:
- "Development grants" to test promising ideas;
- "Validation grants" to establish an evidence base on promising programs;
- "Scale-up grants" to expand promising small-scale programs that have been demonstrated to be effective.

Both programs are in the earliest stages of implementation (the first grants were awarded in March 2010), so it is premature to draw conclusions. However, it stands to reason that the core principles underlying Race to the Top and i3 have large, positive spillover effects for ELLs.

Some of these principles, such as the use of longitudinal data, represent long-recognized effective practices; others, such as performance-based pay for teachers, are at the center of longstanding, but still controversial education policy debates (Laird 2008). Longitudinal data systems, in particular, allow states to hold schools accountable based on student progress over time rather than performance on a specific exam, which can be influenced by a wide variety of exogenous factors. These "growth models" are particularly important for ELLs since successful students exit from the population while newly arriving students constantly enter it, potentially masking trends over time.

In the past, the Department of Education has supported efforts to help states establish longitudinal data (e.g., the Institute for Education Science's Statewide Longitudinal Data System Program) and experiment with performance-based teacher pay (e.g., the Teacher Incentive Fund, which was established in 2006 and is being evaluated). However, participation has been voluntary. Absent severe budget crises (or meaningful federal support), many states have felt little urgency to implement these politically sensitive, but potentially powerful reforms.

Other principles, such as standards-alignment across states and re-thinking how to improve struggling schools, respond to key weaknesses under NCLB. For example, some states and districts quickly identified loopholes in NCLB to minimize their responsibility for reporting ELL student outcomes. Although there is no explicit reference to ELLs, Race to the Top awards states that provide additional funding to schools with large enrollments of disadvantaged students (a practice known as "equalization"), which potentially benefits ELL students, most of whom are poor and many of whom live in concentrated poverty. It also rewards states that include as many students as possible in accountability systems.

On balance, Race to the Top and i3 aim to address the weaknesses of NCLB and make progress toward realizing long-standing education policy objectives without completely eliminating the powerful incentives created by NCLB's assessment and accountability provisions. If the experience of NCLB is taken as a guide, these reforms will gradually improve academic outcomes for ELLs and other disadvantaged students, although better outcomes will not be automatic and will require substantial state investment of time, energy and resources.

Sources: Cf., generally, US Department of Education 2009 and "Investing in Innovation Fund" 2010.

Pending reauthorization of ESEA. The Obama administration recently signaled its intent to reauthorize ESEA in 2010. Details of the proposal remain vague and will likely evolve substantially as Congress considers legislation, but it is already clear that the administration intends to include many of the principles included in ARRA programs, such as the SFSF and Race to the Top (US Department of Education 2010). Many of these principles—such as better tracking and reporting of academic outcomes for all students (including subgroups such as ELLs), incentives for teachers who demonstrate effectiveness for disadvantaged populations, and more meaningful and uniform state standards—are likely to benefit ELLs in addition to other disadvantaged student populations.

States have experienced severe fiscal crises, and most have their cut education budgets. Fiscal crises have forced many states to make dramatic cuts to K-12 education budgets, and falling property-tax revenues suggest further cuts in the months and years ahead. Most decisions on education budget cuts are made at the local level, so the impact of cuts varies widely. For the most part, we do not find evidence that ELL services have been disproportionately targeted for cuts; however, many stakeholders at the state and local levels would argue that this is because few to none of the investments needed in ELL education were being made in the first place.

Education constitutes the largest single expenditure in most state budgets, making cuts inevitable when state revenues decline. According to the Center on Budget and Policy Priorities (CBPP), 29 states and the District of Columbia have enacted budget cuts for K-12 and early childhood education, including California, Florida and Illinois (Johnson, Oliff and Williams 2010). Education spending as a share of total state budgets declined in Nevada, California, Illinois and Texas during the recession, while it increased modestly in Georgia, Arizona and Florida (Roza and Funk 2010). Between 2007 and 2009, California cut its K-12 education budget by over $9 billion (in constant 2009 dollars), or 21 percent, and the governor proposed another $2.4 billion in cuts for fiscal year 2010.[11] Illinois proposed to cut $1.3 billion (17 percent) from its education budget in 2010, and New York's governor proposed to cut $1.1 billion (about 5 percent) from the state's general assistance to schools.

In other states, such as Pennsylvania and Tennessee, governors have explicitly protected education budgets from cuts. Georgia's edu-

---

11 Total K-12 budget as enacted in constant 2009 dollars (California Department of Finance 2010; California Department of Education 2010).

cation system received a smaller budget cut (as a percent of the total budget) than other areas of the state budget, such as transportation. Florida and Texas have not yet enacted meaningful budget cuts to education, although both states provided relatively little funding to schools prior to the recession.

Staff salaries, wages and benefits, which constitute the largest share of state education expenditures, have been the target of budget cuts. Salaries, wages and employee benefits account for about 80 percent of public school expenditures nationwide, so staffing cuts are the most obvious way to implement savings. In California in 2009, over 16,000 teachers were laid off, and about 10,000 classified staff have lost their jobs in recent years. In 2010, the state expected to issue more than 23,000 pink slips to teachers and other education staff in anticipation of possible budget cuts. An estimated 17,000 to 20,000 teachers and administrative staff in Illinois have received notice that they will not be re-hired for the 2010–2011 school year.

School districts have also tried to save on staffing costs by reducing the school week to four days (e.g., in Illinois) and increasing class sizes. Indeed, many states—including California, Florida, Georgia, Oklahoma, Maryland and Nevada—have relaxed minimum-class-size requirements enacted prior to the recession (Tuna 2010). In Virginia's Prince William County, the maximum class size of English as a Second Language (ESL) courses will grow from 29 to 34 in 2010, making ESL classrooms among the largest in the district (Chandler 2010). These changes may well be reversed when the economy improves.

Prior to the recession, ESL and bilingual education programs relied heavily on paraprofessionals and parent-outreach coordinators who may have been more susceptible to cuts. As a result, it is possible that ESL and bilingual education programs have experienced a relative loss of capacity. For instance, in 2009, Maryland cut 120 bilingual paraprofessionals and Latino community liaisons who work with LEP parents (Aizenman and Birnbaum 2010).

Cuts to targeted state funding for ELLs: States typically allocate funds to school districts for both general purposes and through targeted funds (known as "categorical funds") (Kaplan 2008 and 2009).

172

Many states (e.g., California, Colorado, Illinois, Georgia, New Jersey) have created categorical funding streams to support ELL education, while others include ELL enrollment in the state's general per-pupil funding formula (e.g., Florida, Texas). Some states do both (e.g., New York), while other states do not provide any funding tied to ELL enrollment (e.g., Nevada) (Griffith and Hancock 2006). The amount of support available through these funding streams varies widely; in some cases, they only support narrow activities, such as teacher training. As a result, some districts rely heavily on meager federal funds to support the education of ELLs while in other districts, dedicated state funding is available for ELL educational services. When faced with the prospect of education budget cuts, state legislators have faced three choices: (a) cut funding to categorical programs, (b) reduce general funding and allow districts to decide where precisely to cut and (c) temporarily relax restrictions on the use of categorical funding streams, thereby giving districts the option of preserving specific programs and making cuts elsewhere.

Among states that had categorical funding streams for ELLs prior to the recession, Illinois has made cuts, while California and Georgia have not. In particular, Illinois cut bilingual education grants—the state's categorical funding stream to districts to support ESL and bilingual education—from $75.4 million, in 2008, to $68.1 million, in 2009; the governor proposed to cut bilingual education funding more dramatically, to $47.3 million, in 2010.[12] To date, California legislators and the governor have agreed to protect the state's economic impact aid (EIA), which provides categorical state support for both disadvantaged and ELL students. The California legislature is currently considering a bill to allow a three-year study of what would occur if districts were granted greater flexibility in using EIA funds (among other categorical grant programs). This fiscal experiment, which could hold broad implications for ELLs, would be conducted in three high-poverty and high-ELL districts: Long Beach, Garden Grove and Fresno (Legislative Counsel of the State of California 2010). In other

12 Budget data in constant 2009 dollars.

states, such as Florida and Arizona, spending on ELL instruction has been maintained at least in part because service levels have been mandated by long-standing court orders.

Further state budget cuts are likely, particularly as ARRA funding ends. While stimulus funding may have at least partially filled the gap, states are facing renewed fiscal crises as stimulus spending winds down and property-tax revenues decline. Meanwhile, federal formula grants to support the education of disadvantaged children will not take into account deepened child poverty for several years.

Stimulus funding is winding down, while most states' fiscal outlook has not improved. ARRA was clearly a one-time program and, as states draw down their ARRA funds, many will face new rounds of budget cuts. For instance, as of January 22, 2010, Illinois had used 92 percent of the funds available, and California and Arizona had used 90 percent. Other states appeared in better shape: Florida had used only 34 percent of its ARRA funds, New York 10 percent and Texas 16 percent (Government Accountability Office 2010b). At the same time, the fiscal outlook for most state budgets has not improved and, in many cases, has even deteriorated. The California Budget Project estimates that the governor's proposed 2010–2011 budget would reduce K-12 funding for the Los Angeles Unified School District by $183 million, or roughly $307 per student (California Budget Project 2010). However, the cuts appear to hit rural districts much harder than urban districts.

For the most part, state and local government property-tax revenues do not yet reflect the decline in real estate values since the recession began. Property taxes provide an important share of elementary and secondary education revenues in most states and districts. Nationwide, property taxes generate at least 95 percent of local tax revenues for schools in 33 of 50 states (Loeb 2009).

However, it is widely recognized that the economic crisis deflated property values, particularly in parts of the country that had grown rapidly in recent years and experienced both real estate bubbles and rapid immigration, for instance, the inland counties east of Los Angeles as well as Nevada, Arizona, Florida and some suburban Texas areas. For the most part, property-tax revenues do not yet reflect these declines.

Conclusion

It would be premature to draw definitive conclusions, but it is increasingly clear that the economic crisis has prompted a period of both painful adjustment and promising innovation in the nation's schools.

The severe economic crisis that officially began in the United States in December 2007 spread to the K-12 education system primarily through state and local budget crises. This period of public-sector turmoil coincided with major shifts in the US child and student population. Children of immigrants are a growing share of the US child population—accounting for nearly half of all children in California. By some measures, federal education policies to promote greater transparency and data-based decision-making have marginally improved academic outcomes for these vulnerable student populations, but these students continue to lag behind their peers due to new arrivals, persistent inequalities and uneven implementation of federal mandates.

With tax revenues falling, the federal government initiated an unprecedented fiscal stimulus, with education an important focus. Unfortunately, the design of the stimulus funding excluded the major funding stream for ELL students, leaving to chance whether they would receive services from other funding streams. Since children of immigrants and LEP children are more likely to reside in low-income households and communities, they could benefit from this increased federal support if school and district administrators were to use this funding to meet their particular learning needs. However, it is nearly impossible to know whether this has been the case.

Likewise, state and local governments still provide most elementary and secondary education funding, even in districts with large enrollments of disadvantaged and LEP students. State budget cuts—and the prospect of further cuts moving forward—hurt all disadvantaged students. Moreover, while the worst case has not emerged—that is, ELL, LEP and immigrant-student services do not appear to have been singled out for cuts—it is still only a few states that dedicate significant and/or sufficient funding to meet their needs.

Nevertheless, there may also be a silver lining for immigrant and LEP students in the economic crisis: The Obama administration seized upon the crisis as an opportunity to push states into implementing long-standing education-reform objectives. Although these reforms were not expressly targeted at ELLs or immigrant students, they are likely to have positive spillover effects for these subpopulations.

Works Cited

Aizenman, N.C., and Michael Birnbaum. Latinos anxious over end of school liaisons in Pr. George's. *The Washington Post* March 7, 2010. www.washingtonpost.com/wp-dyn/content/article/2010/03/05/AR2010030503028.html (accessed July 7, 2010).

Batalova, Jeanne, and Michael Fix. Children of Immigrants in US Schools: A Portrait. Paper prepared for the conference Students We Share: New Research from Mexico and the United States, January 2010.

California Budget Project. The Governor's Proposed Budget Would Make Deep Cuts in Funding for California's Public Schools. Sacramento: California Budget Project, 2010. www.cbp.org/pdfs/2010/100329_County_%20K-12_Cuts.pdf (accessed July 7, 2010).

California Department of Education. State Schools Chief Jack O'Connell and Members of Education Coalition Announce Number of Pink Slips Issued to Education Personnel. News Release, March 15, 2010. www.cde.ca.gov/nr/ne/yr10/yr10rel30.asp (accessed July 7, 2010).

California Department of Finance. Historical eBudgets. www.dof.ca.gov/budget/historical_ebudgets (accessed July 7, 2010).

Chandler, Michael Alison. Prince William school board approves $760 million budget, job cuts. *The Washington Post* March 25, 2010.

www.washingtonpost.com/wp-dyn/content/article/2010/03/24/
AR2010032402477.html (accessed July 7, 2010).

Chudowsky, Naomi, and Victor Chudowsky. State Test Limits of Federal AYP Flexibility. Washington, DC: Center on Education Policy, 2005. www.cep-dc.org/document/docWindow.cfm?fuseaction=document.viewDocument&documentid=45&documentFormatId=4050 (accessed July 8, 2010).

Chudowsky, Naomi, and Victor Chudowsky. *No Child Left Behind at Five: A Review of Changes to State Accountability Plans.* Washington, DC: Center on Education Policy, 2007. www.cep-dc.org/document/docWindow.cfm?fuseaction=document.viewDocument&documentid=28&documentFormatId=3941 (accessed July 8, 2010).

Chudowsky, Naomi, and Victor Chudowsky. *State Test Score Trends Through 2007–08, Part 6: Has Progress Been Made in Raising Achievement for English Language Learners?* Washington, DC: Center on Education Policy, 2010. www.cep-dc.org/document/docWindow.cfm?fuseaction=document.viewDocument&documentid=305&documentFormatId=4640 (accessed July 8, 2010).

Duncan, Arne. Partners in Reform. Address by the Secretary of Education to the National Education Association, July 2, 2009. 2009a. www2.ed.gov/news/speeches/2009/07/07022009.pdf (accessed July 8, 2010).

Duncan, Arne. Turning Around the Bottom 5 Percent. Address at the National Alliance for Public Charter Schools Conference, June 22, 2009. 2009b. www2.ed.gov/news/speeches/2009/06/06222009.pdf (accessed July 8, 2010).

Duncan, Arne. States Will Lead the Way Toward Reform. Address by the Secretary of Education at the 2009 Governor's Education Symposium, June 14, 2009. 2009c. www2.ed.gov/news/speeches/2009/06/06142009.pdf (accessed July 8, 2010).

Duncan, Arne. Robust Data Gives Us the Roadmap to Reform. Address by the Secretary of Education to the Fourth Annual Institute of Education Sciences Research Conference, June 8, 2009. 2009d. www2.ed.gov/news/speeches/2009/06/06082009.pdf (accessed July 8, 2010).

Fix, Michael (ed.). *Securing the Future: US Immigrant Integration Policy.* Washington, DC: MPI, 2007.

Government Accountability Office. Recovery Act: California's Use of Funds and Efforts to Ensure Accountability, 111th Cong., 1st session. Washington, DC: GAO, 2010. March 5, 2010. 2010a. www.gao.gov/new.items/d10467t.pdf (accessed July 8, 2010).

Government Accountability Office. *Recovery Act: One Year Later, States' and Localities' Use of Funds and Opportunities to Strengthen Accountability.* Report to Congress GAO 10-437. Washington, DC: GAO, 2010. 2010b. www.gao.gov/products/GAO-10-437 (accessed July 8, 2010).

Griffith, Michael, and John Hancock. *A Survey of State ELL/ESL Funding Systems.* Denver, Colo.: Education Commission of the States, 2006. www.ecs.org/clearinghouse/67/70/6770.pdf (accessed July 8, 2010).

Haskins, Ron, and Isabel Sawhill. *Creating an Opportunity Society.* Washington, DC: Brookings Institution Press, 2009.

"Investing in Innovation Fund." *Federal Register* (75) 48: 12004–12071, 2010. www2.ed.gov/legislation/FedRegister/finrule/2010-1/031210a.pdf (accessed July 8, 2010).

Johnson, Nicholas, Phil Oliff and Erica Williams. *An Update on State Budget Cuts: Governors Proposing New Round of Cuts for 2011; At Least 45 States Have Already Imposed Cuts That Hurt Vulnerable Residents.* Washington, DC: Center on Budget and Policy Priorities, 2010. www.cbpp.org/cms/?fa=view&id=1214 (accessed July 8, 2010).

Kaplan, Jonathan. School Finance Facts: How California's School Districts Spend Their Funds. Sacramento: California Budget Project, 2008. www.cbp.org/pdfs/2008/080506_HowDistrictsSpendtheir Funds.pdf (accessed July 8, 2010).

Kaplan, Jonathan. School Finance Facts: How California's Schools Get Their Money. Sacramento: California Budget Project, 2009. www.cbp.org/pdfs/2009/090202_SFF_HowSchoolsGetTheir Money.pdf (accessed July 8, 2010).

Keigher, Ashley, and Kerry Gruber. *Characteristics of Public, Private, and Bureau of Indian Elementary and Secondary Schools in the*

United States: Results from the 2007–08 Schools and Staffing Survey, First Look. Washington, DC: US Department of Education National Center for Education Statistics, 2009. http://nces.ed.gov/pubs2009/2009321.pdf (accessed July 8, 2010).

Kober, Nancy, Naomi Chudhowsky, Victor Chudhowsky and Caitlin Scott. *An Early Look at the Economic Stimulus Package and the Public Schools.* Washington, DC: Center on Education Policy, 2009. www.cep-dc.org/document/docWindow.cfm?fuseaction=document. viewDocument&documentid=299&documentFormatId=4435 (accessed July 8, 2010).

Laird, Elizabeth. Developing and Supporting P-20 Education Data Systems: Different States, Different Models. Washington, DC: Data Quality Campaign, 2008. www.dataqualitycampaign.org/files/meetings-dqc_quarterly_issue_brief_011508.pdf. (accessed July 8, 2010).

Legislative Counsel of the State of California. Senate Bill No. 1396. February 19, 2010. www.leginfo.ca.gov/pub/09-10/bill/sen/sb_1351-1400/sb_1396_bill_20100219_introduced.pdf (accessed July 8, 2010).

Loeb, Susanna. *Local Revenue Options for K-12 Education.* Stanford University, 2009. www.stanford.edu/~slocb/papers/Loca%20 Revenue.pdf.

McNichol, Elizabeth, and Nicholas Johnson. *Recession Continues to Batter State Budgets; State Responses Could Slow Recovery.* Washington, DC: Center on Budget and Policy Priorities, 2010. www.cbpp.org/files/9-8-08sfp.pdf. (accessed July 8, 2010).

Minnesota Population Center. American Community Survey (ACS). www.pop.umn.edu. (accessed July 8, 2010).

Mintrop, Heinrich, and Gail L. Sunderman. *Why High Stakes Accountability Sounds Good But Doesn't Work—And Why We Keep on Doing It Anyway.* Los Angeles: University of California, Los Angeles, The Civil Rights Project, 2009. www.civilrightsproject.ucla.edu/research/esea/study_nclb_sanctions_2009.pdf. (accessed July 8, 2010).

Osorio-O'Dea, Patricia. *Bilingual Education: An Overview.* Congressional Research Service Report for Congress, 98-501 EPW, 2001.

www.policyalmanac.org/education/archive/bilingual.pdf (accessed July 8, 2010).

Ravitch, Diane. *The Death and Life of the Great American School System*. New York: Basic Books, 2010.

Roza, Marguerite, Chris Lozier and Christina Sepe. K-12 Job Trends Amidst Stimulus Funds, Early Findings. Rapid Response Paper, University of Washington Center on Reinventing Public Education, March 2010.

Roza, Marguerite, and Susan Funk. Have States Disproportionately Cut Education Budgets During ARRA? Early Findings. Rapid Response Paper, University of Washington Center on Reinventing Public Education, January 2010.

Ruggles, Steven, J. Trent Alexander, Katie Genadek, Ronald Goeken, Matthew B. Schroeder and Matthew Sobek. *Integrated Public Use Microdata Series: Version 5.0* [Machine-readable database]. Minneapolis: University of Minnesota, 2010. http://usa.ipums.org. (accessed July 8, 2010).

Tuna, Cari. Fiscal Woes Push Up Class Sizes. *Wall Street Journal* February 19, 2010. http://online.wsj.com/article/SB10001424052748 704337004575060030026160638.html (accessed July 8, 2010).

US Census Bureau. Quarterly Summary of State and Local Government Tax Revenues. www.census.gov/govs/qtax/ (accessed July 8, 2010).

US Department of Education. Race to the Top Program, Executive Summary, November 2009. www2.ed.gov/programs/racetothetop/executive-summary.pdf (accessed July 8, 2010).

US Department of Education. *A Blueprint for Reform: The Reauthorization of the Elementary and Secondary Education Act*. Washington, DC: Department of Education, 2010. www.ed.gov/blog/topic/esea-reauthorization/ (accessed July 8, 2010).

US Department of Education. The Federal Role in Education (updated January 29, 2010). www2.ed.gov/about/overview/fed/role.html (accessed July 8, 2010).

Working Group on ELL Policy. Improving Educational Outcomes for English Language Learners: Recommendations for the Reauthorization of the Elementary and Secondary Education Act, 2010. www.cal.org/topics/ell/ELL-Working-Group-ESEA.pdf.

Zehr, Mary Ann. Large Districts to Use Stimulus for ELL Support. *Education Week* March 29, 2009. www.edweek.org/ew/articles/ 2009/05/20/32ell_ep.h28.html (accessed July 8, 2010).

Immigrant Students in OECD Countries during a Recession-Inspired Era of Resource Constraints

Miho Taguma

Introduction[1]

Net migration to Organisation for Economic Co-operation and Development (OECD) countries[2] has tripled since 1960. Some countries have experienced a sudden inflow over recent years, while others have a long-standing history of immigration. By 2006, more than 20 percent of the population in Australia, Canada, Luxembourg, New Zealand and Switzerland was foreign born, as was more than 10 percent in Austria, Belgium, Ireland, the Netherlands, Spain, Sweden, the United Kingdom and the United States (OECD 2008a).

Integration becomes an immediate policy priority, especially into labor markets, in order to ensure social cohesion and sustainable economic growth. As a result, many immigrant-receiving countries now are looking at the relationship between the size and composition of their immigrant populations and the social and economic development of the nation. International comparative research has also been undertaken on immigration policy and labor market integration (OECD 2007 and 2008b). While the integration of immigrants into the labor market has been extensively researched, far less research has been done on

---

1 The opinions expressed in this paper are solely those of the author and do not necessarily reflect those of the OECD or of the governments of its member countries.
2 The 30 OECD member countries are Australia, Austria, Belgium, Canada, the Czech Republic, Denmark, Finland, France, Germany, Greece, Hungary, Iceland, Ireland, Italy, Japan, Korea, Luxembourg, Mexico, the Netherlands, New Zealand, Norway, Poland, Portugal, the Slovak Republic, Spain, Sweden, Switzerland, Turkey, the United Kingdom and the United States.

either outcomes for their children or a review of education policies at the international level.

The challenges and opportunities that immigration poses to education policy vary according to country, as the size and composition of immigrant student populations differ. To examine how policy can respond to the challenges of migration, in January 2008, the OECD Education Policy Committee undertook a policy review of migrant education. The review aimed to compare education outcomes of immigrant students to those of their native peers and, where gaps exist, to determine what actions policymakers could take to close the gaps.[3] Austria, Denmark, Ireland, the Netherlands, Norway and Sweden requested in-depth, country-specific policy reviews along with two country visits (a fact-finding visit and a policy review visit). Other countries have provided country background information, including Finland, Hungary, Italy, Korea, Mexico, Spain, Turkey and the United Kingdom. The project was finalized in December 2009.

This chapter is based on that extensive OECD policy review and summarizes its main findings, focusing on policies that promote successful education outcomes for first- and second-generation immigrant students.[4] It aims to answer the following questions:

- Do immigrant students perform as well as their native peers in OECD countries?
- What can explain the gap *or the absence of a gap* in student performance?
- What are the main tools and policies that can improve immigrant students' performance in school?

Although the review acknowledges the importance of designing policies to help top-performing immigrant students achieve even greater potential, the project focuses on "equity" and, therefore, is most concerned with closing the gap between native and immigrant students

3 For more information about the review, cf. www.oecd.org/edu/migration.
4 The full OECD report, *Closing the Gap for Immigrant Students: Policies and Practices*, was drafted by Miho Taguma, Moonhee Kim, Deborah Nusche, Claire Shewbriedge and Gregory Wurzburg with the editorial assistance of Kelly Mackowiecki.

and ensuring that at-risk students will not be ignored by public policy or further marginalized by the absence of public policy.

Owing to the review's time frame, the current policy context—the postrecession period—has not been fully explored. During our country visits, we asked about implications of the economic crisis for education, especially for immigrant students, when many countries started to fall into recession. Officials in many countries replied that the consequences would hit during the next budget cycle. Ireland, though, faced an immediate challenge in April 2010 as a result of an immediate budget cut for education, particularly for language teachers.

Do Immigrant Students Perform as Well as Their Native Peers?[5]

This section examines whether there is an academic achievement gap between native, first-generation and second-generation students at two different age groups: grade 4[6] and age 15. Grade 4 is an important transition point at which children have learned how to read and are now reading to learn; and age 15 is critical because students in most countries are nearing the end of their compulsory schooling. Student performance can be defined broadly, for instance, to include attitudes toward learning or interpersonal skills; but, for this report, it is defined narrowly, focusing solely on academic achievements, such as reading performance. Given that literacy is a fundamental prerequisite for immigrant students to better integrate into school and society at large, we regard "performance in reading" as a proxy of student performance.

---

5 Due to limited space, this paper focuses on "student performance."
6 The International Association for Evaluation of Educational Achievement review of Grade 4 is of students in the 9–11 age range, generally between 9 and 10 (with requirements for school-starting age varying by country, as well as policies regarding repeating grades).

Reading Performance in Grade 4/Primary Education

Reading ability in primary education is a key measure of student performance. The Progress in International Reading Literacy Study (PIRLS) shows that immigrant students perform less well than their native peers in grade 4 in many OECD countries (see Figure 1).[7] In

Figure 1: Reading performance in primary education (Grade 4) by immigration status, 2006

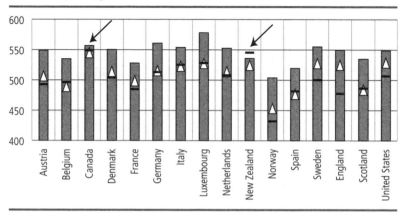

Native students △ Second-generation immigrant students

━━━ First-generation immigrant students

All data in reading scores

Source: International Association for Evaluation of Educational Achievement, PIRLS 2006 database

7 The International Association for Evaluation of Educational Achievement administers the Progress in International Reading Literacy Study (PIRLS). The 2006 data was the most recent data available when the policy review was undertaken. Cf. TIMSS and PIRLS International Study Center, http://timss.bc.edu/. For this immigrant-focused analysis, we have set four criteria: 1) countries had to have a minimum of 3 percent immigrant-student enrollment (including first-generation and second-generation students); 2) at least 3 percent of students in the sample had to speak a different language at home from the language of assessment, except in Ireland, Portugal, Spain and the United Kingdom; 3) countries had to belong to the OECD; and 4) countries had to have at least 100 immigrant students in the sample. According to the criteria, we included Austria, Belgium, Canada, Denmark, France, Germany, Italy, Luxembourg, the Netherlands, New Zealand, Norway, Spain, Sweden, England and Scotland (from the United Kingdom) and the United States.

all countries except Canada and New Zealand, differences are evident between native and immigrant students in average reading performance. No significant gaps can be found in Canada and New Zealand. In fact, in New Zealand, first-generation immigrant students perform better than their native peers.

What can explain the *absence* of a gap in Canada and New Zealand? Some factors include:

- Socioeconomic background: Immigrant children in these countries are from families with higher incomes and levels of parental education than those of their native peers, factors strongly associated with student performance (OECD 2010).
- Native language: These children speak the same language at home as the language of instruction and, therefore, there is almost no disadvantage associated with learning subject matters or general communication with peers and teachers (ibid.).
- The existence of educational programs for second-language learners: These countries have well-established methods and practices in second-language teaching and learning.
- Societal diversity: Both Canada and New Zealand have a long history of and much experience with managing "cultural diversity," as both have indigenous minority populations.

In most countries, however, there is a significant performance gap between immigrants and natives. There is also a performance gap *between* different immigrant groups, as immigrant students are not a homogeneous unit. We might expect the performance of second-generation immigrant students to be comparable to that of their native peers for two reasons: First, these students were born in their host country and, therefore, have been exposed to the language of instruction since birth; and, second, they have gone though the same education system as their native peers. However, there are disparities (see Figure 1):

- Second-generation immigrant students perform less well than their native peers in all countries.

- Despite the observed performance gap, the second generation performs around or above the international average (500 points)[8] in all countries, except Belgium, Norway and Scotland.[9]
- Second-generation students perform better than their first-generation peers in Norway, Sweden, England and the United States; they perform less well in Belgium, Scotland and Spain; and they perform at a similar level in the remaining countries.
- Despite the observed performance gap, the first generation performs around or above the international average except in France, Norway, Spain and the United Kingdom.

Reading Performance at Age 15

We now turn to reading ability at age 15, using comparative data from the Program for International Student Assessment (PISA).[10] The data show that there are marked performance gaps at age 15 in many—but not all—OECD countries (see Figure 2). The exceptions are Australia, Canada, Ireland and New Zealand, where there are no marked differences between native and immigrant students.

Taking a closer look at the countries with performance gaps between immigrant and native students at age 15, we can conclude:

- Second-generation immigrant students perform less well than their native peers in all countries; they perform well below the OECD

8 The international average (500) is the weighted average of national averages of the 35 countries, with a standard deviation of 100.
9 The review and this paper discuss both data as provided from the United Kingdom (inclusive of Scotland and England), and at times separately when the data are available individually from England and Scotland.
10 OECD administers the Program for International Student Assessment (PISA). The 2006 data was the most recent data when the policy review was undertaken. Cf. www.pisa.oecd.org/. For this immigrant-focused analysis using PISA data, we have also used the same criteria used for PIRLS and included Australia, Austria, Belgium, Canada, Denmark, France, Germany, Greece, Ireland, Italy, Luxembourg, New Zealand, Norway, Portugal, Spain, Sweden, the United Kingdom and the United States.

Figure 2: Differences in reading performance at age 15 by immigration status, 2006

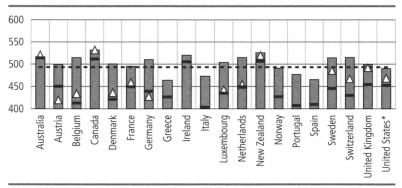

Native students   △ Second-generation immigrant students

—— First-generation immigrant students   - - - OECD average performance in reading

All data in reading scores

Note: A difference of 38 points is roughly equivalent to one year of schooling.
* US data are from PISA 2003.

Source: OECD, PISA 2003 and 2006 database

average (492 points) in all countries except in Sweden and the United Kingdom.[11]

- Second-generation students perform higher than their first-generation peers in Belgium, Denmark, Sweden, Switzerland, the United Kingdom and the United States; they perform less well in Austria and Germany; they perform at a similar level in France, Luxembourg and the Netherlands.

- The first generation performs significantly below the OECD average in all countries.

---

11 PISA uses techniques that set a score range with a mean of 500 and a standard deviation of 100. When a literacy area is the main focus of a cycle, the OECD mean is set at 500 against which performance has since been measured. For example, the reading literacy scale was set at 500 in 2000 when reading was the main focus. For 2006, reading was a minor domain, and the OECD mean score was 492 in comparison with the mean score of scientific literacy, which was the main focus.

Performance in Different Ability Groups at Age 15

Since (as was previously mentioned) immigrants are not a homogeneous body, the "average performance" of immigrant students needs cautious interpretation. Average performance results may mask a range of differences even among immigrant students (see Table 1). It is worth taking a closer look at both high-performing and low-performing groups within the 15-year-old immigrant student population:

- At least 25 percent of first-generation immigrant-students perform above the OECD average in all countries except Denmark, Italy, Portugal and Spain; and they outperform their native peers in Australia and Ireland. However, another 25 percent do not reach the average in the majority of countries.
- At least 25 percent of second-generation immigrant students perform above the OECD average in all countries, where applicable. However, another 25 percent do not reach the average in all countries.

Low-performing students elicit particular concern. Performance below Level 1 on the PISA reading scale (a minimum of 335 points) signals serious deficiencies in students' ability to use reading literacy as a tool for the acquisition of knowledge and skills in other areas (OECD 2008b).

Figure 3 shows us how many students (both immigrant and native) are unable to perform basic reading skills, highlighting the following:

- Only around 5 percent (or fewer) of native students score below proficiency Level 1 in many countries except France, Italy, Norway and Portugal. These exceptions, however, illustrate the need to design universal support measures for low-performing students, regardless of their immigrant status.
- Similarly, only around 5 percent (or fewer) of second-generation students score below Level 1 except in Austria, Belgium, Denmark, France, Germany, Luxembourg, the Netherlands and Switzerland. These exception countries would benefit from special measures targeting second-generation immigrant students, some of which will be discussed later.

190

Table 1: Low- and high-performing students in the reading by immigration status, 2006

	Low performers (1)			High performers (2)		
	Native	Second generation	First generation	Native	Second generation	First generation
Australia	455	463	448	578	585	585
Austria	434	342	367	573	499	538
Belgium	451	367	330	636	563	558
Canada	474	473	448	596	595	585
Denmark	445	375	361	560	503	484
France	431	390	377	568	537	530
Germany	448	350	369	581	515	531
Greece	403	n.a.	362	534	n.a.	497
Ireland	461	n.a.	440	583	n.a.	588
Italy	408	n.a.	324	548	n.a.	491
Luxembourg	448	377	356	566	509	519
Netherlands	457	386	370	582	524	530
New Zealand	460	445	429	597	600	587
Norway	426	n.a.	341	562	n.a.	510
Portugal	414	n.a.	339	546	n.a.	472
Spain	411	n.a.	345	525	n.a.	480
Sweden	454	431	374	580	543	513
Switzerland	460	402	353	575	533	507
United Kingdom	434	434	377	569	553	534

1. Maximum score for the bottom 25 percent of students in each subgroup

2. Minimum score for the top 25 percent of students in each subgroup

Note: The PISA reading scale has a mean of 500 and a standard deviation of 100. Students who score below 407.5 points are only able to complete the simplest reading tasks, and those who score below 335 points are not able to routinely show the most basic reading skills.

Source: OECD, PISA 2006 database

Figure 3: Percentage of students scoring below proficiency Level 1 on reading performance at age 15 by immigration status, 2006

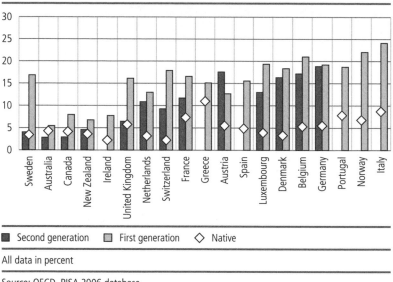

■ Second generation   ▢ First generation   ◇ Native

All data in percent

Source: OECD, PISA 2006 database

- In a majority of countries, more than 10 percent of first-generation students score below Level 1 except in Australia, Canada and New Zealand. Thus, most countries may need targeted measures for the newly arrived.

Drivers of Educational Performance

A number of factors drive educational performance. In this section, we separate them into three categories: *individual-level factors, school-level factors* and *system-level factors* (these variables are derived from PISA; see Appendix). Individual-level factors are those associated with students' arrival age, length of stay, proficiency in the language of instruction and their parents' socioeconomic status and aspirations for their children. School-level factors include whether or not schools provide sufficient language support, group children by ability and re-

192

ceive a high level of immigrant students. System-level factors include whether or not students are classified into different learning paths at a certain age, whether there is a national curriculum or guidelines for linguistic and cultural diversity, and whether student performance—including both that of native and immigrant students—is assessed and monitored. An analysis of these three different factors may help us explain the performance gaps observed in the previous section. This section also introduces a few of the policy solutions that can mitigate these factors and that will be explained in more detail in the next section.

Individual-Level Factors

In many countries—except Australia, Canada, Ireland, New Zealand and the United Kingdom—there is more than a 38-point difference in observed performance levels between native and immigrant students (see Figure 4). This difference accounts for more than one year of schooling. What can explain the gap in these countries?

Family Background

Parents' occupations and educational backgrounds are important factors associated with education outcomes for both native and immigrant students (OECD 2007). Although immigrant students are a heterogeneous group with diverse cultural and socioeconomic backgrounds, 2006 PISA data show that, on average, immigrant students in most countries come from more disadvantaged family backgrounds than their native peers (OECD 2008c). Immigrants have lower economic, social and cultural status (ESCS) than natives and wider distributions (see Figure 5) of ESCS than their native peers except in Australia, Canada and Ireland.[12]

12 ESCS was created for PISA to measure students' family backgrounds. The family background includes such variables as parents' income level and occupational status, parental education level and educational resources at home. For technical definitions, cf. http://stats.oecd.org/glossary/detail.asp?ID=5401.

193

Figure 4: Effects of socioeconomic background on student performance, 2006

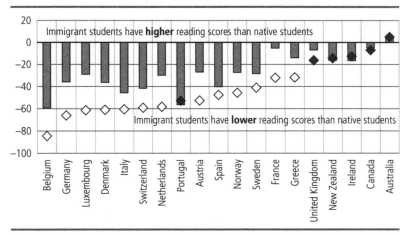

■ Remaining performance difference after accounting for students' socioeconomic background

◇ Observed performance difference between native and immigrant students in reading

All data in number of points difference

Note: Statistically significant differences are marked in darker tones.

Source: OECD, PISA 2006 database

Performance differences are substantially reduced after controlling for socioeconomic factors, such as the occupation and education levels of students' parents. This does not, however, fully explain the observed performance disadvantage for immigrant students. In most countries, substantial performance gaps for immigrant students remain even after accounting for socioeconomic backgrounds.

Speaking a Different Language at Home

Many immigrant students speak a language at home other than the language used at school. This, together with their socioeconomic background, largely explains their comparatively lower performance in many countries (see Figure 6). This indicates that immigrant stu-

Figure 5: Distribution of the index of economic, social and cultural status (ESCS) in PISA 2006

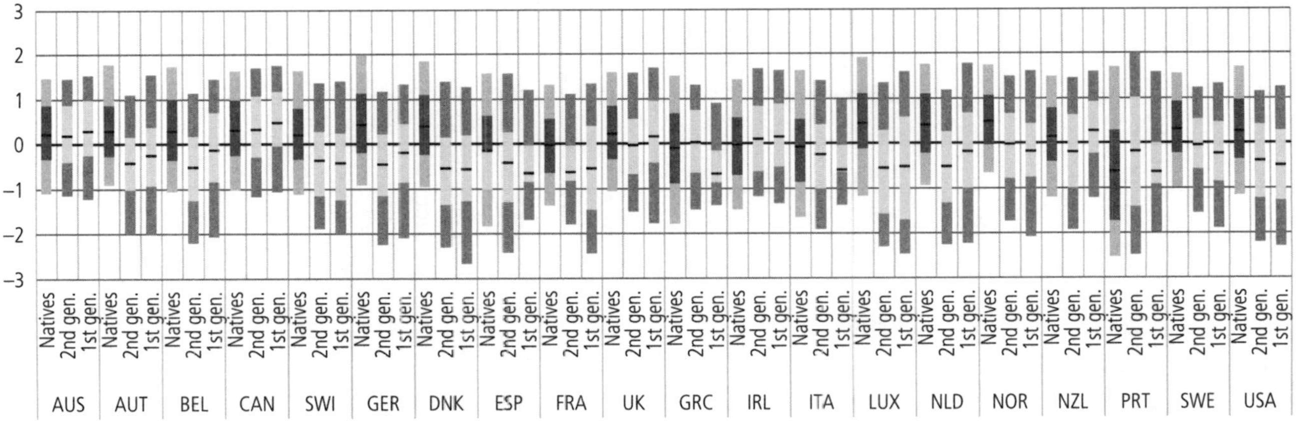

■ Bar extends from 25th to 75th   ■ Bar extends from 5th to 95th   — Mean value

All data in points of ESCS index

Source: OECD, PISA 2006 database

195

Figure 6: Effects of socioeconomic status and language on student performance, 2006

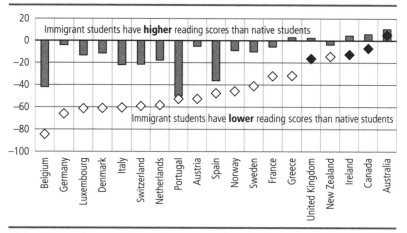

■ Remaining performance difference after accounting for students' socioeconomic background and language spoken at home

◇ Observed performance difference between native and immigrant students in reading

All data in number of points difference

Note: Statistically significant differences are marked in darker tones.

Source: OECD, PISA 2006 database

dents would benefit from language-centric policies as well as ones targeting socioeconomically disadvantaged students.

However, in some countries, the performance gap remains even after accounting for language and socioeconomic background. In Belgium, for example, the gap remains for more than one year of schooling. In Portugal, the gap also remains at the same level even after controlling for both factors. This implies that the lower performance of immigrant students cannot solely be attributed to their background and family characteristics.

Early home reading and learning at home are also associated with better student performance (see Table 2) (OECD 2010). Two things are important to success. First, children must have adequate educational resources available at home, such as a desk, books for school work, a calculator, a computer and a quiet place to study. These are all associated with better performance for immigrant students at age 15 in many countries. Second, families must support children reading at home at a young age. Reading books and telling stories to children prior to primary school are factors positively associated with student performance in primary education in many countries. Therefore, family support for the student's education should be encouraged.

School-Level Factors

School-level factors may influence student behavior and, therefore, may also contribute to explaining the performance gap between native and immigrant students.

Concentration of Immigrant Students

The relationship between educational outcomes and the proportion of immigrant students in a school is a politically sensitive topic, and there is no clear evidence of its existence. Several researchers have found that a high concentration of immigrant students in schools is negatively associated with student performance (Karsten et al. 2006; Nordin 2006). Furthermore, in some countries, immigrant students are clustered in school districts or schools that are less well-resourced, have larger class sizes and have higher teacher-turnover rates, etc. These facts have led to the phenomenon called "white flight" (which indicates that native parents move their children out of such school)

Table 2: Effects of home learning on education outcomes for immigrant students, 2006

Nature of support (as reported by students)				
	Educational resources to learn at home (PISA 2006)		Early home reading activities (PIRLS 2006)	
	2nd generation	1st generation	2nd generation	1st generation
Australia	+	+	n.a.	n.a.
Austria	~~	+	+	+
Belgium	+	+	n.a.	n.a.
Flemish Com.*	+	+	+	+
Canada	+	+	+	+
Denmark	~~	+	~~	n.a.
France	n.a.	n.a.	~~	n.a.
Germany	+	+	+	~~
Greece	n.a.	+	n.a.	n.a.
Ireland	n.a.	+	n.a.	n.a.
Italy	n.a.	+	n.a.	~~
Luxembourg	+	+	n.a.	n.a.
Netherlands	+	~~	+	n.a.
New Zealand	+	+	+	+
Norway	n.a.	+	+	n.a.
Portugal	n.a.	+	n.a.	n.a.
Spain	n.a.	+	n.a.	~~
Sweden	~~	+	~~	+
Switzerland	+	+	n.a.	n.a.
United Kingdom	+	+	n.a.	n.a.
England	n.a.	n.a.	~~	+
Scotland	n.a.	n.a.	~~	n.a.
United States	n.a.	n.a.	+	~~

+ Positive relationship with performance; ~~ No relationship with performance;
n.a. No data available

* The Flemish community in Belgium has a different education system than the French community, and differences in outcomes are masked when viewing Belgium overall. In addition, the Netherlands requested the data so that it could compare its outcomes with those of the Flemish community.

Sources: OECD, PISA 2006 database; International Association for Evaluation of Educational Achievement, PIRLS 2006 database; Progress in International Reading Literacy Study (PIRLS) 2010

or "middle-class flight" (indicating that such a phenomenon is not only for native parents, but also for middle-class immigrant parents).

It can be argued that attending schools with fewer native students may hinder immigrant students' opportunity to develop competencies in the language of instruction and reduce their chance to interact with native students. For instance, Maurice Crul shows that second-generation Turks who are exposed to the majority language and to social networks involving majority members at a young age have better educational outcomes (Crul and Schneider 2009).

However, Reyn Van Ewijk and Peter Sleegers conducted a meta-analysis of several studies and found that the concentration of immigrant students in schools has little effect on the outcomes for immigrant students and no effect for those of native students (Van Ewijk and Sleegers 2009). The PISA analysis shows that, in both Australia and Belgium, about 40 percent of immigrant students attend schools with more immigrant students than native students. The impact of this ratio on educational outcomes differs dramatically between countries. In Australia, the relationship to performance is not statistically significant, whereas, in Belgium, scores dropped between 21 and 40 points, constituting a significant negative effect. This shows that there may be other factors at work.

In schools with higher concentrations of immigrant students, school leaders and teachers need to be better prepared to meet the needs of diverse student groups. Schools should be encouraged to effectively cooperate with families and communities to support immigrant students' learning activities.

School Composition

Table 3, as well as evidence from individual countries (e.g., Denmark), shows that students perform better in schools with a higher average socioeconomic composition regardless of their own socioeconomic background, possibly due to positive peer influences and/or role models (Rangvid 2007).

Table 3: School factors associated with education outcomes of immigrant students, 2006

	More advantaged socio-economic composition of school		More average hours per week spent learning at school	
	2nd generation	1st generation	2nd generation	1st generation
Australia	+++++	+++++	++	++
Austria	+++++	+++++	− − −	− − −
Belgium	+++++	+++++	+++	++
Flemish Com.*	+++++	+++++	+++++	++++
Canada	++++	+++++	+	+
Denmark	++++	~~	~~	~~
Germany	+++++	+++++	~~	~~
Greece	n.a.	++++	n.a.	++
Ireland	n.a.	+++++	n.a.	~~
Italy	n.a.	+++++	n.a.	+++
Luxembourg	+++++	+++++	+++++	+++++
Netherlands	+++++	+++++	~~	~~
New Zealand	+++++	+++++	+++++	++++
Norway	n.a.	+++++	n.a.	+++
Portugal	n.a.	++++	n.a.	++++
Spain	n.a.	+++	n.a.	+++
Sweden	++++	++++	~~	~~
Switzerland	+++++	+++++	++	++
United Kingdom	+++++	+++++	+++	~~

~~ Relationship with performance is not statistically significant

−/+ Less than 20 score point change in reading performance

− −/++ Between 21 and 40 score point change in reading performance

− − −/+++ Between 41 and 60 score point change in reading performance

− − − −/++++ Between 61 and 80 score point change in reading performance

− − − − −/+++++ More than 80 score point change in reading performance

* The Flemish community in Belgium has a different education system than the French community, and differences in outcomes are masked when viewing Belgium overall. In addition, the Netherlands requested the data so that it could compare its outcomes with those of the Flemish community.

Source: OECD, PISA 2006 database

Language Learning in Regular Classes

In many countries, there is a positive correlation between the number of hours spent learning the language of instruction at school and better outcomes for immigrant students (see Table 3). The only exception is Austria, where a negative association was found between more hours of language learning in regular class and student performance. This could be because focusing on the acquisition of the language causes immigrant students to fall behind in subject learning. This reflects the importance of integrating language learning—both communicative and academic language learning—and content learning into a consistent curriculum. Increasing opportunities for students to learn the language of instruction in regular school lessons could be one way to address this. Schools could also increase educational support outside regular school hours.

System-Level Factors

System-level factors may also influence the student and school behavior and, therefore, may contribute to explaining the performance gap between native and immigrant students.

Assessing Student Performance Results

In some countries, there is a positive relationship between academic performance and the existence of assessment mechanisms that evaluate individual student performance against international standards (see Table 4).

At the system level, appropriate data on educational outcomes for immigrant students should be collected, and this data, including data on performance, could be used to identify challenges and offer timely and targeted support. It is also important to stimulate language learning at an early age through institutional arrangements, such as expanded participation in early childhood education, and to provide systematic, continuous language support for children throughout their education.

Table 4: Accountability and education outcomes for immigrant students, 2006

| | School informing parents of children's performance relative to ... | | | | | |
| | National or regional benchmarks | | Other students in the same grade in the school | | Students in the same grade in other schools | |
	Native students	Immigrant students	Native students	Immigrant students	Native students	Immigrant students
Australia	+	~~	++	++	~~	~~
Austria	~~	+++	~~	~~	~~	~~
Belgium	– – –	~~	++	+++	~~	++++
Flemish Com.	~~	+++	++	++++	~~	++
Canada	~~	~~	+	~~	~~	~~
Germany	~~	~~	~~	~~	– –	~~
Greece	~~	~~	++	~~	~~	~~
Italy	++	~~	~~	+++	~~	+++
Luxembourg	++	–	+	– –	++	++
Netherlands	++	++++	~~	~~	~~	~~
Portugal	~~	~~	~~	~~	~~	+++
United Kingdom	~~	– – –	~~	~~	~~	~~

~~ Relationship with performance is not statistically significant

–/+ Less than 20 score point change in reading performance

– –/++ Between 21 and 40 score point change in reading performance

– – –/+++ Between 41 and 60 score point change in reading performance

– – – –/++++ Between 61 and 80 score point change in reading performance

Note: Results are from school principal reports in PISA 2006. The table presents results only for countries where there are significant relationships with performance.

Source: OECD, PISA 2006 database

Which Policies Can Make a Difference for Immigrant Students?

Country policy reviews and qualitative research—while not based on empirical evidence—are important tools as they present information that cannot be found solely through statistical analysis, which is constrained by data limitations. They can offer an insight into potential policy solutions for immigrant students. This section first presents a brief overview of the main government tools for shaping immigrant education policies, followed by key messages in selecting the tools. It then presents some promising school-level policies and system-level policies for closing the performance gap between native and immigrant students based on both policy reviews and statistical analysis from the previous section.

Overview of Main Government Tools for Shaping Immigrant Education Policy

Governments typically use eight tools to shape immigrant education policy at the national, regional and/or local levels. It is important to note that these tools need to be used in combination in order to ensure the maximum impact; each tool alone has limited impact. It is necessary to take into account the political context, challenges and current state of play in each country to understand which tools are most important and in which combination they should be used. The tools are:

- Setting explicit policy goals for immigrant students within broader education policy goals
- Setting regulations and legislation
- Designing effective funding strategies
- Establishing standards, qualifications and a qualifications framework
- Establishing curricula, guidelines and pedagogy
- Building capacity (especially training and teacher support)
- Raising awareness, communication and dissemination
- Monitoring research, evaluation and feedback

To effectively implement these tools, it is essential to recognize heterogeneity among immigrant students, to take a holistic approach and have shared responsibility at all levels and among all key stakeholders, and find the right balance between universal measures for all students and targeted measures for immigrant students.

Key Messages in Selecting Policy-Steering Tools

There are three key messages to bear in mind in selecting one or more of these tools:

- Since immigrant students in many OECD countries are linguistically, culturally, economically and academically diverse, a "one-size-fits-all" immigrant integration policy may fail to meet the needs of individual immigrant students, especially those who are most at risk.
- There should be a balance between designing targeted measures for immigrant students and universal measures from which both native and immigrant students could benefit.
- A holistic approach and shared responsibility at all levels are necessary. This includes national governments—not only of the host country, but often also of sending countries—local governments, schools (principals, language teachers, subject teachers, classroom teachers, etc.), parents, communities and students themselves (OECD 2010).

School Policies That May Close the Gap for Immigrant Students

The growing diversity in early childhood education and care institutions and schools is familiar to some providers and relatively new for others. School leaders and teachers often do not feel qualified or sufficiently supported to teach students with multicultural, bilingual and diverse learning needs.

Proficiency in the language of instruction is a major tool and precondition for learning (Schnepf 2004; Christensen and Stanat 2007). It is essential that school practice be guided by an explicit, coherent language policy that is informed by research and adapted to the different levels of the education system (OECD 2006; Eurydice 2006).

Teachers and school leaders need to establish a positive school and classroom climate that treats diversity as a resource rather than an obstacle for successful teaching and learning and that focuses on nurturing and developing the competencies of all students (Burns and Shadoian-Gersing 2010; OECD 2005 and 2006; Field, Kuczera and Pont 2007; Pont, Nusche and Moorman 2008; Nusche 2009). Such strategies will support school improvement and be beneficial for all students, not only immigrant students. These strategies need to be supported via strong initial training and professional development for teachers and school administrators. With a whole-school approach, support for immigrant students should be provided not only in specialized courses, but also in an integrated way across the curriculum and throughout all school and after-school activities. Schools should develop new ways of communicating and collaborating so as to better engage immigrant parents and communities in school activities. Prioritized support should be given to the most vulnerable immigrant students, namely, those at risk of not achieving basic academic standards.

Parental and community involvement can influence students in the classroom as well as students' learning environments at home (responsive education) (Brind, Harper and Moore 2008; Heckmann 2008). Research shows a positive relationship between parental involvement and students' performance (Henderson and Mapp 2002; Office for Standards in Education 2002; Jeynes 2005). Furthermore, parental involvement is positively related to student achievement regardless of backgrounds, such as immigrant status or ethnicity (Desforges and Abouchaar 2003; Schofield et al. 2006; Smit et al. 2007; Nusche 2009).

Below are some school- and individual-level policies to help address the needs of immigrant students.

Recommendations for strengthening language support:
- Encourage parents to get involved, for example, through reading at home.

- Ensure consistent and continuous support at all levels of education.
- Integrate language and content learning.
- Improve mother-tongue proficiency.

Recommendations for ensuring quality teaching and learning environments:
- Give all teachers diversity training.
- Carry out regular student assessments aimed at improving their performance, and adapt teaching toward that goal.
- Encourage the sharing of "best practices" in school management and the application of research findings in pedagogy (e.g., Denmark's "This Works at Our School" or Sweden's "Idea Schools for Multiculturalism").
- Strengthen school leadership and the whole-school approach by providing school leadership training.

Recommendations for encouraging parental and community involvement:
- Remove linguistic and cultural barriers.
- Educate parents about the host country's educational system, and involve them in classroom instruction (General Teaching Council for England 2007).
- Use the local community's resources, for example, by encouraging those with immigrant backgrounds to become mentors.
- Work with schools to provide extracurricular activities (e.g., assistance with homework and participation in cultural, athletic and academic events) after school and during summer holidays.

System-Level Policies That May Close the Gap for Immigrant Students

Immigrant students may have different educational opportunities depending on where they live and which schools they attend. Policies at all levels of the education system need to ensure that the same quantity and quality of language and other targeted support are consistently offered to immigrant students no matter which school they attend. This requires: strong political leadership; accountability; the sharing of good practices among municipalities, schools and teachers; and the provision of sufficient information about the educational system and schools to immigrant parents.

Review countries (Austria, Denmark, Ireland, the Netherlands, Norway, Sweden) have made significant efforts to improve school system management, and these have apparently had some beneficial effects.

Designing effective funding strategies could be one way to manage inequalities by targeting discrete areas, schools or student groups—or in combination—after careful consideration of educational priorities (Eurydice 2000; Field 2007). Increasing the funding level would require awareness-raising about the importance of migrant education, reallocation from different education programs to migrant education programs, and reallocation from different education levels to early education, from which disadvantaged immigrants would significantly benefit. Generating new sources of funding has also been found in some countries. The examples include funding from nongovernmental organizations and enterprises as part of social corporate responsibilities, such as in the United States and Germany, and support from sending countries, such as educational support through a bilateral government agreement for Turkish students in Germany from the Turkish government. Finding new sources, however, has become restricted during the recession and postrecession period.

Collecting data on student outcomes and monitoring could also help improve school performance by permitting the timely tracking of student outcomes, identifying those who need help and designing appropriate interventions (Herweijer 2009; OECD 2008d). The improvements below could benefit native students as well.

Recommendations for better management of variations across regions and schools:
- Establish a legal and financial framework that governs different regions and schools (Norwegian Ministy of Education and Research 2008).

- Identify what works, and promote knowledge-sharing among regions and schools (Hill and Matthews 2008).
- Improve availability and clarity of information for parents.
- Focus efforts on schools with high concentrations of immigrant students.

Recommendations for designing an effective funding strategy:
- Invest more in early education.
- Earmark funding to target particular groups, areas and schools.
- Target various disadvantaged students based on factors such as low performance, immigrant status, parental income and education level, area of living, etc., to capture not only low-achieving immigrant students, but also native students.
- Monitor the use of extra funding (Department for Education and Skills 2004).

Recommendations for effective monitoring and evaluation:
- Set teaching performance standards, and conduct regular classroom observation.
- Improve data quality and coverage to consolidate evidence on education outcomes for immigrant students (OECD 2001, 2004a, 2006).
- Establish a well-developed system-wide monitoring system (OECD 2004b).
- Train and support teachers to carry out effective monitoring and give feedback in classroom (Irish Department of Education and Science 2009).

Conclusion

Given the different sizes and compositions of their immigrant student populations, each country faces unique challenges. As a result, there is no panacea that will work for all countries to close the performance gap between immigrant and native students. The previous section aimed to provide a "menu" of some of the typical policy options that many countries are using. More comprehensive lists of the various policy options being put in place in many countries are available at www.oecd.edu/migration/policytools.

This chapter concludes with a discussion of policy implications and five priority action points that are most relevant at a time when governments around the world are recovering from a deep recession.

Action Point 1: Ensure affordable access to early childhood education and care for all, and stimulate language learning at an early age.

- When faced with financial pressures during and after the recession, governments or politicians often lose sight of long-term returns on investment or long-term negative consequences of not taking immediate action. However, it is important to continue investing in early years.

- Our statistical analysis showed a strong association between early reading at home and better academic scores at later ages. This is in line with findings of extensive research on human-capital formation. Building a strong foundation for lifelong learning at this stage is of critical importance for educational, social and economic outcomes in later stages, such as better academic scores, fewer dropouts, better salaries, reduced criminal rates, less social-benefit dependency, etc. By investing in early years, especially for disadvantaged immigrant and native children, there will be long-term benefits for society at large, such as more tax revenues resulting from higher salaries from these groups and less spending on social benefits and policing.

Action Point 2: Embed research-based, systemic and continuous language teaching into regular curricula.

- At a time of recession, language teaching is often seen as being of secondary importance, and budgets for language teachers are often threatened by cuts.

- As our research and other literature show, mastering the language of instruction is one of the critical prerequisites for the academic success of immigrant children. Language support should not be affected or threatened by financial constraints that governments may face at any time in their economic cycle. It is important that students have opportunities to learn the language of instruction in regular school lessons. It is also important that research on pedagogy be advanced and that research-based language-teaching practices be promoted, such as integration of language and content learning. To make such practices systemic, it is important that curricula and guidelines be developed and that teachers be trained to effectively implement them.

Action Point 3: Provide training to teachers and school leaders.
- As mentioned above, teachers are the main actors for effective policy implementation. Since they have the longest contact hours with the students, they are the most critical actors in the "change chain" required to make a difference for the students. Providing support and training to teachers and school leaders requires immediate action.
- Training should include not only language-specific teachers, but also subject and mainstream teachers. This would ensure effective support in regular classes as well as help ensure smooth transition from induction classes to mainstream classes in countries that provide language-focused classes to newly arrived immigrant students separate from the rest of the students. This is critically important in countries whose practice is to mainstream immigrant students into regular classes upon arrival.
- Include the following components in the training:
  - Leadership and management in dealing with diversity in classrooms/schools, such as: a) second-language acquisition and integration of content and language learning; b) a whole-school approach, whereby teachers, school leaders, parents and communities need to share responsibility for tackling the challenges; c) how to motivate newly arrived students to do well in class and be integrated into school; and d) management of bullying issues based on cultural stereotypes.

- Carrying out student assessment for improving their perform-ance and ensuring accountability. Based on the results, teach-ers should provide targeted support to the most vulnerable stu-dents (including native students) without stigmatizing them as "failures."
- Effective communication with immigrant parents, such as or-ganizing cultural events, visiting students' homes, suggesting how to help their children with home learning and getting them involved in school, such as with service on the parents' board.
- Effective outreach strategies to communities, such as a) find-ing mentors, role models and mother-language teachers in the immigrant communities; b) exploring opportunities to set up extracurricular activities for after school and during summer holidays; and c) exploring financial or in-kind resources from enterprises and nongovernmental organizations—although this is becoming more difficult in the post-recession period.
- Sharing good practices among teachers and school leaders across different schools.
- Sharing information about students (academic records, family backgrounds, aspirations, etc.) across different education lev-els, such as from primary to lower-secondary grades and from lower-secondary to upper-secondary grades.

Action Point 4: Support immigrant parents.
- In times of recession or postrecession, it is often the low-skilled immigrants—along with women and older workers—who are at risk of being affected in the labor market in many countries.
- As research shows, parents' income level has a strong relationship with their children's academic performance. It is of particular im-portance that policies should help low-skilled immigrants to keep a job or find a new job by a) providing effective career guidance targeted to the low skilled; b) providing flexible learning opportu-nities for adult immigrants, in particular, those with limited edu-cation or language proficiency; c) reinforcing antidiscrimination

laws in the country's labor market (if they exist); and d) ensuring that the most marginalized are targeted for antipoverty measures.

- It is also important to support immigrant parents so they can maintain a good learning environment at home for their children, such as by a) providing classes for parenting skills about children's well-being and learning; b) providing better information and use of libraries and other learning opportunities; and c) implementing home-visiting programs.

Action Point 5: Advance evaluation and monitoring of migrant education.

- When budgets are tight, programs that do not yield immediate outputs are often the target of budget cuts. However, in order to design a cost-effective policy, evaluation of policy interventions is of critical importance.
- Even during a of recession, it is important that policy evaluation and monitoring of target outcomes be continued. With respect to closing the academic gap between immigrant and native students, it is important to collect appropriate data on educational outcomes for immigrant students in countries that have not done so yet, and, if such data are already available in the country, to use them to identify challenges and offer timely targeted support.

Appendix

Table: Factors that may affect student performance

Factors that affect outcome indicators		
Individual level	**School/community level**	**System level**
Student	**School**	**Institutional arrangements**
Academic performance Acculturation Age Age at arrival Aspirations/motivation/ engagement/self-esteem Country of origin/ethnicity/ cultural differences Family size/siblings Family structure Gender Generation Language competencies Learning at home Length of stay	Ability grouping Comprehensive induction and integration program Concentration of immigrants Curriculum adaptation responsive to cultural and linguistic diversity Language support Peers (discrimination, bullying) School composition (average socioeconomic back- ground of students) School-parents-community communication concerning potential dropout students School leaders School resources Teachers expectations; pedagogy; classroom management; stereotypes/discrimination Type of school attended (private/public)	External student assessment Induction and integration program at the system level Longer schooling time (curricular and extra- curricular) National curriculum or teaching guidelines responsive to linguistic and cultural diversity Preschool education and care system School/teacher evaluation Tracking (vocational versus academic; comprehensive versus special needs)
Parent	**Community**	
Aspirations and expectations for children Education resources at home Educational level Involvement in school activities Language competencies Occupational status	Ethnic capital Share responsibility in creating better communication channels between school, parents and community	
	Spatial	
	Belonging to immigrant community Neighborhood	

Works Cited

Brind, Tom, Caroline Harper and Karen Moore. *Education for Migrant, Minority and Marginalised Children in Europe.* New York: Open Society Institute's Education Support Programme, 2008.

Burns, Tracey, and Vanessa Shadoian-Gersing. The Importance of Effective Teacher Education for Diversity. In *Educating Teachers for Diversity: Meeting the Challenge.* Paris: OECD, Centre for Educational Research and Innovation, 2010.

Christensen, Gayle, and Petra Stanat. *Language Policies and Practices for Helping Immigrants and Second-Generation Students Succeed.* Washington, DC: The Transatlantic Taskforce on Immigration and Integration, Migration Policy Institute and Bertelsmann Stiftung, 2007.

Crul, Maurice, and Jens Schneider. *The Second Generation in Europe. Education and the Transition to the Labour Market.* TIES Policy Brief. London: Open Society Institute, 2009. www.tiesproject.eu/component/option,com_docman/task,doc_download/gid,410/Itemid,142 (accessed July 15, 2010).

Desforges, Charles, and Alberto Abouchaar. *The Impact of Parental Involvement, Parental Support and Family Education on Pupil Achievements and Adjustment: A Literature Review.* Research Report No. 433. London: Department for Education and Skills, 2003. www.dfes.gov.uk/research/data/uploadfiles/RR433.pdf (accessed July 15, 2010).

Department for Education and Skills. Aiming High: Supporting Effective Use of EMAG. Working Paper/0283/2004. London, 2004. www.standards.dfes.gov.uk/ethnicminorities/links_and_publications/supportingemag/Efctv_Use_EMAG.pdf (accessed July 15, 2010).

Eurydice. *Key Data on Teaching Languages at School in Europe.* Brussels: Education, Audiovisual and Culture Executive Agency (EACEA), 2008. http://eacea.ec.europa.eu/about/eurydice/documents/KDL2008_EN.pdf (accessed July 15, 2010).

Eurydice. *Key Topics in Education in Europe. Volume 2: Financing and Management of Resources in Compulsory Education.* Luxembourg:

European Commission, 2000. www.europahouse.uz/download/en/education/L0000_inter_cover.pdf (accessed July 15, 2010).

Field, Simon, Malgorzata Kuczera and Beatriz Pont. *No More Failures: Ten Steps to Equity in Education*. Paris: OECD, 2007.

General Teaching Council for England. *Research for Teachers: Multi-agency Working and Pupil Behaviour*. London: GTC, 2007. www.gtce.org.uk/pdf/teachers/rft/behaviour0207 (accessed July 15, 2010).

Heckmann, Friedrich. Education and the Integration of Migrants. NESSE Analytical Report 1, European Union Commission DG Education and Culture, Bamberg: EFMS, 2008. www.efms.uni-bamberg.de/pdf/NESEducationIntegrationMigrants.pdf (accessed July 15, 2010).

Henderson, Anne T., and Karen L. Mapp. *A New Wave of Evidence: The Impact of School, Family, and Community Connections On Student Achievement*. Austin: Southwest Educational Development Laboratory, 2002.

Herweijer, Lex. *Making Up the Gap—Migrant Education in the Netherlands*. The Hague: The Netherlands Institute for Social Research, 2009.

Hill, Robert, and Peter Matthews. *Schools Leading Schools: The Power and Potential of National Leaders of Education*. Nottingham: National College for School Leadership, 2008.

International Association for Evaluation of Educational Achievement. Progress in International Reading Literacy Study (PIRLS). PIRLS Database: www.iea.nl/(accessed July 15, 2010).

Irish Department of Education and Science. *OECD Thematic Review on Migrant Education—Country Background Report for Ireland*. Paris: OECD, 2009. www.oecd.org/dataoecd/8/22/42485332.pdf (accessed July 15, 2010).

Jeynes, William H. Parental Involvement and Student Achievement: A Meta-Analysis. *Harvard Family Research Project*, 2005. www.hfrp.org/publications-resources/browse-our-publications/parental-involvement-and-student-achievement-a-meta-analysis (accessed July 15, 2010).

Karsten, Sjoerd, Charles Felix, Guuske Ledoux, Wim Meijnen, Jaap Roeleveld and Erik Van Schooten. Choosing Segregation or Integration? The Extent and Effects of Ethnic Segregation in Dutch Cities. *Education and Urban Society* (38) 2: 228–247, 2006.

Nordin, Martin. Ethnic Segregation and Educational Attainment in Sweden. Working paper. Lund University, 2006. www.nek.lu.se/ NEKMNO/Ethnic%20Segregation%20and%20educational%20Attainment%20in%20Sweden.pdf (accessed July 15, 2010).

Norwegian Ministry of Education and Research. *OECD Review of Migrant Education – Country Background Report for Norway.* Paris: OECD, 2008. www.oecd.org/dataoecd/8/44/42485380.pdf (accessed July 15, 2010).

Nusche, Deborah. What Works in Migrant Education? A Review of Evidence and Policy Options. Education Working Papers, no. 22. OECD, 2009.

OECD. *Closing the Gap for Immigrant Students: Policies, Practice and Performance.* Paris: OECD, 2010.

OECD. *International Migration Outlook,* Paris: OECD, 2008a. www. oecd.org/document/3/0,3343,en_2649_33931_41241219_1_1_1_ 1,00.html (accessed July 15, 2010).

OECD. *Jobs for Immigrants. Vol. 2: Labour Market Integration in Belgium, France, the Netherlands and Portugal.* Paris: OECD, 2008b.

OECD. Preliminary Findings for Step 1: Establishing Facts in Order to Identify Problems that Policy Ought to Address. Directorate for Education. Paris: OECD, 2008c. www.olis.oecd.org/olis/2008doc. nsf/ENGDATCORPLOOK/NT0000B2A2/$FILE/JT03251858.PDF.

OECD. How Do Countries Take Stock of Progress and Performance in Education Systems? Evidence and Issues. Paris: Directorate for Education, Education Policy Committee, OECD, 2008d. www.dlint. org/arbejdsomraader/OECD/OECD%20test%20og%20evaluering/ HOW_DO_OECD_COUNTRIES_TAKE_STOCK_OF_PROGRESS_ AND_PERFORMANCE_IN_EDUCATION_SYSTEMS_nov2008. pdf (accessed July 15, 2010).

OECD. *Jobs for Immigrants. Vol. 1: Labour Market Integration in Australia, Denmark, Germany and Sweden.* Paris: OECD, 2007.

OECD. *Where Immigrant Students Succeed: A Comparative Review of Performance and Engagement in PISA 2003*. Paris: OECD, 2006a.

OECD. Programme for International Student Assessment (PISA), 2006b. www.pisa.oecd.org/(accessed July 15, 2010).

OECD. *Formative Assessment: Improving Learning in Secondary Classrooms*. Paris: OECD, 2005.

OECD. *Learning for Tomorrow's World: First Results from PISA 2003*. Paris: OECD, 2004a.

OECD. *What Makes School Systems Perform? Seeing School Systems Through the Prism of PISA*. Paris: OECD, 2004b.

OECD. *Knowledge and Skills for Life: First Results from PISA 2000*. Paris: OECD, 2001.

Office for Standards in Education. *Achievement of Black Caribbean Pupils: Three Successful Primary Schools*. Manchester: OfstEd, 2002.

Pont, Beatriz, Deborah Nusche and Hunter Moorman. *Improving School Leadership, Volume 1: Policy and Practice*. Paris: OECD, 2008.

Progress in International Reading Literacy Study (PIRLS), 2010. http://timss.bc.edu (accessed July 15, 2010).

Rangvid, Beatrice S. School Composition Effects in Denmark: Quantile Regression Evidence from PISA 2000. *Empirical Economics* (33) 2: 359–388, 2007.

Schnepf, Sylka V. How Different Are Immigrants? A Cross-Country and Cross-Survey Analysis of Educational Achievement. IZA Discussion Paper No. 1398. Bonn: IZA, 2004.

Schofield, Janet Ward, in cooperation with Kira Alexander, Ralph Bangs and Barbara Schauenburg. *Migration Background, Minority-Group Membership and Academic Achievement: Research Evidence from Social, Educational, and Developmental Psychology*. AKI Research Review 5, Programme on Intercultural Conflicts and Societal Integration (AKI). Berlin: Social Science Research Center Berlin, 2006.

Smit, Friedrich, Gert Dreesen, Roderick Sluiter and Peter Sleegers. Types of Parents and School Strategies Aimed at the Creation of Effective Partnerships. *International Journal about Parents in Edu-*

cation (1) 0: 45–52, 2007. www.ernape.net/ejournal/index.php/
IJPE/article/viewFile/23/13 (accessed July 15, 2010).

Swedish Ministry of Education and Research. *OECD Review of
Migrant Education – Country Background Report for Sweden, 2008.*
www.oecd.org/dataoecd/8/42/42485410.pdf (accessed July 15,
2010).

Szulkin, Ryszard, and Jan O. Jonsson. Ethnic Segregation and Educational Outcomes in Swedish Comprehensive Schools. Working
Paper 2007, no. 2, ISSN 1654-1189. The Stockholm University
Linnaeus Center for Integration Studies (SULCIS): Stockholm,
2007.

Van Ewijk, Reyn, and Peter Sleegers. Peer Ethnicity and Achievement: A Meta-Analysis Into the Compositional Effect. University
of Amsterdam, 2009. http://papers.ssrn.com/sol3/papers.cfm?
abstract_id=1402651 (accessed July 15, 2010).

The Economic Crisis and Funding for Immigrant Integration in the United States

Randy Capps and Margie McHugh with Monica Arciga, Michael Fix and Laureen Laglagaron

Introduction

While national governments have taken responsibility for immigrant integration in many countries, the United States relies more heavily on state and local governments as well as the private sector to incorporate newcomers. Refugees, who comprise less than 10 percent of all US immigrants, are the only group that receives dedicated federal support for their integration. For other US immigrants, integration generally occurs at the local level, with employers, schools, churches and community organizations helping newcomers with everything from learning English to becoming US citizens. States play a major funding role, particularly in the areas of education and social safety-net services, such as cash welfare and public health insurance. The federal government provides substantial funding for education and social safety-net programs as well, but these programs comprise a large share of state budgets, and they are frequently the targets of cuts during times of fiscal crisis. Because immigrants are disproportionately poor, they rely more on public education, health and social services than the native born—and suffer more when these services are cut.

There is substantial variation in the depth and severity of the fiscal crisis across the United States. In general, budgets have been hard hit in the Southwestern states of Arizona, California and Nevada, where the housing market and overall economy have contracted the most. In these three states, the 2010 deficit has been estimated to be more than 45 percent of the budget (McNichol and Johnson 2010). At the same time, some states have thus far avoided a serious fiscal crisis: 2010 deficits were less than 10 percent of the overall budget in six states.[1]

The first section of this report focuses on funding for integration-related programs in the five most populous US states—California, Florida, Illinois, New York and Texas. Together, these states were home to 112 million people, or 37 percent of the US population, according to the 2008 American Community Survey of the US Census Bureau. These five states also accounted for 61 percent of the nation's 38 million immigrants (see Table 1), and immigrants made up a considerable portion of each state's population (see Table 2).

Table 1: Number of immigrants in US states with five largest populations, 2008

State	Immigrant population	Percent of total immigrant population
United States	37,961,000	100
California	9,859,000	26
New York	4,237,000	11
Texas	3,887,000	10
Florida	3,392,000	9
Illinois	1,782,000	5

Source: US Census Bureau 2010

We examine how budget gaps in the five largest states have affected a range of programs serving immigrants and their children: safety-net programs, including cash welfare, food and nutrition assistance, and public health insurance coverage; adult education and literacy programs; citizenship preparation and application assistance; and language-access services. The safety-net programs, while not specifically geared toward immigrant integration, are important for immigrant families because they are disproportionately poor. In the five largest

---

1 These states were Arkansas, Nebraska, South Dakota, Texas, West Virginia and Wyoming.

states, the immigrant poverty rate exceeded the overall poverty rate, with the highest rate for immigrants in Texas (21 percent) and the lowest in Illinois (13 percent). Immigrants made up almost a third of the poverty population in California, a quarter in New York and more than a fifth in Florida and Texas (see Table 2).

Table 2: Immigrant population and poverty figures for the five largest states, 2008

	California	Florida	Illinois	New York	Texas
2008 population					
Total	36,757,000	18,328,000	12,902,000	19,490,000	24,327,000
Immigrant	9,859,000	3,392,000	1,782,000	4,237,000	3,887,000
Percent immigrant	27	19	14	22	16
2008 poverty population					
Total	4,778,000	2,371,000	1,532,000	2,581,000	3,760,000
Immigrant	1,503,000	527,000	224,000	643,000	824,000
Percent immigrant	31	22	15	25	22
2008 poverty rate					
Total (in percent)	13	13	12	14	16
Immigrant (in percent)	15	16	13	15	21

Note: All population numbers are rounded to the nearest thousand. The official US poverty level for a family of four is currently $22,050, lower for smaller families and higher for larger ones

Source: US Census Bureau 2010

In general, unauthorized immigrants are ineligible for federal and state-funded safety-net programs; we describe a few exceptions later in the report. Legal immigrants who have not yet become citizens are generally eligible for safety-net services in some states, but their eligibility is restricted in others—with substantial variation among the five largest states, as we discuss below. Immigrants who entered as refugees and those who have become US citizens are generally eligible for these programs on the same terms as the US-born population.

Moreover, refugees are eligible for a package of federally funded services—including cash welfare, housing assistance, food assistance, health care, education, job training and employment assistance—during their first few months and years in the United States. Other immigrants are generally not eligible for these programs.

Economic conditions, budget deficits and the strength of social safety nets vary considerably across the five states, with California the weakest fiscally and Texas the strongest (see Table 3).

Table 3: Economic and fiscal indicators for the five largest states

	California	Florida	Illinois	New York	Texas
Unemployment rate in percent (seasonally adjusted)[a]					
May 2009	11.3	10.2	10.0	8.4	7.5
May 2010	12.4	11.7	10.8	8.3	8.3
Percent change	+1.1	+1.5	+0.8*	−0.1*	+0.8
2010 state budget deficit[b]					
Deficit	$54.6 billion	$6.0 billion	$14.3 billion	$21.0 billion	$3.5 billion
Percent of budget	64.5	28.5	40.9	38.0	9.8
Projected 2011 state budget deficit[b]					
Deficit	$9.0 billion	$4.7 billion	$13.5 billion	$8.5 billion	$4.6 billion
Percent of budget	9.1	22.2	36.1	15.5	12.8

Notes: Starting and ending months of state budget years vary.

* Unemployment rate change not statistically significant between May 2009 and May 2010.

Sources: a – US Bureau of Labor Statistics 2010; b – McNichol and Johnson 2010

California had the country's third-highest unemployment rate (12.4 percent), behind Nevada and Michigan, in May 2010 (US Bureau of Labor Statistics 2010b). California has one of the most generous safety nets of any state, including programs that target immigrant populations. The state's estimated 2010 budget deficit ($55 billion) was more than a quarter of the value of deficits across all 50 states ($200 billion).

Illinois and *New York* also had relatively high deficits, amounting to 41 percent and 38 percent of their total 2010 budgets, respectively. Like California, these two states spend substantial sums on education and social safety-net services, and both have immigrant integration programs. In February 2010, the Illinois unemployment rate was 10.8 percent, about a percentage point above the national average of 9.7 percent. New York's 8.3 percent unemployment rate was below the national average.

Florida's unemployment rate was almost as high as California's (11.7 percent versus 12.4 percent), but the state has considerably lower taxes than California and spends far less on education and safety-net services. Also, Florida does not have immigrant-targeted programs. In part as a result of lower spending, Florida had a 2010 deficit-to-budget ratio of 29 percent, near the average for all states (McNichol and Johnson 2010).

Texas has one of the strongest state economies and one of the weakest safety nets. As one of the few states without a personal income tax, its budget is relatively less vulnerable to large swings in personal income that result from business cycles. In 2010, the state's unemployment rate was just 8.3 percent, more than a point below the national average. The state's deficit was only 9.8 percent of its budget, sixth lowest across all states (ibid.).

The 2009 Federal Stimulus Law and Immigrant Integration

In response to the economic crisis and the impending fiscal crisis in the states, the US Congress enacted the American Recovery and Reinvestment Act (ARRA) on February 17, 2009 (US Public Law 111-5). ARRA includes substantial federal tax breaks and changes in revenue streams as well as federal spending. ARRA dedicated about half of its new federal spending ($282 billion of $580 billion) to state aid. Although ARRA's $282 billion in state aid exceeds the estimated $200 billion in total state budget deficits in 2010, another $140 billion in shortfalls is predicted for 2011 (Leachman, Williams and Johnson 2010).

ARRA has helped narrow some critical budget gaps, particularly in education, health care and social services, where the recession has increased demand for services by immigrants and other vulnerable populations. One year after the law's passage, $88.7 billion, or 30 percent, of ARRA funding had already reached the states (Government Accountability Office 2010). Federal spending for health, education and training together accounted for 88 percent of ARRA outlays to states in 2009 (ibid.). But ARRA's funding for these services expires at the end of 2010, leaving states vulnerable to much larger budget deficits. Unless the US Congress authorizes additional stimulus funding, states will face renewed and even greater pressure to cut social safety-net and educational programs (Leachman, Williams and Johnson 2010).

Safety-Net Programs

Cash Welfare Programs

Cash welfare has historically been one of the most important resources for US families during economic downturns. But the country's principal cash welfare program has been scaled back dramatically in recent years. The 1996 welfare reform law (US Public Law 104-193) replaced the major US entitlement program for cash welfare with Temporary Assistance for Needy Families (TANF), a block-grant program[2] with lifetime limits on coverage, stringent work requirements and restrictions for immigrants that in practice allow only long-term permanent residents and naturalized citizens to receive benefits in most states. Prior to 1996, legal immigrants were eligible for public benefits on more or less the same terms as citizens. Although spending is now capped, TANF is the largest cash welfare program in the

---

2 Block-grant programs involve fixed-amount grants from the federal government to the states for certain authorized activities, while entitlements are open-ended programs in which funding levels depend on the number of eligible people obtaining benefits and services.

country, costing $14 billion in federal funds and $11 billion in state funds in 2008 (Agency for Children and Families 2009).

The 11 million to 12 million unauthorized immigrants in the United States (Passel and Cohn 2009) are ineligible for TANF-funded assistance or services, although their US-born children, as US citizens, may be eligible. Legal immigrants generally cannot obtain benefits during their first five years in the country, but several states provide cash welfare benefits to legal immigrants during this period, including California and New York (but not the three other states examined in this report).[3] Still, immigrants' participation in TANF plummeted after welfare reform, with only 5 percent of low-income legal immigrant families obtaining benefits in 2004.[4] The overall number of TANF participants fell two-thirds, from 12.8 million in 1996 to 4.1 million at the end of 2009 (National Governors Association and the National Association of State Budget Officers 2009).

ARRA dedicated $5 billion in state aid to TANF and related programs, and it gave states incentives to expand rather than cut their programs. ARRA provides an 80 percent federal reimbursement for increases in state spending on cash benefits, subsidized work programs and short-term assistance programs, such as "back-to-school" grants for school supplies. The additional federal funding has allowed states to serve new or growing populations and devise new programs for cash assistance and work support while spending very little of their own money. This new funding has prevented steep cuts in cash welfare benefits and eligibility for benefits in several states, most notably California. If ARRA state aid for TANF expires, new measures instituted in some states will be in jeopardy, and cuts averted due to the additional funding may take effect.

Across the five largest states, TANF programs vary considerably (see Table 4).

3 Other states include Connecticut, Maine, Maryland, Minnesota, Nebraska, New Mexico, Oregon, Pennsylvania, Tennessee, Utah, Vermont, Washington, Wisconsin and Wyoming (National Immigration Law Center 2002a).
4 This is the share of families with incomes below twice the federal poverty level that reported receiving cash welfare benefits (Capps, Fix and Henderson 2009).

225

Table 4: Cash welfare programs and budget cuts across five largest states

State	Number of TANF participants (2009)	Amount spent on TANF and related programs (2008)	Changes to benefits since recession	Program for *legal* immigrants not covered by TANF?	How states use ARRA funds
California	1.3 million	$6.7 billion	4 percent cut for families	Yes	Cash benefits and more than 15,000 subsidized jobs
Florida	108,000	$948 million	None, but no increase since 1996	No	Goal of 10,000 subsidized jobs
Illinois	55,000	$1 billion	None	Only for those who are victims of domestic abuse	Summer food program, foreclosure relief program, goal of 10,000 subsidized jobs
New York	270,000	$4.4 billion	5 percent increase	Yes	$140 million back-to-school program and 6,000 subsidized jobs
Texas	108,000*	$821 million	None	No	Back-to-school program

* 90 percent are children.

Sources: Agency for Children and Families 2009 (Table A, C1, B1, F) and 2010

California

California has the largest and one of the most generous TANF programs. Over 1.3 million people in California received benefits in 2009, about a third of the national caseload and up substantially since the recession began (Agency for Children and Families 2010). California spent $6.7 billion on TANF and related programs in 2008, or 24 percent of the national total (Agency for Children and Families 2009).

A substantial number of California's TANF participants are children whose parents are ineligible because they are unauthorized, their time limits expired, they failed to meet work requirements or other reasons. California also has a state-funded program for legal immigrants during their first five years of permanent status. In 2009, the state spent $52 million on public assistance outside the TANF program, including the costs of aid for recent legal immigrants (Agency for Children and Families 2009).

In 2009, California reduced the maximum family grant by 4 percent, from $723 to $694 per month, and eliminated its annual cost-of-living adjustment. The state also cut child-care funding and support to help TANF recipients find jobs. Although California's legislature enacted more severe cuts, the additional matching funding in ARRA, along with pressure from state advocates for children, prevented these cuts from being implemented. Governor Arnold Schwarzenegger proposed eliminating the state program for legal immigrants as well as the entire TANF program, but these proposals had not been enacted as of June 2010.

The state has used ARRA funding for cash benefits and more than 15,000 subsidized jobs, a third of them in Los Angeles. Nonetheless, the severity of the state's ongoing financial crisis has many advocates concerned that deeper cuts in public assistance are still to come, especially when the additional TANF funding in ARRA expires.

New York

New York has a much smaller, but also relatively generous TANF program. The recession began later in New York than in other states, unemployment is relatively low and caseloads have grown only modestly. The state spent $4.4 billion on TANF and related cash assistance programs in 2008.

One of those related programs is the constitutionally mandated Safety Net program, which serves legal immigrants, childless adults and other groups ineligible for TANF. In 2008, New York spent $1.8 billion on non-TANF welfare programs, more than any other state. Combined TANF, Safety Net and other public-assistance programs had a caseload of 514,000 in December 2008 (New York Public Welfare Association 2009).

In 2005, New York's maximum monthly benefit level was $577 for a family of three (National Center for Children in Poverty 2009b). In 2009, the state *increased* benefit levels by about 5 percent for TANF- and Safety Net-eligible families with children and used ARRA funding to help pay for this expansion. Similar benefit increases are slated for 2011 and 2012, though there are proposals to roll them back. New York also used ARRA funding to create subsidized jobs, but funding shortfalls for child care prevented some people from getting these jobs.

Florida

Florida has a considerably smaller and less generous cash assistance program than California or New York. The state's maximum grant for a family of three is just $303 per month, an amount that has not increased since 1996. The state has no cash assistance program for legal immigrants who are ineligible for TANF. No major cuts to TANF have been proposed, and the state has used ARRA funding mostly for subsidizing up to 10,000 jobs.

Texas

Like Florida, Texas has a small and historically conservative TANF program. In 2005, the state's maximum monthly three-person grant was $223 per month, one of the lowest in the country (National Center for Children in Poverty 2009c). There are no special programs for legal immigrants or others ineligible for benefits. In fact, the state does not provide TANF for legal immigrants who entered after the welfare reform law was signed in 1996—an eligibility standard more stringent than most states' five-year residency requirement. The Texas legislature only meets every two years, and during its last session, in spring 2009, the state had not yet felt the fiscal impact of the recession. As a result, the legislature did not pass any substantial cuts to social welfare programs. Texas has drawn down very little ARRA funding for TANF benefits.

Illinois

Illinois experienced one of the steepest state-level caseload drops from 1996 to 2009: 91 percent. The state's maximum grant of $396 per month was in the middle range of the states in 2005 (National Center for Children in Poverty 2009a). In 2010, the Illinois legislature increased the amount of income families can earn and still qualify for TANF and made administrative changes that should improve program access. There have been no major proposed cuts or increases in eligibility or benefit levels. The state does not have a special program for ineligible legal immigrants, except for those who are victims of domestic abuse. Like Florida, Illinois has mostly used ARRA funding to create a program for 10,000 subsidized jobs.

Unlike cash welfare, the US government provides all of the funding for its major food- and nutrition-assistance programs, which remain entitlements. Overall spending is not capped, and eligibility requirements and benefit levels are uniform across the states. Because they are not capped, these federal nutrition programs have expanded considerably during the recession.

The largest is the Supplemental Nutrition Assistance Program (SNAP), formerly known as food stamps. SNAP provides vouchers for low-income families to purchase food at grocery stores. Between 2006 and 2009, participation increased 26 percent, from 26.7 million people to 33.7 million (Food and Nutrition Service 2010c). Currently, about eight times as many people receive SNAP as TANF.

ARRA authorized additional SNAP benefits of up to $80 per month for a family of four, raising such a family's maximum monthly benefit to $668 (Food and Nutrition Service 2009). By April 2010, ARRA had contributed an additional $10.2 billion to the SNAP program. Total SNAP benefits issued *almost doubled*, from $30 billion to $50 billion, between 2006 and 2009, with almost half of that increase attributable to ARRA (Food and Nutrition Service 2010d).

The 1996 welfare reform law made most legal immigrants ineligible for SNAP, but a 2002 law restored eligibility for many legal immigrant adults and virtually all legal immigrant children.[5] A handful of states, including California, continue to provide benefits to most legal immigrant adults who are not eligible for the federal program.[6] Unauthorized immigrants are not eligible for SNAP; families with members who are not eligible because they are unauthorized or re-

---

5 The 1996 welfare reform law restricted eligibility to legal immigrants with 10 years of US work experience, refugees, veterans and a few smaller groups. The Farm Security and Rural Investment Act of 2002, US Public Law 107-171, restored eligibility to all disabled legal immigrants, adults with five years of legal residency and virtually all legal immigrant children. Small groups of immigrants with temporary legal status remain ineligible.
6 Other states are Connecticut, Maine, Minnesota, Nebraska, Washington and Wisconsin (National Immigration Law Center 2002b).

cent legal immigrants receive prorated benefits based on the number of eligible members.

In 2005, before the recession, approximately 1.4 million immigrant families with noncitizen parents were receiving SNAP benefits, including almost 400,000 US-citizen children with unauthorized parents (Henderson, Capps and Finegold 2008). In 2004, the share of legal immigrant families receiving benefits was 22 percent, more than five times the share receiving TANF (4 percent) (Capps, Fix and Henderson 2009).

The federal government funds two other major nutrition assistance programs; both serve immigrants regardless of legal status. The Supplemental Nutrition Assistance Program for Women, Infants and Children (WIC) offers food assistance to low-income pregnant women, mothers of infants and children from birth to age 4. Importantly, WIC provides nutritional support for noncitizen mothers and young children who do not qualify for other social programs. Between 2006 and 2009, the total number of WIC participants rose 11 percent from 8.1 million to 9.1 million, and costs for WIC rose from $3.4 billion to $4.6 billion. By April 2010, ARRA had provided an additional $41 million for the WIC program (Food and Nutrition Service 2010e).

The National School Lunch Program (NSLP) offers free and reduced-price lunches to low-income public school students. NSLP served 19.5 million students in 2009, up 10 percent from 17.7 million in 2006 (Food and Nutrition Service 2010b). Over this period, the total cost of these lunches rose from $7.4 billion to $8.9 billion (Food and Nutrition Service 2010a). As of April 2010, ARRA had provided $90 million in additional funding for NLSP.

The numbers of immigrants participating in WIC and NSLP are currently unknown.

The US health-care system is supported by a hybrid of employer-based insurance, insurance individuals buy on the private market and public coverage for seniors, low-income people and other needy groups. Adults age 65 and over—including most legal immigrants—are eligible for the largest national insurance program, Medicare. Since the older immigrant population is small in the United States, we focus here on two other programs, Medicaid and the Children's Health Insurance Program (CHIP). States share funding for these two programs with the federal government, and states set eligibility levels at or above federal minimums. These programs are important sources of coverage for immigrant families with children, as their parents are disproportionately poor and often lack private health insurance. In 2009, over 60 million low-income individuals were insured through Medicaid (about a fifth of the total US population), and the program accounted for about a fifth of all state spending (NGA and NASBO 2009: 10). In 2008, an additional 7.4 million low-income children were enrolled in CHIP (Kaiser Family Foundation, n.d.(a)).

Participation in Medicaid and CHIP varied across the five study states considerably. California had 6.9 million people enrolled in Medicaid in 2009, or 29 percent of the state's entire population (see Table 5). Another 1.7 million children were enrolled in CHIP in California in 2008. New York had nearly as large a share of its population enrolled in Medicaid (27 percent). The share of the population enrolled in the program was substantially lower in the other three states.

Medicaid and CHIP exclude unauthorized immigrants (except for emergency care), and the 1996 welfare reform law excluded most legal immigrants residing in the country less than five years. In 2009, Congress granted states the option to provide federally funded Medicaid and CHIP coverage to virtually all low-income legal immigrant children; 19 states have done so.[7] States have the option to cover re-

---

7   This restoration occurred as part of the Children's Health Insurance Program Reauthorization Act of 2009, US Public Law 111-3.

Table 5: Participation in public health-insurance programs in the five largest states

State	Medicaid enrollment in June 2009	Percent of state population Medicaid covers (2006)	CHIP enrollment in 2008
California	6.9 million	29	1.7 million
Florida	2.5 million	17	354,000
Illinois	2.2 million	19	356,000
New York	4.4 million	27	517,000
Texas	3.1 million	17	732,000

Note: The national average for Medicaid coverage is 20 percent.

Sources: Kaiser Family Foundation, n.d. (a, c and d), 2009

cently arrived legal immigrant adults but receive no federal money for this group.

As of February 2010, 12 states—including California and New York—insured low-income legal immigrant adults regardless of their date of US entry (National Immigration Law Center 2010b). New York and Illinois are also among the handful of states that have established programs providing health insurance for all low-income children, regardless of their citizenship or legal status. Most California counties have also done so but not with state funding; instead they use a combination of county revenues, private foundation support and funding from a settlement with tobacco companies. Florida and Texas generally do not cover recent legal immigrant adults or unauthorized children although Texas covers pregnant women, regardless of immigration status.

A high share of children participated in public health-insurance programs even before the recession. In 2007, 33 percent of legal immigrant children and 23 percent of US-born children were covered by Medicaid, CHIP or another public insurance program (Capps, Rosenblum and Fix 2009). Public coverage of adults was much lower: just 10 percent of legal immigrants and 7 percent of US-born citizens.

Because they comprise such a high share of state budgets, public health-insurance programs become vulnerable during times of fiscal stress. Medicaid expenditures totaled $311 billion in 2008, with the states spending $139 billion and the federal government contributing the balance (Kaiser Family Foundation, n.d. (e)). CHIP spending was more modest, totaling $10 billion, with the states contributing $3 billion (Kaiser Family Foundation, n.d. (f)).

ARRA included about $87 billion to increase the rate at which the federal government matches state-level Medicaid spending, and the five largest states saw their federal match increase by 10 percent to 12 percent (GAO 2010). There was no additional federal funding for CHIP. ARRA prohibited states from reducing eligibility or cutting major services, but it allowed them to cut reimbursement rates for medical providers, as well as vision and dental services. Most states have made cutbacks in these allowable areas. Many states have also cut funding for outreach, potentially reducing enrollment of vulnerable populations, such as immigrants.

In California, ARRA Medicaid funding and pressure from advocates prevented elimination of the CHIP program. Shortfalls in foundation funding and county revenues have led to enrollment freezes in the county programs that insure children regardless of legal status, but only one county has cut back eligibility for its program.

Florida had proposed cutting Medicaid for certain populations, but these cuts were never implemented because of ARRA's higher federal match and prohibitions on eligibility restrictions.[8]

In New York, Texas and Illinois, there have been no major changes to public health-insurance programs except for cuts in provider rates and optional services.

The additional federal funding for Medicaid will expire in December 2010 unless the US Congress reauthorizes it. State officials have described the expiration of ARRA Medicaid funding as a "fiscal cliff"

8 Elderly and disabled people are generally covered through Medicare, but Medicaid provides supplemental coverage for long-term care and other services. Some of the Medicaid services to the elderly and disabled are optional, and cuts in these programs have been considered in several states. Cf. GAO 2010: 11.

with severe consequences for their budgets and programs (Kaiser Commission on Medicaid and the Uninsured 2010). Nonetheless, states are required to maintain eligibility and core services in their Medicaid programs for adults until 2014 and in Medicaid and CHIP for children until 2019, as part of the sweeping health-care reform law enacted in March 2010.[9]

Beyond mandating core Medicaid services, the federal health-care reform law has the potential to improve insurance coverage for legal immigrants, although the unauthorized are excluded. In 2008, about 4 million legal immigrants who had not yet become citizens were uninsured (out of about 12 million legal immigrants overall) (Capps, Rosenblum and Fix 2009). Most of these immigrants—those below a generous income threshold—will be eligible for subsidies to help them purchase their own coverage on the private market in 2014. The unauthorized—the majority of whom have no health insurance—will have to continue to rely on charity clinics, federal health centers and hospitals as their primary sources of care. This health-care safety net may be stretched further in the aftermath of the recession and the reform bill's cost-cutting measures (National Immigration Law Center 2010a).

Adult Education and Literacy Programs

In 2006, an estimated 21.6 million adults in the United States were limited in their English proficiency (LEP).[10] While many LEP adults have both low levels of English proficiency and limited formal schooling, just over half—11.2 million—have at least a high school education, and a significant share has postsecondary degrees.[11]

These numbers underscore the scale of the challenge facing the United States as a whole and the states and localities where immi-

---

9 The Patient Protection and Affordable Care Act of 2010. Cf. Kaiser Family Foundation 2010.
10 Data pooled for 2005–2007. Cf. Capps et al. 2009.
11 Ibid.

grants and their children settle. Proficiency in English and basic education skills are necessary for integration into the US workforce and mainstream society. Numerous studies have documented the lack of sufficient capacity in the existing service system—which includes public, private nonprofit and for-profit providers—to meet instructional demand (Tucker 2006). Creating programs of sufficient scale and quality to address the diverse needs of these adult learners is perhaps the most significant—and unmet—integration policy and funding challenge in the United States.

Through a federal–state funding partnership, adult basic education and English as a Second Language (ESL)/literacy instruction are offered in the United States to adults who do not have a high school diploma or who seek to learn English. The main federal program for these services is contained in Title II of the Workforce Investment Act (WIA) of 1998; these particular provisions are also known as the Adult Education and Family Literacy Act (AEFLA). States receive federal funds under this program and carry primary administrative responsibility to support programs for adults who lack basic skills, a high school diploma or proficiency in English. In recent years, almost half of all individuals served under AEFLA programs were enrolled in ESL programs, and the vast majority of ESL enrollees were immigrants.

AEFLA Federal Funding: Underfunded But Relatively Stable

For years, federal funding authorized under AEFLA has remained stable, albeit meager compared to need (see Table 6). About 80 percent or more of AEFLA grants cover adult basic and literacy education while the remaining smaller portion covers English literacy and civics education. Although it appears that funding significantly increased between 2008 and 2009, the jump is mainly due to an administrative error and a one-time payment of $46 million to states and outlying areas that were underpaid between 2003 and 2008 (US Department of Education, Office of Vocational and Adult Education 2010). It is unclear at the time of this writing whether states will see an increase or a decrease for programs in 2010 and 2011.[12]

Table 6: Adult Education and Family Literacy Act state grants (in thousands of dollars)

	2005	2006	2007	2008	2009	2010 estimate	2011 estimate
National	480,394	497,962	478,969	486,859	555,851	628,221	612,315
California	71,180	64,821	65,919	67,419	81,801	92,269	91,780
Florida	29,063	33,136	40,413	36,522	35,402	43,980	39,672
Illinois	19,650	19,650	20,125	26,600	20,782	21,890	23,001
New York	32,832	36,431	34,346	33,942	38,417	45,347	43,222
Texas	40,877	41,158	41,012	38,819	47,136	52,424	53,106

Source: US Department of Education, Office of Vocational and Adult Education 2010

Additional ARRA Funding: Little or No Help

ARRA provided $5 billion in additional funding for education and allowed local education agencies to use this funding for adult education and literacy programs. Adult education programs, however, received little or no money from ARRA due to the "crowding-out" effect of budget shortfalls in elementary and secondary education. Because local education agencies are judged on the performance of their elementary and secondary school programs, and because budget shortfalls for those programs were generally so severe, local agencies allocated virtually no ARRA funding to adult basic education, literacy or other educational purposes.

12 In 2009, the Office of Vocational and Adult Education switched from the decennial census to the American Community Survey to determine grants to states, which will also change the level of estimated grants.

States must match 25 percent of their federal AEFLA grants with state or local funds, but the five largest states vary greatly in how much they spend on these programs (see Table 7). Since the recession began, all study states except Texas cut their support for these programs. In contrast with the four other states, in recent years, Texas has contributed significantly less to these programs than it has received in federal funds. In fact, Texas does not appear to have met AEFLA's match requirement of 25 percent for receiving AEFLA funds in any of the years shown in Table 7.

Important Changes in California

Lack of comparable data prevents us from analyzing funding changes in the five largest states after 2008. Data are available to allow us to examine California's adult education system, whose funding formula changed significantly in 2009. Until then, California's system of adult schools represented perhaps the most generously funded and comprehensive approach of any state in meeting the needs of adult learners, particularly LEP immigrants. The California adult education system served over 1.2 million adult learners with its more than 450 service providers in 2008–2009 (California Department of Education 2010). Forty-one percent of all California adult education programs at the time were made up of ESL and citizenship courses, which are primarily geared toward immigrants (ibid.). In fact, the most common reason students reported for entering the adult basic education system was to improve their English skills (ibid.).

As a result of California's budget crisis, in 2009, the state incorporated adult education funding into a block grant to local school districts rather than a separate, dedicated funding stream. This conversion to a block grant has allowed school districts to devote a higher share of their state education funding to large shortfalls in primary and secondary education budgets and a lower share to adult educa-

Table 7: WIA Title II funding (in thousands of dollars) across five largest states, 2005 to 2008

	2005		2006		2007		2008	
	Federal	State	Federal	State	Federal	State	Federal	State
Total	480,394	1,385,014	497,962	1,468,572	478,969	1,558,784	486,859	819,861
California	71,180	620,690	64,821	648,064	65,919	707,821	67,419	N/A
Florida	29,063	272,316	33,136	262,382	40,413	244,684	36,522	216,705
Illinois	19,650	34,808	19,650	34,808	20,125	34,808	26,600	27,092
New York	32,832	78,470	36,431	91,810	34,346	93,825	33,942	87,458
Texas	40,877	6,885	41,158	6,890	41,012	6,885	38,819	6,885

Note: N/A = not applicable

Source: US Department of Education, Office of Vocational and Adult Education 2010

tion. The effects of this dramatic change in education funding in California are only now beginning to be understood and chronicled.

Citizenship Preparation and Application Assistance

Due to the 1996 welfare reform law's restrictions on noncitizen eligibility for safety-net programs, acquiring US citizenship has become a gateway to the social safety net. Citizenship is also an increasingly important protection against deportation, as the range of crimes and other factors that can lead to deportation of noncitizens has been expanding in the recent wave of US immigration law enforcement (Fix 2007). Consequently, states such as Illinois, California and New York started using or increased state funds for programs to help legal permanent residents gain US citizenship. Citizenship programs also promote civic engagement and the political integration of new immigrant residents. Extreme pressures on state budgets have resulted in either cuts to or elimination of these programs.

State funding cuts for naturalization programs were announced shortly after the price of applying for US citizenship increased dramatically. In July 2007, the fee increased by 80 percent, from $330 to $595, for adult applicants.[13] The high cost of naturalization can deter immigrants who are unemployed, underemployed or otherwise struggling through the recession from becoming citizens.

At the federal level, support for citizenship programs has actually risen, although the overall amount remains small. In 2010, US Citizenship and Immigration Services provided approximately $7 million to support citizenship-preparation services (US Citizenship and Immigration Services, n.d.). This is a nearly sixfold increase from the $1.2 million available through the Citizenship Grant Program in 2009 (US Citizenship and Immigration Services 2010). The increase

13 This filing fee does not include the required $80 fee charged to all applicants to run requisite background checks based on fingerprints and other biometric information. Cf. Gelatt and McHugh 2007.

is a result of the Obama administration's desire to provide more resources in the area of immigrant integration (Stiefel 2010).

Grants must be used for direct citizenship-preparation services, such as citizenship or civic-focused ESL instruction, citizenship instruction, educational resources (textbooks, language software, computers, etc.) or naturalization-application assistance (including legal services) (ibid.). The Office of Citizenship expects to give out approximately 50 awards (ibid.).

California experienced the most significant cut in funding for citizenship services, eliminating funding for its Naturalization Services Program from the budget for 2008–2009 (see Table 8). Housed within California's Health and Human Services Agency, the Naturalization Services Program contracted with community service providers to furnish citizenship services throughout the state. The program was established in 1998 but had been inactive due to lack of funding. Governor Schwarzenegger revived the program with allocations of $3 million from California's General Fund for 2006–2007 and again in 2007–2008 before the program was eliminated for 2008–2009.

Illinois experienced a more modest decrease in funding for citizenship services. In the 2010 budget, the state's two citizenship programs were reduced by 10 percent as part of across-the-board cuts in the Department of Human Services.

In New York, citizenship services are funded through the state's Bureau of Refugee and Immigrant Assistance, a division of the Office of Temporary and Disability Assistance. The initiative has been funded at roughly $2 million to $2.5 million in recent years, down from a high of $4.5 million before the recession (Hart and Wheeler 2010).

Texas does not fund citizenship services. In Florida, a course designed to prepare legal immigrants for naturalization is taught as part of the Adult General Education Adult ESL program, but no other citizenship services are provided (Florida Department of Education 2010).

Table 8: Naturalization programs across the five largest states

State	Program(s)	Agency responsible	Past budgets	Current budget	Percent cut
California	Naturalization Services Program	California Health and Human Services Agency	$3 million in 2006–2007 and 2007–2008	None	100 percent in 2008–2009 budget
Florida	Naturalization course as part of the adult ESL program	Florida Department of Education	N/A	N/A	N/A
Illinois	Refugee and Immigrant Citizenship Initiative (RICI); the New Americans Initiative (NAI)	Illinois Department of Human Services (NAI run jointly with nonprofit)	RICI: $1.5 million per year, 2006 to 2009; NAI: $3 million per year, 2006 to 2009	$3.1 million	10 percent each for RICI and NAI in 2010
New York	Citizenship services	Bureau of Refugee and Immigrant Assistance	$4.5 million before the recession	$2 million to $2.5 million	45 to 55 percent
Texas	None	N/A	N/A	N/A	N/A

Note: N/A = not applicable

Language Access

One immediate concern for government agency administrators in communities where immigrants settle is the ability of their workers to communicate with individuals who do not speak or understand English. In some jurisdictions, translation and interpretation—or "language access"—services are very controversial and inconsistent; in others, they are routine and comprehensive.

Through an executive order issued by President Bill Clinton in August 2000 (Executive Order 13166 2000), the federal government requires agencies receiving federal assistance to provide LEP individuals with meaningful access to their services. The Coordination and Review (COR) Section, part of the Civil Rights Division of the US Department of Justice, is responsible for federal-level coordination on language access. COR provides technical assistance and guidance on compliance with the law and also investigates complaints of discrimination on the basis of national origin or lack of language access.

While these efforts have helped bolster the provision of language-access services around the country, enforcing the law's provisions is a lengthy and time-consuming process. Some states are hostile to such services and have passed "English-only" laws. Also, the federal executive order does not cover the substantial number of state and local agencies that do not receive federal funds. In part to address these weaknesses in the federal policy regime, legal challenges and legislative efforts at the state and local levels have led to a variety of stricter measures to provide language-access services.

Since the federal government does not directly fund language-access services, it is not possible to measure whether funds for such services have increased or decreased during the recession. However, it is possible to get a sense of how these services are faring by looking at three of the five study states that have language-access laws in some form: California, New York and Illinois. Additionally, we discuss Hawaii and Washington State because they have implemented substantial cuts in their comprehensive language-access services since the recession.

California

California's Bilingual Services Program (BSP) provides guidance, monitoring and technical assistance to state departments in meeting their responsibilities under the Dymally-Alatorre Bilingual Services Act of 1973. The act requires all state and local agencies to ensure that they provide information and services in the various languages of their constituents.

BSP funding has remained fairly consistent since 2006–2007 (Caldwell 2010). In 2008, one position was lost through budget reductions (ibid.). The present budget includes the authority for six general fund positions for 2009–2010 (ibid.). However, the governor has indicated that additional salary savings and general fund reductions will be necessary due to the state's current fiscal crisis. The magnitude of those salary savings and fund reductions is unclear. Moreover, due to California's mandatory furlough program (three days each month), BSP program staff have less time to complete their work (ibid.).

In addition to the state law, in 2001, San Francisco adopted the Equal Access to Services (EAS) Ordinance, which requires city departments to provide services in non-English languages when a certain absolute number or share of either clients served or residents in the office's district are LEP and share a primary language. Local budget cuts have led to an inability to hire multilingual staff, a shift of resources away from language access and the suspension of several bilingual initiatives.[14] Despite these obstacles, the San Francisco Human Services Agency continues to provide language-access services by using available staff and employing outside vendors for translation and interpretation services if a bilingual staff member is not available.[15]

New York

While New York State does not have a language-access law, in 2003, the City of New York passed Local Law 73, which requires all city social service departments, health departments and Workforce Investment Act offices and their subcontractors to provide language-assistance services to LEP clients. Mayor Michael Bloomberg reinforced the 2003 law with Executive Order 120, which, among other things,

14 These include revising the bilingual testing process and designating positions as bilingual (Jung 2010).
15 Ibid.

requires all city agencies to provide services in the city's six most common foreign languages.

A variety of directives have saved New York City's language-access services from being cut during the recession. The Department of Education allocated approximately $6.5 million to eligible schools for translation and interpretation services for LEP parents (Fin 2010). The department's budget director noted that, by making translation and interpretation services available to parents, the department had established an expectation and it would be difficult to roll back this service (ibid.). In fact, this past year, the department added another language to the eight the Translation and Interpretation Unit already covered (ibid.).

Mark Lewis, the director of immigrant services for the city's Administration for Children's Services, had a similar perspective: "At this time, the budget crisis is not having an impact on our provision of language services—these services are viewed as an essential component of our work and there have been no budget cuts" (Lewis 2010). His office spent approximately $1.4 million on in-person and telephone interpretation in 2009.

Illinois

Illinois has a state program for interpretation and translation and, as in New York City, cuts to the Illinois program have been modest. The Immigrant Family Resource Program (IFRP), part of the Illinois Department of Human Services, provides safety-net and interpretation services to immigrant and LEP individuals. IFRP coordinates language-access provision at the state level, providing both translation and interpretation support to state agencies. IFRP also conducts multilingual outreach to immigrant families, informing them about various social services and other resources. As a result of cuts to the Human Services budget, from 2009 to 2010, IFRP's allocation dropped 16 percent from $2.25 million to $1.9 million.

In 2006, Hawaii adopted a language-access law and established the Office of Language Access (OLA) within the Department of Labor and Industrial Relations. In November 2009, OLA laid off four staff members due to budget cuts. Only the executive director of OLA—a position written into the law—remains. Funding for operational expenses was reduced to about $200,000, not including personnel. OLA now employs student interns for most of its work, and some initiatives that were previously under consideration cannot be implemented due to a lack of resources.

Washington State's Department of Social and Health Services (DSHS) established its LEP program as part of a settlement agreement with the Department of Justice's Office of Civil Rights in the 1980s. In 1992, the DSHS developed and implemented its own language-testing and certification program to assess the skills of bilingual employees and contracted interpreters and translators. Other state agencies now also require employees to pass the DSHS test to become certified as bilingual. Recent budget cuts, however, have reduced the number of language-certification testing sites from six to two.

State Executive Orders on Immigrant Integration

In recent years, immigrant leaders in several states have successfully convinced governors to set into motion review processes to determine immigrant integration needs. Illinois was the first state to design and implement one of these "New Americans" executive orders (State of Illinois Executive Order (2005–10) 2005). The Illinois order served as a model for similar efforts that followed in Maryland, Massachusetts, New Jersey and Washington State (see Table 9). As none of the five largest states (except Illinois) have implemented executive orders, we focus here on the states that have done so.

Each executive order created a policy council or advisory panel charged with developing recommendations to improve the integration of immigrants and their family members. The reports and recommendations that emerged from these processes covered multiple areas, including citizenship assistance, adult English instruction, foreign credential recognition and language access. They also raised the profile of immigrant integration programs in state debates and, in most cases, resulted in additional program funding, most often for citizenship initiatives.

Table 9: Demographics of five states with executive orders on immigrant integration

State	Year of executive order	Immigrant population in 2008	Immigrants' share of state population
Illinois	2005	1,782,000	14 percent
Maryland	2008	698,000	12 percent
Massachusetts	2008	937,000	14 percent
New Jersey	2007	1,718,000	20 percent
Washington	2008	804,000	12 percent

Source: US Census Bureau 2010

The executive orders have not entirely prevented integration-service cuts in the states that adopted them. And while these initiatives may build support for future expansions of key services, in most states with executive orders, the recession has forced stakeholders to focus their energies on simply maintaining the status quo or preventing further losses.

Illinois

Signed in November 2005 by then Governor Rod Blagojevich, the Illinois executive order created an Office of New Americans Policy and Advocacy within the governor's office and a public–private taskforce charged with conducting a systematic review of state services to determine how the state could better assist in the integration of immigrants and their family members. In March 2010, Governor Pat Quinn rescinded the Blagojevich order, but his new executive order kept in place important elements of the earlier approach, including a Governor's Office of New Americans (State of Illinois Executive Order (2010-02) 2010).

Prior to the executive order, a New Americans Initiative (NAI) was launched in 2004 with state support of $3 million. Following the 2005 executive order and at the recommendation of the New Americans Policy Council, NAI became a permanent program, and immigrant integration became a budget line item of between $8 million and $10 million, signaling the state's ongoing commitment to immigrants. In addition to NAI and the Immigrant Family Resource Program described earlier in this report, the state's immigrant integration budget includes the Illinois Welcoming Center (IWC), the "We Want to Learn English" program (which seeks to expand vocational ESL classes), an initiative to address the needs of foreign-trained professionals run by the nonprofit Upwardly Global and five suburban Chicago health clinics.

As noted in the earlier discussions of citizenship and language-access services, Illinois cut all human services programs by 16 percent for 2010. An additional line-item cut of 10 percent is expected for 2011 (see Table 10) (Thakkar, Tsao, Jimenez and Jbara 2010; Harley 2010).

Maryland

An executive order creating the Maryland Council for New Americans was signed in December 2008 (Executive Order 01.01.2008. 18). In August 2009, the council issued 15 recommendations in four areas: workforce, citizenship, financial services and governmental access (Maryland Council for New Americans 2009).

The council placed a special focus on the difficulties foreign-trained professionals face in having their education and work credentials recognized by US employers and education institutions. Nevertheless, the Foreign Trained Health Professionals program funded

Table 10: Illinois budget for immigrant integration programs, 2006 to 2011

Program	2006	2007	2008	2009	2010	2011
Immigrant integration budget line item	N/A	N/A	$8,150,000	$10,315,300	$8,997,800	Expected 10 percent cut for the immigrant integration line item.
New Americans Initiative (NAI)			$3 million	$3.1 million	$2.7 million	
Immigrant Family Resource Program (IFRP)	$1.5 million	$1.5 million	$1.5 million	$2.2 million	$1.9 million	
Refugee and Immigrant Citizenship Initiative (RICI)	$2.5 million	$2.5 million	$2.5 million	$2.4 million	$2.2 million	
Illinois Welcoming Center (IWC)	N/A	N/A	$1.2 million	$877,000	$566,000	
Upwardly Global	N/A	N/A	N/A	$145,000	$120,000	
Adult education and ESL (WWLE)	N/A	N/A	N/A	$300,000	$150,000	
Suburban health clinics (five)	$956,000	$978,000	$956,000	$966,000	$833,000	

Note: N/A = not applicable

Source: Harley 2010

under the Maryland Department of Labor, Licensing and Regulation has been substantially reduced. The program began in 2006 as a pilot for Latino nurses and, in 2008, it received a state allocation of $250,000 for expansion. However, the program was eventually funded at $200,000 for 2009, and its budget was reduced in 2010, to $150,000. State funding has been further reduced, to $100,000, in the 2011 budget (Mora 2010); this also eliminated the Maryland Citizenship Promotion Program, which had been funded at between $50,000 and $100,000 over the past several years (Lagdameo 2010). Although the enacted budget differs slightly from the governor's proposed budget, at the time of this writing, final cuts to the programs listed above had not been confirmed (Maryland Budget & Tax Policy Institute 2010).

Massachusetts

The July 2008 Massachusetts executive order entitled "Integrating Immigrants and Refugees into the Commonwealth" called for the development of a New Americans Agenda (Executive Order 503 2008). The agenda, prepared by the Governor's Advisory Council for Refugees and Immigrants, was released in November 2009 and included 131 recommendations in 12 key issue areas (Governor's Advisory Council for Refugees and Immigrants 2009).

In the area of citizenship assistance, one of the recommendations suggested increasing funding for the existing Citizenship for New Americans Program, which received $500,000 in 2008 and $650,000 in 2009. Funding was reduced to $605,000 during mid-year cuts in 2009. The 2010 appropriation for the program dropped further, to $580,000, and the program was cut to only $250,000 midway through the 2010 fiscal year (Tambouret 2010). The proposed 2011 budget was not available at the time of writing.

The Massachusetts New Americans Agenda also sought a dedicated fund for two English instruction programs for adults. According to the Massachusetts Immigrant and Refugee Advocacy Coalition, a nonprofit advocacy organization, $1.4 million was allocated for the fund (MIRA Coalition 2009). An additional $500,000 from the federal Workforce Investment Act was added, making a total of $1.9 million for 2010. Eleven grants were awarded to local service providers through a competitive contracting process (ibid.). The program will likely get funded for 2011 (Green 2010).

Separately from the executive order, Massachusetts has retreated from providing the full cost of health insurance to legally present immigrants. In 2006, the state passed a groundbreaking law that sought to make health insurance accessible to all state residents, including legal immigrants ineligible for federally reimbursed coverage. But, in 2010, coverage for this population was cut, and a new program with restricted coverage and a cap on enrollment was created. The governor has supported restoring coverage to all legal immigrants, but the legislation has yet to be passed.

New Jersey

A New Jersey executive order from January 2010 established a permanent Commission on New Americans that is housed with and provided with staff support from the state's Office of the Public Advocate (New Jersey Executive Order 78, 2007; New Jersey New Executive Order 91, 2007; New Jersey Executive Order 164, 2010). However, the 2011 budget eliminates the Department of the Public Advocate and terminates unclassified employees (effective April 1, 2010) (New Jersey Office of Management and Budget 2010), leaving the Commission on New Americans with no staff support.

This policy reversal came after Republican Chris Christie officially became New Jersey's governor in January 2010, having defeated Democrat Jon Corzine in November 2009. According to the chairman of the Commission on New Americans, its existence and role within the state government is "under review" by Governor Christie (Argote-Freyre 2010). The uncertain status of New Jersey's Commission on New Americans underscores the difficulties of sustaining gains in immigrant integration processes or programs following leadership changes.

Christie opposes key recommendations of the former advisory panel. One is in-state tuition rates for unauthorized immigrant students attending state universities, a proposal that had already failed in the legislature before Christie took office (Tamari 2010). Christie has also cut funding for FamilyCare, a health-insurance program for low-income families that was expanded under Corzine and that provided coverage to many immigrants not eligible for federal programs (Diamant 2010; Governor's Blue Ribbon Advisory Panel, n.d.). On March 1, 2010, enrollment for parents was frozen, generating a projected savings of $24.6 million and affecting an estimated 39,000 adults. In addition, beginning on April 1, 2010, FamilyCare benefits for "restricted aliens" were terminated, saving an estimated $29.8 million (New Jersey Office of Management and Budget 2010). Residents with less than five years of legal immigration status will be cut from the program, which affects about 12,000 legal immigrants (Llorente 2010).

Christie has proposed other cuts in the 2011 budget that would affect immigrants. For example, he would eliminate $3.7 million for the Center for Hispanic Policy, Research and Development (CHPRD), a state agency established in 1975 by executive order (New Jersey Office of Management and Budget 2010). CHPRD coordinates efforts, provides technical assistance and training, and provides grants to local nonprofits that serve Latinos (New Jersey Center for Hispanic Policy, Research and Development, n.d.).

Washington State

Washington's governor signed an executive order establishing the New Americans Policy Council in February 2008 (Executive Order 2008-01, 2008). The following year, the council released a report outlining recommendations in nine key areas (Washington New Americans Policy Council 2009).

The largest program under the initiative, the New Americans Citizenship Program, was funded at $326,000 for 2008. The state legislature provisionally funded the program at $2 million for the 2009–2011 budget cycle.[16] In subsequent budget actions, funding was reduced to $506,000 for the 2009–2011 biennium (Guevin 2010; One America 2010a). Due to the recession, a supplemental budget session was called in 2010. The citizenship program is included in different versions of supplemental budgets in amounts ranging from $250,000 to $280,000 per year. The final 2010 budget for the citizenship program is $283,000 (OneAmerica, n.d.). However, advocates note that funding for the 2011–2013 cycle is not guaranteed and that, if the state's fiscal condition continues to worsen, the citizenship program will likely be targeted for additional cuts or elimination (Guevin 2010).

According to advocates, medical-interpreter services were threatened with $17 million in cuts, but the final 2010 budget maintained funding for this program (OneAmerica n.d. and 2010b). Programs that provide health services for all children (including unauthorized ones) will continue to receive support, though at a level that is greatly reduced in comparison to that of the previous biennium (2007 to 2009). The budgets for these health programs had not yet been finalized at the time of writing.

Conclusion

As we look at large immigrant-receiving states in the United States and key integration programs and services that could be targets for cuts in times of fiscal austerity, we find the following:

There are stark differences across states in the proportion of their needy residents reached by safety-net services, irrespective of the fiscal impacts of the economic crisis.

---

16 Budgets run in two-year cycles in Washington. During these cycles, the budget can be adjusted at supplemental budget sessions of the legislature.

Immigrants—and, in fact, all US residents—are subject to differing state eligibility rules and benefit levels for major safety-net programs. For example, only 12 states—including California and New York but not Texas, Illinois and Florida—allow legal immigrant adults (regardless of their date of entry) to enroll in the Medicaid health insurance program. And only a handful of states, including New York and Illinois, have established health-insurance programs for all low-income children, regardless of their citizenship or legal status.

The proportion of low-income residents receiving cash welfare benefits across states underscores the impact of these varying policies: Only 3 percent to 5 percent of the poverty populations in Texas, Florida and Illinois receive such assistance, while 20 percent in New York and 33 percent in California do.

Significant differences in state policy and funding regimes notwithstanding, federal stimulus spending "maintained the floor" under the state patchwork of key safety-net services, at least temporarily preventing new erosion of key services.

In the 2009 stimulus law, federal policymakers used a variety of strategies to mitigate the disparate impact of state-level rules while coaxing states to maintain or participate with the federal government in providing certain benefits. These included: increasing the federal match of state dollars under certain programs; channeling substantial sums into food-assistance programs, which have more generous and uniform rules across states than cash welfare or health-insurance programs; and prohibiting states from reducing eligibility or cutting services under key programs, such as Medicaid. Where ARRA was less prescriptive, states and localities sometimes shifted funding out of key programs for immigrant integration. For instance, local school districts in California shifted ARRA funding that could have been used for ESL and other adult education programs to cover shortfalls in their primary and secondary education programs.

Significant federal funding, along with sometimes strict and sometimes savvy approaches to obtaining state cooperation, appears to have helped maintain the patchwork of state approaches to immigrant safety-net benefits that existed before the recession—at least when it came to social safety-net services. While, under normal circumstances, one might hesitate to consider this an accomplishment, given the extreme budget pressures states are facing, many observers find it surprising that benefit programs for immigrants by and large have not been singled out for budget cuts.[17]

Integration programs that were funded primarily or solely with state funds were among the most vulnerable, often suffering significant cuts.
Stimulus funding appears to have helped states close what were in many cases gaping holes in their education, health and social-services budgets. However, our survey of states shows that many using state tax-levy funds to support special immigrant services have reduced or eliminated this funding in recent years. For example, citizenship-assistance programs in New York, Illinois, Washington State and Maryland have suffered cuts, while California's was eliminated. Likewise, adult English instruction in California was dealt a double blow of budget cuts and having funding shifted to primary and secondary education.

Additional and more significant cuts may lie ahead, and the results of some cuts and budget policy decisions have yet to unfold.
Governors and state legislatures across the United States were scrambling to close a collective $140 billion gap in their budgets before the July 1 start of the 2010–2011 fiscal year. Budget experts believe that closing the gap this year and next will prove even harder than in earlier years since most states exhausted their reserves or "rainy-day" funds in earlier years. Also, the fees they could increase or the one-time accounting fixes they could implement have already been enacted. In addition, fiscal relief from the federal government will be ending late 2010—as early as September for some programs—well before most types of state revenue will rebound to make up the difference. The prognosis for extension of ARRA supplementary funding

17 In New York, which has particularly generous safety-net provisions for immigrants, these programs enjoy legal protection from the state's constitution and are therefore not as vulnerable to political or economic pressures.

for welfare, health-insurance and other safety-net programs was uncertain in June 2010, when this report went to press.

In a hard-pressed state such as California, ongoing fiscal pressures without offsetting federal supplementary funding will likely heighten the vulnerability of key immigrant services that have narrowly avoided the budget axe in recent years. California had been the most generous state in the nation in its contributions to adult basic education and English classes, which millions of immigrants relied on as they sought to integrate into the labor market and larger society. Allowing elementary and secondary schools facing shortfalls to use adult education funds has most certainly set into motion an erosion of education services for adult immigrants. Without further federal fiscal relief, state-funded safety-net services for immigrants are also likely to erode substantially in the coming years.

Works Cited

Agency for Children and Families. TANF Recipients—through September 2009. Table. January 28, 2010. 2010. www.acf.hhs.gov/programs/ofa/data-reports/caseload/2009/formulas2009_3.xls.

Agency for Children and Families. Fiscal Year 2008 TANF Financial Data. 2009. hwww.acf.hhs.gov/programs/ofs/data/2008/tanf_2008.html.

Argote-Freyre, Frank, chairman, New Jersey Commission on New Americans (Kean University). Telephone interview, April 16, 2010.

Assistant Secretary for Planning and Evaluation. The 2009 HHS Poverty Guidelines: One Version of the US Federal Poverty Measure. Washington, DC: US Department of Health and Human Services, ASPE, 2010. http://aspe.hhs.gov/POVERTY/09poverty.shtml.

Caldwell, Steve, director of legislative and public affairs, State Personnel Board. E-mail correspondence, April 19, 2010.

California Budget Project. An Overview of Recent Cuts to California's Safety Net. Sacramento, Calif.: California Budget Project, 2009. www.cbp.org.

California Department of Education. California WIA Title II Program Year 2008–09.Winter Consortium 2010.

California Health and Human Services Agency. 2008–2009 Budget Facts. Sacramento: California Health and Human Services Agency, 2008. www.chhs.ca.gov/initiatives/CAChildWelfare Council/Documents/2008%20Proposed%20Budget.pdf.

Capps, Randy, Michael E. Fix and Everett Henderson. Trends in Immigrants' use of Public Assistance after Welfare Reform. In *Immigrants and Welfare: The Impact of Welfare Reform on America's Newcomers*, edited by Michael E. Fix. New York: Russell Sage, 2009: 123–152.

Capps, Randy, Michael Fix, Margie McHugh and Serena Yi-Ying. *Taking Limited English Proficient Adults into Account in the Federal Adult Education Funding Formula*. Washington, DC: MPI, 2009. www.migrationpolicy.org/pubs/WIA-LEP-June2009.pdf.

Capps, Randy, Marc R. Rosenblum and Michael Fix. *Immigrants and Health Care Reform: What's Really at Stake?* Washington, DC: MPI, 2009. www.migrationpolicy.org/pubs/healthcare-Oct09.pdf.

Children Now. *California Report Card 2010: Setting the Agenda for Children*. Oakland, Calif.: Children NOW, 2010.

California Department of Community Services and Development. Naturalization. Sacramento: Department of Community Services and Development, 2008. www.csd.ca.gov/documents/Resources% 20tab/Publications%20and%20Reports/Factsheets/Naturalization/ Naturalization%202007-2008%20Fact%20Sheet%20(5-1-08).pdf.

California Department of Community Services and Development. Naturalization Program. www.csd.ca.gov/Contractors/Naturalization/ Naturalization.aspx.

Diamant, Jeff. N.J. immigrant group will likely narrow agenda to fit Gov. Chris Christie's ideals. *New Jersey Star-Ledger* February 16, 2010. www.nj.com/news/index.ssf/2010/02/nj_commission_to_ help_immigran.html.

The Dymally-Alatorre Bilingual Services Act of 1973. California Government Code § 7290 et seq.

Executive Order 13166, "Improving Access to Services for Persons with Limited English Proficiency (LEP)," August 11, 2000, www. justice.gov/crt/cor/eolep.pdf.

Executive Order 1.1.2008. 18, The Maryland Council for New Americans. 2008. www.governor.maryland.gov/executiveorders/ 01.01.2008.18eo.pdf.

Executive Order 2008-01, Washington's New Americans Policy Council. 2008. www.governor.wa.gov/execorders/eo_08-01.pdf.

Executive Order 503, Integrating Immigrants and Refugees into the Commonwealth. 2008. www.mass.gov/Agov3/docs/Executive%20 Orders/executive_order_503.pdf.

Fin, Annie. School Allocation Memorandum No. 65, FY10. Memorandum, New York City Department of Education, March 17, 2010. http://schools.nyc.gov/offices/d_chanc_oper/budget/dbor/ allocationmemo/fy09_10/FY10_PDF/sam65.pdf.

Fix, Michael. Immigrant Integration and Comprehensive Immigration Reform: An Overview. In *Securing the Future: US Immigrant Integration Policy, A Reader*, edited by Michael Fix. Washington, DC: MPI, 2007: iii–xxvi.

Florida Department of Education. Section 6: Adult General Education Courses. 2010. www.fldoe.org/articulation/CCD/files/1011CCD Adult.doc.

Food and Nutrition Service. Federal Cost of School Food Programs. 2010a. www.fns.usda.gov/pd/cncosts.htm.

Food and Nutrition Service. National School Lunch Program: Participation and Lunches Served. 2010b. www.fns.usda.gov/pd/ slsummar.htm.

Food and Nutrition Service. Supplemental Nutrition Assistance Program Participation and Costs. 2010c. www.fns.usda.gov/pd/ SNAPsummary.htm.

Food and Nutrition Service. WIC Program Participation and Costs. 2010d. www.fns.usda.gov/pd/SNAPsummary.htm.

Food and Nutrition Service. WIC Program Participation and Costs, March 3, 2010. 2010e. www.fns.usda.gov/pd/wisummary.htm.

Food and Nutrition Service. Supplemental Nutrition Assistance Program: Applicants and Recipients—Eligibility. 2009. www.fns. usda.gov/snap/applicant_recipients/Eligibility.htm.

Gelatt, Julia and Margie McHugh. Citizenship Fee Increases in Context. Washington, DC: MPI, 2007. www.migrationpolicy.org/ pubs/FS15_CitizenshipFees2007.pdf.

Government Accountability Office. Recovery Act: One Year Later, States' and Localities' Uses of Funds and Opportunities to Strengthen Accountability. Washington, DC: GAO, 2010. www. gao.gov/products/GAO-10-437.

Governor's Advisory Council for Refugees and Immigrants. Massachusetts New Americans Agenda. Boston: Governor's Advisory Council for Refugees and Immigrants, 2009. http://miracoalition. org/uploads/No/t7/Not74NYLXkWOUWgfDGbFRQ/MIRA_ NAA_FullReportSMALL.pdf.

Governor's Blue Ribbon Advisory Panel. Report to Governor Jon S. Corzine, Governor's Blue Ribbon Advisory Panel On Immigrant Policy, Executive Summary. New Jersey: Governor's Blue Ribbon Advisory Panel, n.d. www.state.nj.us/publicadvocate/home/pdf/ Executive%20Summary_final.pdf.

Green, Claudia, director of workforce development and English for New Bostonian, Massachusetts Immigrant and Refugee Advocacy Coalition, telephone interview, June 24, 2010.

Guevin, Toby, state policy and legislative manager, OneAmerica. E-mail correspondence, March 25, 2010, and April 22, 2010.

Harley, Christine, project manager, Illinois Department of Human Services. E-mail correspondence, April 19, 2010.

Hart, Tom, and Dorothy Wheeler, Bureau of Refugee and Immigrant Affairs, telephone interview, April 21, 2010.

Henderson, Everett, Randy Capps and Kenneth Finegold. Impact of 2002–03 Farm Bill Restorations on Food Stamp, Use by Legal Immigrants. Washington, DC: US Department of Agriculture, Economic Research Service, 2008. http://ddr.nal.usda.gov/dspace/ handle/10113/32784.

Jung, Wanda, former program director of Medi-Cal Health Connections, San Francisco Human Services Agency, telephone interview, April 16, 2010.

Kaiser Commission on Medicaid and the Uninsured. Medicaid's Continuing Crunch In a Recession: A Mid-Year Update for State FY 2010 and Preview for FY 2011. Washington, DC: Kaiser Family Foundation, 2010. www.kff.org/medicaid/upload/8049.pdf.

Kaiser Family Foundation. Summary of New Health Reform Law. Washington, DC: Kaiser Family Foundation, 2010. www.kff.org/healthreform/upload/8061.pdf.

Kaiser Family Foundation. Estimated Number of Children Enrolled in CHIP and Monthly Medicaid Enrollment (in thousands). 2009. www.statehealthfacts.org/.

Kaiser Family Foundation. Estimated Number of Children Enrolled in CHIP with Family Income at or Below 200 % Federal Poverty Level (FPL) and Above 200 % FPL, FY 2008. n.d. (a). www.statehealthfacts.org/.

Kaiser Family Foundation. Health Insurance Coverage of Nonelderly 0-64, states (2007–2008), US (2008). n.d. (b). www.statehealthfacts.org/.

Kaiser Family Foundation. Medicaid Enrollment as a Percent of Total Population, 2006. n.d. (c). www.statehealthfacts.org/.

Kaiser Family Foundation. Monthly Medicaid Enrollment (in thousands), June 2009. n.d. (d). www.statehealthfacts.org/.

Kaiser Family Foundation. State Medicaid Expenditures (in millions), SFY 2008. n.d. (e). www.statehealthfacts.org/.

Kaiser Family Foundation. Total CHIP Expenditures, FY 2008. n.d. (f). www.statehealthfacts.org/.

King, Loretta. Prepared remarks at the April 20, 2009 meeting of the Federal Interagency Working Group on Limited English Proficiency. 2009. www.lep.gov/Kingremarks4_20_09.pdf.

Lagdameo, Angela, policy and faith-based director, Governor's Office of Community Initiatives, telephone interview, March 31, 2010.

Leachman, Michael, Erica Williams and Nicholas Johnson. Failing to Extend Fiscal Relief to States Will Create New Budget Gaps, Forcing Cuts and Job Loss in at Least 34 States. Washington, DC: Center on Budget and Policy Priorities, 2010. www.cbpp.org/files/6-8-10sfp2.pdf.

Lewis, Mark, director of immigrant services, Administration for Children's Services. E-mail correspondence, April 8, 2010.

Llorente, Elizabeth. Critics warn dropping immigrant health care coverage could backfire. *The Record,* March 8, 2010. www.north jersey.com/news/health/other_health/86789007_Dropping_ legal_immigrants___a_disgrace_.html.

Maryland Budget & Tax Policy Institute. Maryland Budget Summary Fiscal Year 2011. Baltimore: Maryland Budget & Tax Policy Institute, 2010. www.marylandpolicy.org/documents/budgetover viewenactedfy11.pdf.

Maryland Council for New Americans. A Fresh Start: Renewing Immigrant Integration for a Stronger Maryland. Baltimore: Department of Labor, Licensing, and Regulation and Governor's Office of Community Initiatives, 2009. www.newamericans.maryland. gov/documentsNA/2009Report.pdf.

Massachusetts Immigrant and Refugee Advocacy Coalition. State Launches $1.4 Million Workplace Education Fund. News release, November 4, 2009. www.miracoalition.org/press/press-releases/ press-statement-state-launches-1.4-million-workplace-education- fund.

McNichol, Elizabeth, and Nicholas Johnson. Recession Continues to Batter State Budgets; State Responses Could Slow Recovery. Washington, DC: Center on Budget and Policy Priorities, 2010. www.cbpp.org/cms/?fa=view&id=711.

MIRA Coalition, "State Launches $1.4 Million Workplace Education Fund". News release, November 4, 2009. www.miracoalition.org/ press/press-releases/press-statement-state-launches-1.4-million- workplace-education-fund.

Mora, Sonia, program manager, Latino Health Initiative, and administrator, Suburban Maryland Welcome Back Initiative, Montgomery County, telephone interview, April 20, 2010.

National Center for Children in Poverty. Temporary Assistance for Needy Families (TANF) Cash Assistance: Illinois. 2009a. www. nccp.org/profiles/IL_profile_36.html.

National Center for Children in Poverty. Temporary Assistance for Needy Families (TANF) Cash Assistance: New York. 2009b. www. nccp.org/profiles/NY_profile_36.html.

National Center for Children in Poverty. Temporary Assistance for Needy Families (TANF) Cash Assistance: Texas. 2009c. www. nccp.org/profiles/TX_profile_36.html.

National Governors Association and the National Association of State Budget Officers. The Fiscal Survey of the States. Washington, DC: National Governors Association and the National Association of State Budget Officers, 2009.

National Immigration Law Center. How Are Immigrants Included in Health Care Reform? Patient Protection and Affordable Care Act (H.R. 3590). Washington, DC: National Immigration Law Center, 2010a. www.nilc.org/immspbs/health/immigrant-inclusion-in-HR3590-2010-03-22.pdf.

National Immigration Law Center. Table: Medical Assistance Programs for Immigrants in Various States. Washington, DC: National Immigration Law Center, 2010b. www.nilc.org/pubs/guideupdates/med-services-for-imms-in-states-2010-02-24.pdf.

National Immigration Law Center. Table 8: State-Funded TANF Replacement Programs. (Updated 2008). In *Guide to Immigrant Eligibility for Federal Programs.* Washington, DC: National Immigration Law Center, 2002a. www.nilc.org/pubs/guideupdates/tbl8_state-tanf_2004-03_2008-10.pdf.

National Immigration Law Center. Table 12: State-Funded Food Assistance Programs. (Updated 2007). In *Guide to Immigrant Eligibility for Federal Programs.* Washington, DC: National Immigration Law Center, 2002b. www.nilc.org/pubs/guideupdates/tbl12_statefood_2007-07.pdf.

New Jersey Center for Hispanic Policy, Research and Development. About the CHPRD. n.d. www.state.nj.us/dca/chprd/aboutthechprd.shtml.

New Jersey Executive Order 78, Establishes the Governor's Blue Ribbon Advisory Panel on Immigrant Policy. 2007. www.state.nj.us/infobank/circular/eojsc78.htm.

New Jersey New Executive Order 91, Governor's Blue Ribbon Advisory Panel on Immigrant Policy. 2007. www.state.nj.us/infobank/circular/eojsc91.htm.

New Jersey Executive Order 164, Establishes the Commission on New Americans. 2010. www.state.nj.us/infobank/circular/eojsc 164.htm.

New Jersey Office of Management and Budget. Fiscal 2011: Budget in Brief. Trenton: Office of Management and Budget, 2010. www.state.nj.us/treasury/omb/publications/11bib/BIB.pdf.

New York Public Welfare Association. Grappling with Safety Net Assistance for Single Adults. Albany: NYPWA, 2009. www.nypwa.com/NYPWA%20Safety%20Net%20Policy%20Paper%2002-09%20E2.pdf.

OneAmerica. Invest in the Future, Invest in Citizenship: Support the Washington New Americans Program. Seattle: OneAmerica, 2010a. www.weareoneamerica.org/sites/weareoneamerica.org/files/New%20Americans%20Fact%20Sheet%202010%20FINAL.pdf.

OneAmerica. OneAmerica's Agenda for 2010 Legislative Session. Seattle: OneAmerica, 2010b. www.weareoneamerica.org/sites/weareoneamerica.org/files/OA%20Leg%20Agenda%202010.pdf.

OneAmerica. Policy Analysis and Advocacy. www.weareoneamerica.org/policy-analysis-and-advocacy.

Passel, Jeff, and D'Vera Cohn. A Portrait of Unauthorized Immigrants in the United States. Washington, DC: Pew Hispanic Center, 2009. http://pewhispanic.org/files/reports/107.pdf.

State of Illinois Executive Order (2005–10). Creating New Americans Immigrant Policy Council, November 2005. www.illinois.gov/gov/execorders/docs/execorder2005-10.pdf.

State of Illinois Executive Order (2010-02), Creating Governor's Office of New Americans, March 2010. www.illinois.gov/gov/execorders/docs/execorder2010-02.pdf.

Stiefel, Nathaniel, division chief, Policy and Program, US Citizenship and Immigration Services, telephone interview, April 27, 2010.

Tambouret, Nicole, state policy director, Massachusetts Immigrant and Refugee Advocacy Coalition. E-mail correspondence, April 7, 2010.

Tamari, Jonathan. N.J. legislature denies in-state tuition for illegal immigrants. *Philadelphia Inquirer* January 12, 2010. www.philly. com/philly/news/local/81206887.html.

Thakkar, Lisa, Fred Tsao, Flavia Jimenez, Ahlam Jbara, Illinois Coalition for Immigrant and Refugee Rights, interview, March 31, 2010.

Tucker, J.T. Waiting Times for Adult ESL Classes and the Impact on English Learners. Los Angeles: National Association of Latino and Appointed Officials, 2006. www.naleo.org/downloads/ESLReport LoRes.pdf.

US Citizenship and Immigration Services. USCIS Announces $1.2 Million Citizenship Grant Program: Up to 12 Grants Offered to Community-Based Organizations Serving Immigration Population. News release, March 12, 2010. www.uscis.gov/portal/site/ uscis/menuitem.5af9bb95919f35e66f614176543f6d1a/?vgnext channel=68439c7755cb9010VgnVCM10000045f3d6a1RCRD& vgnextoid=eba4cccdcebff110VgnVCM1000004718190aRCRD.

US Citizenship and Immigration Services. Citizenship and Integration Grant Program. n.d. www.uscis.gov/portal/site/uscis/menu item.eb1d4c2a3e5b9ac89243c6a7543f6d1a/?vgnextoid=ea0e0b 89284a3210VgnVCM100000b92ca60aRCRD&vgnextchannel= ea0e0b89284a3210VgnVCM100000b92ca60aRCRD.

US Bureau of Labor Statistics. Regional and State Employment and Unemployment Summary. Economic News Release, March 26, 2010a.

US Bureau of Labor Statistics. Regional and State Employment and Unemployment Summary. Economic News Release, June 18, 2010b. www.bls.gov/news.release/laus.nr0.htm.

US Census Bureau. *2008 American Community Survey*. Washington, DC: US Department of Commerce, 2010.

US Department of Education, Office of Vocational and Adult Education. Program Memorandum–FY2010–01. 2010. http://ed.gov/about/offices/list/ovae/pi/AdultEd/estimated-adult-education-fy2010.pdf.

US Public Law 104-193. The Personal Responsibility and Work Opportunity Reconciliation Act of 1996.

US Public Law 111-5. American Recovery and Reinvestment Act of 2009.

Washington New Americans Policy Council. *A Plan for Today, A Plan for Tomorrow: Building a Stronger Washington Through Immigrant Integration.* Olympia, Wash.: Washington New Americans Policy Council, 2009. www.governor.wa.gov/priorities/diversity/report.pdf.

Government Investment in Integration and Fiscal Uncertainty: Reactions in Europe

Elizabeth Collett with Sheena McLoughlin

Introduction

The financial crisis affected public budgets across Europe, from the fiscally conservative to the unsustainably expansive. Some countries, such as Latvia and Greece, are more clearly in crisis than G-6 countries, such as Germany and France. While doomsayers announce the end of the mythical European social model, the rising debt levels of all European countries will catalyze difficult public spending decisions in the near future. Already, several countries have announced severe austerity plans (Her Majesty's Treasury 2010), and several more have announced deep budget cuts.[1]

Immigration has been at the forefront of many debates about the effects of the economic crisis. Just as immigration fed economic growth in numerous European countries in the early 21st century—not least Ireland, Spain and the United Kingdom—the economic downturn has deeply affected immigrants across the Continent (see Table 1 for an overview of demographic and economic indicators in EU countries). Perceptions of immigration's role have had both policy and political ramifications: A number of countries have tightened immigration policies over the past two years, and others—even established immigration countries, such as the Netherlands and the United Kingdom—have seen populist parties capitalize on the idea that immigra-

---

1   Shortly after taking office in May 2010, the new UK government announced a £6.2 billion budget cut as a first step to tackling the mounting national deficit. Cf. Her Majesty's Treasury 2010.

Table 1: Data on immigrants, unemployment and government budgets in EU Member States

| Country | 2008 | | Unemployment rate, annual average (2009) | Government deficit/ surplus, debt and associated data (2009) |
	Total foreign citizens (in thousands)	Percent of total population	Percent	Percentage of GDP
European Union (27 countries)	30,779	6.2	8.9	−6.8
Austria	835	10.0	4.8	−3.4
Belgium	971	9.1	7.9	−6.0
Bulgaria	24	0.3	6.8	−3.9
Cyprus	125	15.9	5.3	−6.1
Czech Republic	348	3.3	6.7	−5.9
Denmark	298	5.5	6.0	−2.7
Estonia*	229	17.1	13.8	−1.7
Finland	133	2.5	8.2	−2.2
France*	3,674	5.8	9.5	−7.5
Germany (including ex-GDR from 1991)	7,255	8.8	7.5	−3.3
Greece*	906	8.1	9.5	−13.6
Hungary	177	1.8	10.0	−4.0
Ireland	554	12.6	11.9	−14.3

* Eurostat estimate.

Source: Eurostat 2010

Country	2008		Unemployment rate, annual average (2009)	Government deficit/surplus, debt and associated data (2009)
	Total foreign citizens (in thousands)	Percent of total population	Percent	Percentage of GDP
Italy	3,433	5.8	7.8	−5.3
Latvia	415	18.3	17.1	−9.0
Lithuania	43	1.3	13.7	−8.9
Luxembourg (Grand-Duché)	206	42.6	5.2	−0.7
Malta	15	3.8	6.9	−3.8
Netherlands	688	4.2	3.4	−5.3
Poland	58	0.2	8.2	−7.1
Portugal	446	4.2	9.6	−9.4
Romania	26	0.1	6.9	−8.3
Slovakia	41	0.8	12.0	−6.8
Slovenia	69	3.4	5.9	−5.5
Spain	5,262	11.6	18.0	−11.2
Sweden	524	5.7	8.3	−0.5
United Kingdom*	4,021	6.6	7.6	−11.5

* Eurostat estimate.

Source: Eurostat 2010

tion is fueling future economic uncertainty and undermining the solidarity inherent in national social models.

Immigrant integration policy has so far avoided extensive public debate, though it is clearly on the minds of politicians. Several have noted the need to reinforce rather that cut funding for integration, and they have characterized integration policies as being in a zero-sum battle against alternatives, such as return migration. But what has actually happened to the budgets of national programs for the integration of immigrants?

This chapter takes a first look at government reactions to integration organization, financing and programming across Europe and identifies areas of potential concern over the coming decade with respect to sustainable investments in integration. The analysis is based on desk research and responses to a Transatlantic Council on Migration (TCM) questionnaire sent to selected representatives of the European Union's National Contact Points on Integration and members of the Eurocities' Working Group on Migration and Integration during February and March 2010.[2]

Contrary to what might be assumed from the headlines highlighting drastic budget revisions in the hardest-hit countries, EU Member States have had highly diverse reactions, not all of which have been negative. Furthermore, a number of countries have sought to use integration policy to mitigate the recession's impacts on more vulnerable migrant populations. This chapter outlines some of those reactions and makes a tentative analysis of the factors driving such a broad range of responses. It then suggests a few potential "danger areas" for future immigrant-integration programming.

For several reasons, caution is needed when reviewing the available evidence regarding public finances for integration. First, the evidence itself is scattered. Almost all integration strategies involve multiple budget lines across a range of ministries. A review of the institutional organization of integration policy reveals a number of constel-

2 Eurocities is a network of over 140 cities across 30 European countries. Based in Brussels, the organization seeks better inclusion of urban needs in EU policies as well as shares best practices across a range of issues. Cf. www.eurocities.eu.

lations, sometimes under the aegis of one central authority, but more often spread over three or four ministries responsible for areas including home affairs, employment, education and health. While such arrangements demonstrate that governments have taken the concept of "mainstreaming" integration policy to heart, they also make a simple aggregation of integration funding difficult to formulate and impossible in a comparative sense.

Second, some programs target immigrants but also other groups as part of social-inclusion strategies. It would be impossible to demonstrate that immigrants received a specific portion of money.

Third, the definition of "immigrant group" complicates budget lines. For example, are education initiatives targeting the children of immigrants considered integration programming? For some countries, such programs are a central tenet of integration while others see them as part of a broader education strategy.

This chapter thus limits itself to highlighting shifts in integration funding that can be clearly identified. The survey of EU Member States and European cities specifically asked respondents to limit themselves to programming for newly arrived, or "first-generation," immigrants. Changes with a broader focus are highlighted where appropriate, but the central foci for discussion are language programs, courses for newcomers, labor market integration programs for migrants, education and training programs for migrants, and, to a lesser extent, funding for other actors, such as nongovernmental organizations (NGOs) and local authorities.

A second cautionary note relates to the political cycle. For many Member States, cutting budgets has been an immediate and necessary first step; but, for many others, the trimming has yet to take place. Several respondents to the TCM survey noted that they expect cuts to be made later in 2010 and in 2011, and at the time were preparing themselves for programmatic change. Thus, while a number of interesting observations can be made, it is too early for a systematic review of budget changes in response to the economic crisis.

Instead, we look at how Europe is beginning to respond and the initial policy conclusions that may be drawn. What evidence is there that Member States are responding to the crisis in terms of integration? What impact might this have on integration programming and outcomes in the future?

Funding Sources before the Crisis

In the majority of European countries, integration funding is decided and coordinated at the national level. Priorities are set, for the most part, through multiannual strategies. Examples include the Portuguese National Plan of Immigrant Integration (second iteration) and the Estonian Integration Strategy (2008–2013), both of which set a ballpark budget for activities over the relevant period.

Despite strong national control over spending on integration, several developments have taken place in recent years. First, since the majority of migrants settle in urban areas, one can see increasing focus on integration from city and regional governments within each Member State. For some countries, regional autonomy is longstanding. In Germany, the federal government is responsible for providing introduction programs. The states (*Länder*) oversee broad areas like education, while integration policies in Belgium are almost entirely devolved to the country's three language communities (Flemish, French and German), with very little strategic direction from the federal government. However, in others, the local focus is new. In the United Kingdom, the Department for Communities and Local Government was created in 2006, and integration policies moved across from the Home Office (Somerville 2007).

Second, city authorities have become aware of their increasingly diverse communities. According to a recent review of local policies, many cities have established units within their administrations to develop integration strategies (Eurocities 2009), though financial resources tend to be deployed through existing mainstream service providers in areas such as education, housing and employment.

Third, cities have received money directly from various EU funds to support specific integration projects and initiatives. As cities usu-

ally depend on funding from both national and regional governments, which can limit their ability to develop projects, the EU money
has made it possible to develop projects with a specific integration focus and to connect with other cities across Europe. Relevant EU-level
funds range from the European Social Fund—€75 billion ($92.3 bil-
lion) aimed at improving employment, social cohesion and social inclusion, which is administered nationally by region—to PROGRESS,
a €628 million fund ($772.4 million) based on the goals of the Euro-
pean Employment Strategy (social inclusion, living and working conditions, nondiscrimination and gender equality).[3] In addition to these
thematic funds, several streams are based on geography, such as UR-
BACT and the Regional Development Fund.

Fourth, the European Union has created stable, dedicated funding
for integration policy over the past decade. A preparatory fund (Integration of third-country nationals, or INTI) was put in place between
2002 and 2006; INTI funded a number of cross-border activities on
integration, including two editions of the *Integration Handbook.*[4] In
2007, a European Integration Fund (EIF) was established, comprising
€825 million ($1 billion) over the seven-year period 2007–2013. While
a small portion of EIF is reserved for pan-European projects managed
at the EU level, 93 percent (€768 million; $944.6 million) is devolved
to the 26 participating Member States (Denmark has opted out of the
fund). Each participating state receives money based on its number
of legally resident third-country nationals (immigrants from outside
the European Union) and its multiannual programming strategy.
The remaining €57 million ($70.1 million) are for pan-European
projects similar in scope to the original INTI fund.[5]

The first amounts were announced in late 2008 and early 2009,
and it is immediately clear that the sums vary widely (see Table 2). In
addition, as will become clear, these amounts vary in proportion to

---

3 Exchange rate used is 1 euro = 1.23 US dollars.
4 Cf. http://ec.europa.eu/justice_home/funding/2004²007/inti/funding_inti_en.htm
   for details of projects granted over the four-year period.
5 For details of how funds are disbursed, cf. European Commission, Justice and
   Home Affairs 2010.

Table 2: Allocation of funding to Member States from the European Integration Fund

Member State	EIF budget (in millions of euros)[6]
Austria	17.25
Belgium	n/a*
Bulgaria	3.70
Cyprus	n/a*
Czech Republic	16.75
Denmark	OPT OUT
Estonia	7.90
Finland	2.50
France	67.62
Germany	132.36
Greece	n/a*
Hungary	13.00
Ireland	7.87
Italy	96.00
Latvia	11.20
Lithuania	5.70
Luxembourg	3.90
Malta	3.70
Netherlands	17.70
Poland	15.80
Portugal	15.20
Romania	6.95
Slovakia	4.60
Slovenia	5.50
Spain	122.90
Sweden	13.40
United Kingdom	129.49

* Information is unavailable, but allocations to Belgium, Cyprus and Greece total €47 million.

Source: European Commission 2008

6   Community contribution of the European Integration Fund 2007–2013 to Member States, together with the Annual Programs of 2007 and 2008, based on IP Memos (press releases) published by the European Commission.

the total amount spent in each country. For recipients of relatively smaller amounts, including newer Member States Poland and Slovakia, EIF money accounts for most of the integration activity in that country (co-funded by the national government). But some of the larger allocations are merely a drop in the ocean for Member States with well-developed integration strategies, such as the Netherlands, whose overall integration budget is upwards of €500 million ($615 million).

Finally, private foundations have begun to develop pan-European approaches to funding integration strategies. The European Foundation Center hosts a Diversity, Migration and Integration Interest Group (DMIIG), which brings together 18 foundations, including many of the biggest philanthropic organizations, to discuss national trends and needs in nongovernmental funding (cf. European Foundation Center 2010). All of these foundations devote significant resources to funding organizations that provide services in the area of immigrant integration.

The Network of European Foundations, in turn, has created the European Program for Integration and Migration, pooling donations from 12 foundations to fund projects on the basis of shared pan-European objectives. The program was created in 2005 and funds projects in three-year cycles, and the organization is currently mid-way through the second phase (2008–2011). The current cycle has three main themes: preventing illegal immigration, promoting migrant voices and developing the role of migrants and the portrayal of migration in the media. Public institutions tend to underfund these areas. In addition to these themes, the program has a strategic focus on networking organizations and building their capacity to influence the European political agenda (cf. European Program for Integration and Migration 2010).

Effects of the Crisis on Integration Programming

Given the diversity in the scale and range of funding across Europe, the response to the economic crisis has not been singular. In several countries, the economic crisis has brought about political change. For example, in March 2009, the Czech government suffered a vote of no confidence over its handling of the state economy, which led to a change in ministers, including the minister of interior and the minister of labor and social affairs (Ministry of the Interior of the Czech Republic 2010). In Estonia, the three-party government coalition collapsed in May 2009 because it failed to agree on state budget cuts. As a result, three ministers from the Social Democrat Party were removed, including Urve Palo, minister for population and ethnic affairs, responsible for integration policy. Rather than appoint a new official to the position, the government shut down the ministry and shifted integration responsibility to the Ministry of Culture and a newly merged Integration Foundation (Estonian National Contact Point for the European Migration Network 2010).

The crisis has also directly affected integration programming. Greece, Spain and Ireland had the three highest average deficits as a percentage of gross domestic product (GDP), with Greece registering 10.6 percent, Ireland 10.1 percent and Spain 8.7 percent in the second quarter of 2009 (Eurostat 2010). As a result, all three countries have made severe budget cuts across the board, including to integration policy, which will be elaborated upon below.

Every country in the European Union, with the exception of Malta, experienced a drop in surplus or an increase in deficit (as a share of GDP) between 2008 and 2009. However, many have not reduced spending on integration. In some cases, this is because of an explicit intention to continue investing in integration. At the most recent Ministerial Meeting on Integration, in Zaragoza, Spain, several countries called for sustained financing of integration strategies.

For other countries, however, not reducing the integration budget merely reflects the fact that the investment is insignificant compared to other areas of public finance. Poland undertook a consultation process in 2009 but made no changes to integration policy or funding as a result of the crisis. However, almost all integration activities in Poland are reserved for refugees, of which there were about 15,300 in January 2010 (United Nations High Commissioner for Refugees 2010).

A number of Member States have stated that the crisis has had no effect on integration programming, such as Austria (Austria National Point of Contact for the European Migration Network 2010), Germany (TCM questionnaire response from Germany 2010) and Slovenia (TCM questionnaire response from Slovenia 2010). The Portuguese government has explicitly stated that investments in integration are more, rather than less critical at such a volatile point in the economic cycle. So far, the main agency responsible for implementing integration policies in Portugal, the High Commission for Immigration and Intercultural Dialogue (ACIDI), has only seen a slight reduction in its budget (see Box 1) (High Commission for Immigration and Intercultural Dialogue 2010).

Box 1: High Commission for Immigration and Intercultural Dialogue (ACIDI), Portugal

The High Commission, created in 2007 and known as ACIDI, took over responsibilities for integration policies from ACIME, a consultative body for immigration and integration issues. ACIDI's National Immigrant Support Centers serve as one-stop shops for integration services provided by representatives of numerous ministries and government departments, from housing information to recognition of qualifications.

During its short life, ACIDI's budget has more than doubled, from just over €6 million in 2007 to €13.5 million by 2009 (about $7.4 million to $16.6 million), reflecting the importance of integration policy in Portugal. However, this rise comes from more than an increase in national funding. EU funds represented 40 percent of the total in 2009 (€5.4 million, or $6.6 million), up from 1 percent in 2007.

ACIDI's 2010 budget is slightly smaller, at €12.1 million ($14.9 million), and EU funding represents more than half of the projected spending. Despite severe budget constraints, the Portuguese government does not expect any major changes to ACIDI's budget in 2011. In addition, it is worth noting that ACIDI transferred approximately half its funds (€6 million, or $7.4 million) to nonprofit organizations that work directly with immigrants in 2009, and it expects to do the same in 2010.

The United Kingdom has also kept integration funding intact. The Ministry for Communities and Local Government, where integration policy is located, was asked to make cuts of £1.16 billion ($1.74 billion) for the 2010–2011 fiscal year.[7] While several of the budget lines focused on community cohesion were cut, the £70 million Migration Impacts Fund ($105 million), which is financed via a levy on migrants and aims to reduce pressure on local public services, remains unscathed.

Among the countries that have adjusted their integration programming, four trends can be observed at this early stage: direct budgetary cuts, institutional changes, refocused policy support and additional programs.

Direct Budgetary Cuts

The most obvious effect is a direct reduction in the overall budget for integration programming. Here, Spain provides a clear example. In 2004, the Spanish government began disbursing funding to autonomous communities, such as Madrid, reaching a plateau of €200 million ($246 million) annually by 2007 (Davis 2008). Regional communities took the lead on many aspects of integration and co-funded integration policies from their own budgets. As early as February

---

7   Exchange rate used is 1 pound = 1.50 US dollars.

2009, the Spanish government attempted to reduce the amount spent nationally on integration—from €200 million ($246 million) to €100 million ($123 million)—due to budget constraints. Protests, primarily from the regions, prompted the federal government to restore the full amount. In March 2010, the government announced a deeper cut— this time from €200 million ($246 million) to €70 million ($86.1 million)—though the proposed cut has not been finalized. To some degree, additional money given to the autonomous communities based on population estimates counterbalances the smaller budget; however, this money is fed into the general budget, and it is up to each region to determine how much is earmarked for specific integration policies.

A second clear example can be seen in Ireland, where funding for specific programming has been reduced. The Department of Education's budget for employing special tutors to teach English as a Second Language was reduced from €120 million ($147.6 million) to €98 million ($120.5 million) in the last budget, while the Equality Authority's budget has been cut by 43 percent since the fall of 2008 (see the Ireland case study for more examples) (McLoughlin 2010).

Finally, some countries expect cuts to occur in the future. The Netherlands, for example, anticipated cuts of up to 20 percent in the next financial year to the entire immigration, asylum and integration budget. The government is currently conducting an internal review to identify which areas of integration programming might be adjusted (TCM questionnaire response from the Netherlands 2010). Similarly, in Norway, the government has begun calculating the 2011 state budget, and it has signaled to all ministries that there will be a need for cuts in all areas (TCM questionnaire response from Norway 2010). Given the necessity of maintaining some immigration and asylum policies regardless of budgetary constraints, integration is a comparatively "soft" target. It may also be possible that governments will find it hard to justify bolstering integration services while cutting support for other policies that affect vulnerable native-born populations.

Institutional Changes

Several new Member States have changed which institutions are responsible for integration policy, as was the case with Estonia (detailed above).

In Latvia, the Office of Citizenship and Migration Affairs was restructured in 2009 to improve delivery and reduce expenditures (Siliņa-Osmane and Safonova 2009). Similarly, in Lithuania, the Migration Policy Department in the Ministry of the Interior was dissolved in November 2009 and replaced with a new Division of Migration Affairs, which has 50 percent less staff. At the same time, within the Ministry for Employment, the Economic Migration Division was dissolved entirely. These changes, made in light of tight budgetary constraints, reflect the fact that, in the Baltic region, emigration is rising while return migration is decreasing. No institution is responsible for integration and, with the current budget crisis, none is foreseen (National Contact Point for the Republic of Lithuania 2010).

Still, this phenomenon is not limited to new Member States. In 2008, the Irish Office of the Minister for Integration published a new integration strategy, *Migration Nation: Statement on Integration Strategy and Diversity Management*. However, much of the infrastructure associated with the strategy has yet to emerge. A Commission on Integration (to review progress) and a Task Force on Integration (for future policy development) are no longer going ahead, but the Ministerial Council on Integration (a consultative body) is expected to be funded. At the same time, the National Consultative Committee on Racism and Interculturalism, a central player in the development of integration policies over the past decade, has been abolished (TCM questionnaire response from Ireland 2010; McLoughlin 2010).

Refocused Policy Support

The landscape is not entirely bleak. In some countries, the economic crisis has caused governments to shift integration programming toward employment access. This is particularly the case in Scandinavia.

In Finland, while no change in policy is foreseen as a result of the crisis for the time being, there is generally a greater focus on helping immigrants find jobs (Asa, Kivilehto and Koljonen 2010) In Norway, participation in the labor market is still the overall goal for integration, and additional financing has been given to a program for immigrants who are experiencing long-term unemployment (TCM questionnaire response from Norway 2010).

Sweden has accelerated a planned reform of integration policy due to the economic crisis; the focus is now on labor market introduction. Examples include supplementary courses for foreign professionals, language courses and mentoring programs. These reforms are expected to increase costs by 920 million crowns (€95 million; $117 million) (TCM questionnaire response from Sweden 2010; Ministry of Integration and Gender Equality 2009).

Additional Programming

Finally, in some countries, integration programming is reported to have increased, with particular attention to employment and language courses. In Germany, for example, an additional €44 million ($54.1 million) have been allocated for integration courses (TCM questionnaire response from Germany 2010). Alongside wholesale cuts in integration programming, Ireland has almost doubled funding for the Employment of People from Immigrant Communities Program (EPIC) from €276,700 ($339,500) in 2008 to €512,568 ($630,460) in 2009. The program is focused on employment, education and training for non-EU adult migrants (TCM questionnaire response from Ireland 2010).

The Czech Republic responded to the recession by introducing a voluntary return program in May and September 2009 to address the problem of unemployed migrants. Of the 27,700 third-country nationals who lost their jobs in 2008–2009, it is thought that around 8 percent (mostly from Mongolia) left through this program, which covered the plane ticket home and some accommodation costs as well as paying returnees up to €500 ($615) (McCabe et al. 2009).

However, for the vast majority who remained, the Ministry of the Interior began emergency integration programs in cooperation with Czech municipalities. These included social and legal counseling, language training and support for further education. In addition, the Czech Republic is putting in place Integration Support Centers for foreign nationals in its regions (six were established in 2009; and four more are expected in 2010). According to the Czech government, "integration becomes more important and visible" due to the crisis and, for this reason, financial spending has been increased since 2008 along with support from the European Integration Fund and European Social Fund (TCM questionnaire response from the Czech Republic 2010).

Regions and Cities

For regions, changes in national budgets have had an impact as was the case with the Spanish cuts detailed above. At the same time, regions and cities have experienced the economic crisis in vastly different ways, with some being under more strain than others.

A survey conducted by the Council of European Municipalities and Regions in August 2009 found that 76 percent of local and regional authorities felt that the situation had worsened during 2009 and that 94 percent expected the situation to continue or worsen in 2010. Specifically, 63 percent of the regions' own-source tax revenues decreased, and national government transfers and grants dropped by 56 percent. Nevertheless, pressures to provide public services and increase spending either remained constant or increased (Council of

European Municipalities and Regions 2009). Broadly, newer members of the European Union seem to be in greater crisis than those in Northwest Europe.

A survey conducted by Eurocities in August 2009 found that 43 percent of the 12 cities responding had already experienced budget decreases since January 2008, but that over 50 percent expected future decreases during 2010 (Eurocities 2010b). Turning to specific integration cuts, a separate Eurocities survey of 13 European cities in March 2010 revealed a range of concerns related to the economic crisis (Eurocities 2010a). For those who responded, higher unemployment and negative perceptions of migrants were key concerns, with some highlighting that less money will be available for social services and voluntary-sector activities. Indeed, several cities have cut NGO funding since the beginning of the economic crisis, while one made specific cuts to newcomer courses and education and training programs. Given these circumstances, several cities increased funding for labor market initiatives, mirroring national policymakers. The responses to the questionnaire were neither numerous nor detailed enough to draw any conclusions. Generally, many cities expected further cuts in integration funding while several highlighted that the European Integration Fund might buffer national cuts.

Despite similar responses at the local and national levels, several policymakers have highlighted the tension between levels of government at a time when resources are limited yet in greater demand (Discussion during TCM Plenary May 2010). This tension is particularly evident when the divisions of responsibility for providing support—for example, employment or housing—are unclear. In these situations, municipalities find themselves shouldering a burden for which they do not have the resources to cope.

As detailed above, allocations from the European Integration Fund and related funds, such as the European Social Fund, will remain stable until 2013. For some countries, this is a relatively insignificant amount compared to their annual expenditure on integration policies. But for countries like Latvia and Lithuania, the Integration Fund is the main source (Siliņa-Osmane and Safonova 2009). Indeed, the Latvian government's integration information portal for immigrants, www.integration.lv, was developed and funded with EU money. A number of Member States—particularly those in Central and Eastern Europe, such as Estonia—follow the established Common Basic Principles for European Integration[8] (CBPs) closely, and their integration strategies follow the same timeline as the Integration Fund.

Shortly after launching in 2007, the European Integration Fund highlighted four key priorities, and Member States were asked to highlight which of the four strategic priorities they would focus on:

1. Putting into practice the CBPs.
2. Developing indicators and evaluation methodologies to assess progress, adjust policies and measures, and facilitate coordination of comparative learning.
3. Building policy capacity coordination and intercultural competence across the different levels and departments of government in Member States.
4. Encouraging the exchange of experience, good practices and information on integration between Member States.

For countries that stated different priorities, these four priorities are proving constraining.

The European Integration Fund also has no mechanism for releasing additional funds, where necessary, to support shifts in need and national financing. Several Member States have indicated that

8   In 2004, EU Member States agreed on a total of 11 so-called Common Basic Principles to jointly serve as the basic framework for European policies on integration. Cf. Council of the European Union 2004.

they would like to make precisely this change. Another limitation is the fact that such money can only be applied to legally resident third-country nationals, although many countries in Western Europe would like to target EU citizens. In this respect, since the European Social Fund is focused broadly on social inclusion, it is a more useful and flexible tool.

Foundations and Philanthropic Organizations

Briefly, two points may be made concerning the role of European foundations. First, the crisis has significantly shrunk the endowments of most foundations. This means that budgets for funding NGO integration activities have been reduced and that fewer new projects can be financed at the national and local levels.

At the same time, less government funding for NGOs means that foundations play a more critical role than ever before. In certain countries, notably Ireland, philanthropic organizations are filling the gaps left by public budget cuts.

Conclusions and Recommendations

As data from many countries of immigration have shown, migrants are particularly vulnerable in times of economic crisis (Papademetriou, Sumption and Terrazas 2010). Yet the data the Transatlantic Council on Migration collected from several European governments in March and April 2010 suggests that the European integration landscape is not entirely bleak. A number of countries have retained their core integration objectives and, in some cases, bolstered integration policies in critical areas, such as access to employment.

It is important to remember that, at this early stage, it is difficult to understand how the economic crisis will impact governments' approaches to funding integration and setting policy priorities in the future.

Some initial observations can be made:

- *High degree of fiscal constraint.* Governments are being forced to make cuts across the board, and they will continue to come under pressure to do so.
- *Commitment to long-term policy priorities.* Despite pressure, many governments have remained committed to funding immigrant integration and have not adjusted national priorities. This commitment was reinforced at the most recent European Ministerial Conference on Integration, held in Zaragoza in April 2010. Furthermore, by addressing immigrants' access to the labor market, several governments have turned their attention to one of the most immediate effects of the recession.
- *Greater importance of European funding.* For many countries, particularly those with limited independent resources for integration programming, the European Integration Fund has become ever more critical (although the fund's inflexibility could undermine its potential to help). Projects falling under the aegis of the fund must be co-funded, which secures a minimum of national government support.
- *More coordination and comparison of policies.* Governments are beginning to discuss how to increase the impacts of programs and how to run them at sustainable levels of funding.

What impact might these trends have on integration programming and outcomes in the future?

- *Highest impact at the local level.* Initial analysis suggests that integration funding has a trickle-down effect. While national governments respond primarily to overall fiscal constraints and national politics, actors lower down the food chain may be more deeply affected by the crisis, yet unable to cut programming given the rising demand for services. The ongoing tension between the Spanish Ministry of Employment and Immigration and Spain's autonomous communities highlights the fact that, for regions, high immigrant unemployment has local effects that communities cannot ignore. In this context, clear programmatic responsibility is critical.

- *Reduction in civil-society activities.* Similarly, although NGOs are often the central service providers at the grassroots level, they depend on stable sources of funding for their own institutional survival. Drops in government and foundation support for NGOs leaves these organizations in a deeply vulnerable position.

- *Need for greater flexibility within stable European funding streams.* To be most effective in a period of fiscal volatility, the European Integration Fund needs to be more flexible. Two ways to ensure that the fund helps governments through the crisis would be creating a mechanism for shifting priorities on a more frequent basis and establishing a pool of emergency funding within the fund.

- *More meaningful evaluation.* As long as money is tight, there will be calls for evaluation of policies, and government actors will come under pressure to find the most efficient paths to integration. While core policies for employment and training are being reinforced, there is little spare money for policy experimentation or innovative approaches to integration. Evaluations should be welcomed as an investment, but they should not be pursued to the exclusion of new ideas.

- *Sustainable funding and mainstreaming.* Integration policymakers fear they will lose influence if integration is mainstreamed into other policy areas, such as employment, education or health. However, current budget constraints may make mainstreaming the best option for governments looking to sustain integration investments. Infusing mainstreamed policies with expert oversight is a necessary trade-off between expensive targeted policies and the need to find economies of scale.

Integration Programming Postcrisis:
Ireland Case Study

Sheena McLoughlin

Introduction

After decades of mass emigration, Ireland quickly became a country of immigration over the last 15 years. As such, the Irish government had begun developing a strategy to address the integration needs of its immigrant population when the financial crisis catalyzed a significant and serious economic recession.

The government's integration strategy—*Migration Nation: Statement on Integration Strategy and Diversity Management*—was published in May 2008, just months before Ireland suffered the biggest drop in GDP growth of any Organisation for Economic Co-operation and Development country. This case study examines the recession's impact on Ireland's integration plans and the future of integration policy given recent changes.

Background

Soaring growth rates from the early 1990s in Ireland prompted a demand for workers that the indigenous population could not satisfy. As a result, Irish abroad began returning, and migrants from elsewhere in the European Union and from third countries began working and living in towns and cities all over the country, shifting net emigration flows to net immigration flows by the mid-1990s. By 2006, more than 420,000 non-Irish nationals were living in Ireland, an estimated 12 percent of the population, according to the Irish census. The great bulk of these migrants came from new EU Member States in Eastern Europe, as these EU citizens could work in Ireland as soon as their countries joined the European Union, in 2004.

For the most part, political leaders publicly acknowledged that migrant labor helped the Irish economy expand during the boom years. However, they had little experience with large-scale immigration or immigrant integration.

The first integration initiatives were introduced only a decade ago to address the needs of refugees. Slowly, politicians and state officials realized that immigration was not temporary and that the integration of all immigrants needed to be addressed.

In 2007, the government created the position of Minister of State with Special Responsibility for Integration Policy. The minister is supported by the Office of the Minister of State for Integration (OMI), which was launched with an €8 million ($9.8 million) budget and has become the lead governmental body with responsibility for developing Ireland's overall integration policy approach. *Migration Nation* articulates this approach, which emphasizes that integration is a two-way process. The strategy makes it clear that integration initiatives are underpinned by "whole-of-government" and mainstreaming approaches. Both of these ideas draw from the European Union's Common Basic Principles, drafted and adopted in 2004. In practice, this means that integration policies form part of the government's overall social cohesion effort and use existing structures and systems, where appropriate, to implement those policies.

Funding of Integration Initiatives before the Crisis

Aside from managing the two major EU funds for third-country nationals—the European Integration Fund and the European Refugee Fund—OMI also has a budget for supporting certain bodies that deal with migrants' needs on a daily basis. As noted in the main part of this chapter, this is not the only source of funding for migrants, but it is difficult to disaggregate mainstream funding that supports migrants as one part of a broader target group. OMI groups its major funding streams into three categories (Office of the Minister of State for Integration 2010a).

- *Local authorities* promote integration through activities they run themselves or that local groups/associations organize.
- *Major national sporting organizations* receive funding because the government believes that being part of a sporting organization is a good way to get newcomers involved in Irish society.
- *Faith-based groups* may apply for OMI funding for integration-related activities subject to receiving proposals for projects they deem "suitable." However, the criteria for these "suitable projects" are not clear.

OMI granted some funding to bodies concerned with migrant integration via other schemes, including the Fund for Initiatives to Support the Integration of Legally Resident Immigrants, which granted €1.4 million ($1.7 million) in 2008, mainly to NGOs. OMI also oversees funding to NGOs from the European Integration Fund (EIF). EIF-funded projects usually require NGOs to provide at least part of the funding requested themselves or obtain it from a private funder. Foundations such as Atlantic Philanthropies and the One Foundation have been major sources of this funding since long before the economic crisis. According to the foundations and their partners, this demand has not dissipated and has become even more pronounced over the past few years.

The Impact of the Recession on Integration Initiatives

Considering the three main recipients of OMI funding, the picture is mixed, though some direct budget cuts can be seen in the short term:
- *Local authorities.* Funding did not appear to decrease from 2008 to 2009, according to OMI figures. Some local authorities even received more (Dublin City Council received €260,000 [$320,000] in

2009, up €10,000 [$12,300] from the previous year) (for a list of OMI funding beneficiaries, cf. Office of the Minister of State for Integration 2010b). However, the Dublin City Council's integration unit—often singled out as an example of good practice—has lost one of its 3.5 full-time employees in the last year, and the person will not be replaced.

- *National sporting organizations.* In 2009, the government gave €429,000 ($528,000) to five different national bodies—15 percent less than in 2008.
- *Faith-based groups.* In 2008, the Inter-Church Committee on Social Issues received €77,300 ($95,100), but OMI gave out no funding in this area in 2009.

Beyond OMI, the government has targeted language and antidiscrimination funding for cuts.

Indeed, the biggest victim has been the language support given to newcomer children in primary and secondary schools around the country. The Department of Education's budget for employing special tutors to teach English as an additional language was reduced from €120 million ($147.6 million) to €98 million ($120.5 million) in the last budget.[1] Widely reported in the media, this decision has concerned many schools and civil-society groups.

Although the government does not organize language courses for adults, immigrants can take optional English language classes at government-funded Vocational Educational Committee (VEC) schools throughout the country. Some of these are free, while others charge a small fee. According to the government, approximately €10 million ($12.3 million) are spent annually in this area.

Beyond language, the government decided to abolish the National Consultative Committee on Racism and Interculturalism, which received a core funding of approximately €500,000 ($615,000) from the state, and slash the budget of the Equality Authority by 43 percent and that of the Irish Human Rights Commission by 24 percent.

1   Figure provided by OMI.

Meanwhile, the government has not announced a follow-up strategy to its 2005–2008 National Action Plan Against Racism, which provided strategic direction to combat racism and to develop a more inclusive, intercultural society in Ireland (Department of Justice, Equality and Law Reform 2005).

Finally, and perhaps most significantly, many of the initiatives outlined in the *Migration Nation* integration strategy have been slow to come to fruition. In some cases, this is due to the crisis; in others, it is because the strategy did not provide a budget.

One bright spot is the increased funding for the Employment of People from Immigrant Communities Program (EPIC), which rose from €276,700 ($339,500) in 2008 to €512,568 ($630,460) in 2009. Targeting legally resident EU and non-EU adult migrants, the program assists the unemployed find jobs, get training and increase their level of education.

The Future of Integration in Ireland

In its first three years, OMI pursued a number of initiatives. These include the publication and implementation of an intercultural health strategy, the development of local antiracism and intercultural plans and other intercultural initiatives within education and policing.

Although OMI says it is not considering a review of integration funding priorities and policies, a report of the Special Group on Public Service Numbers and Expenditure Programs, published in mid-2009, recommended that OMI be discontinued. In its place, each government department would be required to report annually on the promotion of cultural integration. It also proposed significant staffing cuts in the Department of Justice units that look after immigration and perhaps even further cuts to the number of English-language support teachers in schools across the country. OMI has experienced some changes in 2010, though they are not as drastic as those recommended in the 2009 report. First, the office moved from the Department of Justice, Equality and Law Reform to the Department of Community, Rural and Gaeltacht Affairs. Second, OMI's overall budget allocation was cut to €5.4 million ($6.6 million) in 2010, or one-third less than when the office was set up.

Some politicians from mainstream parties have indicated that they would prefer to see migrant workers leave Ireland than to have to worry about their long-term integration.[2] The public appears to agree, according to an *Irish Times*/Behaviour Attitudes opinion poll from November 2009, which reported that 72 percent of people want to see a reduction in the number of non-Irish people living in Ireland (O'Brien 2009).

In parallel, most politicians realize they need to ensure that social tensions do not rise during times of recession (Crowley 2010). The government announced some measures in August 2009 intended to help newly unemployed migrants. These include extending from three to six months the time non-EU migrants have to find new employment and giving non-EU migrants who have fallen out of the work-permit system and become unauthorized (due to unexpected redundancy or exploitation) the opportunity to apply for temporary residence permits for four month during which time they can attempt to reenter the work-permit system (ibid.).

However, the willingness of the Irish government to cut funding and dismantle institutions at such a critical moment should raise alarm bells. Not only are core policies facing cutbacks, but investments in future thinking—through a taskforce or commission on integration both of which the Migration Nation strategy foresaw—are being set aside.

---

2 For example, the Mayor of Limerick Kevin Kiely, from the main opposition party Fine Gael, called publicly in 2009 for any non-EU migrants living in Ireland who cannot afford to pay for themselves to be deported after three months. Cf. Hayes 2009.

Works Cited

Asa, Riikka, Mirkka Kivilehto and Tuomas Koljonen. *Annual Policy Report 2009*. Helsinki: Finnish National Contact Point for the European Migration Network and the European Migration Network, 2010. http://emn.sarenet.es/Downloads/download.do; jsessionid=9C4724FC020A7CB06A847063715653E9?fileID=978 (accessed July 12, 2010).

Austria National Point of Contact for the European Migration Network. *Austria: Annual Policy Report 2009*. Vienna: Austrian Federal Ministry of the Interior and the European Migration Network, 2010. http://emn.sarenet.es/Downloads/download.do;jsessionid= 6DA632F46803DD4C1E04DB1F85BAD5C5?fileID=1019 (accessed July 12, 2010).

Council of European Municipalities and Regions. *The Economic and Financial Crisis: Impact on Local and Regional Authorities, Second Survey*. Brussels: Council for Municipalities and Regions, 2009. www.ccre.org/docs/second_survey_ec_crisis_en.pdf (accessed July 12, 2010).

Council of the European Union. Common Basic Principles for Immigrant Integration Policy in the European Union. Council of Europe Press Release 14615/04 (Presse 321), 2618th Council Meeting, Justice and Home Affairs, Brussels, November 19, 2004. www.consilium.europa.eu/ueDocs/cms_Data/docs/pressData/ en/jha/82745.pdf (accessed July 12, 2010).

Davis, Andrew. *Multi-nation building? Immigrant integration policies in the autonomous communities of Catalonia and Madrid*. London: The Cañada Blanch Centre for Contemporary Spanish Studies, London School of Economics and Political Science, 2008. www.sps.ed.ac. uk/__data/assets/pdf_file/0017/13094/Andrew_Davis_Multi nation_building_Madrid_Catalonia.pdf (accessed July 12, 2010).

Estonian National Contact Point for the European Migration Network. *Estonia Annual Policy Report 2009*. Tallinn: Estonian National Contact Point for the European Migration Network and the European Migration Network, 2010. http://emn.sarenet.es/Downloads/

download.do;jsessionid=9C4724FC020A7CB06A847063715653E9?
fileID=970 (accessed July 12, 2010).

Eurocities. Eurocities' Working Group on Economic Migration and
Migration & Integration. *Integration Policies After the Economic
Crisis*. Brussels: unpublished, May 2010. 2010a.

Eurocities. *Eurocities Survey: Recession and Recovery in Cities*. Brussels:
Eurocities, January 2010. 2010b. www.eurocities.eu/main.php

Eurocities. Benchmarking Integration Governance in Europe's Cities:
Lessons from the Inti-Cities project. Brussels: Bourg, 2009.

European Commission, Justice and Home Affairs. The European
Fund for the Integration of Third-Country Nationals. Brussels,
2010. http://ec.europa.eu/justice_home/funding/integration/
funding_integration_en.htm#part_2 (accessed July 12, 2010).

European Foundation Centre. Diversity, Migration and Integration.
2010. www.efc.be/Networking/InterestGroupsAndFora/DMIIG/
Pages/DiversityMigrationIntegration(Default).aspx (accessed July
12, 2010).

European Program for Integration and Migration. The Project. Brussels, 2010. www.epim.info/theproject.php (accessed July 12 2010).

Eurostat. *Financial Turmoil: its impact on quarterly government accounts*.
Statistics in Focus 5/2010. Luxembourg: Eurostat, 2010.

Her Majesty's Treasury. Reducing the Government Deficit. May 24,
2010. www.hm-treasury.gov.uk/psr_reducing_government_
deficit.htm (accessed July 12, 2010).

McCabe, Kristen, Serena Yi-Ying Lin, Hiroyuki Tanaka and Piotr
Plewa. Pay to Go: Countries Offer Cash to Immigrants Willing to
Pack Their Bags. Migration Information Source, November 2009.
www.migrationinformation.org/Feature/display.cfm?ID=749.

McLoughlin, Sheena. Integration Programming Postcrisis: Ireland
Case Study. In *Prioritizing Integration*, edited by the Bertelsmann
Stiftung and Migration Policy Institute. Gütersloh: Verlag Bertels-
mann Stiftung, 2010.

Ministry of the Interior of the Czech Republic. *EMN Annual Policy
Report 2009: Czech Republic*. Prague: Ministry of the Interior of the
Czech Republic and the European Migration Network, 2010.

http://emn.sarenet.es/Downloads/download.do;jsessionid= 9C4724FC020A7CB06A847063715653E9?fileID=967 (accessed July 12, 2010).

National Contact Point for the Republic of Lithuania. *Annual Policy Report: Migration and Asylum in Lithuania in 2009*. Vilnius: National Contact Point for the Republic of Lithuania and the European Migration Network, 2010. http://emn.sarenet.es/Downloads/ download.do;jsessionid=9C4724FC020A7CB06A847063715 653E9? fileID=974 (accessed July 12, 2010).

Papademetriou, Demetrios G., Madeleine Sumption and Aaron Terrazas. Recovering from Recession: Immigrants and Immigrant Integration in the Transatlantic Economy. In *Prioritizing Integration*, edited by the Bertelsmann Stiftung and Migration Policy Institute. Gütersloh: Verlag Bertelsmann Stiftung, 2010.

Siliņa-Osmane, Ilze, and Diāna Safonova. *Policy Report on Migration and Asylum Situation in Latvia: Reference Year 2009*. Riga: Latvian National Contact Point of the European Migration Network and the European Migration Network, 2009. http://emn.sarenet.es/ Downloads/download.do;jsessionid=9C4724FC020A7CB06A847 063715653E9?fileID=979 (accessed July 12, 2010).

Somerville, Will. *Immigration under New Labour*. London: Policy Press, 2007.

Swedish Ministry of Integration and Gender Equality. *FactSheet: Government Program to Speed up Integration of New Arrivals in Sweden*. Stockholm: Swedish Ministry of Integration and Gender Equality, 2009.

TCM questionnaire response from Germany on file with the Migration Policy Institute, received on April 12, 2010.

TCM questionnaire response from the Netherlands on file with the Migration Policy Institute, received on March 22, 2010.

TCM questionnaire response from Sweden on file with the Migration Policy Institute, received on March 16, 2010.

TCM questionnaire response from the Czech Republic on file with the Migration Policy Institute, received March 15, 2010.

TCM questionnaire response from Norway on file with the Migration Policy Institute, received on March 12, 2010.

TCM questionnaire response from Ireland on file with the Migration Policy Institute, received on March 10, 2010.

TCM questionnaire response from Slovenia on file with the Migration Policy Institute, received on March 9, 2010.

United Nations High Commissioner for Refugees. Poland. Geneva: UNHCR, 2010. www.unhcr.org/pages/49e48df06.html (accessed July 12, 2010).

Works Cited for Ireland Case Study

Central Statistics Office. Census 2006. Dublin: CSO, 2006. www. cso.ie/releasespublications/documents/labour_market/current/ qnhs.pdf (accessed July 12, 2010).

Crowley, Niall. Hidden Messages, Overt Agendas. Dublin: Migrant Rights Centre Ireland, 2010. www.mrci.ie/news_events/ documents/HIDDEN_MESSAGES_OVERT_AGENDAS_000.pdf (accessed July 12, 2010).

Department of Justice, Equality and Law Reform. *Immigration and Residence in Ireland: outline proposals for an immigration and residence bill*. Dublin: Department of Justice, Equality and Law Reform, 2005a.

Department of Justice, Equality and Law Reform. *Planning for Diversity: National Action Plan Against Racism, 2005–2008*. Dublin: Department of Justice, Equality and Law Reform, 2005b. www. nccri.ie/pdf/ActionPlan.pdf.

Department of Justice, Equality and Law Reform. *Integration: A Two Way Process. Dublin: Department of Justice, Equality and Law Reform, 1999*.

Hayes, Kathryn. Mayor of Limerick's comments branded 'racist.' *Irish Times* November 12, 2009. www.irishtimes.com/newspaper/ireland/2009/1112/1224258655436.html (accessed July 12, 2010).

Immigrant Council of Ireland. *Coordinating Immigration and Integration: Learning from the International Experience*. Dublin: Immigrant Council of Ireland, 2007.

International Organization for Migration. *Managing Migration in Ireland: A Social and Economic Analysis*. Dublin: National Economic and Social Council, 2006.

O'Brien, Carl. Poll shows hardening of attitude towards immigrants. *Irish Times* November 24, 2009. www.irishtimes.com/newspaper/frontpage/2009/1124/1224459339934.html (accessed July 12, 2010).

Office of the Minister of State for Integration. OMI Funding Policy, 2010a. www.integration.ie/website/omi/omiwebv6.nsf/page/funding-omipolicy-en (accessed July 12, 2010).

Office of the Minister of State for Integration. Lists of Beneficiaries of OMI Funding, 2010b. www.integration.ie/website/omi/omiwebv6.nsf/page/funding-omiamounts-en (accessed July 12, 2010).

Office of the Minister of State for Integration. *Migration Nation: Statement on integration strategy and diversity management*. Dublin: Department of Justice, Equality and Law Reform, 2008. www.integration.ie/website/omi/omiwebv6.nsf/page/AXBN-7SQDF91044205-en/$File/Migration%20Nation.pdf (accessed July 12, 2010).

Papademetriou, Demetrios G., Madeleine Sumption and Aaron Terrazas. Recovering from Recession: Immigrants and Immigrant Integration in the Transatlantic Economy. In *Prioritizing Integration*, edited by the Bertelsmann Stiftung and Migration Policy Institute. Gütersloh: Verlag Bertelsmann Stiftung, 2010.

The Relationship Between Immigration and Nativism in Europe and North America

Cas Mudde

Introduction

Migration is as old as mankind itself, yet it has increased dramatically in scope and consequences in recent decades. Millions of people migrate or have migrated as transportation has become affordable, opportunity has expanded and countries have become increasingly connected.[1] While the vast majority of migrants stay fairly close to their homeland, a growing group sets out for farther shores, most notably Western Europe and North America.

This report focuses primarily on the effects of migration on political extremism in three industrialized regions: North America, Western Europe and Central and Eastern Europe. Although all three regions are internally diverse, they share some key features that are relevant: In North America, both Canada and the United States have long traditions as countries of immigration; Western Europe has seen mass immigration since the end of World War II (although some countries, France and the United Kingdom among them, experienced it much earlier than others, such as Ireland and Spain); and Central and Eastern Europe have only been confronted in recent dec-

---

1 The reasons for migration are diverse and are influenced by so-called push and pull factors. Push factors are those that push the migrants away from their own country, which are mostly economic (e.g., poverty) or political (e.g., civil war). Pull factors are those that pull the migrants toward their new country, which are also mostly economic (e.g., high standard of living) and political (e.g., safety and security), although much recent migration to Western Europe has been personal (e.g., family building and reunion).

ades with generally low levels of immigration and higher levels of emigration.

The focus of this chapter will be on the political extremism of the host population, or "the native born" not of the immigrants. While extremism among some immigrant groups—ranging from Turkish nationalist groups to Arab jihadists—has increased, this will only be addressed indirectly, in the ways in which it has influenced the immigration debate in the host country. The chapter primarily focuses on the various nativist reactions to immigration. Nativism—a combination of nationalism and xenophobia—is "an ideology, which holds that states should be inhabited exclusively by members of the native group ("the nation") and that non-native elements (persons and ideas) are fundamentally threatening to the homogeneous nation-state" (Mudde 2007).

The first section defines and introduces the main nativist actors by region. It also highlights the different ways in which nativists mobilize in the different regions and their respective strengths and weaknesses. The second section discusses the importance of migration to the identity and political relevance of the nativist actors, and it analyzes how these actors frame migration and how central it is to their discourse and electoral success. The third section shifts the focus onto how nativist actors have affected migration policies in their country. The fourth section broadens the focus by looking into the public effects of nativist actors. The fifth section focuses on the various ways in which states and societies have tried to counter the nativist actors. The sixth section touches briefly on the effects that the recent economic crisis has had on immigration and nativism in the three regions. The final section summarizes the main findings and addresses some best practices for dealing with anti-immigrant extremism.

The Main Nativist Actors

The extremists discussed here go by many different, if often related, names. Academics and journalists use terms like "xenophobes," "nativists," "racists," "right-wing populists," the "radical right," "radical right-wing populists," the "extreme right," "(neo-)fascists" and "neo-Nazis" (Hainsworth 2008; Mudde 2007; Decker 2004; Schain, Zolberg and Hossay 2002; Betz 1994; Elbers and Fennema 1993). While the intrinsic details of the definitional debates don't concern us here, it is important to provide at least some broad clarifications of the main terms used. As mentioned previously, the overarching category we are concerned with is nativism, as defined above.

There are two fundamental distinctions that are relevant here: right-left and radical-extreme.[2] However, these relative terms don't help us much in a broad interregional comparison. At the same time, the socioeconomic distinction between a pro-state left and a promarket right seems at best secondary to the main concern of this chapter. Therefore, for the purposes of this chapter, the distinction between left and right is in line with that of Italian philosopher Norberto Bobbio, who differentiates on the grounds of the attitude toward (in)equality (Bobbio 1994). In this interpretation, the left considers the key inequalities between people to be artificial and wants to overcome them by active state involvement, whereas the right believes the main inequalities between people to be natural and outside the purview of the state (Mudde 2007).

The distinction between extreme and radical is not merely of academic importance but can have significant legal consequences. For example, in Germany, extremist organizations can be banned whereas radical groups cannot (Backes 2003). To keep things simple, this chapter defines extremism as antidemocratic, in the sense that the

---

2 The distinction between left and right goes back to the French Revolution (1789–1799), when supporters of the Revolution would be seated on the left side of the French parliament and opponents on the right. More generally, the term left has been associated with "progressive" forces, while the right is deemed "conservative."

key aspects of democracy—majority rule and one person, one vote—are rejected. Radicalism, on the other hand, accepts the basic tenets of democracy but challenges some key aspects of liberal democracy, most notably minority protections. Hence, there is a fundamental difference between radical and extreme forces, which have significant consequences for the way (liberal) democracy can deal with them.

The main groups dealt with here belong to the radical right (Mudde 2007). Although these groups accept both inequalities and basic democracy, they espouse an ideology that challenges minority protections. The most important representatives of the radical right, at least throughout Europe, are political parties; in Europe, parties dominate politics. Radical-right parties share an ideology that includes core features, such as nativism, authoritarianism and populism (ibid.). In addition, we look at nonparty organizations, both of the radical and extreme right. The most important groups, at least in terms of physical threats to immigrants, are violent extreme-right groups, such as neo-Nazi organizations and skinhead gangs.

Western Europe

Since the early 1980s, there has been a third wave of postwar radical-right parties that has been much more successful in electoral terms than the previous two waves. That said, the development and success of radical-right parties in Western Europe has been quite uneven.

The *pater familias* of the contemporary radical right is the French National Front (FN), founded in 1972 as a collection of radical- and extreme-right groups. Under the charismatic leadership of Jean-Marie Le Pen, it gained its electoral breakthrough in the mid-1980s and although its parliamentary representation would be mostly minimal because of the French electoral system, FN has become the leading example for most contemporary radical-right parties in (Western) Europe (Rydgren 2003). Many parties have adopted FN propaganda and slogans, and some have even copied their name and logo (e.g., the Belgian National Front).

302

While most contemporary radical-right parties are relatively new, having been founded since the 1980s, some have much longer institutional legacies although often not as radical-right parties. The most important, in terms of gaining electoral success and political power, are the Austrian Freedom Party (FPÖ) and the Swiss People's Party (SVP). The former developed from a small national(ist)-liberal party into one of the biggest radical-right parties after Jörg Haider took over the leadership in 1986. The latter originated as a farmers' party and changed into a mainstream conservative party in the 1970s; new Zurich-based leader Christoph Blocher transformed it into a full-fledged radical-right party in the 21st century.

Radical-right parties have been electorally successful (winning over 15 percent in two or more elections since 1980) in only a few Western European countries (notably Austria and Switzerland). In about one-third of the countries (e.g., Belgium, Denmark, France, Italy), they have had moderate electoral success, receiving between 5 percent and 15 percent of the national vote. However, in most Western European countries, radical-right parties have never had serious electoral support and have polled below 5 percent (see Table 1).

In addition, many of the (once) successful radical-right parties passed their peak in the late 1990s. In fact, the prototype, FN, itself seems to be close to a meltdown, with no clear successor to its aging leader, Le Pen. Even Flemish Interest (VB) seems destined for a decline, having lost fairly substantially in the local and regional elections of 2006 and 2009, respectively. The only three real powerhouses are: Austria's FPÖ, which has bounced back from internal strife and electoral defeat; the Danish People's Party (DFP), which is providing essential support for the minority government for the second time in a row; and Switzerland's SVP, which, despite no longer taking part in the Swiss government, is the most popular party in the country in terms of public support.

There are a few parties that could be counted as radical right but, at least for the purposes of this chapter, are borderline cases. Most notably, the Norwegian Progress Party has been an ideologically eclectic and chaotic party, which at times has supported a strong anti-

Table 1: Support in parliamentary elections for radical-right parties in Western Europe, 1980 to 2010

Country	Party	Highest Ever	Most Recent
Austria	Alliance for the Future of Austria	10.7 (2008)	10.7 (2008)
	Austria Freedom Party (FPÖ)	26.9 (1999)	17.5 (2008)
Belgium	National Front (Belgian) (FNb)	2.3 (1995)	2.0 (2007)
	Flemish Interest (VB)	12.0 (2007)	12.0 (2007)
Britain	British National Party (BNP)	0.7 (2005)	0.7 (2005)
Denmark	Danish People's Party (DFP)	13.8 (2007)	13.8 (2007)
France	National Front (FN)	14.9 (1997)	4.3 (2007)
Germany	The Republicans (REP)	2.1 (1990)	0.4 (2009)
Greece	Popular Orthodox Rally (LAOS)	5.6 (2009)	5.6 (2009)
Italy	Northern League (LN)	10.1 (1996)	8.3 (2009)
Netherlands	Centre Democrats (CD)	2.5 (1994)	–
Portugal	National Renovator Party (PNR)	0.2 (2009)	0.2 (2009)
Spain	New Force (FN)	0.5 (1982)	–
Sweden	Sweden Democrats (SD)	2.9 (2006)	2.9 (2006)
Switzerland	Swiss People's Party (SVP)	28.9 (2007)	28.9 (2007)

Source: Álvarez-Rivera 2010

immigrant agenda. With 22.9 percent of the national vote in 2009, it was the second-largest party in Norway. Another party that is sometimes considered radical right is the Dutch Party of Freedom (PVV) of Geert Wilders. The party was founded in 2005, gaining 5.9 percent in the 2006 parliamentary elections and 15.5 percent in the 2010 parliamentary elections. As the third-biggest party in the Dutch parliament, the PVV has become a courted, if contested, coalition partner. Although the PVV takes some very strong anti-immigrant positions, the party differs from the (real) radical right by virtue of its exclusive focus on Muslim immigrants and relative openness to non-Muslim immigrants.[3]

Central and Eastern Europe

Although the parties and party systems of Central and Eastern Europe are not yet as institutionalized as in the western part of the Continent, political parties are also the main actors in the former communist part of Europe. While received wisdom holds that Central and Eastern Europe is a hotbed for nationalist extremists, radical-right parties are hardly more successful there than they are in "Old Europe" (Mudde 2005b) (see Table 2).

Only in four countries have radical-right parties ever gained over 15 percent of the vote. However, in two of them, the respective parties have since lost most of their support (the Liberal Democratic Party of Russia, or LDPR, and Greater Romania Party, or PRM) and, in the third, the party has recently split (the Serbian Radical Party, or SRS). The newest star on the radical-right front is the Hungarian Movement for a Better Hungary (Jobbik), which started with a bang but still has to prove its longevity. In only four countries was the most recent score also the highest support score for parliamentary elections since 1990; in two other countries, the parties no longer have independent parliamentary representation (Croatia and Po-

3   In addition to these political parties, there are various extreme and radical-right non-party organizations. Many are sectarian and cater to a few hundred people (at best) in their country (e.g., the various neo-Nazi *Kameradschaften* in Germany or small radical student groups, such as the Union Defense Group, in France). A few groups work in Europe or even worldwide (e.g., the infamous neo-Nazi skinhead organization Blood & Honour, which has [small and often barely active] branches in all three regions, or the esoteric International Third Position). Some of the most notable organizations have developed only recently, focusing almost exclusively on Muslim migrants (e.g., the English Defence League [EDL] or the organization Stop the Islamification of Europe). However, this latter group is mainly successful because of the tight connection to politicians from radical-right parties (including the DFP and VB).

Table 2: Radical-right parties in Eastern Europe with the largest share of support in parliamentary elections, 1990 to 2010

Country	Party	Highest Ever	Most Recent
Bulgaria	National Union Attack (NSA)	9.4 (2009)	9.4 (2009)
Croatia	Croatian Party of Rights (HSP)	5.0 (1995)	3.5 (2007)
Czech Republic	Assembly of the Republic – Republican Party of Czechoslovakia (SPR-RSĖ)	8.0 (1996)	–
Hungary	Hungarian Justice and Life Party (MIÉP)	5.5 (1998)	0.0 (2010)
	Movement for a Better Hungary (Jobbik)	16.7 (2010)	16.7 (2010)
Latvia	Popular Movement for Latvia-Zigerista Party (TKL-ZP)	15.0 (1995)	–
Poland	League of Polish Families (LPR)	8.0 (2005)	1.3 (2007)
Romania	Greater Romania Party (PRM)	19.5 (2000)	3.2 (2008)
Russia	Liberal Democratic Party of Russia (LDPR)	22.9 (1993)	8.8 (2007)
Serbia	Serbian Radical Party (SRS)	29.5 (2008)	29.5 (2008)
Slovakia	Slovak National Party (SNS)	11.7 (2006)	11.7 (2006)

Source: Álvarez-Rivera 2010; Wikipedia

land).[4] In other words, as in the western part of the Continent, radical-right parties are without significant electoral support in a majority of Central and Eastern European countries.

Central and Eastern Europe does seem to have a stronger non-party radical right, which includes: old mainstream nationalist organizations like Slovak Motherland (Matica Slovenská) in Slovakia, revisionist organizations like the Marshal Antonescu League in Romania or orthodox-religious organizations like Radio Maria in Poland (Mudde 2005a; Ramet 1999). However, in most cases, their political relevance has been closely related to the electoral strength of the domestic radical-right party or to their relationships with idiosyncratic postcommunist parties, such as the Movement for a Democratic Slo-

4 In Croatia, HSP is still represented in parliament but as part of a larger, not-radical-right electoral coalition.

vakia (HZDS) or the Socialist Democratic Party of Romania (PDSR), both of which have lost most of their power since the 1990s. Finally, several Central and East European countries have significant neo-Nazi groups and extreme-right skinhead gangs, most notably Russia and Serbia (Pilkington, Garifzianova and Omel'chenko 2010; Anti-Defamation League 1995). Unlike in much of the West, these groups are still growing and are seldom confronted with strong state or anti-racist resistance.

North America

The United States and Canada have very different political systems from each other, so it is unsurprising that the structures of their nativist movements also differ significantly. They do share two main features though: (1) there are no significant nativist political parties; (2) nativists confront strong proimmigration forces in the political and public debates.

Canada has no nativist political parties. The Nationalist Party of Canada is a tiny white-supremacist organization that is not registered to contest elections, although some members have run in local elections (with very marginal returns). Some people consider Canada Action a nativist party because it wants to halve the level of immigration to Canada. However, this would bring it down to US levels, which are among the highest in the world; therefore, this is hardly a nativist position. In recent years, there has been a toughening of the discourse on immigration in elections in Quebec under pressure from the Democratic Action of Quebec (ADQ), but the effects seem marginal in terms of policy and short-lived and regional in terms of discourse (Kymlicka 2010). Moreover, the ADQ's call for "reasonable accommodation" might be radical within the very pro-multicultural context of Canada but is far removed from the policies supported by nativist parties in Europe.

There are some groups that try to lobby mainstream parties and the public to support a drastic decrease in migration. Arguably the most prominent is Immigration Watch Canada, though even its own party members do not want to do away with immigration entirely. Instead, the groups wants to bring immigration levels back to 50,000 a year; according to the organization, this would constitute "about 20 percent of the current annual 260,000 intake" (Immigration Watch Canada 2010). In addition, there are some small neo-Nazi and white-supremacist groups, which are often Canadian branches of US-based groups.[5]

Although the United States boasted some of the first nativist parties in the world—notably the Know-Nothing Party or American Party in the mid-19th century (cf., e.g., Higham 1955)—they have been nonexistent or irrelevant throughout the 20th century. The only recent example of a notable nativist party was the Reform Party under Patrick J. Buchanan in 2000. Since then, the Reform Party has supported nonnativist politicians for the US presidency.

The United States does count a broad variety of nativist nonparty organizations, however, most of which are politically marginal at the federal level. This includes virtually all white-supremacist groups, including the various incarnations of the formerly powerful Ku Klux Klan, and neo-Nazi and skinhead gangs. It should be noted, though, that while these groups have no relevance in the political arena, their often highly local presence does at times adversely influence the life of immigrants in the area.

The most prominent organization of anti-immigration politicians is arguably the House Immigration Reform Caucus (IRC), which, according to its website, is "an organization dedicated towards identifying legislative solutions to address the issue of illegal immigration" (House Immigration Reform Caucus 2010a). Although the IRC was created, among other reasons, "to create a much-needed forum in Congress to address both the positive and negative consequences of immigration," it almost exclusively focuses on the negative aspects, and all the legislation it supports is aimed at restricting illegal immi-

5   One of the few significant groups still active is the National Alliance, in Ontario, now that the Heritage Front (1997–2005) and the Aryan Guard (2006–2009) have been dissolved.

gration (Building Democracy Initiative 2007). The outspoken anti-im-migration politician Tom Tancredo, a Colorado Republican who sought the Republican presidential nomination in 2008 on an immigration-control platform, founded the caucus in 1999 and was its first chair-man. Representative Brian Bilbray (R-CA) has run the caucus, which has 95 members (all but four of whom are Republicans), since 2007 (House Immigration Reform Caucus 2010b). Despite its clear anti-immigration stand, the IRC is careful in its wording and does not use an openly nativist discourse.

The most important anti-immigration actors in the United States are single-issue groups that are able to connect to mainstream media and politicians. This includes the various organizations linked to John Tanton, a retired Michigan ophthalmologist who has been instrumen-tal in creating a host of anti-immigration organizations (Southern Pov-erty Law Center 2009). Among the most active and influential Tanton organizations are the grassroots group NumbersUSA and the lobbying group Federation for American Immigration Reform (FAIR). In cer-tain regions, notably in the South, more openly racist groups like the Council of Conservative Citizens and various neo-Confederate groups like the Heritage Preservation Association also are active in the immi-gration arena and have connections to some mainstream politicians (cf., e.g., Southern Poverty Law Center 2004).

Immigration and the Radical Right

The rise of radical-right parties is considered to be closely linked to the phenomenon of mass migration, particularly in Western Europe. Indeed, the German political scientist Klaus Von Beyme defined the "third wave" of "right-wing extremism" as a response to mass immi-gration and the consequent development of multicultural societies in Western Europe (Von Beyme 1988). But while there clearly is a rela-tionship, it is not as straightforward as is often assumed. Moreover, immigration plays much less of a role in elections in North America and, particularly, in Central and Eastern Europe.

Much of the literature on the radical right in Western Europe considers the phenomenon to be first and foremost a majority response to the perceived threat of mass immigration. In fact, some authors go even a step further and consider radical-right parties by and large as single-issue parties, referring to them as "anti-immigrant parties" (Van der Brug, Fennema and Tillie 2005; Gibson 2002; Fennema 1997). However, the single-issue thesis is inaccurate on at least two counts: First, radical-right parties have a broader ideology and stress different issues. And, second, people vote for radical-right parties on the basis of different issues (Mudde 1999).

Radical-right parties share a core ideology of nativism, authoritarianism and populism (Mudde 2007). The three core ideological features are closely linked to three major political issues: immigration, crime and corruption. Hence, radical-right parties are clearly not single-issue parties. That said, immigration features prominently in both the internally and externally oriented literature of these parties (cf. Mudde 2000; Hainsworth 2008: 70–77). In line with their nativism, these parties view migration and migrants as multifaceted threats.

At least four frames are used in the propaganda of nativist movements in Western Europe. The predominant frame is *cultural*, in which migration is seen as a threat to the cultural homogeneity of the home nation. Depending on how strictly the nativist ideology is interpreted, migrants are considered to be either unable or unwilling to assimilate in the host culture. And, as the nation is flooded by a "tsunami" of migrants,[6] the core of its culture is viewed as threatened. Some parties even go so far as to speak of a "bloodless genocide" (BBC News 2009a).

At least since the horrific terrorist attacks of 9/11, a *religious* frame has accompanied the cultural one. Increasingly, the immigrant is seen as a Muslim rather than as a Turk or Moroccan. While Muslims

---

6   Dutch PVV leader Geert Wilders often refers to a "tsunami of Islamization" (cf., e.g., *De Volkskrant* October 7, 2006).

have been migrating to Western Europe since the 1960s, their numbers and visibility have increased significantly since the 1980s, in part as a consequence of family reunification and growth in the number of asylum seekers. Today, by conservative estimates, approximately 13 million Muslims live within the European Union (an estimated 2.5 percent of the EU population). Virtually all Muslims live in Western Europe, most notably in France (3.5 million), Germany (3.4 million) and the United Kingdom (1.6 million). Countries with the largest Muslim populations in relative terms include France (5 percent) and the Netherlands (6 percent) (European Monitoring Centre on Racism and Xenophobia 2006). In many Western European countries, the Muslim population is relatively young and growing much faster than the non-Muslim population. For example, in both Austria and Switzerland, the Muslim population quadrupled between 1980 and 2000 (Dolezal, Helbling and Hutter 2010).

While much of Islamophobia is in fact cultural xenophobia, the religious angle adds important aspects to the debate. Most importantly, nativists consider Islam a fundamentalist religion; VB leader Filip Dewinter, for example, flat out denied the possibility of a moderate Islam (*Metro* June 15, 2005). Painting the average Muslim immigrant as an Islamic extremist, they argue that Muslims threaten key aspects of Western democracies, such as the separation of church and state, the equal position of women and gay rights (although many radical-right parties are themselves too homophobic to take up this point).

The third-most-important theme is *security*, in which immigration and (petty) crime are linked. Some parties argue, in line with ethnopluralist ideology, that immigrants become criminals because they have been uprooted from their natural environment. Radical-right magazines are full of short news articles about criminal offenses, such as murder and rape, committed by "aliens." They argue that immigrants are much more likely to commit criminal acts than the host population and that the real level of crime is being kept from the public by politically correct politicians. Moreover, they decry the allegedly soft way in which the state deals with these criminals, preferring them to be either expelled or punished more severely. As in the case of the religious frame, the security frame is used not just by the radical right. Particularly after 9/11, the immigration debate in Europe and North America has become "securitized"—that is, immigration policy is increasingly made in light of national security (cf., e.g., Chebel d'Appolloni and Reich 2008; Rudolph 2006).

In recent years, the security frame has come to include the link between migration and terrorism. With the migrant increasingly defined in religious terms, and the various Islamist attacks on the public radar, nativists create a dark picture in which Muslim immigrants are considered the "fifth column" of the Muslim empire. The ultimate goal, they warn, is "Eurabia," a Euro-Arab axis that is connected by Islam and will be fiercely anti-American and anti-Zionist (Ya'Or 2005).

Oddly enough, while the Eurabia thesis is limited to the margins of the radical right in Europe itself, it is widely popular within mainstream conservative circles in the United States. It is popularized in the books of people like Bruce Bawer, with telling titles like *While Europe Slept: How Radical Islam is Destroying the West from Within* and *Surrender: Appeasing Islam, Sacrificing Freedom*, both of which are published by highly respectable publishing houses (Random House and Doubleday, respectively) and reviewed positively in even liberal publications, such as the *New York Times* (Pollard 2009). *While Europe Slept* was even nominated for a National Book Critics Circle award, which did raise some critique (Cohen 2007).

The fourth frame employed in nativist discourse is *economic*. Here, immigrants are depicted as a financial burden to the host society for allegedly taking jobs away from the natives and/or draining social benefits. A popular slogan among radical-right parties is "xxx,xxx unemployed, why are there xxx,xxx immigrants?" This is often combined with a welfare-chauvinist agenda, in which welfare programs are supported, but only for the natives. The argument is that, if immigrants are sent back to their own country, there will be enough money to provide decent services to natives.

The fifth and final frame is *political*, in which immigrants are seen as mere tools of sinister political forces. With varying degrees of conspiracy theories—some more anti-Semitic, others more anticapitalist—mass immigration is presented as a willing plot of (inter)national politicians, business leaders and trade union leaders to strengthen their own position at the expense of the "regular guy." Moreover, in line with the populism of those espousing these views, the elite (seen as a homogenous, corrupt entity) are accused of covering up the real costs of immigration and of muffling the people through antidiscrimination laws and political correctness.

Many studies have looked into the relationship between the number of immigrants and the number of votes for radical-right parties in Western Europe. So far, the results have been highly contradictory, in part becuse different datasets, indicators and units of analysis are used. For example, some authors have found a clear, positive correlation between the number of foreign-born citizens and the electoral success of a radical-right party in a country (cf., e.g., Golder 2003) while others have not (Messina 2007; Wendt 2003; Kitschelt and McGann 1995). Similarly, some studies show a significant positive correlation with the number of new immigrants (Swank and Betz 2003; Lubbers 2001; Knnige 1998) or asylum seekers (Wendt 2003) at the national level, while others find a negative (cor)relation or none at all (Dülmer and Klein 2005; Jesuit and Mahler 2004; Kitschelt and McGann 1995; Kriesi 1995).

This is not to say that immigration and immigrants do not play an important role in the electoral success of radical-right parties. But the relationship is not as simple as is often assumed—that is, the more immigrants in a country, the higher the electoral success of a radical-right party. Immigration is not inherently a political issue; in fact, while mass immigration started in most West European countries in the 1960s or 1970s, it only became a salient political issue in the 1980s or 1990s. To become a salient political issue, immigration has to be (made) visible to a significant section of the population. Once this has happened, different narratives will emerge, and there will be a political struggle over the right narrative.

In many countries, notably the Netherlands and the United Kingdom, the hegemonic narrative—which saw multiculturalism as an enrichment of national culture—was for a long time a positive one (Messina 2007). Only since the late 1980s has this started to change, with more and more leading political and societal actors subscribing to various interpretations of the multiculturalism-as-problem/threat narrative (see below).

Central and Eastern Europe

In Central and Eastern Europe, immigration levels are still very low. According to a recent Eurostat report, virtually all Central and Eastern European countries had fewer non-EU immigrants per 1,000 inhabitants than the EU average in 2006 (Herm 2008: 2). The only two exceptions were the Czech Republic and Slovenia. Moreover, while immigration into Central and Eastern Europe is still relatively low, emigration from Central and Eastern Europe, particularly into western EU countries, has been rather high since 2004, when most of the countries joined the European Union. For example, in 2006, an estimated 290,000 Polish and 230,000 Romanian migrants lived in other EU countries (ibid.: 3).

Consequently, few political actors, radical right or otherwise, have made immigration an important issue in their propaganda. Although the number of immigrants has been rising slowly but steadily in recent years and immigrants have become more visible in many of the larger cities in the region, including Budapest and Prague, radical-right parties tend to focus on indigenous minorities (notably the Roma) rather than on immigrants. And while anti-immigrant attitudes are at least as widespread in the eastern as the western parts of the Continent (Mudde 2005a), so far, few Central and East European voters have considered immigration a key concern.

One of the few exceptions is Slovenia, where the radical right responded to the influx of Bosnian and Serbian refugees from the Yugoslav civil war in the early 1990s (Kuzmanic 1999). However, even here, the impact was relatively modest and only short-lived despite continuously high levels of former-Yugoslav immigrants. In later years, the Slovenian National Party (SNS) moderated its ideology and shifted its primary focus to Croatians and Roma (Trplan 2005).

The most recent exception is Russia, where the single-issue party Russian Movement against Illegal Immigration (DPNI) was founded in 2002. While electorally irrelevant, its emergence does signify the rising salience of the immigration issue in Russia. Most interesting is the striking similarity between its anti-immigration positions and those of the radical right in Western Europe. The group links migrants to societal problems and even shares their Islamophobia. For example, the DPNI states that "migrants from the Caucasus states and from Central and South-Eastern Asia are the first part of the foreign expansion" (Mudde 2007).

North America

North America, finally, has a much longer history of mass immigration. Unlike the European countries, Canada and the United States are officially immigration countries. This means that they not only accept relatively large groups of immigrants annually but they also (try to) regulate the influx of immigrants. Consequently, the annual number of new (legal) immigrants is fairly constant, which makes it less explosive as a political issue. That said, illegal immigration—estimated to be in excess of 10.8 million people as of January 2009 (Department of Homeland Security 2010), particularly from Latin America—will at times explode onto local and national public agendas in the United States, not least through the advocacy of anti-immigration organizations and politicians.

The discourse on immigration in the United States is quite similar to that in Western Europe. In fact, there is contact between nativists in both regions. For example, British National Party (BNP) leader Nick Griffin spoke in Virginia in 2006 at the annual meeting of the magazine *American Renaissance,* while Pat Buchanan met with VB leaders Filip Dewinter and Frank Vanhecke in Washington, DC, in 2007 (Anti-Defamation League 2009). As in Western Europe, cultural, reli-

315

gious, security, economic and political themes are prevalent. There are some subtle differences, though, which are described below.

First of all, in many cases, the cultural theme is more racial in the United States. This is in part a linguistic matter: Apart from in the United Kingdom and United States, the term "race" is no longer used in European languages. Whereas Americans might be taught that all races are equal, Europeans are taught that there is only one race, the human race. Consequently, much of the racial nativism in the United States (e.g., that of Pat Buchanan) is very similar to the cultural nativism found in Europe. Still, classic racist ideas that are limited only to the absolute neo-Nazi fringes in Europe are found in some nativist groups in the United States, particularly in white-supremacist and neo-Confederate ones.

Second, with regard to security, Islam plays a less dominant role among US nativists. Oddly enough, it seems to be most present among neo- and paleoconservatives, who see the threat as predominantly being in Europe. As mentioned earlier, a good example is the Islamophobic book *While Europe Slept: How Radical Islam is Destroying the West from Within* by Bruce Bawer. While this book has some popularity among European nativist groups, it seems to be the American conservative's bible on contemporary Europe and has received positive reviews in many mainstream media sources. Interestingly enough, few neoconservatives write such alarmist essays on the United States, while most paleoconservatives consider the "Mexican threat" more pressing.

The most prominent and prolific writer on "alien invasions" of the United States is Pat Buchanan, whose nativist books can be found in all major bookstores. In his book *State of Emergency*, he argues that Mexico is slowly but steadily taking back the American Southwest (Buchanan 2006). This is the key threat, according to American nativists. They refer to it as the "Aztlan Plot" for "*la reconquista*," or the recapture of the lands lost by Mexico in the Texas War of Independence and the Mexican-American War. While these ideas are far removed from those of mainstream political actors in the United States—most notably, the two main political parties—they were expressed in Lou Dobbs' program on CNN and by various right-wing talk-radio hosts. Moreover, Buchanan himself is a well-known pundit on the national TV network MSNBC.

Effects of Political Extremism

While public attitudes and, particularly, political violence are important aspects of politics, the true test of power is in whether or not nativist actors have influenced policies. It is worth distinguishing two different types of influence: direct and indirect.

Direct influence means that nativist groups directly influence immigration policy, either by implementing it themselves or by (directly) making other actors implement it. Indirect influence works more slowly and unclearly; nativist actors influence nonnativist actors, who would then implement anti-immigrant policies. Establishing "influence" here is obviously problematic.

Direct Effects

Overall, there are very few cases of nativist actors directly affecting immigration policy in all three regions. The reason is simple: Only in a few cases have nativist actors been part of government (see Table 3). Moreover, most of these cases were in Eastern Europe, where immigration has so far not been a major issue, not even for nativist parties. Where nativist parties have been represented in the parliament but not in the government, their legislative initiatives have mostly been boycotted by the governmental (and even most other oppositional) parties. In other words, nativist parties have had relatively few direct effects on politics, even on immigration politics.

In Western Europe, only four nativist parties have made it into government so far: the Northern League (LN) in Italy (2000–2005, 2008–present); the FPÖ and the Alliance for the Future of Austria (BZÖ) in Austria (2000–2006); and the SVP in Switzerland (2005–

317

2007). However, the few academic studies of radical-right parties in office all agree on one thing: They have been "instrumental" in introducing more restrictive immigration policies (Fallend 2004; Zaslove 2004; Heinisch 2003; Minkenberg 2003).

Table 3: Nativist parties in European national governments since 1980

Country	Party	Period(s)	Coalition partners (party ideology)
Austria	FPÖ	2000–2002	ÖVP (Christian democratic)
		2002–2005	ÖVP
	BZÖ	2005–2007	ÖVP
Croatia	HDZ	1990–2000[1]	
Estonia	ERSP	1992–1995	Isamaa (conservative)
Italy	LN	1994	FI (neoliberal populist) and AN (conservative)
		2001–2005	FI and AN and MDC (Christian democratic)
		2008–	PdL (right-wing)
Poland	LPR	2006–2008	PiS (conservative)and Samoobrona (social populist)
Romania	PUNR	1994–1996	PDSR (diffuse) and PSM (social populist)
	PRM	1995	
Serbia	SRS	1998–2000	SPS (social populist) and JUL (communist)
Slovakia	SNS	1994–1998	HZDS (diffuse) and ZRS (communist)
			Smer (social populist) and HZDS
Switzerland	SVP	2005–2007	SPS (social democratic), FDP (liberal) and CVP (Christian democratic)

Notes: 1 HDZ changed into a conservative party after 2000.
The SVP only became a full-fledged radical-right party in/around 2005.

Source: Mudde 2007

Both Austria and Switzerland tightened their asylum laws at the initiative of the radical right in 2003 and 2006, respectively. Interestingly, the Austrian radical-right governments did not introduce stricter general immigration laws; previous mainstream governments had already done so (Gächter 2008). The most notable examples in the Italian case are the Bossi-Fini Law, which came into force in August 2002 and was named after the LN and National Alliance (NA) leaders who proposed the bill. The bill aimed to curb immigration, except for highly skilled workers, although it also included a limited amnesty for some unauthorized immigrants (Colombo and Sciortino 2003). A more recent law, adopted in August 2009, goes much further by, among other things, making illegal presence a criminal offense (Lewis 2009).

Although most countries will allow nongovernmental parties to submit proposals for legislation, in very few cases does this lead to actual laws. This is even more apparent with proposals from the radical right, which tend to be shunned by the other parties in the parliament (e.g., the VB in Belgium). There are two important exceptions, however: the DFP in Denmark and the SVP in Switzerland. Although the DFP has never been an official part of the Danish government, it has been the major support party in right-wing minority governments since 2001. As a consequence, the party played a crucial role in drafting the immigration law of 2002 for the government, which, among other things, limited grounds for political asylum and stipulated financial requirements for marrying a foreigner (CNN 2002). This law is described as "one of Europe's strictest immigration laws" by the United Nations High Commissioner for Refugees (UNHCR 2009). Since leaving the Swiss government in 2007,[7] the SVP no longer has direct access to the legislative drafting process. However, because of Switzerland's strong system of direct democracy, which includes referendums initiated by the public, the SVP still plays a significant role in influencing both public opinion and the implementation of Swiss legislation. A recent example of this—which gained much attention and condemnation around the world—was the referendum that banned the construction of minarets, which was passed by 57 percent of the voters and in 22 of the 26 Swiss cantons in November 2009 (BBC News 2009b).

While Central and Eastern Europe has seen more radical-right government participation, only a small minority of governments have

---

7 Technically, SVP leader and Justice Minister Christophe Blocher was ousted from the cabinet in 2007 in favor of one of his more moderate party colleagues, who was then kicked out of the SVP.

included the radical right. Furthermore, this has not had an effect on immigration policies. As said before, immigration is simply a nonissue in the region, even for the radical right, which focuses instead primarily on indigenous minorities, such as Hungarians, Russians and "Gypsies" or Roma. In fact, most pressure to implement tougher border regimes came from the European Union, which was worried that Central and Eastern European states did not exert sufficient control of their borders, which were soon to become and now are EU borders (Lavanex 1999).

The situation in North America is more complex. Canada has no nativist party with parliamentary, let alone governmental, representation. But while the United States does not currently have any successful nativist parties, unlike in the 19th century (e.g., the Know Nothing Party), there are some powerful nativist voices within the main parties, most notably the Republican Party. None have made it into prominent positions within Republican administrations, however. Hence, nativist actors have had at best only indirect effects.

The situation is different at the local and regional levels. Various US communities have tried to limit the effects of illegal immigration by pushing through a broad variety of legislation. Much of this legislation seeks to punish businesses that use or cater to unauthorized immigrants or to exclude unauthorized immigrants from local community services (ranging from schools to hospitals). While in many cases these changes were pushed through by mainstream actors, groups like FAIR have provided technical assistance to several state legislators in passing bills that curtail immigrant rights (e.g., requiring proof of citizenship to get a driver's license, mandating employer verification, restricting immigrant access to public benefits). Similarly, groups like FAIR and Save Our State (SOS) have been instrumental in pushing for versions of the so-called Illegal Immigration Relief Act, which aims to exclude unauthorized immigrants from housing, in a number of communities. Moreover, there are other state actors that can foster anti-immigrant sentiment in a particular area (Massa and Abundis 2007). A key example here is Sheriff Joe Arpaio in Arizona, who now faces a Department of Justice civil-rights complaint alleging that he discriminated against Latinos while enforcing federal immigration law (cf., e.g., James 2009).

One of the states that has seen the most polarized debates about such measures is California, which—despite its progressive image and Democratic legislative majorities—has seen significant nativist campaigns and legislative successes (particularly through referendums) (cf., e.g., Ho-Sang 2010). The most (in)famous of these was Proposition 187, listed on the ballots as the "Save our State Initiative," which called for strict and punitive measures against unauthorized immigrants. The initiative was cosponsored by the nativist California Coalition for Immigration Reform (CCIR) and was passed in 1994 by an overwhelming 59 percent of the votes, though it was ruled unconstitutional by a federal court and never implemented (Building Democracy Initiative 2007).

However, while there are many examples of successful anti-immigration measures at the subnational level, with or without pressure from nativist actors, there are also countless examples of successful proimmigration mobilization, particularly at the local level (cf., e.g., Hanley, Ruble and Garland 2008). For example, since the 1980s, a growing group of cities has banned city employees and police officers from asking people about their immigration status. Although the number of cities involved is not very impressive (ca. 30), it does include practically all major cities in the United States (e.g., Chicago, Dallas, Los Angeles, Miami, New York, San Francisco, Washington, DC) (Ridgley 2008).

Indirect Effects

Obviously, governments do not make policies in total isolation. They are influenced by the media, public opinion, international organizations and other competing political parties. Both opponents and supporters of the radical right have argued that mainstream parties have implemented anti-immigration legislation under pressure from radical-right electoral success. In a few cases, the respective governments

321

have acknowledged this. In some of these cases, governments have been criticized for offering what sounded like a convenient excuse rather than a credible explanation. For example, British Prime Minister Tony Blair, German Chancellor Gerhard Schröder and Spanish Prime Minister José María Aznar all called for stricter immigration laws to prevent the rise of the radical right despite the fact that their countries have very marginal radical-right parties (Hooper, Tremlett and Henley 2002).

While there are many national and regional differences, one can detect some general shifts in the debate on immigration in Western Europe. First and foremost, there *is* a debate on immigration. Up until the 1980s, the established parties in most Western European countries were engaged in a "conspiracy of silence" (Messina 2007) or has an explicit or implicit agreement to keep immigration outside of the public debate. Mainly due to public pressure—often expressed loudly by the tabloid media—the mainstream parties reluctantly started to address immigration as a political issue while nativist parties further heightened the salience of the issue.

Second, the consensus in the debate has shifted in most countries from a (implicit or explicit) proimmigration to an anti-immigration standpoint. Nowadays, virtually all but a few radical-left and green parties consider immigration a fundamental challenge to their society at best and a threat at worst (Zaslove 2004; Heinisch 2003; Minkenberg 2001). Hence, whereas mainstream parties in the Netherlands or the United Kingdom tended to sing the praises of the many enrichments of multiculturalism in the 1970s and 1980s, they now ponder the ways in which "Dutchness" and "Britishness" can be protected against outside influences (Kymlicka 2010). Overall, right-wing parties have co-opted radical-right positions more often and more radically than left-wing parties; the best examples include Britain's Conservative Party, the Netherlands' People's Party for Freedom and Democracy and France's Union for a Popular Movement. That said, there are many examples of social democratic, and even communist, parties that have adopted anti-immigration positions in their programs, from the Netherlands' Labour Party to the French Communist Party.

Third, the debate has shifted from immigration to integration since, in most countries, no significant party calls for more immigration. As Western European countries do not typically present themselves as immigration countries, and mainstream politicians do not want to encourage immigration, they still have few integration policies in place—despite several decades of immigration. Hence, from Belgium to Norway and from Spain to Denmark, countries are debating what the rights and duties of the host population and immigrants are, with an increasing emphasis on the duties of the immigrants.

Fourth, the immigration debate has shifted from the cultural to the religious. For example, the typical Dutch or German immigrant was traditionally seen as a Turk; but, after 9/11, s/he had become a Muslim. This has had significant influence on the debate, most notably on the anti-immigrant position. Initially, immigration could only be opposed on the basis of economic and cultural grounds. In most countries, cultural opposition was outside of the realm of the respectable, as it linked to (ethnic) nationalism. The struggle against Islamist terrorism has shaped the post-9/11 debate about immigration, linking it to religion and security and widening the scope for anti-immigration positions. Nowadays, parties will oppose immigration on the basis of mainstream liberal-democratic arguments rather than marginal nationalist positions. A good example was the infamous Dutch politician Pim Fortuyn, who framed his attacks on Muslim immigrants in terms of his defense of gay rights, equality of men and women, and the separation of church and state (Akkerman 2005). Similar arguments have been made by right-wing Italian Prime Minister Silvio Berlusconi as well as left-wing Scandinavian feminists (Akkerman and Hagelund 2007).

The relationship between the strength of radical-right parties and the adoption of anti-immigrant positions by mainstream parties is not always clear, however. For example, while countries such as Denmark and France exemplify the received wisdom that strong radical-right parties have pushed mainstream parties "to the right," other countries do not. The best counter-example is Belgium (De Decker et al. 2005), where most mainstream parties are among the most proimmigrant in Europe, precisely *because of* the strong VB. And then there are many mainstream parties—from Britain's Labour Party to Germany's Christian Social Union—that have adopted relatively strong anti-immigration positions despite the lack of a successful radical-right party in their country.

A similar point can be made about immigration policies in Western Europe. As far as cross-national comparative studies of immigration laws are available, they show that European immigration policies are increasingly converging, not least because of cooperation within the European Union (Messina 2007; Givens and Luedtke 2004). Recent developments indicate that this will only increase in the future:[8] "During the last decade, the need for a common, comprehensive immigration policy has been increasingly recognised and encouraged by the European Commission and the EU's Member States. The Commission is therefore now proposing concrete principles and measures—accompanied by a new strategy on immigration governance— on which to base the further development of the common immigration policy over the coming years" (European Commission 2008).

That said, at this moment, the level of convergence is still rather limited. And while there are some important changes that might facilitate further convergence (e.g., the Stockholm program 2010–2015 and the introduction of Qualified Majority Voting under the Lisbon Treaty), progress is glacial, and the European Commission might be an unreliable barometer of such progress (Faist and Ette 2007). Most importantly, given their marginal role in the European Parliament and in the European Council, radical-right parties will most likely not play an important role in these initiatives.

The finest hour of the nativist movement in the United States was in 2007, when a major bipartisan immigration reform package—proposed by Senators Edward Kennedy (D-MA) and John McCain (R-AZ) and backed by President George W. Bush—was defeated. While various factors played a role—not least the internal divisions within ma-

8 An overview of EU-wide immigration initiatives can be found on the EU's website: European Commission 2010a.

jor progressive forces, such as the trade unions—a key factor in the defeat of the bill was the mobilization by nativist organizations, such as Numbers USA. Indeed the phone system of the US Congress reportedly collapsed under the weight of more than 400,000 calls (Southern Poverty Law Center 2009). Moreover, in recent years, representatives of nativist, and sometimes outright racist, organizations have become mainstream in the media—appearing most notably on CNN's *Lou Dobbs Tonight*.[9] They also repeatedly testified as experts to Congress; indeed, FAIR claims it has testified to Congress "more than any other organization in America" (Southern Poverty Law Center 2009).

While there is no doubt that the "nativist lobby" has access to the mainstream media and politics, its influence should not be exaggerated. Even the defeat of the "amnesty" bill in 2007 was a defensive victory. From their point of view, they prevented the situation from becoming worse. With regard to implementing new legislation, nativists have been much less successful, at least at the federal level. While they have been able to profit from the securitization of the immigration debate after 9/11, most notably with the construction of the border fence, they have also faced a powerful proimmigration lobby that includes big business, immigrant groups and libertarians (Tichenor 2002). This is in sharp contrast to the situation in Western Europe, where proimmigration forces have been almost invisible in the debate (see below).

---

9 In return, Dobbs was awarded the 2004 Eugene Katz Award for Excellence in the Coverage of Immigration by the anti-immigration Center for Immigration Studies (CIS). In November 2009, Dobbs left CNN after a campaign by immigrant-rights advocates to get him removed and allegedly because of growing unease over his right-wing agenda, and *Lou Dobbs Tonight* is no longer aired on television. Dobbs continues his radio work, which includes *Lou Dobbs Radio* and *Lou Dobbs Financial Report*.

Public Effects of Nativism

Effects on policies and other political parties are arguably the most important possible effects of nativist actors, though certainly not the only ones. Nativist actors can also affect the public directly. For example, back in 1955, the famed American sociologist Seymour Martin Lipset argued that "radical-right agitation has facilitated the growth of practices which threaten to undermine the social fabric of democratic politics" (Lipset 1955). Over the years, this belief has become received wisdom, uttered at strategic times in political debates and repeated in the mainstream media. With regard to immigrants, two alleged phenomena have received most attention: an increase in anti-immigrant violence and an increase in anti-immigrant public sentiment.

So far, these assertions have not been supported by academic research, although this is to a large extent thanks to a lack of reliable cross-national data. This might change in the near future, as several organizations have started to collect reliable cross-national data, most notably the European Union Agency for Fundamental Rights, formerly the European Monitoring Center on Racism and Xenophobia (EUMC), in Vienna, Austria.

Racist Violence

There are two strains of thought regarding the relationship between radical-right parties and anti-immigrant violence. The majority view holds that "the xenophobic rhetoric [of radical-right parties is] often spilling over into violence" (Marcus 2000). One of the few studies that has provided empirical evidence for this thesis was a pilot study in Switzerland in the 1984–1993 period (Altermatt and Kriesi 1995). In addition, some other studies have found a slight positive correlation between the electoral success of radical-right parties and the level of anti-immigrant violence (Mudde 2005a; Eatwell 2000; Björgo and Witte 1993).

There is a minority that holds the opposite view, that is, that successful radical-right parties actually channel the frustrations of would-be perpetrators away from anti-immigrant violence (Minkenberg 2003; Wilensky 1998). The first cross-national study on the topic, by Ruud Koopmans, concludes that, "(i)n general, strong extreme right parties serve to limit the potential for extreme right and racist violence" (Koopmans 1996). This conclusion was confirmed in a more recent study based on EUMC data (Backes 2003).

The problem with all these studies is their lack of reliable cross-national data on anti-immigrant violence. Most countries do not have a central agency responsible for collecting such data. Sometimes the information is only registered at the local level, and local police officers by and large determine whether a crime is logged as racist or not. But even if countries do use a centralized and standardized way to register anti-immigrant violence, different countries use different definitions of anti-immigrant violence (Oakley 2005). For example, in some countries, such as Hungary, a crime becomes registered as "racist" only after the police or a judge has ruled it a racist crime; whereas, in other states, such as the United Kingdom, the victim can declare whether the crime is racist or not. Obviously, the huge differences in implementation will lead to substantial differences in levels of "racist violence."

Anti-Immigrant Attitudes

Another argument is that the electoral success of radical-right parties has "infected" the public discourse with anti-immigrant sentiments, which has in turn led to a "tolerance for intolerance" (Schain, Zolberg and Hossay 2002b). Because of a lack of reliable cross-time and cross-national data, there is little empirical evidence for this thesis.[10] A comparative study of seven Western European countries found that electoral success of radical-right parties does correlate with ethnic

10 An exception is Westin 2003.

prejudice within countries but has a fairly limited impact on other authoritarian values (Andersen and Evans 2004). Yet, other studies have found an increase in tolerance toward immigrants in countries with strong radical-right parties (Bjørklund and Andersen 2002).

Again, a simple causal relationship should hardly be expected. First of all, radical-right parties reflect existing prejudices as much as they create or unleash new ones. While data are sketchy for the pre-1990s period, various authors have noted long-standing anti-immigrant sentiments in Western Europe and North America that are virtually unrelated to the number of immigrants in the country (Messina 2007; Schain 2008). Moreover, while the success of radical-right parties might heighten the visibility of anti-immigrant discourse, it has often also given way to popular and state antinativist initiatives (see below).

It is crucial to note that there are many more people with anti-immigrant sentiments than there are anti-immigrant voters. As far as data are available, anti-immigration sentiments were already widespread before the rise of radical-right parties in the late 1980s (Messina 2007; Schain 2008). Even in countries with highly successful radical-right parties, such as Austria or Switzerland, the majority of people with anti-immigration sentiments vote for nonnativist parties across the political spectrum (Mudde, forthcoming).

In summary, the success of radical-right parties probably doesn't change many opinions. Rather, it brings existing anti-immigrant attitudes to the fore. Undoubtedly, this process is helped by the behavior of mainstream parties, which legitimize the radical-right discourse by borrowing (slightly watered-down versions of) it. Simply stated, radical-right parties do not make people nativist; they make people aware of their nativist sentiments and of the importance of these sentiments.

Also, while most Western European countries had fairly strong social and legal pressures against expressing nativist sentiment at least until the late 1990s, the success of radical-right parties helped undermine the strength and effectiveness of this "political correctness." That said, radical-right parties were, at best, one of several factors that undermined the proimmigration consensus. Among some of the other important factors are the (sometimes imagined) crises with asylum seekers, "scandals" involving immigrants (framed in nativist terms by the tabloid media) and, of course, 9/11 and the subsequent "War on Terror."

Antinativist Reactions

In the previous sections, we discussed how nativist actors have been able to influence political parties, policies and publics in order to bring them closer to their own position. This is only one side of the coin, however. The rise of nativism has also provoked antinativist reactions, both at the societal and state levels.

Societal Responses

The success of radical-right parties might heighten the visibility of anti-immigrant discourses, but it has also given way to popular anti-racism movements that put forward proimmigration discourses. The most famous examples are the British Anti-Nazi League, which was founded in reaction to the (moderate) electoral successes of the National Front in the 1970s, and the French SOS Racism, a direct reaction to the breakthrough of Le Pen's National Front in Dreux in 1983 (Lloyd 1998). In addition, in many countries, governments at all levels started to sponsor antiracist and pro-multicultural activities in response to radical-right electoral victories. As most important media were either state-controlled or close to mainstream political parties, this meant that the dominant discourse remained antinativist or, in many cases, changed from implicit antiracist to explicit antiracist. Even where tabloid media would advance nativist arguments—as in the case of Britain's *Sun* newspaper or Germany's *Bild* tabloid daily— they would equally strongly come out against nativist actors, ranging from political parties (e.g., the BNP and NPD) to neo-Nazi groups and violent racist youths (Mudde 2007).

Hence, some authors have argued that the successes of radical-right parties "provoke a backlash among those with liberal attitudes" (Andersen and Evans 2004; Kitschelt and McGann 1995). This seems an overstatement, however. While the antiracist backlash might have mobilized large groups of people at certain times, it is most likely that it rallied people who were already antiracist and pro-multicultural. Similarly, it is doubtful that antiracist mass mobilization has played a big role in hindering the electoral success of radical-right parties (Mudde 2007: 247).

There is one area in which antiracist groups have played an important role: law. Throughout Europe—in both its western and eastern parts—a broad coalition of nongovernmental organizations has pushed for stricter antidiscrimination laws and the better enforcement of these laws (see below). In the United States, groups such as the Southern Poverty Law Center (SPLC) have gone even further, taking nativist groups to civil court and, at times, even bankrupting them (Michael 2003). The most famous case is *Berhanu v. Metzger,* which led to the bankruptcy of Tom Metzger's infamous White Aryan Resistance group.

The situation in the United States is markedly different from that in Europe. Here, the so-called populist backlash against mass migration has often been met by a powerful proimmigration movement. Moreover, the movement brings together a broad variety of actors, ranging from some of the richest businessman in the country (e.g., former Republican presidential candidate Steve Forbes) to Latino groups from the poor inner cities (Freeman 2001). Some of the largest demonstrations in the United States in recent years have been those in favor of comprehensive immigration reform, that is, they have had a clear proimmigration message. For example, in March 2006, some 500,000 people demonstrated in favor of immigrant rights in Los Angeles, while smaller groups demonstrated all over the country (Associated Press 2006). And, in March 2010, tens of thousands of people participated in the "March for America" in Washington, DC, urging President Obama to make good on his promise for immigration reform (Preston 2010).

State Responses

At least initially, most countries have treated radical-right parties negatively. A broad variety of state responses to nativist actors have been implemented, from the ideological to the legal. As indicated above, many local and national governments have spent millions of dollars on antinativism/pro-multicultural initiatives in direct reaction to the rise of nativist actors. On various occasions, local and national authorities have hindered nativist groups from freely demonstrating and organizing (Van Donselaar 2005). In some cases, such as in Germany, they were merely enforcing existing laws that prohibited certain organizations from demonstrating and organizing; but, in other cases, the legal basis was at best shaky. For example, in the Netherlands, many radical-right demonstrations were forbidden because of the alleged threat of a confrontation with antifascists, who had announced a counter-demonstration (rather than simply keeping the two groups apart or banning the counterdemonstration).

The focus here will be on the most important *legal* state responses to nativist actors. These regions have fairly strong antidiscrimination laws in place, even though the implementation differs significantly between countries and even regions. In particular, Northwestern Europe and Canada have developed very elaborate antidiscrimination laws that are strictly enforced, some of which directly target nativist actors. The United States has a more permissive legal framework although the introduction of the concept of "hate crimes" and the easier procedures in civil laws (see above) provide state and nonstate actors with significant avenues for legal action. Central and Eastern Europe, as well as much of Southern Europe, have similar legal frameworks to the rest of the European Union; but, in many countries, the implementation of antidiscrimination legislation is lacking (Mudde 2005b).

This is not the place to discuss the ins and outs of antidiscrimination legislation. What is most important is the observation that antidiscrimination legislation has increasingly been used against nativist actors, ranging from individuals to organizations. The most famous case was in Belgium in 2004, when the VB was effectively convicted for incitement to racial hatred. While this didn't directly lead to a ban on the party, it did make it practically impossible for the party to continue. That said, the successor party, Flemish Interest, is almost an exact copy of its predecessor (Erk 2005).

Other countries have banned or withheld registration of political parties on the basis of a variety of laws, including antidiscrimination and explicitly antiextremist legislation. Some of the most notable cases include the National Democratic Party in Austria, the National Socialist Block in the Czech Republic and the Centre Party '86 in the Netherlands. Currently, Geert Wilders' PVV, the third-biggest party in the Netherlands, is facing trial for incitement to racial hatred. Another example is the recent legal case brought against the BNP by the Equality and Human Rights Commission in the United Kingdom, which forced the BNP to amend its constitution and accept non-whites as members (Hamilton 2009).

In most countries, since political parties enjoy special legal protections, they are more difficult to ban. A good example of this is Germany, which has failed to ban the radical-right National Democratic Party of Germany, despite the fact that it has the most suppressive legal system regarding "nondemocratic" actors. At the same time, Germany's Interior Ministry has banned more than 50 "extreme-right" groups in the last two decades. Similarly, in several Central and Eastern European countries, nonparty organizations have faced much more legal pressure than radical-right parties (Mudde 2005b).

Finally, nativist individuals have been taken to court by both state and nonstate actors. These individuals have included radical-right politicians who have gone on to lose their political rights. For example, in France, various leading members of the National Front have been convicted on the basis of antidiscrimination and historical-revisionism legislation (including Bruno Gollnisch, Bruno Mégret and even Jean-Marie Le Pen). In other countries, radical-right politicians have also been convicted for inciting racial hatred, but they have kept their political rights (e.g., FPÖ parliamentarian Susanne Winter in Austria and Centre Democrats leader Hans Janmaat in the Netherlands).

The effects of state actions against nativist groups or individuals go much further than the relatively few convictions, however. First of all, these actions have an impact on the public discourse. Second, they affect the organizational capabilities of nativist groups. In countries with governments that work to curtail nativist activities and where such activities also often have more social stigmatization, nativist groups can have a hard time attracting qualified members and leaders. Third, it leads to debates about how far liberal democracies can go in their struggle against their enemies without undermining their own liberal-democratic values.

The Economic Crisis, Immigration and Nativism

The association of crisis and extremism goes back more than a century. For example, in 1919, the famous German scholar Max Weber argued that charismatic leaders benefit from crisis situations (Weber 1987). But it was particularly the rise of Adolf Hitler and his National Socialist Party of Germany in the wake of the Wall Street crash of 1929 that has linked economic crisis and the rise of political extremism. In fact, most contemporary studies of the radical right link its emergence to some form of crisis—though not always (exclusively) economic—connected to some type of modernization process (cf., e.g., Berezin 2009; Kitschelt and McGann 1995).

Despite the strength of this received wisdom, the empirical evidence is very thin. For example, while the Great Depression did lead to the rise of extremist parties in Germany, it did not in many other countries in Europe (e.g., the Netherlands and the United Kingdom) or the United States. Similarly, neither the oil crisis of the 1970s nor the democratic transition in Central and Eastern Europe in the 1990s, which involved massive economic hardship for large portions of the people, led to the clear rise of extremist politics.

So far, the recent economic crisis seems to follow this pattern. If one looks at the national elections in European countries that have been conducted since the global recession really hit, in mid-2008, there is no clear trend toward the rise of "extremist" parties (i.e., radical-right parties). While some radical-right parties have gained some striking gains in recent elections—most notably the Hungarian Jobbik in 2010—others have lost, e.g., the VB in Belgium. And even though various radical-right parties have done well in national and local elections (e.g., Austria's FPÖ and France's FN), they are nowhere near their peaks in the 1990s.

The lack of a clear trend toward radical-right electoral success can also be seen in the results of the elections for the European Parliament in June 2009. Against the striking victory of Jobbik in Hungary (gaining 14.8 percent in its first European election) stands the complete implosion of the League of Polish Families (LPR) in Poland (which had gained 15.2 percent in 2004 but didn't even contest in 2009). Similarly, while much attention in Western Europe went to the large gains of the British National Party (+3.5 percent) and the Dutch PVV (+17 percent), few noted the clear losses of the Belgian VB (–3.4 percent) and French FN (–3.5 percent) (cf., among many others, Waterfield, Samuel and Squires 2009). Moreover, in most European countries, radical-right parties did not contest the European elections or they didn't make it into the European Parliament (e.g., in the Czech Republic, Germany, Finland, Ireland, Latvia, Luxembourg, Spain and Sweden).

Although it is too early to discern clear trends, data from the Organisation for Economic Co-operation and Development (OECD) show that immigration to Europe and North America has actually decreased since the beginning of the economic crisis (Barta and Hannon 2009). Some anecdotal evidence even indicates that return migration from the United States has increased in recent years (Papademetriou and Terrazas 2009). At the same time, immigration has become a less salient issue for Europeans. Whereas 15 percent of Europeans considered immigration to be one of the two most important issues facing their country in September 2007, this had dropped to 9 percent by August 2008 (European Commission 2010b). This has stabilized since; in October/November 2009, 9 percent was still the EU average, though with some striking national variations (European Commission 2010c). Most importantly, in the United Kingdom, the figure was 29 percent, which served as a reflection and a reason for the sharply increased salience of immigration in the campaign preceding the May 2010 parliamentary elections.

The situation in the United Kingdom seems to be exceptional, however. In most European countries, the debate is fully focused on the dire economic situation and the worrying increase in unemployment, and immigration plays only a minor role. In the United States, the political debate in 2010 was dominated by health care and the country's financial system and rising debt load. However, with health-care reform by and large concluded and President Obama's promise to propose comprehensive immigration reform, immigration will undoubtedly move to the center of the political debate in the coming months. It remains to be seen how immigration reform will impact the further development of the Tea Party movement although it seems plausible that it could further strengthen already clearly present nativist tendencies in the United States.

Conclusion

As has been demonstrated, many of the assumptions about the relationship between immigration and nativism are based upon feeble empirical evidence. In many cases, academic research is inconclusive, not least because of a lack of reliable cross-national data. Hence, it is absolutely vital that more cross-national data projects be created and supported over longer periods of time. Recent developments, such as the EUMC and the European Social Survey, are important steps forward. Nevertheless, it is critical that policymakers base their assumptions about policy and law on what we do know. Policy-relevant findings from the literature include:

The most extreme reactions to migration and migrants are fomented by the radical or extreme right rather than the left, though their popularity is highly circumscribed across North America, Western Europe and Central and Eastern Europe.

The most important extremist reaction to immigration comes from radical-right parties in Western Europe. However, radical-right parties are successful in only a minority of European countries and not at all in North America. In the United States, the most important nativist actors are nonparty organizations that are at times well connected to mainstream media and politicians. In addition, extreme-right violence against immigrants is a significant problem in some countries, including Germany and Russia. Research shows that this violence is not directly related to radical-right parties; when the perpetrators are active within political organizations, these are small neo-Nazi groups and skinhead gangs.

Migration patterns do not drive radical-right voting, although immigration as a political issue has contributed to their electoral success.
There is no straightforward relationship between immigration patterns and radical-right voting. Immigration has to be *translated* into a political issue, which involves many different steps. And while immigration is certainly not the single issue of the radical right, it clearly plays an important role in their propaganda and electoral success.

There is no clear relationship—either way—between rising numbers of immigrants and extremist incidents.
Logically, with the growth of the immigrant population, anti-immigrant crimes have increased, too. However, there is no clear relationship between the electoral strength of a radical-right party in a country and its level of anti-immigrant violence. Since the EUMC started to collect reliable cross-national data several years ago, future research might find more conclusive evidence on the exact relationship between the two factors.

Have the largely negative public attitudes toward immigrants led to increasing support for radical-right parties? Is globalization rather than immigration a better explanatory variable for support for right-wing extremists?
Mass attitudes toward immigration and immigrants have always been relatively negative, in the sense that, at the very least, a large mi-

nority in every country will hold nativist attitudes. While radical-right groups have clearly profited from this, they tap into only a minority of the nativist population.

The radical right frames the immigration debate consistently across countries focusing on two main themes: a cultural threat (recently amalgamated as a cultural-religious threat) and a security threat (recently amalgamated as a criminal-terrorist threat). Secondary themes include economic competition and an antielite/antipolitics narrative.

Although individual parties will emphasize specific points more than others in their discourse, all share a roughly similar set of themes. The key theme is cultural: Immigrants are considered a threat to the cultural homogeneity of the nation because of their alleged inability or unwillingness to assimilate. In recent years, the cultural has been accompanied by a religious theme, according to which (radical) Islam is seen as a threat to liberal-democratic values. All parties also share a strong security theme, which links immigration to (petty) crime and, increasingly, terrorism. Two secondary themes are the economic one (immigration is seen as a threat to the wealth of welfare of the nation) and the political one (a corrupt elite is accused of using immigration for its own financial and political gains). Of all these themes, the security, religious and economic ones have been most adopted by mainstream actors, though often in watered-down versions.

States have tightened immigration policies, but the radical right is only one causal factor; furthermore, counterforces, particularly state-sponsored anti-discrimination laws, have blunted the rise of more extremist parties.

There is no doubt that European countries have tightened their immigration policies in recent decades. However, the electoral pressure of radical-right parties has been only one of many important factors behind this. In many cases, the most important policies were implemented well before the radical right became successful. Moreover, European integration complicates the distinction between domestic and international factors. There is an increasing pressure on developing an EU-wide migration policy; while this has yet to be implemented, national policies have already started to converge significantly.

Still, not everything has gone the radical right's way. In various countries, antiracist and proimmigrant groups have sprung up in direct reaction to radical-right success, pushing through an alternative, proimmigration discourse. These initiatives have often been subsidized and expanded by local and national governments. Finally, many states have used antidiscrimination legislation, including the banning of political parties, to hinder the development of the radical right.

There is a complex relationship between immigration and extremism where some parties have profited, especially in Western Europe, though many countries do not have a relevant party—and not at all in Central and Eastern Europe.

In conclusion, the relationship between immigration and extremism is unclear and complex. Increased levels of immigration have given rise to nativist reactions in Europe and North America but not yet in Central and Eastern Europe. While immigration has helped some radical-right parties obtain moderate electoral success, most European and North American countries do not have a politically influential nativist movement. Moreover, while nativist sentiments and organizations have played a role in the tightening of immigration laws, particularly those regarding asylum, they have lost the big battle as both Western Europe and North America are increasingly true multicultural societies.

Works Cited

Akkerman, Tjitske. Anti-Immigration Parties and the Defense of Liberal Values: The Exceptional Case of the List Pim Fortuyn. *Journal of Political Ideologies* (10) 3: 337–354, 2005.

Akkerman, Tjitske, and Anniken Hagelund. 'Women and Children First!' Anti-Immigration Parties and Gender in Norway and the Netherlands. *Patterns of Prejudice* (41) 2: 197–214, 2007.

Altermatt, Urs, and Hanspeter Kriesi. *Rechtsextremismus in der Schweiz. Organisationen und Radikalisierung in den 1980er und 1990er Jahren.* Zurich: Verlag Neue Zürcher Zeitung, 1995.

Álvarez-Rivera, Manuel. Election Resources on the Internet: Western Europe. 2010 (accessed July 5, 2010).

Andersen, Robert, and Jocelyn A.J. Evans. Social-Political Context and Authoritarian Attitudes: Evidence from Seven European Countries. Working Paper No. 104, CREST, Glasgow, 2004.

Anti-Defamation League. Pat Buchanan: Unrepentant Bigot. New York: ADL, 2009. www.adl.org/special_reports/Patrick_Buchanan2/extremists.asp (accessed July 5, 2010)

Anti-Defamation League. The Skinhead International: A Worldwide Survey of Neo-Nazi Skinheads. New York: ADL, 1995.

Associated Press. Immigration Issue Draws Thousands Into the Streets. March 26, 2006.

Backes, Uwe. Extremismus und politisch motivierte Gewalt. In *Demokratien des 21. Jahrhunderts im Vergleich: Historische Zugänge, Gegenwartsprobleme, Reformperspektiven*, edited by Eckhard Jesse and Roland Sturm. Opladen: Leske & Budrich, 2003: 341–367.

Barta, Patrick, and Paul Hannon. Economic Crisis Curbs Migration of Workers. *Wall Street Journal* July 1, 2009. http://online.wsj.com/article/SB124636924020073241.html (accessed July 5, 2010).

Bawer, Bruce. *While Europe Slept: How Radical Islam is Destroying the West from Within.* New York: Anchor, 2006.

Bawer, Bruce. *Surrender: Appeasing Islam, Sacrificing Freedom.* New York: Doubleday, 2009.

BBC News. BNP Leader Defends Policy on Race. April 23, 2009. 2009a. http://news.bbc.co.uk/2/hi/uk/politics/8011878.stm (accessed July 5, 2010).

BBC News. Swiss Voters Back Ban on Minarets. November 29, 2009. 2009b. http://news.bbc.co.uk/2/hi/8385069.stm (accessed July 5, 2010).

Berezin, Mabel. *Illiberal Politics in Neoliberal Times: Cultures, Security, and Populism in a New Europe.* New York: Cambridge University Press, 2009.

Betz, Hans-Georg. *Radical Right-Wing Populism in Western Europe.* Basingstoke: Macmillan, 1994.

Björgo, Tore, and Rob Witte. Introduction. In *Racist Violence in Europe,* edited by Tore Björgo and Rob Witte. New York: St. Martin's, 1993. 1–16.

Bjørklund, Tor, and Jørgen Goul Andersen. Anti-immigration Parties in Denmark and Norway: The Progress Parties and the Danish People's Party. In *Shadows over Europe: The Development and Impact of the Extreme Right in Western Europe,* edited by Martin Schain, Aristide Zolberg and Patrick Hossay. New York: Palgrave, 2002. 107–136.

Bobbio, Norberto. Rechts und Links. Zum Sinn einer politischen Unterscheidung. *Blätter für deutsche und internationale Politik* (39) 5: 543–549, 1994.

Buchanan, Patrick J. *State of Emergency: The Third World Invasion and Conquest of America.* New York: Thomas Dunne, 2006.

Building Democracy Intiative. Nativism in the House: A Report on the House Immigration Reform Caucus. Chicago: Center for New Community, 2007.

Chebel d'Appollonia, Ariane, and Simon Reich (eds.). *Immigration, Integration, and Security: America and Europe in Comparative Perspective.* Pittsburgh, Penn.: University of Pittsburgh Press, 2008.

Cheles, Luciano, Ronnie Ferguson and Michalina Vaughan (eds.). *Neo-Fascism in Europe.* London: Longman, 1991.

CNN. Denmark Passes Tough Migrant Laws. May 31, 2002. http://archives.cnn.com/2002/WORLD/europe/05/31/denmark.immigration (accessed July 5, 2010).

Cohen, Patricia. In Books, a Clash of Europe and Islam. *New York Times* February 8, 2007. www.nytimes.com/2007/02/08/books/08circ.html (accessed July 5, 2010).

Colombo, Asher, and Giuseppe Sciortino. The Bossi-Fini Law: Explicit Fanticism, Implicit Moderation, and Poisoned Fruits. In *Italian Politics: The Second Berlusconi Government*, edited by Jean Blondel and Paolo Segatti. New York: Berghahn, 2003: 162–179.

Decker, Frank. *Der neue Rechtspopulismus*. Opladen: Leske & Budrich, 2004.

De Decker, Pascal, Christian Kesteloot, Filip De Maesschalck and Jan Vranken. Revitalizing the City in an Anti-Urban Context: Extreme Right and the Rise of Urban Policies in Flanders, Belgium. *International Journal of Urban and Regional Research* (29) 1: 152–171, 2005.

Department of Homeland Security, Office of Immigration Statistics. *Estimates of the Unauthorized Immigrant Population Residing in the United States: January 2009*. Washington, DC: DHS Office of Immigration Statistics, 2010. www.dhs.gov/xlibrary/assets/statistics/publications/ois_ill_pe_2009.pdf (accessed July 5, 2010).

"Wilders bang voor 'tsunami van islamisering.'" *De Volkskrant* October 6, 2006. www.volkskrant.nl/binnenland/article356420.ece/Wilders_bang_voor_tsunami_van_islamisering (accessed July 5, 2010).

Dolezal, Martin, Marc Helbling and Swen Hutter. Debating Islam in Austria, Germany and Switzerland: Ethnic Citizenship, Church-State Relations and Right-Wing Populism. *West European Politics* (33) 2: 171–190, 2010.

Dülmer, Hermann, and Markus Klein. Extreme Right-wing Voting in Germany in a Multilevel Perspective: A Rejoinder to Lubbers and Scheepers. *European Journal of Political Research* (44) 2: 243–263, 2005.

Eatwell, Roger. The Extreme Right and British Exceptionalism: The Primacy of Politics. In *The Politics of the Extreme Right: From the Margins to the Mainstream*, edited by Paul Hainsworth. London: Pinter, 2000: 172–192.

Elbers, Frank, and Meindert Fennema. *Racistische partijen in West-Europa. Tussen nationale traditie en Europese samenwerking.* Leiden, Netherlands: Stichting Burgerschapskunde, 1993.

Erk, Jan. From Vlaams Blok to Vlaams Belang: Belgian Far-Right Renames Itself. *West European Politics* (28) 3: 493–502, 2005.

European Commission. Freedom, security and justice. Brussels, 2010. 2010a. http://ec.europa.eu/justice_home/fsj/immigration/fsj_immigration_intro_en.htm (accessed July 5, 2010).

European Commission. *Standard Eurobarometer 70*, June 2010. 2010b. http://ec.europa.eu/public_opinion/archives/eb/eb70/eb70_full_en.pdf.

European Commission. *Eurobaromètre Standard 72*, February 2010. 2010c. http://ec.europa.eu/public_opinion/archives/eb/eb72/eb72_vol1_fr.pdf.

European Commission. Common Immigration Policy. Press release, June 17, 2008. http://europa.eu/rapid/pressReleasesAction.do?reference=MEMO/08/402&format=HTML&aged=0&language=EN&guiLanguage=de (accessed July 5, 2010).

European Monitoring Centre on Racism and Xenophobia. *Muslims in the European Union: Discrimination and Islamophobia.* Vienna: European Monitoring Centre on Racism and Xenophobia, 2006.

Faist, Thomas, and Andreas Ette (eds.). *The Europeanization of National Policies and Politics of Immigration: Between Autonomy and the European Union.* New York: Palgrave, 2007.

Fallend, Franz. Are Right-Wing Populism and Government Participation Incompatible? The Case of the Freedom Party of Austria. *Representation* (40) 2: 115–130, 2004.

Fennema, Meindert. Some Conceptual Issues and Problems in the Comparison of Anti-immigrant Parties in Western Europe. *Party Politics* (3) 4: 473–492, 1997.

Freeman, Gary P. Client Politics or Populism? Immigration Reform in the United States. In *Controlling a New Migration World*, edited by Virginie Guiraudon and Christian Joppke. London: Routledge, 2001: 65–95.

Gächter, August. Migrationspolitik in Österreich seit 1945. Working Paper No. 12, Migration und soziale Mobilität, 2008.

Gibson, Rachel. *The Growth of Anti-Immigrant Parties in Western Europe.* Ceredigian: Edwin Mellen, 2002.

Givens, Terri, and Adam Luedtke. European Immigration Policies in Comparative Perspective: Issue Salience, Partisanship and Immigrant Rights. *Comparative European Politics* (3) 1: 1–22, 2005.

Givens, Terri, and Adam Luedtke. The Politics of European Union Immigration Policy: Institutions, Salience, and Harmonization. *The Policy Studies Journal* (32) 1: 145–165, 2004.

Golder, Matt. Explaining Variations in the Success of Extreme Right Parties in Western Europe. *Comparative Political Studies* (36) 4: 432–466, 2003.

Hainsworth, Paul. *The Extreme Right in Western Europe.* London: Routledge, 2008.

Hamilton, Fiona. British National Party Forced to Admit Non-Whites. *The Times* September 4, 2009. www.timesonline.co.uk/tol/news/politics/article6820847.ece (accessed July 5, 2010).

Hanley, Lisa M., Blair A. Ruble and Allison M. Garland (eds). *Immigration and Integration in Urban Communities: Renegotiating the City.* Baltimore: Johns Hopkins University Press, 2008.

Heinisch, Reinhard. Success in Opposition – Failure in Government: Explaining the Performance of Right-Wing Populist Parties in Public Office. *West European Politics* (26) 3: 91–130, 2003.

Herm, Ann. Recent Migration Trends: Citizens of EU-27 Member States Become Ever More Mobile While EU Remains Attractive to Non-EU Citizens. *Eurostat* 98, 2008.

Higham, John. *Strangers in the Land: Patterns of American Nativism, 1860–1925.* New Brunswick: Rutgers University Press, 1955.

Hooper, John, Giles Tremlett and John Henley. Immigration the key as left faces loss of power. *The Guardian* May 16, 2002.

Ho-Sang, Dan. *Racial Propositions: Genteel Apartheid in Postwar California.* Berkeley: University of California Press, forthcoming 2010.

House Immigration Reform Caucus. 2010a. www.house.gov/bilbray/irc (accessed July 5, 2010).

House Immigration Reform Caucus. Membership. 2010b. www.house.gov/bilbray/irc/members.shtml (accessed July 5, 2010).

Immigration Watch Canada. Who are we? Why have we organized? www.immigrationwatchcanada.org/ (accessed July 5, 2010).

James, Randy. Sheriff Joe Arpaio. *Time* October 13, 2009. www.time.com/time/nation/article/0,8599,1929920,00.html (accessed July 5, 2010).

Jesuit, David, and Vincent Mahler. Immigration, Economic Wellbeing and Support for Extreme-Right Parties in Western European Regions. Paper presented at the conference "Immigration in a Cross-National Context: What are the Implications for Europe?" Bourlingster, Luxembourg, June 20–22, 2004.

Kitschelt, Herbert, and Anthony McGann. *The Radical Right in Western Europe. A Comparative Analysis.* Ann Arbor: University of Michigan Press, 1995.

Knigge, Pia. The Electoral Correlates of Right-wing Extremism in Western Europe. *European Journal of Political Research* (34) 2: 249–279, 1998.

Koopmans, Ruud. Explaining the Rise of Racist and Extreme-Right Violence in Western Europe: Grievances or Opportunities. *European Journal of Political Research* (30) 2: 185–216, 1996.

Kriesi, Hanspeter. Bewegungen auf der Linken, Bewegungen auf der Rechten: Die Mobilisierung von zwei neuen Typen von sozialen Bewegungen in ihrem politischen Kontext. *Swiss Political Science Review* (1) 1: 9–52, 1995.

Kuzmanic, Tonci A. *Hate-Speech in Slovenia: Slovenian Racism, Sexism and Chauvinism.* Ljubljana: Open Society Institute-Slovenia, 1999.

Kymlicka, Will. *The Current State of Multiculturalism in Canada and Research Themes on Canadian Multiculturalism 2008–2010.* Ottawa: Minister of Public Works and Government Services Canada, 2010.

Lavanex, Sandra. *Safe Third Countries. Extending EU Asylum and Immigration Policies to Central and Eastern Europe.* Budapest: Central European University Press, 1999.

Lewis, Aidan. Italian Migration Policy Draws Fire. *BBC News* March 7, 2009. http://news.bbc.co.uk/2/hi/europe/7880215.stm.

Lipset, Seymour Martin. The Radical Right: A Problem for American Democracy. *British Journal of Sociology* (6) 2: 176–209, 1955.

Lloyd, Cathie. Antiracist Mobilization in France and Britain in the 1970s and 1980s. In *Scapegoats and Social Actors: The Exclusion and Integraion of Minorities in Western and Eastern Europe*, edited by Danièle Joly. Basingstoke, UK: Macmillan, 1998: 155–172.

Lubbers, Marcel. *Exclusionistic Electorates: Extreme Right-Wing Voting in Western Europe*. Ph.D. diss., Radboud University Nijmegen, 2001.

Marcus, Jonathan. Exorcising Europe's Demons: A Far-right Resurgence? *The Washington Quarterly* (23) 4: 31–40, 2000.

Massa, Justin, and Cecelia Abundis. The New Battleground: Anti-Immigrant Ordinances Attack Housing Rights. *Building Democracy Monthly* February 2007.

Messina, Anthony W. *The Logics and Politics of Post-WWII Migration to Western Europe*. Cambridge: Cambridge University Press, 2007.

Metro. "Multicultureel betekent multicriminee." June 15, 2005.

Michael, George. *Confronting Right-Wing Extremism and Terrorism in the USA*. London: Routledge, 2003.

Minkenberg, Michael. The West European Radical Right as a Collective Actor: Modeling the Impact of Cultural and Structural Variables on Party Formation and Movement Mobilization. *Comparative European Politics* (1) 2: 149–170, 2003.

Minkenberg, Michael. The Radical Right in Public Office: Agenda-Setting and Policy Effects. *West European Politics* (24) 4: 1–21, 2001.

Mudde, Cas. The Populist Radical Right: A Pathological Normalcy. *West European Politics*. Forthcoming.

Mudde, Cas. *Populist Radical Right Parties in Europe*. Cambridge: Cambridge University Press, 2007.

Mudde, Cas (ed.). *Racist Extremism in Central and Eastern Europe*. London: Routledge, 2005a.

Mudde, Cas. Racist Extremism in Central and Eastern Europe. *East European Politics and Societies* (19) 2: 161–184, 2005b.

Mudde, Cas. *The Ideology of the Extreme Right*. Manchester: Manchester University Press, 2000.

Mudde, Cas. The Single-Issue Party Thesis: Extreme Right Parties and the Immigration Issue. *West European Politics* (22) 3: 182–197, 1999.

Oakley, Robin. *Policing Racist Crime and Violence: A Comparative Analysis.* Vienna: EUMC, 2005.

Papademetriou, Demetrios G., and Aaron Terrazas. *Immigrants and the Current Economic Crisis: Research Evidence, Policy Challenges, and Implications.* Washington, DC: MPI, 2009. www.migration policy.org/pubs/lmi_recessionJan09.pdf.

Pilkington, Hilary, Al'bina Garifzianova, and Elena Omel'chenko. *Russia's Skinheads.* London: Routledge, 2010.

Pollard, Stephen. The Appeasers. *The New York Times* July 24, 2009. www.nytimes.com/2009/07/26/books/review/Pollard-t.html.

Preston, Julia. At Rally, Call for Urgency on Immigration Reform. *The New York Times* March 22, 2010. www.nytimes.com/2010/03/22/us/politics/22immig.html.

Ramet, Sabrina P. (ed.). *The Radical Right in Central and Eastern Europe since 1989.* University Park: Pennsylvania University Press, 1999.

Ridgley, Jennifer. Cities of Refuge: Immigration Enforcement, Police, and the Insurgent Genealogies of Citizenship in U.S. Sanctuary Cities. *Urban Geography* (29) 1: 53–77, 2008.

Rudolph, Christopher. *National Security and Immigration: Policy Development in the United States and Western Europe since 1945.* Palo Alto, Calif.: Stanford University Press, 2006.

Rydgren, Jens. Meso-level Reasons for Racism and Xenophobia: Some Converging and Diverging Effects of Radical Right Populism in France and Sweden. *European Journal of Social Theory* (6) 1: 45–68, 2003.

Schain, Martin. *The Politics of Immigration in France. Britain and the United States: A Comparative Study.* New York: Palgrave, 2008.

Schain, Martin, Aristide Zolberg and Patrick Hossay (eds.). *Shadows over Europe: The Development and Impact of the Extreme Right in Western Europe.* New York: Palgrave, 2002a.

Schain, Martin, Aristide Zolberg and Patrick Hossay (eds.). The Development of Radical Right Parties in Western Europe. In *Shadows* over Europe: The Development and Impact of the Extreme Right in Western Europe, edited by Martin Schain, Aristide Zolberg and Patrick Hossay. New York: Palgrave, 2002b: 3–17.

Southern Poverty Law Center. The Nativist Lobby: Three Faces of Intolerance. Montgomery, AL: SPLC, 2009.

Southern Poverty Law Center. Communing with the Council: When a race hate scandal engulfed a right-wing group in 1998, politicians ran for cover. They didn't stay away long. Montgomery, AL: SPLC, 2004. www.splcenter.org/get-informed/intelligence-report/browse-all-issues/2004/fall/communing-with-the-council (accessed July 5, 2010).

Swank, Duane, and Hans-Georg Betz. Globalization, the Welfare State and Right-wing Populism in Western Europe. Socio-Economic Review (1) 2: 215–245, 2003.

Tichenor, Dan. Dividing Lines: The Politics of Immigration Control in America. Princeton, NJ: Princeton University Press, 2002.

Trplan, Tomas. Slovenia. In Racist Extremism in Central and Eastern Europe, edited by Cas Mudde. London: Routledge, 2005: 225–246.

United Nations High Commissioner for Refugees (UNHCR). Freedom in the World 2009 – Denmark. www.unhcr.org/refworld/docid/4a6452bfc.html (accessed July 5, 2010).

Van der Brug, Wouter, Meindert Fennema and Jean Tillie. Why Some Anti-immigrant Parties Fail and Others Succeed: A Two-step Model of Aggregate Electoral Support. Comparative Political Studies (38) 5: 537–573, 2005.

Van Donselaar, Jaap. De staat paraat? De bestrijding van extreem-rechts in West-Europa. Amsterdam: Babylon-De Geus, 2005.

Von Beyme, Klaus. Right-Wing Extremism in Post-War Europe. West European Politics (11) 2: 1–18, 1988.

Waterfield, Bruno, Henry Samuel and Nick Squires. European Elections 2009: Far-Right and Fringe Parties Make Gains across Europe Amid Low Turnout. Daily Telegraph June 8, 2009.

Weber, Max. Politik als Beruf. Berlin: Duncker & Humblot, 8th edition, 1987.

Wendt, Christopher. Toward a Majoritarian Model for Western Europe. Paper presented at the 99th annual APSA meeting, Philadelphia, August 28–31, 2003.

Westin, Charles. Racism and the Political Right: European Perspectives. In *Right-Wing Extremism in the Twenty-First Century*, edited by Peter H. Merkl and Leonard Weinberg. London: Frank Cass, 2003: 97–125.

Wilensky, Harold L. Migration and Politics: Explaining Variation among Rich Democracies in Recent Nativist Protest. Working Paper No. 87, Berkeley, Institute of Industrial Relations, 1998.

Ya'Or, Bat. *Eurabia: The Euro-Arab Axis*. Madison, NJ: Fairleigh Dickinson University Press, 2005.

Zaslove, Andrej. Closing the Door? The Ideology and Impact of Radical Right Populism on Immigration Policy in Austria and Italy. *Journal of Political Ideologies* (9) 1: 99–118. 2004.

Investing in School and Labor Market Preparedness: A Silver Lining to the Economic Crisis?

Maurice Crul

Introduction

In all the doom and gloom of the economic crisis, an unexpected silver lining has emerged for higher education trends across Europe and the United States. There are increasing media reports of record new student enrollments in colleges and universities (Bolwijn 2009; Jaschik 2009).

Some universities and colleges report an enormous enrollment increase for first-year students. At the Amsterdam Academy for Higher Vocational Education (HvA), introductory-week attendance has increased by 88 percent over the last three years. In the Netherlands, the increase in first-year enrollment for this year alone is 18 percent. At the University of Amsterdam, record enrollment created a shortage of classrooms and facilities (Weeda 2009; Kamran 2009).

Suddenly, despite a decade of lagging progress, the Lisbon targets[1] for higher education in EU countries are coming within reach almost effortlessly. To date, this important but unexpected outcome of the economic crisis has received little attention.

---

1 In 2000, the heads of state and government of the EU Member States endorsed common objectives for education and training in Europe for the subsequent decade, known as the Lisbon Objectives. EU ministers of education agreed to: (a) improve the quality and effectiveness of EU education and training systems; (b) ensure that education and training systems are accessible to all residents; and (c) open up education and training systems to the wider world. They set 2010 as a deadline for realizing these objectives. Cf. European Commission, Directorate General for Education and Culture 2009.

In Europe, the protracted labor market stagnation of the 1980s taught policymakers that keeping individuals active in education or work is essential to avoiding a "lost generation" of unproductive or inactive workers. But the tendency to pursue lifelong educational opportunities is more common among highly educated than among less-educated workers. The well-educated usually have sufficient savings to fund tuition and forego labor income while studying. Similar to the 1980s, the real challenge for policymakers is to promote continuing education and job training among the less-educated and often poorer strata of society.

Governments across the countries that belong to the Organisation for Economic Co-operation and Development (OECD) reacted to the recent economic crisis by enacting unprecedented fiscal stimulus measures to spur growth. Largely reflecting the desires of the general population, education figured high on the list of stimulus spending priorities. But where higher education is financed by local governments that are unable to fund countercyclical spending—one recent example is the University of California system in the United States[2]— higher education has suffered. Moreover, governments are starting to withdraw stimulus spending, and sovereign debt crises loom large in several European countries, thus limiting the scope for future spending.

The crisis has given governments a unique opportunity to rapidly expand higher education with a focus on the less fortunate. But the outcomes must be meaningful. Making the less fortunate and the next generation of workers competitive in the postrecession labor market is the most pressing challenge currently facing the education systems in the United States and Europe.

---

2   California cut funding for the University of California (UC) system by hundreds of millions of dollars in its 2008–2009 budget and again in 2009–2010. The UC system regents responded with a number of cost-saving measures but agreed in November 2009 to raise tuition 32 percent starting in the summer of 2010, prompting student protests across UC campuses.

The Tools Needed to Boost Competitiveness

Two recent research projects—the Europe-wide Integration of the European Second Generation (TIES) project and the transatlantic Children of Immigrants in School (CIS) project—both came to the same conclusion: Inclusion of the most vulnerable socioeconomic groups in Europe depends on how prepared the children of immigrants are for school and the labor market.[3]

Evidence shows that the labor market prospects of immigrant children improve dramatically with prolonged schooling and on-the-job training. Children who spend more hours in school are better prepared for high-stakes testing, and children who are given an opportunity to take a longer route to postsecondary education are more likely to succeed (Crul et al., forthcoming 2010). Similarly, additional on-the-job experience—for instance, through internships—prepares students to make a smooth transition to the labor market (ibid.).

These two parallel observations—people's willingness to (re)enter higher education during an economic crisis and the documented need for extra time in school among second-generation youth—suggest that the economic crisis could become an advantage for the children of immigrants with the right policies. The crisis has granted second-generation youth extra time by delaying their entrance into the labor force. It is now up to governments to use the extra time to appropriately prepare these youth to meet future labor market demands.

Who Are the Most Vulnerable Groups in Europe?

The recent global recession is different than earlier economic crises because it affects people in low-level service jobs on temporary contracts as well as people in high-skilled managerial jobs. We highlight both groups below.

3 For further information on the research projects, cf. www.tiesproject.eu/.

At-Risk Youth

The European Union has defined early school leavers (students who have left school with a lower-secondary school diploma at most) as the group most at risk in entering the labor market. A comparable group in US statistics is those without a high school diploma. To get an idea of the early-school-leaving trends among children of immigrants across Europe, we present findings for second-generation youth in Austria, Belgium, France, Germany, the Netherlands, Switzerland and Sweden. The analysis is based on the results of a unique Europe-wide survey, TIES, coordinated by the Institute for Migration and Ethnic Studies at the University of Amsterdam (see Appendix for more details on TIES). The analysis focuses on second-generation Turks between the ages of 18 and 35, as this population allows for the greatest comparison across European countries.

The data that stands out (as shown in Table 1) is that almost one-third of all second-generation Turks in Germany and the Netherlands

Table 1: Second-generation Turks: early school leavers (ESL), 2007–2008

	Share of ESL among second-generation Turks *not* in education (total N)	Share of ESL among all second-generation Turkish respondents (total N)	Share of ESL among all respondents with native-born parents (total N)
Austria	33.5 (334)	24.5 (458)	10.3 (484)
Belgium	10.0 (468)	7.8 (602)	3.4 (553)
France	24.6 (284)	14.2 (500)	2.0 (351)
Germany	34.2 (438)	29.7 (505)	13.5 (503)
Netherlands	48.4 (304)	29.4 (500)	10.0 (512)
Sweden	11.4 (201)	9.2 (251)	3.6 (250)
Switzerland	17.3 (277)	10.3 (468)	4.5 (467)

All data in percent

Notes: "Early school leavers" includes youth with a lower-secondary diploma or less. In Belgium, we took the first cycle as the end of lower-secondary school.

Source: TIES Survey 2007–2008

were early school leavers, as were about one-quarter in Austria. Second-generation Turks in France, Switzerland, Sweden and Belgium showed lower rates of early school abandonment.

When we examine how early school leavers performed in the labor market in the countries with the highest rates of early school abandonment, several trends emerge:

- Even before the crises, only half of the early school leavers in the *Netherlands* were working. About a quarter were unemployed and looking for a job, while another quarter were unemployed and not looking for a job (because they were looking after children or their family). The working population was mostly employed in the private sector, especially in wholesale, transport and food businesses, all sectors severely hit by the crises. Only half had a permanent contract.
- In *Germany,* we see the same pattern as in the Netherlands, with only half of the early school leavers in a paid job before the economic crisis. One in five was unemployed and looking for a job. More than 90 percent of those who were working were employed in the private sector, and two-thirds had a permanent contract.
- Early school leavers in *Austria* resemble their peers in Germany. A slightly higher share were employed in the public sector (about one in five), and they were more likely to have permanent contracts than second-generation Turks in Germany or the Netherlands.

The TIES survey also asked early school leavers their reasons for abandoning their studies. The attraction of the labor market was an important reason for one-quarter to one-third of the population (see Table 2). Presumably, youth who left school early to work can be easily attracted back to education when they lose their jobs, a likely scenario as many reported having temporary contracts. However, large shares of second-generation Turks in Austria (42.9 percent) and Germany (52.0 percent) reported no interest in further studies because they did not like school. It will be more difficult to convince this group to return to school. Thus, on-the-job training is likely a more suitable option for them. To target mothers of young children, courses organized in their children's school can provide an instrument to draw them back to education.

Table 2: Second-generation Turks: reasons for early school abandonment, 2007–2008

	Austria	Netherlands	Germany
Satisfied with study	18.0	14.4	12.8
Don't like to go to school anymore	42.9	19.7	52.0
Work	21.4	34.1	24.3
Marriage (women only)	5.3	22.6	14.7

All data in percent

Note: Respondents were permitted to select more than one response.

Source: TIES Survey 2007–2008

Higher Education Students of Immigrant Descent: A New At-Risk Group?

Many second-generation Turks in Europe leave school early, but a growing number are succeeding in school as well: One-quarter (852) of the 3,275 respondents we interviewed in seven European countries made it into higher education.[4] Entering higher education represents an enormous advantage for the second generation. This is especially true if we compare daughters with their mothers. A considerable group of second-generation Turkish women in our study entered higher education while their mothers were practically illiterate.

Policymakers tend to focus on the most problematic groups within immigrant communities. However, the group of successful students is growing. In many countries, the number of immigrant students entering higher education has doubled in the last 10 years. This is

4 This includes students who are studying for, or already have, a bachelor's or master's diploma.

354

partly the result of the second generation's reaching the age to enter higher education and partly the result of the better performance of the second generation compared to the first and 1.5 generations. In normal economic times, policymakers have few motivations to focus on successful second-generation Turks. But during a recession, this upwardly mobile population may face unique challenges.

As described in the introduction, many young people have coped with the economic crisis by delaying their entrance into the labor market and continuing their studies. Others who lost their jobs chose to return to school. Are second-generation Turks in Europe behaving similarly? The data suggest that this is not the case. Largely due to their less advantageous financial situation, lower levels of enrollment in higher education and higher dropout levels, second-generation Turks were less likely than natives to return to school upon losing their jobs during the recession. This finding, examined below in more detail, has obvious implications for their long-term socioeconomic mobility.

Financial Situation

Among second-generation Turks who were enrolled in higher education in 2007–2008, the majority had a student job to support themselves (and, in some cases, to support their families). But especially temporary part-time jobs (e.g., telemarketing and working in retail as a shop assistant) suffered from the economic crisis (Sharp 2008; Nutting 2009; Statistics Netherlands 2010). Without their own income, many students depend on their low-income families. As a result, more students will have to apply for study loans to study. Building debt in a period of economic recession is a risky investment. It will also put more pressure on current students to finish their studies quickly or to quit if they experience delays.

Enrollment in Higher Education

In some European countries (e.g., the Netherlands), the educational system is designed so that secondary students on an academic track can automatically attend an institution of higher education, usually a "higher school" or university; nearly all such students continue on to higher education. Elsewhere (e.g., Belgium, Sweden), a large portion of academic-track secondary students of immigrant background enter the labor market directly. In countries where large numbers of academic-track students do not continue on to higher education, there is a potentially large pool of academic-track students who are at risk of becoming unemployed.

Dropout Rates

Second-generation Turks who have managed to enter higher education may face unique difficulties. The economic crisis has caused a dramatic rise in higher education enrollment without a concomitant increase in resources allocated to institutions of higher education. Dropout rates among children of immigrants in higher education were already high prior to the recession. In the Netherlands, Belgium and France, about one-third of the second-generation Turkish student population dropped out of higher education after enrolling (see Figure 1). Scarce resources could potentially drive this number further up.

Lessons Learned

The data thus far point to the unique challenges of both low-performing and high-performing second-generation Turkish youth in Europe. Perhaps unsurprisingly, second-generation Turkish youth who left school early are among the populations most vulnerable to the effects of the economic crisis in Europe. Even prior to the recession, they suf-

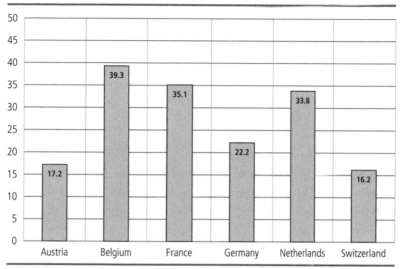

All data in percent

Source: TIES Survey 2007–2008

fered from high unemployment rates, and it is safe to assume that many more have since lost their jobs since (a) they tended to work in the sectors of the economy that were most affected by the crisis and (b) they were more likely than other workers to have temporary contracts.

However, this vulnerable population has been the focus of policymakers for some time now. More unexpectedly, better-educated second-generation Turkish youth may also be vulnerable. While returning to school is an obvious coping strategy for high-performing youth from middle- and high-income families, students of low-income families face more challenges because of their greater dependency on study loans and part-time jobs to support their studies. Also, at a time when demand for education exceeds supply, institutions of higher learning may not have the capacity to absorb larger numbers of students. Those who do enroll may not receive the quality of education and support they need.

If the best and brightest in immigrant communities are unable to enter or succeed in higher education, it could send a devastating message that European societies have few opportunities for the children of immigrants. To do nothing for this particular group could potentially set back the integration process for many years.

Policy Options for Promoting School and Labor Market Preparedness

Public policies are not yet fully in place to address the needs of second-generation students in Europe—both those at the top and bottom of the educational system. This section explores several policy options for improving the academic and labor market outcomes of the most vulnerable students during the "waiting period" created by the recession (i.e., the current lull in job creation). It includes options for both immediate and short-term investments as well as longer-term ideas.

Immediate and Short-Term Policies and Investments

Subsidies for On-the-Job Training Targeting (Potential) Early School Leavers

The current "waiting period" should be used to raise the skill level of the most vulnerable youth so as to ensure better access to the labor market once jobs become available. To do this, governments could subsidize on-the-job training schemes for early school leavers. The training should prioritize the social and language skills necessary in order to function well in a work environment.

Where real job-training positions do not exist, early school leavers should be encouraged to either reenter education or be placed in job-training centers that simulate work situations as used in vocational training. The best moment to intervene is directly before they leave school, when they should immediately be placed in job-training schemes.

Outreach programs for higher education targeted at children of immigrants (especially in countries, such as Belgium and Sweden, where students do not automatically transfer to college or university after completing the academic track of secondary school) would help to increase enrollment. Pupils in the final level of academic-track secondary school could, through academic counseling, be informed about the current labor market and the opportunities for them to enter higher education.

Individualized Coaching or Mentoring to Prevent Dropouts

As enrollments rise rapidly in universities and colleges, first-year students who need extra guidance and counseling will likely be the first to drop out. Temporary, unorthodox solutions to the understaffing in higher education should be taken into consideration. Individualized coaching or mentoring by older students is an already established and effective practice that could offer a low-cost solution.

Long-Term Policies and Investments

The transition to apprenticeships also presents important challenges for second-generation students in vocational education programs. The TIES survey shows that, in Germany, half of second-generation Turks fail to successfully transition from lower-secondary school (*Hauptschule*) to an apprenticeship. The Swiss education system faces similar challenges. One in three second-generation Turks completing lower-secondary education in Switzerland does not find an apprenticeship. However, in Switzerland, they do not drop out of the system altogether. Rather, they are placed in a bridging course known as *Brückenangebot*, where pupils receive assistance choosing careers and selecting appropriate training, as well as vocational work experience and personal development coaching. Research suggests that these bridging courses for early school leavers are effective: Three-quarters of the pupils find an apprenticeship after completing the program (Crul and Schneider 2009).

Promoting Access to Higher Education

The TIES survey shows two main pathways to higher education: (1) the "traditional" pathway through academic-track secondary school or (2) the "long" or "alternative" route through the vocational track, which means moving from lower-vocational education to middle-vocational education and then to higher-vocational education. The second possibility is especially important in countries where there is early tracking. The "long" or "alternative" pathway through vocational education programs is an important strategy for children of immigrants to move up the educational ladder.

As Figure 2 illustrates, this is particularly true in the Netherlands and Austria. In countries with strong vocational education programs (e.g., Belgium, Germany), there is still room for improvement. At the time of the TIES survey (prior to the recession), youth reported abandoning vocational studies mainly because they wanted to work. In the present economic climate, many more youth may decide to take the long route and continue on to higher education. This trend toward more time in school could prove to be one of the most dramatic and positive effects of the economic crisis on educational systems across Europe. We advocate investments and changes in school systems as well as in different support systems.

Investments and Changes in School Systems

Prevention of Early School Leaving

Early school leaving among second-generation Turks is particularly high in countries where students are forced to select specialized tracks before age 14 and where the transition to apprenticeships proves problematic for children of immigrants (e.g., Austria, Germany). Therefore, programs that prepare the most vulnerable children for apprenticeship positions should form a key element in programs in countries where apprenticeships serve as gateways to the labor market.

Policymakers often assume that early-selection systems are advantageous, and may even prevent dropouts, because a student's coursework is designed to match his or her abilities from a young age. How-

Figure 2: Share of second-generation Turkish immigrants in higher education who started on the vocational pathway, 2007–2008

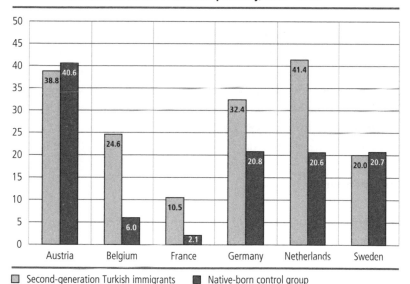

Second-generation Turkish immigrants   Native-born control group

All data in percent

Source: TIES Survey 2007–2008

ever, the outcomes of the TIES survey suggest otherwise. Early specialization often leads to marginal, segregated schools where high concentrations of difficult students reinforce underperformance and increase dropout rates. This seems especially true for the children of immigrants in the Netherlands and Belgium who were placed in vocational tracks.

Rethinking Education Systems

The TIES survey revealed clear best practices to promote participation in higher education by second-generation youth. School systems that start education early (at ages 2 and 3) and specialization late (at age 15) show dramatically larger groups (up to 10 times as many) of second-generation Turks in preacademic tracks than school systems where children start school much later (ages 5 or 6) and specialize earlier (ages 10 or 12).

Enlarging the preschool system seems an obvious policy to pursue. This would create new jobs and raise the educational level of the most vulnerable groups in the long term. But the focus on preschool should not be an excuse to overlook secondary education. Since middle- and higher-education institutions are the strongest link between students and the labor market and should therefore be a priority area for countries as they recover from the crisis.

Support Systems

Immigrant parents are key to success in school. Teachers across the European countries studied, however, hold two widespread assumptions about Turkish immigrant parents:
1. They are not supportive or engaged in the academic success of their children.
2. They cannot help their children with homework due to their low levels of formal education.

As Table 3 shows, the first assumption is not true. Although the share of second-generation Turkish students who said their parents did not support their school achievement is higher than among students with native-born parents, they were still a small minority of students. The majority of the second-generation youth said their parents had been "somewhat important," "important" or "very important" for their academic achievement. Mothers and fathers were considered almost equally important.

When we take a closer look at how parental support influences academic outcomes, there is clear support for the idea that better-performing students in all countries have more supportive parents. Children whose parents talk about school with them are less likely to leave school early and are more often continuing on to higher education (Crul et al. forthcoming 2010).

It is true that most parents are not able to give practical help (between half and three-quarters of Turkish parents). But the aggregate figures hide a smaller group of younger parents, many of whom immigrated at young ages themselves and have been partly educated in Europe. We can illustrate this with the case of Germany. The results suggest that these parents were much more involved with their children's schooling and more capable of supporting their children's academic progress. Two-thirds of the children whose mothers studied partly in Germany say their parents helped with homework, while this was only true for a bit more than one-fourth of the students with mothers who were schooled entirely in Turkey. The children who are now in elementary school often have parents who are of the 1.5 generation or the second generation. Many European schools (and education policymakers) still make decisions based on antiquated stereotypes of the first generation, but the next generation of parents—which is willing and able to contribute—is still often ignored.

Table 3: Importance of parents' academic support, Turkish second generation (percent), 2007–2008

	Not important at all	Not important	Some-what important	Impor-tant	Very impor-tant	Missing	Total number
Mother's support							
Austria	14.6	18.6	21.2	27.3	11.4	7.0	458
France	24.2	16.0	13.8	23.4	21.2	1.4	500
Germany	14.1	17.8	14.7	22.8	28.9	1.8	505
Netherlands	6.4	7.4	14.2	30.2	39.8	2.0	500
Sweden	8.8	3.8	10.9	32.4	43.3	0.8	238
Switzerland	21.9	23.7	12.5	18.9	13.5	9.5	465
Father's support							
Austria	13.3	17.2	18.6	28.9	11.6	9.4	458
France	24.4	16.8	18.6	19.8	18.2	2.2	500
Germany	6.9	14.3	17.2	24.8	35.0	1.8	505
Netherlands	7.6	11.0	16.4	29.2	30.2	5.6	500
Sweden	11.8	3.8	12.2	29.4	39.1	3.8	238
Switzerland	20.9	25.6	14.0	17.6	11.2	10.8	465

Note: This question was not asked in Belgium.

Source: TIES Survey 2007–2008

Policy Options for Parental and Community Engagement

Most policies to promote academic achievement among second-generation youth focus on school resources and targeted support to students. However, these school-based efforts should be accompanied by policies to promote a culture of success in migrant communities. Above all, this means focusing on students' immediate family—including parents, siblings and other close kin.

Having received part of their education in Europe, many parents of elementary-school-age, second-generation immigrants have the necessary skills to help their children succeed and can also serve as intermediaries between schools and communities. If trained as paraprofessionals or employed by welfare organizations, these parents could play an important role in boosting student success. Many immigrant women who were raised and educated in Europe do not work during the years they bear and raise children. As part-time mediators in schools, such women could help establish a better relationship between schools and parents, for instance, through low-key meetings (e.g., coffee mornings, home visits).

A Europe-Wide Student Mentor Scheme

The TIES survey revealed the importance of support from older siblings with higher education degrees—particularly with homework assistance and goal setting (see Table 4). In general, elder siblings in migrant families provide twice as much support as their counterparts in native families. Many of these successful youth not only serve as mentors for their younger siblings, but also work while studying, in part to pay for school.

Table 4: Share of second-generation Turkish youth receiving homework help from highly educated siblings (percent), 2007–2008

	Frequently	Regularly	Occasionally	Seldom	Never
Austria	28.6	19.0	31.0	14.3	7.1
Germany	12.0	30.0	36.0	12.0	10.0
Netherlands	8.1	27.0	33.3	14.4	17.1

Note: This question was not asked in Belgium, France, Sweden and Switzerland.

Source: TIES Survey 2007–2008

As many student jobs have disappeared, employing successful youth from immigrant communities as student mentors could address both of these challenges. Mentor schemes provide an institutionalized form of social support similar to older siblings. The mentors are knowledgeable about the school system, speak the language of the children and the parents, and can show by example that it is possible to succeed in school. Moreover, mentor schemes that enroll students can exempt them from paying tuition in higher education or could pay them a student-job wage for their efforts. Many successful mentor programs already exist in the United Kingdom, the Netherlands, Sweden and Germany.

Accordingly, the European Union could consider developing a Europe-wide student mentor program in which national and local programs would be funded to develop programs with student immigrant organizations, universities and secondary schools.

Conclusion

We described a wide range of policies, short and long term, that could turn the economic recession into an advantage for children of immigrants. School and labor market preparedness is at the heart of effective policymaking in this arena. With respect to the recession, the most important priority is to prepare students for apprenticeships. Without training in apprenticeships, immigrant students are extremely vulnerable in the labor market. Smoothing the transition with an additional training and coaching year, as is the case in Switzerland with the *Brückenangenbot*, proves to be effective.

The more long-term aim is to direct more students into academic tracks, which reduces the risk of early school leaving and increases their labor market opportunities. Many German states already have undertaken reforms that provide greater emphasis on preschool, full-day elementary schools and later selection. These reforms will—not unimportantly in this era—create more jobs in the educational sector. The above policy recommendations are already on the agenda in many countries. It is mostly the special urgency resulting from the recent economic crisis that needs to be stressed.

Two other policy areas outlined in this chapter are much newer and maybe also more thought-provoking. The economic crisis hit when the first big wave of children of immigrants moved into higher education. That is a very positive development that can be further advanced by offering more alternative-access possibilities to higher education through the vocational column. The global recession, however, has put a huge strain on resources in higher education and, at the same time, affected the financial situation of students from immigrant families. This makes this group especially vulnerable for dropout for both financial reasons and due to a lack of student support staff.

We recommend policy awareness of the special situation affecting these students, particularly since the "successful" group is often overlooked in the political arena. Additional investment for this group is important to ensure its future success. One way to do this is to capitalize on earlier groups of successful students by hiring them as mentors for this younger generation. Subsidized mentor schemes can accomplish two goals: Financially assist the older students and provide support to freshman students in a time of scarce staff resources.

The other new and much-overlooked trend is that of young parents of the 1.5 and second generations. For decades, schools have tried—and often failed—to bring immigrant parents into schools and further connect them with the educational lives of their children and institutions. A new generation of parents has arrived that is willing to participate and work together with teachers and school boards. Local governments and schools should jump to the occasion to invest in this new generation of parents.

Investments in school and labor market preparedness, if undertaken in the short term, could serve as a silver lining to the economic crisis.

Appendix: International TIES Survey

The Integration of the European Second Generation (TIES) project is a collaborative and comparative research project on the descendants of immigrants from Turkey, the former Yugoslavia and Morocco in eight European countries: Austria, Belgium, France, Germany, the Netherlands, Spain, Sweden and Switzerland. All respondents belong to the "second generation" (defined as persons who were born in the country of residence to immigrant parents) and were ages 18 to 35.

The centerpiece of the project is the first systematic and rigorously collected common European dataset executed in 15 European cities with almost 10,000 face-to-face interviews. The participating cities include Paris and Strasbourg in France, Berlin and Frankfurt in Germany, Madrid and Barcelona in Spain, Vienna and Linz in Austria, Amsterdam and Rotterdam in the Netherlands, Brussels and Antwerp in Belgium, Zurich and Basel in Switzerland, and Stockholm in Sweden.[5]

The fact that each of these groups shares very similar starting positions in the different countries offers the unique opportunity to look at the effects of specific *city and national contexts.* TIES also differs from previous international surveys because it not only records the final outcomes of education or labor market transitions; it also looks at full educational trajectories and professional career development. This long-term approach makes it possible to reconstruct the most important selection- and decision-making points in the lives of second-generation immigrants and to relate them to the institutional and structural arrangements in the different cities and countries.

---

5 The TIES survey was carried out by survey bureaus under supervision of the eight TIES partner research institutes: the Institute for Social and Political Opinion Research (ISPO), University of Leuven, Belgium; the National Institute for Demographic Studies (INED), France; the Swiss Forum for Migration and Population Studies (SFM), University of Neuchâtel, Switzerland; the Centre for Research in International Migration and Ethnic Relations (CEIFO), University of Stockholm, Sweden; the Institute for Migration Research and Intercultural Studies (IMIS), University of Osnabruck, Germany; the Institute for European Integration Research (EIF), Austrian Academy of Sciences, Austria; The National Interdisciplinary Demographic Institute (NIDI) in The Hague and the Institute for Migration and Ethnic Studies (IMES) in Amsterdam, the Netherlands.

The TIES Survey in Sweden, Germany, Belgium, France, Austria and Switzerland

Table A-1 shows the final numbers of interviewees per city and "ethnic" category. Note that all groups were sampled according to a technical demographic criterion—that is, one or both parents were born in Turkey, the former Yugoslavia or Morocco—and that all respondents were born in the country of residence. For the comparison group, two criteria were relevant: (a) both parents were born in the country where the survey was executed and (b) the youth lived in the same neighborhoods or city areas as the respondents from the three second-generation groups.[6]

The international TIES project team interviewed second-generation youth according to the same selection criteria. Sampling strategies, however, had to be (slightly) different (according to the available information in the register data in the countries) but could not compromise our aim to select a representative population. For the first time, both naturalized as well nonnaturalized second-generation youth were interviewed in a Europe-wide survey. Since most countries do not have a comparable survey, the representativeness of our sample is difficult to check. Therefore, some caution is necessary in generalizing the findings.

We chose to survey at the city rather than the country level because the second generation largely resides in big cities. Also, immigration is typically a big-city phenomenon that has usually resulted in local policy reactions. Our study, therefore, does not claim any national representativeness. For convenience, we use only the country names in published tables. Strictly speaking, this is misleading because it is only a sample in two cities and not a national survey.

---

6 An exception in the second criterion is Stockholm, where the comparison group is a representative sample of the group in the entire city.

Table A-1: Number of interviews for TIES, per city and group

		Turkish	"Former Yugo-slavian"	Moroccan	Comparison group	Total
Austria:	Vienna	252	253	–	250	755
	Linz	206	242	–	234	682
Belgium:	Brussels	250	–	257	271	778
	Antwerp	358	–	312	303	973
France:	Paris	248	–	–	174	422
	Strasbourg	252	–	–	177	429
Germany:	Berlin	255	202	–	250	707
	Frankfurt	250	204	–	253	707
Netherlands:	Amsterdam	237	–	242	259	738
	Rotterdam	263	–	251	253	767
Spain:	Madrid	–	–	250	250	500
	Barcelona	–	–	250	250	500
Sweden:	Stockholm	250	–	–	250	500
Switzerland:	Zürich	206	235	–	202	643
	Basel	248	191	–	266	705
TOTAL		**3,275**	**1,327**	**1,562**	**3,642**	**9,806**

Source: TIES Survey 2007–2008

Background Characteristics of the Parents of the Turkish Respondents

An important departure point of the TIES project design is the hypothesis that the background situation of second-generation Turks of a particular age group is actually comparable across different European countries. The parents' background characteristics are central to testing this hypothesis. We analyzed these characteristics in three domains: reason for migration, rural versus urban origin and the level of education of both parents.

Two-thirds of the fathers came as labor migrants. The second and third most-mentioned reasons were family reunion and marriage. The exception is Sweden, which has fewer labor migrants and more humanitarian migrants (refugees or asylum seekers). The parents of our second-generation respondents mostly came from small villages or towns in the countryside and arrived with low levels of education. In Austria, Sweden and Switzerland, they were somewhat better educated than in Germany and France (more often having some secondary schooling). Sweden had a higher share of Kurdish and Assyrian refugees than the other countries. Based on these background characteristics of the parents, we would expect the second generation to do a bit better in Austria, Switzerland and Sweden.

Works Cited

Bolwijn, Marjon. Hbo Verwacht Recordaantal Studenten [Hbo Expects a Record Number of Students]. *Vkbanen* August 2009. www.vkbanen.nl/onderwijs/748359/Hbo-verwacht-recordaantal-studenten.html (accessed July 7, 2010).

Crul, Maurice, and Jens Schneider. The Second Generation in Europe. Education and the Transition to the Labour Market. Paper presented at the TIES Policy Brief for the Stakeholders' Conference held in Amsterdam, May 11–13, 2009. www.tiesproject.eu/component/option,com_docman/task,cat_view/gid,45/Itemid,142/(accessed July 7, 2010).

Crul, Maurice, and Richard Wolff. *Talent gewonnen. Talent verspild? Een kwantitatief onderzoek naar de instroom en doorstroom van allochtone studenten in het Nederlandse Hoger Onderwijs (1997–2001).* Utrecht: ECHO, 2002.

Crul, Maurice, Philipp Schnell, Maren Wilmes, Marieke Slootman, Barbara Herzog-Punzenberger, Helga De Valk and Gulseli Baysu. Which school systems provide the best opportunities for success? School careers of second generation youth in Europe. In *How the integration context makes a difference. The second generation in Eu-*

rope, edited by Maurice Crul and Jens Schneider. Amsterdam/
New York: Amsterdam University Press/Russell Sage Publications, forthcoming 2010.

Dienst Maatschappelijke Ontwikkeling. Goal. 2010. www.goal.
amsterdam.nl (accessed July 7, 2010).

European Commission, Directorate General for Education and Culture. Progress towards the Lisbon Objectives in Education and
Training. Brussels: European Commission Directorate General
for Education and Culture, 2009. http://ec.europa.eu/education/
lifelong-learning-policy/doc1522_en.htm (accessed July 7, 2010).

Hackney Schools' Mentoring Programme. London, 2005. www.hsmp.
org.uk/index.asp. (accessed July 7, 2010).

Jaschik, Scott. Defining the Enrollment Boom. *Inside Higher Ed* December 2009. www.insidehighered.com/news/2009/12/18/enroll
(accessed July 7, 2010).

Junge Vorbilder. Mentoring mit Migrationshintergrund [Young role
models. Mentoring with a migration background]. http://verikom.
de/junge_vorbilder.htm (accessed July 7, 2010).

Kamran. UvA-bestuurder: 'Laat Studenten Lekker Kiezen' [UvA-
driver: 'Let Students Choose Good']. *Campus TV*, September 2009.
www.campus.tv/tag/uva/page/2/(accessed July 7, 2010).

Nutting, Rex. Biggest Job Loss Ever for Retail Sector: Retailing May
Never Recover Fully as Consumers Begin to Save Again. *Market-
Watch* (News Release), February 12, 2009. www.marketwatch.com/
story/retail-jobs-disappearing-fast-wont-come (accessed July 7,
2010).

Sharp, Meghan. As Jobs Disappear, Education Beckons. *Foxbusiness*,
December 5, 2008. www.foxbusiness.com/story/personal-finance/
lifestyle-money/career-center/jobs-disappear-education-beckons
(accessed July 7, 2010).

Statistics Netherlands. Employment down. News release, February 12,
2010. www.cbs.nl/en-GB/menu/themas/dossiers/conjunctuur/
publicaties/conjunctuurbericht/inhoud/kwartaal/archief/2010/
2010-02-12-k02.htm?Languageswitch=on (accessed July 7, 2010).

The Integration of the European Second Generation. TIES Project. www.tiesproject.eu (accessed July 7, 2010).

Weeda, Martijn. Recordaantal Studenten Tijdens Introductie [Record Number of Students During the Introduction]. *ASVA Studenten-unie*, August 2009. www.asva.nl/ASVA/Persberichten/tabid/144/ctl/Details/mid/526/ItemID/634/Default.aspx (accessed July 7, 2010).

Part III: Discussion Summary

Fourth Plenary Meeting of the Transatlantic Council on Migration

Transatlantic Council on Migration

Immigrant Integration: Priorities for the Next Decade[1]

Bellago, Italy

May 5–7, 2010

This fourth plenary meeting of the Transatlantic Council on Migration analyzed the global recession's effects on immigrant integration and developed several recommendations for effectively investing in immigrants during the long recovery from the crisis. The meeting examined how immigrants might have lost ground, looking at socioeconomic indicators (changes in educational and labor market attainment), political indicators (trends in extremism, discrimination and public opinion) and material indicators (reductions in funding for integration programs and practices). The discussion also touched upon ways in which the crisis might have benefited immigrants.

This systematic look at where and how the crisis has affected immigrants allowed participants to engage in in-depth deliberations on how governments can use meaningful, targeted integration investments during the recovery. Well-considered actions could boost economic competitiveness, in large part by increasing investments in upgrading the human capital of immigrant populations and, by extension, improving social cohesion.

1 Meetings of the Transatlantic Council on Migration take place under the Chatham House Rule to foster an open and candid debate. Accordingly, participants are not identified by name, title or country, and the discussion summary is a compilation of the broad range of discussions.

Participants concluded by determining the integration-related investments that transatlantic national and local governments should prioritize in the coming decade.

Session I:
Setting the Stage: The Recession and Immigrant Integration

The meeting began with an overview of the recession's impact on immigrants and a preliminary discussion of the main challenges facing politicians.

The most distinctive feature of what has been dubbed the Great Recession has been the diversity of its effects across countries. Disparities in unemployment among countries are extremely wide (ranging from 3 percent in Norway and 10 percent in the United States to nearly 20 percent in Spain, as of the first quarter of 2010). However, though immigrants (and particularly certain groups, such as African-born migrants) have fared poorly in some places, we cannot say this has been the experience across the board; indeed, in some countries, immigrants have gleaned some benefits from the financial crisis. Immigrant women, for instance, fared much better than immigrant men, as they tended to work in the hospitality and care sectors, which were less affected by the crisis. Despite the huge variety in what has happened to immigrants, we can draw some commonalities among countries. First, the recession has hit youth hardest. Among them, minorities and migrants have been hit harder yet. Second, though many countries saw a large influx of immigrant flows during economic booms, we haven't seen any evidence of "buyer's remorse," in that transatlantic governments have not drastically slashed flows in response to the crisis.

"Our data is on the recession, but policies should focus on the recovery."

In terms of immigrant flows, the "unregulated margins" have responded in a way that makes sense: illegal migration has decreased in response to the recession, as has temporary migration. And, in Europe, immigrants who have secure legal status and an explicit right to return also have more flexibility: They are more likely to go home if they face economic hardship (unless the situation in their country of origin is markedly worse). In contrast, this flexibility does not exist in the United States or Canada, where lawful residents are *penalized* for leaving the country for too long. This means that these immigrants delay making long-term decisions during periods of high uncertainty and, for this reason, most have decided to stay put. The question becomes: How long will they wait it out?

"There is competition between natives and immigrants, and it has increased dramatically during the recession."

Policymakers need to be aware of several potential consequences of the recession:

First is the danger of economic scarring: If migrants arrive during a downturn and are either unable to find a job or lose their job, they will have a much harder time catching up than if they had come during any other time. The long-term disadvantages in the labor market are especially felt by immigrant youth.

Second, though the peak of the global crisis has passed, national and subnational fiscal crises are far from over. While public spending boosted growth during the crisis, this stimulus is now being withdrawn and, in some cases, newly deficit-conscious governments are trimming existing programs. Also, there has been very little immigrant-specific spending to cope with the effects of the crisis. In fact, there have been cuts to integration budgets, and these will continue—especially where deficits have become untenable.

Third, the recovery will be long, and jobs must be created at an extraordinary pace to make up for both crisis-driven unemployment and regular population growth. Key questions: How will immigrants access these new jobs? And will they have the necessary skills (including language abilities) to succeed in the labor market?

"In the recovery, there can be a potential clash between immigrants in low-paying jobs and jobless natives who may suddenly be prepared to take jobs they would never have considered."

Participants pointed out that a key challenge is compelling policymakers to think beyond the crisis. This will not be automatic for them, as most are spending their energy and resources putting out fires in order to stave off an even bigger disaster.

Session II:
Perspectives from the Reflection Group on the Future of Europe

The opening day of the Transatlantic Council meeting included a brief presentation on the conclusions of the Reflection Group on the Future of Europe, which outlined the demographic challenges facing a Europe "at the forefront of population decline."[2] The main question posed was how policymakers can adapt to the needs (and abilities) of an aging population, of which only 240 million are currently "economically active"—a number forecasted to drop by another 70 million in the next 30 years (in the absence of immigration). As Europe's productive age groups shrink and its dependent groups grow, how will policymakers avoid constraining the benefits and services to which their citizens have become accustomed?

"If we do nothing, benefits and wages will decrease by themselves. So 'doing nothing' is not on the table."

The presentation outlined several potential solutions to fill this workforce gap. Necessary measures include integrating more women into the workforce, increasing the retirement age and bringing in more

---

2　The European Council established an independent "Reflection Group" in December 2008 with the goal of helping the European Union better anticipate and meet its long-term challenges, looking specifically at 2020 to 2030. The 12-member group presented its official report to the European Council in June 2010.

immigrants—but these, on their own, would still fall short in meeting Europe's human capital needs. It is clear from a research perspective that Europe needs fundamental labor market reforms to integrate both older people and migrants. Indeed, you can't bring more people in or tell people to work for 10 more years, if you don't have the capacity to employ them! Still, from a political perspective, it is unclear whether citizens are ready to accept these difficult changes.

"How can you sell politically unpalatable messages to European electorates, especially under the current circumstances?"

Session III:
Extremism and Discrimination: Status Quo or Razor's Edge

Mass migration and the economic crisis are thought to have combined to help drive the popularity of the radical right as well as spur a rise in discrimination. But these interrelationships are not as straightforward as assumed. Higher levels of immigration do not automatically correlate with greater prejudice or with more votes for radical-right parties, though this might be one of the manifestations of how societies and communities are grappling with the rapid pace of change.

Participants considered several important variables governing these trends. First, the scale and nature of immigration matters: Specific national contexts and the speed with which immigration occurs are important factors. Unlike other issues, trends in discrimination and extremism are conditioned to a large extent by national histories and cultural traditions. The second point is that the way leaders talk about immigration—or avoid talking about it—can actually cause greater instability and friction. The far-right has succeeding in mobilizing anxious publics by claiming to address contentious issues, such as immigration, head-on. Migrants themselves—and their leadership—must also take responsibility for informing the debate.

One case study examined was that of the Netherlands, where economic difficulties have not actually increased support for the radical right (the success of the latter began during an economic boom period). However, legislation—in good times or bad—that is perceived as "only" benefiting migrants will be less palatable to the public, especially when natives also face difficulties, such as unemployment. Particularly in times of crisis, it is necessary to take people's fears seriously; denying them will fuel extremist success.

"Migration is the vehicle through which people see the changes precipitated by globalization."

Elsewhere in Europe, we can see that trends in far-right voting have not pointed in a single direction, even during the recession. The rise of Jobbik in Hungary, for instance, is counterbalanced by the demise of the Polish far-right party. The advances are also not perfectly correlated to the recession; other contributing factors, such as the modernization of far-right parties themselves, have played a role. The success of the British National Party, for example, can be partly attributed to its superior organization and diligent door-to-door campaigning.

Immigration is just *one* of the frames used by the far right; crime and corruption are also important parts of the message. And while the political success of far-right parties can lead to immigration restrictions, the impact on broader politics might include countermobilizations, such as antiracism movements. Similarly, there is no empirical evidence that the rise in far-right parties correlates to greater violence; in fact, it might reduce violence toward immigrants by channeling those feelings into the political arena.

Although comparative tools for measuring discrimination are scarce, the 2009 EU-MIDIS survey offers insights into perceived levels of discrimination across Europe. The survey revealed disturbing trends, including the fact that 76 percent of North African respondents considered discrimination to be "widespread" and that 67 percent said ethnic minorities and immigrants are at a disadvantage in getting a job. Significant percentages of minorities surveyed did not know that antidiscrimination legislation existed or where they could go to lodge a complaint. Many labor migrants believed there were no laws against discrimination in employment (including 74 percent of Romanians in Spain). Not surprisingly, the survey found rampant underreporting of discrimination. Most people said they did not report incidents of discrimination because nothing would change if they did. And the majority said they did not even report serious crimes, mostly because of lack of confidence in the police or because they would rather deal with it themselves.

"Discrimination occurs in the gap between 'comparable' and equal."

One question that participants repeatedly returned to was why certain groups seem to fare better than others, for example, ex-Yugoslavs versus North Africans in Europe. At the same time, there are huge differences between the *same* groups in different countries in terms of levels of discrimination as well as awareness of their rights (for example, Turks in Germany versus Turks in Bulgaria or North Africans in France versus North Africans in Spain), suggesting that national context plays a decisive role. One participant noted that anxiety is exacerbated by the perception of *difference* in communities rather than the volume of flows to a country. But these perceptions can shift (and be shaped) over generations, which suggests that education and information campaigns can play a role in changing the status quo.

These issues bring up the question of how to conceptualize "ownership" in a nation; if the claim to ancestry or roots is emphasized, then immigrants can be left out of the national narrative. Leaders need to strike a balance between preserving identity and making cultural compromises. Far-right parties have had success presenting this "clash of civilizations" view that mainstream parties do not want to address. Thus, even symbolic gestures—and what policymakers *appear* to do about immigration—become tremendously important.

"We have to understand the impact of symbolism. No one thinks 200 women wearing the burka is an actual threat, but it does matter."

New thinking on these trends led to a discussion of the role of civil society and the private sector in mitigating discrimination and anti-immigrant sentiment. We sometimes assume these are problems solely for local government and municipalities to solve on their own, but this dialogue needs to exist in the workplace, too, not just in neighborhoods. Labor unions, for instance, could have a role in informing migrants about their labor rights.

Session IV:
Current Evidence on Immigrant Employment

This session explored how immigrants have fared in the labor market during the crisis, and it quickly disproved the assertion that immigrants have done worse than natives across the board. While some categories of immigrants have fared poorly, immigrants have actually outperformed natives in some Organisation for Economic Co-operation and Development (OECD) countries.

The underlying conclusion was that the effects of the economic crisis on employment have been extraordinarily diverse: The crisis disproportionately affected men, youth and minorities, particularly African-born migrants, who fared badly in virtually every country examined.

This recession has been different than past crises. Whereas the low-skilled group once suffered the most, it is now the middle-skill group (with an upper secondary education) that has been hardest hit. There is a real risk that this unemployment will be stubborn and long-lasting. Yet one silver lining to the immigrant mantra of "first hired, first fired" is that, when the economy takes off again, the temporary jobs typically filled by immigrants might be the ones filled first and, thus, immigrants might do better earlier in the recovery.

"The crisis reveals a lot about the state of labor markets in our countries."

While there is some consensus about which groups are being hit the hardest, there is little agreement on what policy interventions work best to address these trends. Governments have pursued very different strategies, depending largely on the structure of their labor markets and whether they chose to invest most of their resources in creating jobs or in bolstering unemployment benefits.

Many European countries have chosen to make adjustments to the number of hours worked rather than decrease the number of jobs (depending on factors such as the bargaining power of unions and the degree to which employers wish to retain skilled workers). Some countries have had no choice but to make certain workers redundant, while others (e.g., Germany) have had the luxury of implementing part-time work initiatives subsidized by the government, thereby allowing private employers to preserve jobs. Such programs have soared in popularity: While only half of OECD countries had such initiatives before the crisis, 24 countries have now introduced some version of flexible hours.

"No major political party wants to address labor market reforms because this will translate into lost votes."

In conclusion, while the crisis has aimed a spotlight on labor market shortcomings across the Atlantic, it also affords a unique opportunity to implement much-needed labor market reforms (particularly in countries like Spain). The question is whether countries are prepared to avail themselves of this window of opportunity.

Session V: Understanding Education Trends

This session determined recommendations on how to ensure that children of immigrants do not fall further behind during periods of budget uncertainty and spending cuts.

Schools are dealing with a growing, extraordinarily diverse population of immigrant students, who are placing a strain on existing educational structures. In the United States, the children of immigrants have doubled in number between 1990 and 2008, from 8 million to 16 million. In the majority of OECD countries, there is a worrisome academic performance gap between first- and second-generation children of immigrants, on the one hand, and native students, on the other (with some notable exceptions, e.g., Canada and New Zealand). The recession has exacerbated the pressure on educational systems; but, at least in the United States, it has also created a unique opportunity to push an education reform agenda. In the United States, stimulus spending not only forestalled more severe budget cuts but also promoted accountability by linking funding to outcomes.

The Transatlantic Council's two-day Education Symposium, held earlier in the week, helped synthesize three important factors that can lead to substantial improvements in student outcomes:

First, researchers agree that early-childhood education is one of the most critical ingredients of success, as it is able to "inoculate" children against the consequences of subpar schooling later in life. Yet it is one of the areas made most vulnerable by the recession. A comparison across countries shows that it is already not offered widely enough (or at a high enough quality), mostly due to lack of resources.

A second critical variable in student achievement is parent engagement. This does not mean that the burden is only on parents; it is also the responsibility of schools and communities to proactively support parents and teach them what their children need at home.

A third variable is teacher quality, which arguably has the highest impact on educational outcomes (when you control for socioeconomic factors). In particular, there is a vast shortage of teachers trained specifically to work with immigrant children, though demographic trends show that most teachers will soon have migrant children in their classrooms.

"Equality-driven reforms have not concentrated enough on excellence."

Participants agreed that governments and societies can make certain changes to meaningfully improve education for vulnerable students.

First, countries must place a higher premium on teaching and elevate its status in society if they want to recruit the best and brightest to the profession. The most highly qualified teachers should be working with the neediest children, as part of an approach that does not require more resources, but simply a smarter allocation of them.

Second, school curricula should strike a balance between the needs of society and those of immigrant children. As with most aspects of integration, this is a two-way street: Children need to be integrated into the culture of the host country, but curricula should also be responsive to the specific needs, values and *assets* of immigrant children. Furthermore, curricula should integrate language learning with subject matter content so that nonnative speakers do not fall behind in school.

Third, innovative methods should be explored, including focusing on apprenticeships or vocational training, so that students graduate with the skills they need to succeed in the labor market.

"Are students failing to perform well in school, or are schools failing students?

Participants made it clear that accountability is viewed differently across the globe. Canada, the United States and the United Kingdom subscribe to a "performance-based" model for making decisions about programs and funding, whereas Germany, Greece and other European countries felt this was a "punitive" approach. However, participants agreed that evaluating student progress over time is important and that better data were needed for this. There was also broad agreement that insufficient education funding affects all populations, not just immigrants.

"We haven't yet begun to see the real impact of the economic crisis on education."

In conclusion, participants agreed that including the needs of immigrant children under mainstream, systemic reforms—and thereby making states accountable for their performance—is an effective way to improve outcomes while also "flying under the radar" of those reluctant to devote resources to immigrants in times of crisis. There are no silver bullets in education reform; it is a long-term challenge requiring continuous change and adaptation. In times of budget cuts, it is wise to look for resources outside of government, while capitalizing on engagement from parents and communities.

"If we had tried to say we were passing a law that improves the outcomes of immigrant children, it never would have passed."

Session VI:
Public Perceptions, the Recession and Immigrant Integration

The central questions guiding this session were whether public opinion on immigration has shifted as a result of the crisis and how this will affect reform efforts.

Contrary to expectations, public opinion on this issue fluctuated very little as a result of the recession, with views on immigration, integration and legalization remaining largely unchanged. Voters' attitudes changed somewhat with the worsening of their financial situation, but the economic crisis did not drum up greater support for statements like "immigrants take jobs" or "immigrants bring down wages" (except in the United Kingdom, an outlier). And although the public continues to say that immigration is an important concern, it falls below the economy in terms of importance.

Public opinion on immigration is marked by internal ambiguity: Voters might both oppose reform while also expressing displeasure with the status quo. This paradox lies at the heart of the political challenge. Public perceptions can be "primed" if leaders assuage public anxiety by emphasizing enforcement, as voters generally feel more comfortable with immigration when there are certain "requirements" for immigrants residing in the country.

Participants considered whether public sentiments can change faster than they are measured and whether the status quo reflects a false confidence. Just as with budget cuts, the situation might only get worse as the recovery continues. Although we have not seen drastic changes yet, it does not mean we are out of the woods yet.

Session VII: Investments in Immigrant Integration: What Do We Know That Works and What Does Not Work?

This session outlined some of the long-term integration policy priorities for governments, focusing on more flexible funding mechanisms and greater policy accountability.

"Whatever the effect of cuts at the national level, they are significantly more critical at the local level."

In the United States, the recession has had a huge impact on state and local budgets, resulting in significant cuts to many important immigrant integration services and programs. However, while some programs have been cut entirely, others have emerged largely unscathed, mostly because the US system is comprised of a "patchwork" of decentralized programs at the state and local levels. Yet, despite these differences among states, federal stimulus spending temporarily prevented the erosion of key services and shielded immigrants' safety-net benefits from the ravages of the recession. By and large, benefit programs for immigrants have not been singled out for budget cuts. However, the worst may be yet to come: As fiscal relief from the federal government dries up, legislators will be forced to make cuts in order to maintain a balanced budget (a state requirement in 49 of the 50 states), which could mean disaster for immigrant services.

"We're approaching a cliff in the US, when all the state budgets are being passed and all the stimulus money has already been spent."

One concern shared by many European governments was accountability. It is hard to determine how much money is actually spent on integration at each level of government or what effect this money has had. Funding for immigrant integration is not differentiated from general employment budget lines, and many integration responsibilities (such as second-language learning) are carried out by municipalities—and, thus, not supported by states.

Another question posed is whether to extend integration services to intra-European migrants, who might actually face the same hurdles as third-country migrants (e.g., language acquisition, credential recognition), yet are not covered by European integration funds.

"We have a long history of funding for integration, but we do not know much about the impact of that funding."

There is one common thread that ties disparate national experiences together: Integration is a huge investment. Participants commented on the terminology itself: An "investment" implies a two-way street, in that immigrants are expected to make their own investment in society in return (e.g., learning the host language and customs). Participants agreed that we need contributions from everyone—migrants and natives alike—to emerge from the crisis with good integration results. Also, governments must commit to long-term investments, as integration takes time and the results will not appear immediately.

"Even if governments don't have all the answers—and can't measure the effectiveness of their investments—the results are clear when no investment is made at all: disaster."

One of the major political hurdles for policymakers is countering the perception that the government spends too much money on immigrants and ignores natives, which has particular salience in a downturn. One strategy to overcome this barrier is to invest in disadvantaged groups of all types and not appear to target immigrants.

Participants mentioned that the Spanish government, facing growing fiscal pressures, has tried on several occasions to cut immigrant integration funds for autonomous regions—a move that sparked widespread protests. While political opposition has staved off the worst cuts, funds have still been reduced, and there is no mechanism for ensuring that the remaining money is spent on immigrants.

The challenge for communities is that they must deal with the trickle-down effects of national immigration policies, which tend to be more interested in immigrant admissions than integration. Cities can be a platform for success in this area, as urban economies can promote the need for migrants. Local decisionmakers must assure national policymakers that integration policy does not end with entry controls, but must continue once immigrants are here to develop social cohesion.

Session VIII:
Charting a Forward Course: The Major Policy and Strategic Questions on Immigrant Integration in the Next Decade

The meeting concluded with a discussion on how to invest *smartly* in immigrant integration without losing momentum—or, worse, losing ground—due to recession-induced budget cuts.

One conclusion was that integration "should become a habit." It should become ingrained in government activities as well as in the national consciousness. Governments cannot actively admit immigrants in order to fill labor needs and then become passive when the time comes to integrate them into society. The ultimate sign of success will be when it is so mainstream that we no longer need meetings to discuss it.

"Immigration is all about social engineering: building and rebuilding communities and societies every day."

Participants proposed three overarching lessons for governments and communities to absorb:
1. *Adaptating and evaluating.* Integration programs are not static; they should instead be the product of constant, ongoing experimentation. For this, we need a feedback mechanism so that governments know what they are doing right (and wrong) and can act nimbly to make necessary changes. Independent evaluations—to which governments must adapt and respond—are critical for producing dynamic, adaptive systems.

391

2. *Learning from others.* Governments should think in terms of "clear-inghouses," where experts collect innovative ideas, examine and vet them dispassionately and come up with good practices useful to policymakers. While "mindless copying" from one country to the next will not work, certain ideas can be "decontextualized." An important piece of this puzzle is to look at outcomes: The key is not just how many people passed the test but, rather, how many people were helped by the test to function better in the labor market.

3. *Planning for budget cuts.* Money is not going to be as plentiful as it was in the past, yet integration needs will either stay the same or increase. Thus, we need to make the money count. This means thinking innovatively about the complexities of integration—that is, not only all the different categories of people who need to be incorporated into our investments but also programs that actually respond to these needs.

"We're going to have to work harder, faster, smarter—with fewer dollars."

The group also discussed specific lessons for how to accomplish these goals:

First, governments need to pay attention to newcomers. First-generation immigrants have different needs than established immigrants or national minorities, who may require different policy inputs and investments. This formula must be constantly examined, adapted and readapted. Predeparture integration schemes, when implemented correctly, may provide an innovative avenue for improving outcomes.

Second, governments must be more strategic about whom their investments are targeting. Should governments only invest in permanent migrants? While some temporary migrants (e.g., seasonal workers) are truly temporary, some may transition into permanent status down the road. In most countries, there are dramatic differences in outcomes both between immigrant groups and between immigrants and natives. Investments should specifically target these gaps—not just as a humanitarian impulse but because it is the only way to build a truly competitive society with the proper human capital.

Third, we need to hone in on what we really mean when we say "integration." If political leaders, urged by demographic imperatives, find themselves arguing that more immigration is necessary, they must be able to demonstrate to their electorates that they have succeeded at the other end: immigrant integration. What are the goals, and what defines success? Are we emphasizing economic integration (i.e., when people are successful in jobs) or cultural integration? Is it a never-ending process, or is there a point when we consider people to be fully integrated?

"We're no longer thinking tactically about migration."

There are three primary areas on which governments should concentrate: The first is education. Allowing the second generation to become entrenched at the bottom of society will have the most negative long-term consequences, with a ripple effect on other areas. Second, societies must not only prevent discrimination but also work to actively *regress* this trend and prevent anti-immigrant animus from exploding. "Beggar thy neighbor" incidents can catch fire when resources are scarce. Third, leaders need to better understand—and even mold—public opinion in order to allocate resources to integration without public contempt.

In order to succeed, a "whole of society" approach is needed. Participants repeatedly argued that we spend too much time and effort on the rights and entitlements of immigrants and not enough on the benefits of this relationship to the whole of society. We need to think broadly. Governments lack both the capacity and funds to individualize policies for specific categories of people; instead, the policies apply to multiple groups at once (e.g., establishing literacy programs for all children, not just those of migrants). How governments manage illegal immigration will also affect this debate: Publics want to stop this perceived "cheating" before they agree to allocate more benefits to migrants. Thus, the biggest consequence of the recession will not be unemployment; instead, it will be the "rationing" of limited infrastructure and goods, such as education, transportation and housing.

Immigration and Integration Resources

More details about the Transatlantic Council on Migration, convened by the Migration Policy Institute and supported by its policy partner, the Bertelsmann Stiftung, can be found at their websites:
The Transatlantic Council on Migration:
www.migrationpolicy.org/transatlantic
The Migration Policy Institute: www.migrationpolicy.org
The Bertelsmann Stiftung: www.en.bertelsmann-stiftung.de

The Transatlantic Council's Published Works

Visit here to learn more about the Transatlantic Council's three earlier books:

- *Delivering Citizenship* examines how citizenship has become a dynamic policy vehicle for promoting the political incorporation of immigrants and, by extension, their more complete integration: www.bertelsmann-stiftung.de/cps/rde/xchg/bst_engl/hs.xsl/publikationen_90776.htm
- *Talent, Competitiveness and Migration* analyzes two opposing policy pressures confronting policymakers: While there is strong popular and political outcry to protect jobs at home as a result of the economic crisis, policymakers also face midterm demographic challenges: www.bertelsmann-stiftung.de/cps/rde/xchg/bst_engl/hs.xsl/publikationen_94735.htm.

- *Migration, Public Opinion and Politics* explores a critical policy issue that has often been underestimated in the migration policy debate: the media and public opinion. The volume contains expert analysis of how our publics perceive immigration and immigrants— from their effects on the job market to their impact on culture and society to their prospects for integration: www.bertelsmann-stiftung.de/cps/rde/xchg/SID-33E0B94A-58033FCC/bst_engl/ hs.xsl/publikationen_98119.htm

Other Related MPI Resources

MPI's Labor Markets Initiative is undertaking a comprehensive, policy-focused review of the role of immigration in the labor market. Its work can be found at: www.migrationpolicy.org/lmi.
Program on European Migration:
www.migrationpolicy.org/research/europe.php
Program on US Immigration Policy:
www.migrationpolicy.org/research/usimmigration.php
Program on US Immigrant Integration:
www.migrationpolicy.org/integration

About the Transatlantic Council on Migration

The Transatlantic Council on Migration was launched in 2008 as a new initiative of the Migration Policy Institute (MPI) in Washington, DC. The Council's principal policy partner in this effort is the Bertelsmann Stiftung. The Council is a unique deliberative body that generates, studies and evaluates practical ideas about immigration and integration in order to promote more thoughtful, evidence-based migration policies across the Atlantic community. Its approach is evidence-based, progressive yet pragmatic and ardently independent. Council members and their guests combine exceptional political and public influence with profound interest and experience in issues related to migration.

The Council has a dual mission:

- To help inform, and thus influence, the transatlantic immigration and integration agendas by proactively identifying critical policy issues, analyzing them in light of the best research and mature judgment wherever they exist, and bringing them to the attention of the public. In so doing, the Council's work will also build the applied, comparative, international, analytical infrastructure—a virtual and easily accessible library—that promotes better-informed policy-making on these issues.
- To serve as a resource for governments as they grapple with the challenges and opportunities associated with international migration. Council members representing governments (and other governments, as appropriate) are encouraged to bring policy initiatives to the Council so that they can be analyzed, vetted and improved

before implementation—and/or evaluated after they have been executed.

Support and Membership

The Council is generously supported by the Carnegie Corporation of New York, the Open Society Institute, the Bertelsmann Stiftung, the Rockefeller Foundation, the Ford Foundation, the Barrow Cadbury Trust, the Luso-American Development Foundation, the Calouste Gulbenkian Foundation and the governments of Germany, the Netherlands and Norway.

The permanent Council members are: Giuliano Amato, former Prime Minister and Minister of the Interior in Italy; Xavier Becerra, Member of the US House of Representatives and Vice Chairman of the House Democratic Caucus; Mel Cappe, President of the Institute of Research on Public Policy and formerly Canada's High Commissioner to the United Kingdom; Armin Laschet, Minister for Intergenerational Affairs, Family, Women and Integration in North Rhine-Westphalia, Germany, and a former Parliamentarian of the European Union; Ana Palacio, Senior Vice President for International Affairs and Marketing for AREVA and formerly Parliamentarian of the European Union, Foreign Minister of Spain and Senior Vice President and General Counsel of the World Bank; Trevor Phillips, Chairman of the UK Commission on Equality and Human Rights; Rita Süssmuth, former President (Speaker) of the German Bundestag (1988–1998) and twice leader of Germany's Independent Commissions on Immigration and on Integration in the first half of this decade; Henriette Westhrin, State Secretary of the Norwegian Ministry of Children, Equality and Social Inclusion; and Antonio Vitorino, partner in the international law firm Gonçalves Pereira, Castelo Branco & Associados and former European Union Commissioner for Justice and Home Affairs (1999–2004) and former Deputy Prime Minister of Portugal.

The Council is convened by MPI President Demetrios G. Papademetriou and staffed by Gregory A. Maniatis, Senior European Fellow, MPI.

The Council's Approach

The Council's work is at the cutting edge of policy analysis and evaluation, and is thus an essential tool of policymaking. Among the policy fields that the Council explores are: (a) advancing social cohesion and social justice through more thoughtful citizenship and integration policies; (b) enhancing economic growth and competitiveness through immigration; (c) encouraging and facilitating greater mobility through better security; and (d) understanding better the complex links between migration and development. The Council's work is informed by: a belief in adhering to the rule of law across the board; commitment to a rights-sensitive agenda rooted in fairness; and the determination that the increasing diversity that migration has brought about—covering virtually the entire advanced industrial world—can be managed smartly and to one's advantage.

The policy options placed before the Council for its deliberation are analyzed and vetted by some of the world's best specialists organized in a virtual think tank that generates, studies and evaluates practical ideas about immigration and integration policies. MPI, together with members of the Management Board and its policy partner, the Bertelsmann Stiftung, systematically promote Council findings and decisions.

The Council is transatlantic at its very core because policymakers in Europe and North America face increasingly similar migration-related issues. As a result, policymakers find themselves coordinating more closely in areas that, only a few years ago, were considered to be sovereign prerogatives, especially concerning mobility and security matters. They are more interested in exchanging policy ideas and good practice across the entire migration policy and practice continuum: expanding legal migration channels across skills and types (permanent, temporary, contract, project-tied, etc.) of movements; fostering more effective integration and better relations between newcomers and established communities; and exploring the idea of forging an agenda on migration and development. Furthermore, there is a growing awareness that the actions of governments on both sides of the

Atlantic have implications for each other in areas such as the prevention of terrorist travel, responses to radicalization, the evolution (some say "subversion") of the idea of citizenship and the risk that popular (but poorly reasoned) ideas of migration management will spread across the Atlantic.

The Council aims to help policymakers map the landscape with robust, analytically anchored ideas and thereby inform, and even shape, the transatlantic policy agenda on migration.

Council Meetings

The full Council meets twice annually, and all meetings are held under the Chatham House Rule. Smaller preparatory and expert sessions are held prior to each meeting. Extraordinary meetings of interested Council members are convened in the capital of the country that is consulting the Council at any one time. Such meetings focus on issues of particular concern to the host country and/or are in response to an immigration crisis.

Papers commissioned for the May 2010 Council meeting are presented in this book, and an abbreviated summary of the Council's discussion is included elsewhere in this book.

More information about the Council's membership, operations and publications can be found at:
www.migrationpolicy.org/transatlantic.

About the Authors

Monica Arciga is Policy Analyst/Program Coordinator for MPI, where she works for the National Center on Immigrant Integration Policy. Prior to joining MPI, she was Management and Program Analyst for the District of Columbia Public Schools, where she coordinated and monitored federally funded district-wide educational programs for Title I students. She also spent four years working as Outreach Coordinator at the Center for Iberian and Latin American Studies at the University of California, San Diego.

Ms. Arciga holds a Master's of Pacific International Affairs (MPIA), with a Latin America focus, from the School of International Relations and Pacific Studies at the University of California, San Diego. She has a BA in Economics and Latin American Studies from the University of Illinois.

Carola Burkert has headed the working group "Migration und Integration" at the Institute for Employment Research (IAB) since March 2008.

She studied social sciences in Nuremberg and Bath (UK) and did her doctorate at the Department of Statistics and Empirical Economics of the University of Erlangen-Nuremberg. From 2002 to 2004, she was on the staff of the German Federal Agency for Recognition of Foreign Refugees (economic aspects of migration) and, from 2003 to 2004, was a researcher on the Council of Experts on Immigration and Integration.

Dr. Burkert has been a member of the research staff of IAB Hesse since 2005.

Randy Capps, a demographer with substantial expertise in immigrant populations, is a Senior Policy Analyst at the Migration Policy Institute. He has analyzed data on immigrants, from a wide variety of sources, at the national, state and local levels. Dr. Capps has participated in federally funded studies of: the integration of immigrants in rural areas; immigrant participation in public nutrition programs; implementation of immigrant-eligibility restorations to nutrition programs; access of immigrants to welfare, health-care and other public benefit programs; the impact of the 1996 welfare reform law's benefits restrictions on immigrant families; and employment services provided by the refugee resettlement program. His recent work at the state and local level includes: an analysis of immigrant workers and families in Maryland; a demographic profile of immigrants in Arkansas; a study of immigrant integration in Louisville, Kentucky; a description of the unauthorized population in California and Los Angeles; a study of tax payments by immigrants in the Washington, DC metropolitan area; an assessment of immigrants' health-care access in Connecticut; and an analysis of the involvement of children of immigrants in the Texas child welfare system. He also recently co-authored a report on the potential impact of US health-care reform on the insurance coverage of immigrants. Prior to joining MPI, Dr. Capps was a Senior Research Associate at the Urban Institute, where he studied immigrant integration and social programs for needy US populations. He holds a BA in Political Science from Williams College (1987), a Master's of Public Affairs from the University of Texas at Austin (1992) and a PhD in Sociology from the University of Texas (1999).

Elizabeth Collett is European Policy Fellow at the Migration Policy Institute and Senior Advisor to MPI's Transatlantic Council on Migration. She is based in Brussels and works on the International Program, with a particular focus on European policy.

Prior to joining MPI, Ms. Collett was a Senior Policy Analyst at the European Policy Centre, an independent, Brussels-based think tank, and responsible for its migration program, which covered all aspects of European migration and integration policy. During her time at EPC, she produced numerous working papers and policy briefs focused on the future of European Union immigration policy. She has also worked in the Migration Research and Policy Department of the International Organization for Migration, in Geneva, and for the Institute for the Study of International Migration, in Washington, DC.

Ms. Collett holds a Master's in Foreign Service (with Distinction) from Georgetown University, where she specialized in foreign policy and earned a certificate in refugee and humanitarian studies, and a bachelor's degree in law from Oxford University.

Maurice Crul is a Senior Researcher at the Amsterdam Institute for Social Science Research of the University of Amsterdam. He has published on school careers of children of immigrants in a comparative European and transatlantic perspective.

He is the international coordinator of the TIES (The Integration of the European Second Generation) Project, which compares second-generation Turkish, Moroccan and former Yugoslavian youth in 15 cities in eight European countries. More about the project can be found at www.tiesproject.eu/.

Currently, he is a visiting scholar at the Russell Sage Foundation, in New York.

Ruth Ferrero-Turrión is Associate Professor of Political Science at the Universidad Complutense of Madrid. She has been a visiting scholar at the London School of Economics, Columbia University, Babes-Bolyai University (Cluj-Napoca, Romania) and the Hungarian Institute of International Affairs (Budapest, Hungary). Her field of research includes minority rights, national minorities, the Balkans and migration policies in Spain and Europe.

Michael Fix is Senior Vice President and Director of Studies at the Migration Policy Institute (MPI) as well as the Co-Director of MPI's National Center on Immigrant Integration Policy. His work focuses on immigrant integration, citizenship policy, immigrant children and families, the education of immigrant students, the effect of welfare reform on immigrants and the impact of immigrants on the US labor force.

Mr. Fix, who is an attorney, was previously at the Urban Institute, where he directed the Immigration Studies Program from 1998 through 2004. His research at the Urban Institute focused on immigrants and integration, regulatory reform, federalism, race and the measurement of discrimination.

Mr. Fix is a Research Fellow at the Institute for the Study of Labor (IZA), in Bonn, Germany. He served on the National Academy of Sciences' Committee on the Redesign of US Naturalization Tests and is a member of the Advisory Panel to the Foundation for Child Development's Young Scholars Program. In November 2005, Mr. Fix was a New Millennium Distinguished Visiting Scholar at Columbia University's School of Social Work.

His recent publications include: *Immigrants and Welfare* (editor); *Los Angeles on the Leading Edge: Immigrant Integration Indicators and Their Policy Implications; Adult English Language Instruction in the United States: Determining Need and Investing Wisely; Measures of Change: The Demography and Literacy of Adolescent English Learners*; and *Securing the Future: US Immigrant Integration Policy, A Reader* (editor). His past research explored the implementation of employer sanctions and other reforms introduced by the 1986 Immigration Reform and Control Act.

Mr. Fix received a JD from The University of Virginia and a BA from Princeton University. He did additional graduate work at the London School of Economics.

Laureen Laglagaron is a Policy Analyst at the Migration Policy Institute and Director of MPI's Internship Program. Her work focuses on initiatives of the National Center on Immigrant Integration Policy, including language access, state and local governance, and enforcement of federal immigration law at the state level. Prior to joining MPI, Ms. Laglagaron, an attorney, practiced immigration and family law in San Francisco as an Equal Justice Works Fellow at Asian Pacific Islander (API) Legal Outreach. Ms. Laglagaron has trained community groups, law students, consular staff and pro bono attorneys on the basics of immigration law, citizenship, human trafficking and domestic violence. Ms. Laglagaron received her JD from the University of California, Los Angeles, School of Law, where she received a certificate from the Program in Public Interest Law and Policy. She also holds a BA in Economics and Sociology/Anthropology from Swarthmore College.

Dr. Steven Loyal is a Senior Lecturer in the School of Sociology, University College Dublin. His research interests include migration, ethno-racial processes and dynamics, sociological theory and class and stratification. He has recently completed a book on immigration in Ireland to be published by Manchester University Press.

Margie McHugh is the Co-Director of the National Center on Immigrant Integration Policy at the Migration Policy Institute.

Prior to joining MPI, Ms. McHugh served for 15 years as the executive director of The New York Immigration Coalition, an umbrella organization for over 150 groups in New York that uses research, policy-development and community-mobilization efforts to achieve landmark integration policy and program initiatives. During her time with the NYIC, Ms. McHugh oversaw research, writing and publication of over a dozen reports dealing with issues such as the quality of education services provided to immigrant students in New York's schools, the lack of availability of English classes for adult immigrants, the voting behavior of foreign-born citizens and barriers faced by immigrants seeking to access health and mental health services.

Prior to joining the NYIC, Ms. McHugh served as deputy director of New York City's 1990 Census Project and as the executive assistant to NYC Mayor Ed Koch's chief of staff. She is the recipient of dozens of awards recognizing her successful efforts to bring diverse constituencies together and tackle tough problems, including the prestigious *Leadership for a Changing World* award. She has served as a member and officer on the boards of directors for both the National Immigration Forum and Working Today as well as on the editorial board of *Migration World Magazine*, and she has held appointive positions in a variety of New York City and State commissions, most notably the Commission on the Future of the City University of New York and the New York Workers' Rights Board.

Ms. McHugh is a graduate of Harvard and Radcliffe Colleges.

Sheena McLoughlin is a Junior Policy Analyst at the European Policy Centre, in Brussels, where she works on immigration and asylum policy and minority and integration issues. She coordinates EPC's Migration and Integration Forum, which analyses immigration, asylum and integration policies in Europe, assesses their economic and social impact, and considers the issues raised by increasingly multicultural societies. She also provides support to the Muslims in Europe Forum.

Cas Mudde is the Nancy Schaenen Visiting Scholar at the Janet Prindle Institute for Ethics and a Visiting Associate Professor at the Department of Political Science of DePauw University. Previously, he taught at the Central European University, in Budapest, the University of Edinburgh and the University of Antwerp. He has also been a Visiting Scholar at Universita Karlova (Czech Republic), Academia Istrapolitana Nova (Slovakia), University Jaume I (Spain) and, in the United States, at New York University, the University of California-Santa Barbara, the University of Oregon and the University of Notre Dame.

The bulk of his academic work has been in the broad field of "extremism and democracy," and he is involved in various projects on populism, focusing particularly on the relationship between various types of populism and liberal democracy worldwide. He is co-directing an international collaborative project, provisionally entitled "Populism: Corrective or Threat to Democracy?", which investigates the conditions under which populism becomes a corrective or threat to liberal democracy (drawing upon case studies from Eastern and Western Europe as well as North and South America). He is also working on a new project that looks at how liberal democracies can defend themselves against extremist challenges without undermining their core values.

Dr. Mudde is the author of *The Ideology of the Extreme Right* (Manchester University Press, 2000) and *Populist Radical Right Parties in Europe* (Cambridge University Press, 2007). He has edited or co-edited five volumes, including *Racist Extremism in Central and Eastern Europe* (Routledge, 2005), *Western Democracies and the New Extreme Right Challenge* (Routledge, 2004) and *Uncivil Society? Contentious Politics in Post-Communist Europe* (Routledge, 2003).

He received his MA and PhD from Leiden University in the Netherlands.

Demetrios G. Papademetriou is the President and Co-Founder of the Migration Policy Institute (MPI), a Washington-based think tank dedicated exclusively to the study of international migration. He is also the convener of the Transatlantic Council on Migration and its predecessor, the Transatlantic Task Force on Immigration and Integration (co-convened with the Bertelsmann Stiftung). Dr. Papademetriou is Co-Founder and International Chair Emeritus of *Metropolis: An International Forum for Research and Policy on Migration and Cities*. He also serves as Chair of the World Economic Forum's Global Agenda Council on Migration.

Dr. Papademetriou holds a PhD in Comparative Public Policy and International Relations (1976) and has taught at the University of Maryland, Duke University, American University and the New School for Social Research. He has held a wide range of senior positions that include Chair of the Migration Committee of the Paris-based Organisation for Economic Co-operation and Development (OECD); Director for Immigration Policy and Research at the US Department of Labor; Chair of the Secretary of Labor's Immigration Policy Task Force; and Executive Editor of the *International Migration Review*.

Dr. Papademetriou has published more than 250 books, articles, monographs and research reports on migration topics and advises senior government and political party officials in more than 20 countries, including numerous EU Member States while they hold the rotating EU presidency.

Madeleine Sumption is a Policy Analyst at the Migration Policy Institute, where she works on the Labor Markets Initiative and the International Program.

She holds a master's degree with honors from the University of Chicago's School of Public Policy. There, she focused on labor economics and wrote a thesis on the development of social networks among Eastern European immigrants and their labor market implications. Her recent publications include: *Migration and the Economic Downturn: What to Expect in the European Union* (co-authored); *Social Networks and Polish Immigration to the UK*; *Immigration and the Labour Market: Theory, Evidence and Policy* (co-authored); and *Aligning Temporary Immigration Visas with US Labor Market Needs: The Case for a New System of Provisional Visas* (co-authored).

Miho Taguma is Policy Analyst at the Education and Training Policy Division of the Directorate for Education at the Organisation of Economic Co-operation and Development (OECD), a position she has held since 2006.

She is the Project Manager of the OECD Policy Review of Migrant Education. She is also the Project Manager for the OECD Network on Early Childhood Education and Care and the OECD research project "Encouraging Quality in Early Childhood Education and Care." She also worked on the OECD Policy Review of Recognition of Non-Formal and Informal Learning.

Prior to joining the Education and Training Policy Division, she worked at the Center for Educational Research and Innovation of the OECD (2003–2005). During her post at the center, she worked on "E-learning in Tertiary Education." She was also involved in the UNESCO-OECD Policy Review of Education Sector for Mauritius as a review team member.

Prior to joining OECD, she worked in the Education Sector of UNESCO (2002–2003), where she focused on intercultural dialogue and education projects.

Aaron Terrazas is a Policy Analyst at the Migration Policy Institute, where he focuses on immigrant integration and education, migration and development, and the role of immigrants in the workforce.

His recent publications include *The Binational Option: Meeting the Instructional Needs of Limited English Proficient Students* (co-authored); *Immigrants and the Current Economic Crisis* (co-authored); and *Gambling on the Future: Managing the Education Challenges of Rapid Growth in Nevada*.

Mr. Terrazas holds a BS with honors from the Edmund Walsh School of Foreign Service at Georgetown University, where he majored in International Affairs and earned a certificate in Latin American Studies. He was awarded the William Manger Latin American Studies Award for his senior thesis. He also studied at the Institut d'Etudes Politiques in Paris and has completed postgraduate coursework in statistics and econometrics.